John Lennon

Printed in the United Kingdom by MPG Books Ltd, Bodmin

Published by Sanctuary Publishing Limited, Sanctuary House, 45–53 Sinclair Road,
London W14 0NS, United Kingdom

www.sanctuarypublishing.com

Distributed in the US by Publishers Group West

ISBN: 1-86074-517-2

John Lennon

Alan Clayson
Sanctuary

Contents

1 "Who Am I To Regard
As Mother?"

At 6:30pm on Wednesday 9 October 1940, John Winston
Lennon was prised into the world at Liverpool's Oxford Street
Maternity Hospital. The BBC Home Service weatherman had
forecast that the night and the next day would be dull but
mild, which they were. Dull but mild it remained for more or
less the next fortnight. But one evening before the baby was
brought home, wailing sirens and flares illuminated the sky
as the Luftwaffe dropped ton upon booming ton of death and
destruction in and around the slip-slapping wharfs of the
docklands where the Mersey sweeps into the Irish Sea.

The following morning, brick dust crunched beneath the
hooves of dray horses dragging coal through mean streets to
rusty ships, but Julia Lennon's firstborn was destined for a
comfortable middle-class home – with a fitted dining-room
carpet, not lino – in Menlove Avenue, one of the main
thoroughfares of Woolton, a village-like suburb that aligned

itself more with rural Lancashire than Merseyside, embracing mock-Tudor colonies, golf clubs and boating lakes.

After his father, Freddie, a seaman of Irish extraction, vanished to all intents and purposes when John was five, so soon did the concept that there is no God but Mummy, and Daddy is the prophet of Mummy. With Freddie represented – perhaps unfairly – as the villain of the piece, the subsequent complications of his wayward mother's love-life and domestic arrangements made it more convenient for the child to grow up in Mendips, the semi-detached villa of Julia's childless sister, Mary Smith (whom John would always call by his cradle articulation "Mimi") and her ex-serviceman husband, George, once an infinitesimal cog in the global hostilities but now running his late father's dairy business. George was to die suddenly when his nephew by marriage was 14.

As John was to discover, Julia lived nearby with her second family, and bound by the invisible chains that shackle child to parent he used her council house as a bolthole whenever strait-laced Mimi's rearing methods became oppressive. The innate confusion of "Who am I to regard as mother?" affected John's ability to trust adult authority figures, whom he mocked and abused as a defence against being rejected by them – particularly after Julia was killed in July 1958 by a car with a policeman, late for his shift, at the wheel.

Moreover, despite the extenuating circumstances, he felt that he'd been cast out by his mother as well as by Freddie, having had enough experience of her to know what he was missing, hence the bitterness inherent in outbursts against teachers, friends and his devoted aunt. She usually blamed doubtful company for John's mischief when, short-trousered and gaberdine-raincoated, he began his formal education on 12 November 1945 in the kindergarten at Moss Pits Lane Infant School, a few streets' dawdle from Mendips.

The following April, John was expelled for disruptive behaviour and, chastened by this disgrace, commenced a less wild career at Dovedale Road Primary School. For a while, he modelled himself on "William Brown", Richmal Crompton's outrageous 12-year-old from a well-to-do rural family, whose first exploit, *Just William*, was published in 1917. Lennon, however, was to go beyond the rough-and-tumble of acceptable boyhood larks on passing his Eleven Plus and gaining a place at Quarry Bank, a grammar school nicknamed "the Police State" by the Liverpool Institute, Prescot Grammar, the newer Liverpool Collegiate and other more liberal seats of learning for its pretentious affectations and Draconian rigmarole. An Eton-like house system was in full force there and so was corporal punishment, administered as often as not with the swish of a bamboo cane on buttocks or outstretched palm.

It didn't take long for John to transform from a capable if uninvolved pupil to a C-stream hard case, hanging onto his place at Quarry Bank by the skin of his teeth. By the end of his second year there, he had become a sharer of smutty stories and magazines of female lingerie, and a mainstay of the smoking club behind the bicycle sheds. Indeed, the adult Lennon would be tearing the cellophane off up to three 20 packs a day.

As well as overt offences, John was a more insidiously bad influence on others. Leading by example, Lennon had some kind of vice-like grip on his allies in delinquency, some of whom weren't so much friends as disciples whom he could usually persuade to do almost anything. "I used to beat them up if they were small enough," John was to admit, not especially ruefully, "but I'd use long words and confuse them if they were bigger. What mattered was that I stayed in charge."

The attitude of that Lennon boy – lazy, destructive, narcissistic and, as far as he dared, a bully – was also reflected in further extra-curricular activities that had little bearing on what he was supposed to be learning at school. Absorbing a hidden curriculum, he'd developed a messy aptitude as an illustrator and writer of comic verse and stories since Dovedale Primary. On a par with this at Quarry Bank, however, was his interest in the guitar, the instrument that Elvis Presley hung around his neck. Lennon didn't only like Presley; he worshipped him – no other word would do. John Lennon worshipped Elvis Presley – the Hillbilly Cat, the Memphis Flash, the King Of Western Bop – from the moment he heard 'Heartbreak Hotel', the Tennesseean's debut entry in the newly established *New Musical Express* record charts, and saw the first photograph of him published in Britain as a hybrid of nancy boy and amusement-arcade hoodlum.

John Lennon had acquired a guitar as a result of the skiffle craze, but the fascination of holding down an E major chord didn't interfere with his work on the visuals and he got all the Elvis Presley moves off too, even though there wasn't room in his bedroom for feigning a collapse and crawling to the edge of an imaginary stage. The chief motivation for his efforts, of course, was connected with the fleeting flashes of knickers as girls jived in gingham whenever he went to a dance.

A hard-won mastery of basic musical and choreographic techniques, combined with the rising sap of puberty, therefore found him at the central microphone – indeed, the only microphone – with The Quarry Men, as a perk of being in a skiffle group was, so he understood, readier licence to talk to girls, at least, than most of the other chaps who'd paid to shuffle about in the gloom beyond the stage with a built-in sense of defeat. The outfit was still functional after Lennon left Quarry Bank in July 1957.

When the predictably poor results of his GCE O-levels fluttered onto the doorstep a few weeks later – he'd failed all of them – Aunt Mimi made an appointment to discuss her charge's future with the headmaster, Mr William Pobjoy, who informed her that John's most legitimate contribution to school affairs had been when The Quarry Men performed during the interval at the sixth form's end-of-term party.

The outcome of a rather fraught discussion was that John was to be enrolled at Liverpool's Regional College of Art that

September. Entry standards for the establishment were particularly lax, to the point of being non-existent beyond evidence of a slight artistic turn.

The Quarry Men survived their leader's transfer to the higher-education establishment in the city centre, although by then he had come to seek the particular company of a lad named Paul McCartney, enlisted into The Quarry Men in July 1957. The fact that his elder son was joining a group fronted by that John Lennon was a severe test of paternal support, but McCartney's widowed father accepted Paul's case for the defence, that John had been a square peg in a round hole at Quarry Bank and that he was a fine fellow when you got to know him.

Moreover, for all his loutish affectations, Lennon knew how he was supposed to behave when introduced to other boys' parents. McCartney, forever rejoicing in his council-estate origins, "never realised John put on this 'working-class hero' stuff. Nobody had a set of Winston Churchill books. Nobody had an aunt, 'cause we called 'em 'aunties'. 'Aunt' was very posh. Nobody had relatives who were dentists or worked at the BBC, as two of John's Scottish relatives did. Nobody had relatives in Edinburgh, my dear! This was a middle-class structure in which John was very much part of."

The Quarry Men's new pianist, John Duff Lowe, was in the same form as Paul at Liverpool Institute and met John in the McCartney living room in the city suburb of Allerton. "It wasn't a particularly momentous encounter," he recalled, "though when you're 16, anyone 18 months older is often a bit intimidating. John also used to dress in what you'd loosely describe as teddy-boy gear. Paul's father – like all parents – was paranoid that his children were going to turn into teddy boys, pushing bottles into people's faces and creating mayhem in the clubs. The uniform indicated someone who was looking for trouble. John gave the impression of being like that but was actually quite a nice guy.

"George Harrison came into the group a week or two after me. Prior to us, the band had Rod Davis on banjo, Pete Shotton on washboard, Eric Griffiths on guitar, Colin Hanton on drums, Len Garry on tea-chest bass, John Lennon and, right at the end of the skiffle era, Paul McCartney."

Without the others, Paul and John began to practise and even write songs together, sometimes truanting to do so. They even lugged their instruments with them when, on the spur of the moment, they went hitch-hiking in the south of England one Easter holiday. That was when they'd really become friends.

Although their style was based on blues, hillbilly and further subdivisions of North American folk music, the pre-McCartney Quarry Men also embraced rock 'n' roll, and it was this element that had impressed Paul when he'd attended a performance in 1957 at the Woolton summer fête. So began one of the most crucial liaisons in pop. Not long afterwards, George Harrison deputised for and then superseded original lead guitarist Eric Griffiths, who, like most of the other personnel, regarded skiffle as a vocational blind alley, a trivial pursuit to be thrust aside on departure to the world of work, marriage or National Service.

Hundreds more than could actually have been there were to reconjure a night within the Mersey hinterland at maybe a church youth club with a wholesome, self-improving reek about it. They'd handed over the sixpence (2½p) admission to a with-it vicar in a cardigan, who'd booked The Quarry Men to perform in a playing area with a solitary white bulb as the lightshow and a microphone and two of the three guitars plugged perilously into one amplifier via two shared jacks. The other was fed through something soldered together from a kit advertised ("with a ten-watt punch") in *Melody Maker*.

This latter arrangement was the work of George Harrison, a bus driver's son, happy just to be around the beery breathed John, three years his senior and a fully fledged rock 'n' roller who boasted about how he'd tilted successfully for the downfall of some girl's underwear. An educated guess, however, is that John Lennon at 17 was probably still a virgin, like the vast majority of his adolescent peers. In days before the birth-control pill and the Swinging Sixties, pre-marital sex was a much bigger issue. Nevertheless, through some undignified fumblings, Lennon discovered that even a youth club's most arch proto-feminist – the sort who looked as if she couldn't wait for a game of ping-pong, followed by a chat about life after death over an orange squash – her whole tweedy, earnest being was screaming for sex just as much as any bloke.

Although George Harrison was the most heterosexual of males too, his heart would feel like it had burst through its ribcage whenever the great Lennon lowered himself to actually speak to him, no matter how nastily. Yet while George was looked down upon by John, this was balanced by the former's freshly acquired skills as a trainee electrician, notably ensuring that overloaded amps with naked wires were rendered less lethal and less likely to cut out halfway through a number. George had also taught himself ripostes to counter John's sarcasm, his callous teasing and, more recently, the near-impossibility of having a sensible conversation with him.

Of all The Quarry Men, John Lennon was the loudest in praise of BBC radio's *The Goon Show*, which ushered in that stratum of fringe-derived comedy that culminated in the late 1960s with *Monty Python's Flying Circus*. Aspects of the Goons became apparent, too, in the stylistic determination of such as Scaffold, The Bonzo Dog (Doo-Dah) Band and, less directly, The Beatles, particularly in their first two films. It was also evident in Lennon's associated slim volumes, *In His Own Write* and 1965's *A Spaniard In The Works*. Many of the assorted oddments that filled these books dated from the first broadcasts of *The Goon Show* and John's habit of scribbling nonsense verse and surreal stories supplemented by Milligan-esque cartoons and caricatures, a habit that intensified with exposure to the programme.

John was also among those irritating people who re-enacted *Goon Show* sketches the next day during the

JOHN LENNON

programme's high summer, which was reflected in spin-off
double-A-side hit-parade entries in the UK in 1956 for 'I'm
Walking Backwards For Christmas'/'Bluebottle Blues' and
'The Ying Tong Song'/'Bloodnok's Rock 'n' Roll'. While these
singles were released on Decca, solo records by Milligan,
Sellers and Bentine, as well as two album anthologies entitled
The Best Of The Goon Shows, came to be issued by
Parlophone, a subsidiary of EMI, another of Britain's four
major record labels. The discs were produced by George
Martin, elevated to headship of Parlophone in 1954 at the
age of only 29.

To The Quarry Men, George Martin was an unknown
figure in an unknown future in 1958, when the group was a
vehicle for John Lennon's self-projection as an aspirant Presley.
Because John imagined himself a firm enforcer of his own
discipline at rehearsals, there had been disenchantment
amongst certain of the others, exemplified by premature
departures motivated by his ruthlessness in sticking to the job
in hand. Over-sensitive souls walked out, mortally offended,
to dissect his character and musical ability with bitter intensity.

Yet middle-aged ex-Quarry Men from the Woolton fête
era would reunite and perform again for fun and profit.
Moreover, hardly a day would go by without them
remembering with doleful affection one who had been the
Woolton Flash as surely as Elvis had been the local equivalent
light years away in Memphis.

2 "There Was Something Slightly Worrying About Him"

Lennon's preoccupation with a fragmenting Quarry Men –
soon to rename themselves Johnny And The Moondogs –
took its toll on his art studies. What did stereoplastic colour,
tactile values and Vorticism matter when the group was filling
the intermission spot that evening at, say, Stanley Abattoir
Social Club or the Morgue Skiffle Cellar in Oak Hill Park?

A new-found college friend of Lennon's by the name of
Bill Harry "put forward the proposal that the Students' Union
used its funds to buy PA equipment for John's band to use".
This seemed a practical suggestion as Lennon, McCartney,
Harrison and a turnover of other musicians were also being
engaged as a recurring support act at college shindigs
headlined by the likes of The Merseysippi Jazz Band, then
Liverpool's pre-eminent combo, and fully mobilised a decade
before traditional jazz permeated the Top Ten via the toot-
tooting of Acker Bilk, Kenny Ball et al. "In 1958, it was all

jazz bands," sighed John Duff Lowe, "and we played mostly intervals during their beer breaks. We were always warned not to play too loudly."

The Quarry Men's only concession to the impending trad-jazz craze was Louis Armstrong's 'When You're Smiling', albeit with John singing in Harry Secombe's "Neddy Seagoon" voice and inserting cheeky references to college staff into its lyrics. Otherwise, nearly every item in the metamorphosing Quarry Men's repertoire now was a salaam to Elvis Presley, Gene Vincent, Jerry Lee Lewis, Chuck Berry, Little Richard and further behemoths of classic rock.

As it had always been, Lennon tended to be singled out as "leader" by both the casual listener and those Quarry Men still in terrified admiration of one who, as Philip Hartas, in charge of foundation sculpture, soon realised was "like a fellow who'd been born without brakes. His objective seemed to be somewhere over there that nobody else could see, but he was going, and in that process a lot of people got run over. He never did it to me, but he had this very sarcastic way of talking to people."

When Lennon, in his first term at art college, attempted to change from a lettering course to graphics like Bill Harry, the head of that department, George Jardine wouldn't have it. Like some other members of staff, he regarded Lennon as a nightmare of a young man, although it was recognised that many fellow students vied for John's attention, just as they had at Quarry Bank. Partly, it was to do with his strong personality, but also because The Quarry Men, if not the wildest act going on Merseyside, were starting to be noticed outside the comparative security of Students' Union bookings, having become adept at bypassing potentially ugly moments, often via Lennon's instinctive if indelicate crowd control.

With the music itself, the bars that linked choruses and bridges were cluttered and arrangements often shot to pieces, despite bawled off-mic directives. Yet every now and then, the group would be home and dry long before they reached the final number, in which either Lennon or McCartney on lead vocals might pull out every ham trick in the book, guarding a *pro tempore* stardom with the passionate venom of a six-year-old with a new bike.

However, it was enough that The Quarry Men/Johnny And The Moondogs survived at all at a time when a hick outfit's only way forward was via the growth of a substantial fan following via regular performances in youth clubs, coffee bars, pub functions rooms and so forth. From one of the toughest districts in Liverpool, Gerry Marsden's Skiffle Group had worked a similar circuit to The Quarry Men, although Gerry confessed, "I didn't see them until Paul joined. Their sound was rubbish, but he and John stood out as talented. Somehow whatever John did was just *different*. He seemed to have absorbed all the rock 'n' roll influences and then come out the other side with entirely his own variation on them."

At a higher position in the local pop hierarchy than Lennon, Marsden's outfit had slipped into a routine of maybe two or three bookings a week within easy reach and with the occasional side trip into the next county. Meanwhile, the outer reaches of Johnny And The Moondogs' stamping ground didn't extend beyond the environs of Liverpool, at least until autumn 1959, when the group – which had by now boiled down to just John, George and Paul – made it through to the final regional heat of Carroll Levis's *Search For Stars* – the spiritual forerunner of *Opportunity Knocks* – under the proscenium at the Hippodrome Theatre in Manchester, "Entertainment Capital of the North", some 50km (30 miles) to the east.

The ultimate prize was the spot on Levis's ITV series. However, an obligation to catch the last train back to Liverpool put the tin lid on Lennon, McCartney and Harrison's chances, as it left too early for the three to be judged (by volume of applause) at the show's finale. Yet this crestfallen headway mattered more to John than any progress he was making at college.

John's career there was seeming to trace much the same ignominious trajectory as it had at Quarry Bank. Failure seemed inevitable from the start. In preparation for The Entrance on the very first morning, John had risen early to spend an inordinate amount of time combing his hair into a precarious quiff, gleaming with Brylcreem. For quick adjustments, he stuck a comb in the top pocket of a concessionary sports jacket buttoned over a lilac shirt that Mimi detested. He walked to the bus stop in approved Cavalry twills, but when he alighted he had a slightly pigeon-toed gait, having changed somehow during the jolting journey into the contentious drainpipe jeans, so tight that it looked as if his legs had been dipped in ink. Thus attired, he stood at the college portals and narrowed short-sighted eyes. He was too vain to be seen wearing the spectacles he'd needed for chronic short-sightedness since Dovedale Primary.

The undergraduate's self-image was at odds with the only subject he kept quiet about: his privileged upbringing in Woolton. An inverted snob, he'd already embraced the *machismo* values of both teddy boys and proletarian Merseyside males and generally came on as the Poor Honest Wacker – a working-class hero, in fact, although the only paid work he ever did, apart from as a musician, was as a labourer at local waterworks Scaris & Brick for a month during a summer recess. Nevertheless, by the end of his first term at college, he had started speaking in florid Scouse, laced with incessant swearing.

He'd also latched onto the notion that northern women were mere adjuncts to their men. John's overwhelmed new girlfriend – and future wife – Cynthia Powell seemed to tolerate this role, as well as the jealous anxieties that made him turn pale, clench his fists and make exasperating scenes if she said as much as a civil hello to a male not on his mental list of those that he considered to have no romantic interest in Cynthia.

And yet, however much he showered her with kisses and sweet nothings in private, Cynthia, a lass from over the river in Cheshire, was otherwise just one of an entourage in danger of being lost in his shadow as he continued to establish himself as a lecture-disrupting clown, and lunaticked around the city centre with his Moondogs and college sidekicks.

Lennon's buffoonery would sometimes deteriorate into a nonsensical (and frequently alcohol-fuelled) frenzy and soon would come the antics that would get him barred from pubs. "I just knew I'd never see him grow old," remarked Gerry Marsden with the benefit of hindsight. "Even as a young guy, there was something slightly worrying about him. It was like he was racing through life. He didn't have the look of a man who'd be happy in maturity."

Back in class, John's tutors could not help but imagine that he did very little reading. "You had the feeling that he was living off the top of his head," said Philip Hartas. It was a veneer of self-confidence, rather than any heavily veiled air of learning, that enabled John Lennon to bluff his way through prolonged discussion on art. His bluff was often called by the late Arthur Ballard, an artist who might have gained national renown had he chosen not to remain a big fish in the small pool of Merseyside culture.

Germane to this discussion are Ballard's swim across the Seine for a bet, as well as his Art College seminars conducted in a nearby pub. A strategy regarded as unorthodox even now, in the early 1960s it verged on lunacy – as to a lesser degree did Arthur's defence of Lennon in the faces of those who wanted his expulsion. Ballard insisted that, if John was "a bloody nuisance and totally uninformed in every kind of way", he possessed more than mere talent.

"You could see in his written output the heritage of Lewis Carroll," reckoned Bill Harry. "John also reminded me of Stanley Unwin – his malapropisms, etc – but there was an Englishness about it when everyone else was copying the Americans."

Located within earshot of the bells of both the Anglican and Roman Catholic cathedrals, bohemian Liverpool was, so Harry reaffirmed, "a pallid imitation derived from what the Americans were doing". Nevertheless, it was enough like Greenwich Village, New York's vibrant beatnik district, that newshounds from the muck-raking *Sunday People* were sent to Liverpool Art College to root out what would be headlined "THE BEATNIK HORROR!". Lashing those present in a student abode in nearby Gambier Terrace with drinks, the journalists assured everyone that it was to be a feature on the difficulties of surviving on student grants.

It certainly was, agreed John Lennon. As their nicotine-stained fingers scribbled, the hacks from *The Sunday People* steered such discussions towards more pragmatic matters, smiling in sympathy when – so his friend Rod Murray remembered – John told them that "he had to go home and scrounge food off his relatives". Inwardly, however, they were feeling dubious about the assignment. The situation wasn't up to scratch – or, to be precise, down to scratch. Murray's room, in which they were sipping coffee, was mildly untidy but quite clean and agreeably decorated. One so-called beatnik flatmate had just come home from an honest day's toil in a suit, while a female tenant had said she had no qualms about inviting her parents around for a candlelit dinner.

Nevertheless, with others eager to get their pictures in the paper, John Lennon obeyed an instruction to dress down and make the place more higgledy-piggledy, chucking some household waste about to make it more photogenic. You want the readers to think you're poor, starving students, don't you?

On 24 July 1960, two million people read *The Sunday People*'s beatnik piece, which was printed alongside a photograph, the first Britain at large saw of John Lennon. With sideburns now past his earlobes and sporting sunglasses, Lennon had pride of place, lolling about on the littered floor amongst Bill Harry, Rod Murray and other self-conscious "beatniks". He looked as if he probably slept in his vest.

From THE BEATNIK HORROR! surfaced the enduring legend that John Lennon slept in a coffin at Gambier Terrace, although he actually lived there only for brief spells, until it made abrupt sense to look homeward again to Mendips, where the sugar was in its bowl, the milk in its jug and the cups unchipped on their saucers and set on an embroidered tablecloth. There he would make short work of the meal Aunt Mimi prepared for him as he watched a cowboy film on television prior to soaking himself in the hot, scented water of the aqua-coloured bath before going to sleep in his own little room again.

3 "His One Saving Grace Was That Stuart Liked Him"

There was a new mood at college – for a while. It was pleasing for both Aunt Mimi and his tutors to note how industriously a suspiciously subdued Lennon was applying himself to at least aspects of his coursework. John's yardstick of "cool" was now as much the Impressionist painter Amedeo Modigliani as Elvis Presley.

Lennon's new wonderment at Modigliani was down to his best pal at college, Stuart Sutcliffe, a painter whose lecture notebooks were as conscientiously full as Lennon's were empty. Indeed, when written or practical assessment was pending, John would cadge assistance from Stuart – and Cynthia – just as he would a cigarette. "Lennon's no hero of mine," glowered Johnny Byrne, now a TV scriptwriter but then one of Liverpool's arch-beatniks. "His one saving grace was that Stuart – who I respected enormously – liked him, and Stuart knew Lennon in a way that perhaps no one else did at the time."

There will remain division over whether Stuart was gifted – even brilliant – in absolute terms or whether he was just a minor talent peripheral to the fairy tale of John, Paul, George and Ringo, after his purchase of one of these new-fangled electric bass guitars enabled him to be in Lennon's group from 1960 until just the wrong side of the 'Love Me Do' watershed.

Although they were the same age, John was in the academic year below Stuart. Because of this and their greatly contrasting attitudes towards coursework, many college lecturers were surprised later that they even knew each other, let alone became the best of mates. "Stuart was a totally different character in the sense that he was a very reflective chap," maintained Philip Hartas. "He would fall into quiet moods and he'd be thinking a lot or he'd go off and he'd come back in, that sort of thing. There were things going on in his head, and he wasn't living at the tempo that Lennon was living at."

While the differences between Stuart and John consolidated their friendship, so equally did all that they had in common. For instance, they both needed spectacles and each found vague enchantment in the idea of aping self-destructive Modigliani – starving in a garret apartment, burning his furniture against the cold of a Parisian winter and going to an early grave for his art. However, a less uncomfortable option might have been the happy(ish) ending in *The Horse's Mouth*, a light film comedy that the pair saw in 1958. Starring Alec Guinness, it was about an obsessive artist, a social liability who might have been Modigliani's frightfully refined English cousin. He's frightful to live with too, but his friends stick by him. In a way, this antedated what one college contemporary was to say of Lennon: "He was a terrible fellow, really, but I liked him."

John had learned at least as much about self-immolation from his drunken exploits with more footloose lads from college than from his discussions about Modigliani with Stuart. Furthermore, John was basically lazy. Yet, with Stuart showing him how, he grew less cautious about the marks he made on the canvas. "It was Stuart who nurtured an interest in John to want to know more about things than he knew," said Arthur Ballard. "In other words, he was educating him. Lennon wouldn't have known a Dada from a donkey. He was just so ignorant."

Conversely, Stuart was often content to be a passive listener as John, angry or cynically amused by everything, held forth during their wanderings along street and corridor, giving his lightning-bright imagination its ranting, arm-waving head.

Occasionally, Stuart would let slip a seemingly uncontroversial comment, which might spark off a sudden and inexplicable spasm of rage in John. He'd take a long time to calm down. Then again, Lennon would mock his comrade for no tangible reason at all. "Hanging's too good for it" was his view of one of Stuart's early abstracts.

"I can imagine John taking the mickey out of Stuart mercilessly in private," reflected Bill Harry. "He'd try it on, and if you stood up to it, fine. If you put up with it, he'd keep on." Although Stuart struck back occasionally, nothing John said or did could belittle him in Stuart's eyes, and vice versa. Outlines dissolved and contents merged. They started to dress similarly and copy each other's mannerisms; John, for instance, took to flicking his cigarette away just like Stuart always did. Without purposely snubbing anybody, they evolved a restricted code that few outsiders could crack. Ballard would cite Stuart as source of "a lot of that goofy kind of Dadaist sort of humour. It's entirely Stuart's influence on John Lennon that introduced that Dada element."

In turn, Sutcliffe's fascination with Lennon extended to spectating during his rehearsals with George Harrison and Paul McCartney whenever the college's Life Room was vacant. Alternatively, John, Stuart and the other two might sit at one of the kidney shaped tables for hours in the local Jacaranda coffee bar, a convenient stone's throw away. The café was owned by Allan Williams, who began acting in a quasi-managerial capacity for Johnny And The Moondogs – though, with John, Stuart originated a more attention-grabbing name, The Silver Beetles, although John added that it should be spelled Beatles, as in beat music.

What they needed more, however, was the drummer that had been lacking since the last days of The Quarry Men. Early in 1960, they found one in Tommy Moore – although it was assumed that, with his heart in jazz, 26-year-old Tommy would suffice only until the arrival of someone more suitable for an outfit derided as "posers" by certain personnel in fellow local bands Cass And The Cassanovas, Rory Storm And The Hurricanes, Derry And The Seniors and other more workmanlike city outfits. John and Paul's pretensions as composers caused comment, too, because neither a teenager in a dance hall nor the BBC Light Programme's director would be interested in their home-made songs.

Nevertheless, The Silver Beatles were developing into a more credible attraction than The Quarry Men, having moved up from youth clubs and Students' Union supports to welfare institutes, far-flung suburban palais, Lancashire village halls, working men's clubs and, indeed, any venue that had embraced regular "beat" sessions.

Moreover, Lennon had spat out the nicely spoken Lancashire plum in his singing as well as in his speaking and now had a baritone that was bashed about and lived-in – in other words, the voice of a great rock 'n' roll vocalist. His voice grew more strangled as he broke sweat and his adolescent spots rose through the lacto-calomine lotion and turned red. He was probably nothing without the PA system, but when he became intense, every sound he dredged up was like a brush-stroke on a painting. Backing off until the microphone was at arm's length, just a sandpapery quiver during a dragged-out note could be as loaded as a roar with it halfway down his throat.

Yet The Silver Beatles failed to feature among the local fare advertised low on the bill when, on 3 May 1960, legendary US rock 'n' roller Gene Vincent headlined a three-hour extravaganza at Liverpool Boxing Stadium, promoted by Allan Williams and celebrated pop Svengali Larry Parnes. A last-minute addition to the bill, Gerry Marsden's ensemble – now rechristened Gerry And The Pacemakers – arrived in the first division of regional popularity.

In the Jacaranda after the show, Parnes thought aloud about a further, less ambitious joint venture with Allan Williams. He wanted, he explained, an all-purpose backing outfit for use by certain of the singers on his books. A name he kept mentioning was Billy Fury, a Liverpudlian then on the crest of his first Top Ten breakthrough.

Fury was more comfortable as an English Elvis than the more popular Cliff Richard, who had entered the 1960s by following the wholesome all-round-entertainer path. Nonetheless, Richard's backing ensemble, The Shadows, were respected generally as Britain's top instrumental act – although not by John Lennon, who affected to despise the showbiz polish and now-period charm of their big smiles and intricately synchronised footwork.

Larry Parnes told Allan Williams that Billy Fury was looking for an outfit who could rival The Shadows as he did Cliff, and that Larry would bring Billy along if Allan could hurriedly assemble some Liverpool groups for him to take a look at.

Although John Lennon was also present in the Jacaranda that night, he couldn't summon the courage to approach the Great Man himself, but two nights later he asked Williams if The Silver Beatles could audition for the job. Allan assented, but he pointed out that they'd be up against Derry And The Seniors, Cass And The Cassanovas, Gerry And The Pacemakers, you name 'em – the very upper crust of Liverpool pop.

That morning, John fiddled with his hair prior to donning the current group-costume of jeans, short-sleeved black shirt, two-tone tennis shoes and apposite mock-silver pendant. Then he and the other Silver Beatles – minus a latecoming Tommy Moore – joined the midday queue of hopefuls at the Wyvern Social Club, with its essence of disinfectant and faint whiff of last night's alcohol, tobacco and food.

George tried to locate the source of a buzz from an amplifier while John paced up and down, smoking furiously and cursing the still-absent Moore. When it was The Silver Beatles' turn to show what they could do, Lennon implored Johnny Hutchinson of the Cassanovas to step in until the interruption of Tommy's eventual arrival and the consequent delay while he settled behind the kit.

Yet The Silver Beatles gained the day, insofar as Parnes scribbled on his notepad, "Silver Beetles [sic] – very good. Keep for future work." Less than a fortnight later, John, Paul, George, Stuart and Tommy were off on a string of eight one-nighters in Scotland, backing not Billy Fury but

Johnny Gentle, a Parnes luminary less likely to give Cliff Richard cause for nervous backwards glances.

The spurious thrill of thus "going professional" manifested itself in John purportedly assisting Johnny with the composition of a song entitled 'I've Just Fallen For Someone'. Lennon was to be uncredited, however, when the number was issued by Parlophone in 1963, when Gentle had assumed another *nom du théâtre*, 'Darren Young', and when it was recorded by Adam Faith on his eponymous debut album two years earlier.

This creative diversion was atypical of the prevalent mood of stoic cynicism during the trek around Scotland. This was typified when, via shameless manoeuvring, John eased himself between the sheets of the only single bed available at one bed and breakfast while out-of-favour Tommy spent as comfortable a night as was feasible in sleeping bags on the floor.

Well before they steamed back to Liverpool, a disgusted Moore – with only £2 left to show for his pains – had had enough of washing in streams, shaving in public-convenience hand basins, and staring across a wayside café's formica tabletop as Lennon tunnelled into a greasy but obviously satisfying chips-with-everything fry-up – and especially the van, that mobile fusion of lunatic asylum and death cell.

A beat group without a drummer was no use to anyone. Into the bargain, Britain's take on traditional jazz was now midway through a golden age. This trend had spread across the English Channel, where The Dutch Swing College Band, Germany's Old Merrytale Jazz Band and other pre-eminent outfits on the continent had absorbed their music from British 'dads' like Chris Barber, Kenny Ball and Acker Bilk rather than its US originators.

Trad-jazz bands were therefore more numerous than they'd ever been when John, Paul and George were Quarry Men, and so were the places in which they could play. In the Cavern, for instance, Liverpool's main jazz stronghold, there were specific designations about what should and shouldn't be heard there. The place had put up with skiffle in the past, but what could not be tolerated was lowbrow rock 'n' roll. It was detrimental to the club's reputation.

4 "Aggressive Restraint, A Brando Type"

Bruno Koschmider owned the Kaiserkeller and the Indra – night clubs off the Reeperbahn ("Rope Street") in the heart of Hamburg's Grosse Freiheit ("Great Freedom"), where a red-light district had developed since the pillaging French had passed through in 1814. The entertainment in the Kaiserkeller had been mostly coin-operated, but a German group had been hired for the evening when, on an visit to Hamburg in spring 1960, professional interest found Allan Williams seated at one of the club's tables. When the music got under way, he moaned quietly to his companion, Harold Phillips (nicknamed "Lord Woodbine" after the cheap cigarettes he chain-smoked), another whose association with The Beatles eventually made him better known than he might have otherwise been.

Aided and abetted by Woodbine – Williams was soon spieling in top gear about the marvellous Liverpool outfits he could procure for the fellow in charge. Outside the USA, whose rock 'n' rollers Bruno Koschmider couldn't afford, Allan's groups were rated as the finest by no less than Larry Parnes, manager of Billy Fury. The parley ended, nonetheless, on a sour note when it transpired that Allan's tape of the acts under discussion had been rendered a cacaphonous mess, possibly through demagnetisation somewhere *en route*.

Yet, following Williams and Woodbine's deflated departure, Bruno had to sample British pop for himself. Not in Liverpool, however, but Soho, the closest London came to having a red-light area. Familiar smells of multi-mega-tar tobacco, real coffee and Greek and Italian restaurants were lacing the evening air when, down Old Compton Street, he found what he'd been assured was still the epicentre of British pop.

The 2I's coffee bar was small, smaller than the Indra, and it was obvious that it had known better days. Nevertheless, Koschmider snatched a ragbag of London-based players to be reassembled as the Kaiserkeller's house band, named The Jets and put to work six nights a week on the club's rickety stage for an exploratory period.

On their opening night, the Englishmen's devil-may-care exuberance – particular that of singing guitarists Ricky Richard and Tony Sheridan – brought them safely into harbour. "We had a Midas touch," said Sheridan with quiet pride. "There was no question of failure. It was nothing like we'd ever experienced in England. Our repertoire was about 50 per cent rocked-up skiffle, 50 per cent rock 'n' roll."

However, by the late summer, the Kaiserkeller needed a comparable draw to The Jets, who were now administering their powerful elixir at a rival establishment, the Top Ten. Bruno remembered and made contact with Allan Williams, who sent Derry And The Seniors. Within days, the Kaiserkeller was thriving again and Koschmider's thoughts turned to his sleazier Indra. With few customers for its gartered erotica most evenings, it could be only more profitable to put on pop there too. Koschmider then requested another Derry And The Seniors from his man in Liverpool, who wondered about the group now trading as just plain Beatles. After the Scottish expedition with Johnny Gentle, they'd been back on the trivial round of recurring and diminishing local engagements. It was likely that the battle to stay afloat would force them back to the youth clubs from whence they'd come, particularly as they hadn't yet recruited a full-time drummer since the exit of Tommy Moore.

It was small wonder, therefore, that the lads were open to an offer of work in Germany, on the proviso that they could enlist a drummer. At the Casbah, a teenage haunt where they'd played as Quarry Men, they understood that proprietor Mona Best's son, Pete, was beating the skins with the club's resident quartet, The Blackjacks. With the information that The Blackjacks were about to disband, there was no harm in The Beatles asking if he fancied a trip to Hamburg. Pete packed his case with Mona's full approval, but 19-year-old John had to jump the highest hurdle of parental opposition. Tight-lipped Mimi washed her hands of the whole business and she would not acknowledge – as her son did – that his Art College studies were over.

On 17 August 1960, John breathed foreign air for the first time when the night ferry docked at the Hook of Holland and Lord Woodbine took over at the wheel of an overloaded minibus, which was carrying the five Beatles, Allan Williams, his wife and brother-in-law – who was to snap a much-syndicated photograph of the passengers, minus Lennon, too comfortable in a prime seat at the Arnhem War Memorial.

Williams and Woodbine's eyes were bloodshot with nigh-on two solid days' driving when Bruno Koschmider took charge of their human freight, and conducted them around the dingy Indra and then to three small, windowless rooms adjoining a toilet in a cinema over the road. This was where The Beatles would sleep. Even Lennon was too nonplussed to joke about Stalag 13, Red Cross parcels and forming an escape committee.

In 1960, however, nearly all newcomers from Britain wished that they were in hell rather than Hamburg at first, but they couldn't wait to get back there when their sojourn was over. There might have been better ways of breaking a group in, but The Beatles weren't to know of any. Musically, they came to know each other in an almost extra-sensory way whilst ascertaining how to "read" an audience. The five scruffy Liverpudlians had good and bad nights, of course, but there were moments when they were truly tearing it up, the most wailing combo on the planet.

After hours, they had been guided around the city's diversions by members of both The Seniors and, nearing the end of their Top Ten run, The Jets. Ricky Richards had accompanied John Lennon to the Musikhaushummel shop for the handing-over of crumpled deutschmarks for a short-armed Rickenbacker Model 1996 guitar. Later, on a flying visit to Hamburg in 1961, Richards was to join The Beatles on stage, borrowing John's expensive instrument to give 'em his 'I Go Ape' and 'C'mon Everybody' party pieces.

While the band fraternised with dyed-in-the-wool rock 'n' rollers like Richards, as well as the Kaiserkeller's formidable team of waiter-cum-bouncers, the fact that the five Beatles who'd arrived in Hamburg were ex-grammar school and, therefore, supposedly of Britain's academic elite might have been a subliminal lure for Hamburg's existentialist crowd – the "Exis" – of which Jurgen Vollmer, Klaus Voorman and Astrid Kirchherr were leading lights.

"Lennon, the obvious leader, was like a typical rocker," estimated Jurgen Vollmer, "cool, no gestures except for pushing his body slightly in rhythm to the music. Aggressive restraint, a Brando type." Yet Lennon wasn't all sullen magnetism, as he had few qualms about using coarse language in heated moments on the boards and would attack, say, 'Hound Dog' with the blood-curdling dementia of one in the throes of a fit.

John's off-duty rampaging gave foundation to many of the embellished tales that would unfold in later trips to Hamburg. Golden rain squirted from Lennon's bladder onto the wimples of three promenading nuns, and foul-mouthed "sermons" were preached by him from the same balcony. While he was a popular leader rather than a follower, even his customary Rosencrantz and Guildenstern, Paul and George, cried off at the last fence during an attempt to mug a pie-eyed sailor who'd just stood them a meal.

When he was on stage at the Kaiserkeller, John was also full of *sieg heils* and "You zhink you play games mit der Master Race!" and so forth, goosestepping with a Hitler salute and a finger across his upper lip. This didn't go down very well with Bruno Koschmider, who had fought in a Panzer division during the war. He had grown rather leery of The Beatles in general of late. "*Ist gut,*" he'd exclaim – with a scowl that said it wasn't – after interrogating them about a tale he'd been told about them planning to defect to the hated Top Ten. The Jets' contract there was about to expire and the retinue set to scatter like rats disturbed in a granary, with Tony Sheridan opting to stay on with no fixed backing unit, using instead whoever happened to be around – such as The Beatles.

Acting swiftly, Bruno gave the Liverpudlians a month's notice while withdrawing whatever immunity he'd sorted out with the police concerning the youngest Beatle's nightly violation of a curfew forbidding those under 18 from frequenting Grosse Freiheit clubland after midnight. George Harrison's deportation was arranged by late November.

As for the others, who had decided to muddle on without Harrison, Bruno looked into the middle distance and intimated that an open-all-night city crawling with human predators might not be safe for them if they dared to commence the Top Ten residency. At a distance from safety measurable less in the miles from England than how they were going to get back there, while serving their notice at the Kaiserkeller, The Beatles pondered whether the journey might begin in an ambulance or a hearse. Violence, however, proved unnecessary – within a fortnight of George's removal, Bruno had Pete Best and Paul McCartney handcuffed, bundled into a Peterwagon (Black Maria) and, after questioning, ordered out of the Fatherland on a trumped-up charge of arson.

So then there were two and both were forbidden to seek employment as freshly unearthed paperwork revealed that The Beatles had had no work permits for their months at the Kaiserkeller. While Stuart – now engaged to Astrid Kirchherr – chose to remain in Germany, John had little choice but to go home.

He dumped his luggage in the hallway of Mendips and tramped straight upstairs with a mumbled "Never again". To Mimi, he looked just like a refugee from the war-torn Europe of the 1940s. Yet he seemed fundamentally undamaged the next morning, as he lay propped up in bed, stuffed with his favourite "cowboy's breakfast" of bacon and beans and basking in winter sunshine and the sound of a faraway pneumatic drill.

The way he told it, time that hung heavy between one night onstage and the next had been spent just resting and practising guitar. On days off, he'd seen the sights, boated on the lake and visited the zoo, art galleries, museums and a couple of folk fayres. The only trick he'd missed was doing brass rubbings in Hamburg's older churches. Mimi wasn't impressed. Uncle George had served three wartime years in the army, and she had gleaned that travellers' tales about the fleshpots of Germany were hard fact.

Cynthia couldn't ask how or why, but she may have guessed what he'd been up to from signals that penetrated the tacit vow of silence that has persisted among bands of roving minstrels for as long as *omertà* has among the Mafia.

In any case, the group's future was more important than what might or might not have happened abroad. They had turned into a hard act to follow. It was there for all to see on the first post-Hamburg date back at the Casbah on 17 December 1960, promoted via Mona Best's posters – boasting the "Return Of The Fabulous Beatles" – and via word-of-mouth. The full house remained spellbound until the final chord, and there was a long moment of shell-shocked hush before clapping crescendoed to a bombardment of whistling, cheering, stamping pandemonium.

5 "Which Way Are We Going, Boys?"

When the British beat boom was yet two years away, it was sufficient for the act destined to spearhead it to be on a par with Rory, Gerry and other of Liverpool's most popular rock 'n' rollers – and for Pete Best's mum to co-ordinate the operation from the Casbah. It was thanks largely to her dogged efforts that The Beatles became fixtures at the Cavern. Otherwise, their stock-in-trade was regular one-nighters at the Casbah, Aintree Institute, the Cassanova Club and like venues mentioned in the celebrated *Mersey Beat*, the brainchild of Bill Harry, John Lennon's college chum.

The bi-weekly journal was responsible for innovations later adopted by the national music press – including the first "gig guide" – as well as publishing John Lennon's Goonish early prose. "One of the things I was trying to do with *Mersey Beat*," explained Bill, "was get the musicians to express themselves, and bring a flavour of their world across to the readers – because I was always interested in dragging the potential out of creative people. That's why I used to have John writing his 'Beatcomber' columns."

That each of the first pressings of *Mersey Beat* sold out within a morning demonstrated the strength of demand for venue information and news coverage as well as other activities, professional and otherwise, of a veritable host of key personalities who were as much stars in Liverpool as Cliff Richard and Billy Fury were in the charts.

During the previous unseasonably cold summer, its second issue had made a lot of a Beatles record date that had taken place in Germany when, after much fuss involving the West German Immigration Office and Hamburg's chief of police, they'd been allowed to return to Germany for a season at the Top Ten. Among their duties there was backing Tony Sheridan, who'd become the city's undisputed rock 'n' roll king – and he remains the name that trips most readily off the tongue whenever British musicians in Hamburg are discussed. "I was an ingredient in the pudding," the man himself would concede. "I don't think that I was any more important than anyone else – except that I was a bit more experienced. That was my plus point."

Learning the tricks of the trade from one now nicknamed "The Teacher", Gerry And The Pacemakers had preceded The Beatles at the Top Ten – where their front man's fretboard skills had been fine-tuned through paying acute attention to Sheridan. Indeed, Gerry – and John Lennon – were to share the same high-chested guitar stance with Tony.

As Stuart had, to all intents and purposes, left the group by then, it was John, Pete, Paul and George who were hired by Bert Kaempfert, freelance producer for Polydor, Deutsche Grammonphon's pop subsidiary, to accompany Sheridan on half his debut album, *My Bonnie* – including the title song which, as a spin-off single, was to enter the German chart briefly. The remaining tracks were taped with other UK musicians in Hamburg.

"Bert had been trying rock 'n' roll with young Germans," Tony elucidated, "but it had sounded ludicrous. He was impressed by what he thought was our authenticity. I was doing most of the lead guitar – though if John, say, took a solo, it was halfway good because it came out of the rawness of him. Because the drummer wasn't that good, rhythm guitars had to compensate for the lack of a strong beat. Bert made no comment about this and was quite happy to leave it the way it was when we recorded."

In a perhaps wrong-headed attempt to capture the *au naturel* power that they and Tony generated on the boards, The Beatles were hastened to a session mere hours after the last major sixth of the night at the Top Ten had reverberated so that their adrenalin could be pumped more profitably onto a spool of tape, a phonographic equivalent of bottling lightning – albeit adulterated by the clinical exactitudes of the studio.

All the numbers were punched out in three takes at most, and there was time in hand for Kaempfert to lend critical ears to items from The Beatles' repertoire without Tony. He was impressed particularly with their arrangement of the ragtime standard 'Ain't She Sweet' – with John on lead vocal – and 'Cry For A Shadow', a Harrison–Lennon instrumental.

Neither would be issued outside Germany until they had acquired historical interest, but even being a backing group on a foreign disc was a yardstick of achievement for The Beatles back home – and, after so beginning their commercial discography, Lennon would assume Sheridan's lead vocal when it was incorporated into the act when, describing themselves for a while as "Polydor Recording Artists", he, Paul, George and Pete recommenced an itinerary in and around Liverpool. The spectrum of work had broadened – and they'd always have Hamburg – but there was a creeping sense of marking time. They'd taken their impact on Merseyside to its limit, but no one understood how to advance to the step between consolidation of a regional following and the threshold of the Big Time. "Which way are we going, fellows?" Lennon would shout when spirits were low.

"To the top, Johnny!" was the Pavlov's Dog response.

"What top?"

"To the toppermost of the poppermost!"

Progress towards that goal had been slight since 'My Bonnie'. On aggregate, an individual Beatle's income was a fraction of that of a dustman, even after they won the first readers' poll in *Mersey Beat*. Down in the dumps because of a letter from the HP firm threatening to repossess his amplifier,

John spoke half-seriously of packing it in. Aunt Mimi often reminded him that it wasn't too late to make a proper go of it as a commercial artist. Recently, she'd undergone a descent down the worn, slippery stairwell to the Black Hole of Calcutta that was a Beatles lunchtime session in the Cavern, fighting a desire to flee the enveloping fug of mould, perspiration and cheap perfume, not to mention the prickly heat that grew by the minute as more jabbering teenagers joined the massed humanity bobbing up and down before a wooden stage beneath bare light bulbs.

Minutes after her arrival, John and the rest of those dreadful fellows sauntered on – and he was smoking! – to hit all their instruments at once to a staccato "Right!". Mimi clapped her hands to her ears with a moan of agony. What first struck her in every sense was the deafening din, and how dissimilar it was to anything pop she'd ever seen on television. Cliff Richard had indulged in a little scripted playfulness on *Sunday Night At The London Palladium*. This was fine, but John was belching into the microphone, and saying things like the f-word. Indeed, she was more profoundly shocked by his language than she was by the "music".

Nonetheless, she restrained herself – or was prevented – from wriggling through to the front to drag John off the stage and out. Instead, Mimi contented herself instead with trying to glare him out of countenance, but then Paul stepped up for a sentimental ballad, something she actually recognised. Moreover, his pleasant-enough warbling stayed in key, and a claque screamed when he finished. Amongst them when John waved George Harrison forward to sing Buddy Holly's 'Crying Waiting Hoping', a jocose, middle-aged woman was clapping and cheering as voraciously as everyone else.

When the sweatbath was over, this person – who turned out to be George's mother – was there already when Mimi decided to confront John with this latest and most heinous folly the minute that he stumbled into what might be described as a changing room.

"Weren't they great!?" exclaimed Mrs Harrison.

Mimi was glad someone thought so. If that was entertainment, let's have a great deal less, said she.

More insidiously, John drove his mystified aunt nervous for weeks by dirgeing "A-wimoweh a-wimoweh a-wimoweh a-wimoweh…" round the house, *sotto voce* like a mantra. It was the background chant of 'The Lion Sleeps Tonight', a song that milkmen were whistling as incessantly towards the end of 1961.

Surprisingly, the British cover version, albeit using a different title – by The Karl Denver Trio – had risen higher in the Top 20 than the US template by The Tokens. That there were further signs of resistance to the dominance of North American pop was one reason for The Beatles, in optimistic moments, to at least pretend that they'd ascertained from a buzz in the air that they were almost there.

Another was that they'd acquired someone with more clout than Mona Best. If he wasn't a born manager, Brian

47

Epstein was as determined as her to do whatever willingness and energy would do to push The Beatles further up the ladder of success, all the way up if the time came. Unlike others of his age – 27 – he didn't behave as if all he liked about pop was the money it could generate. Neither was he intending to sell The Beatles like tins of beans – with no money back if they tasted funny.

He was also too much of a gentleman to stand outside on the pavement and bark the show to passers-by. Neither would he demean himself by, say, sitting with the back of the chair against the stage, holding up the central microphone on the end of a broomstick as Cynthia Powell had done in the first flush of wonderment at John, when once a mic-stand hadn't been available.

This Mr Epstein had been lost in wonder too. The group had been vaguely aware of him as a privately educated Jewish businessman who had followed his father into the family firm, which had grown since the turn of the century into a prominent Merseyside department chain, specialising in electrical goods and furniture. By 1961, Brian was a bored and frustrated sales manager at the city centre branch of NEMS – North End Music Stores – and heir apparent to the prominent firm that had sprung from a grandparent's small suburban shop.

By coincidence, Epstein had been attending a seminar in record retailing management in Hamburg the same month that his future clients were working at the Top Ten, but The

Beatles first impinged on his consciousness via *Mersey Beat*. "At NEMS, Brian Epstein took a dozen," confirmed Bill Harry, "but he rang me, astonished, to say they'd all gone just like that, and ordered a gross of the next issue – which had on the front cover a picture and the complete story of The Beatles recording in Germany. He knew all about the group months before a reputed guy came into NEMS and asked for 'My Bonnie', and Brian asked me to fix for him to go down the Cavern to see them."

Epstein didn't feel quite so out-of-place in the Cavern as Aunt Mimi, but he went through a brief phase of dressing down from his usual conservative suit, shirt-and-tie and sensible shoes to go there and to other venues where he was observed looking round so frequently to assess how well The Beatles were going down that observers guessed he had a vested interest. Funny, no one had ever noticed him around them before.

Much has been written about Brian's homosexuality – often the butt of unpleasant jibes by John over the years – and his erotic attraction to The Beatles, particularly Lennon. Yet in his first autobiography, *Beatle!*, Pete Best states that Brian propositioned him one evening in 1962, "but there had been nothing nasty about it, nothing obscene, nothing dirty. It was a very gentle approach."

When the group – then without Pete – took a fortnight's break from a hectic schedule between 27 April and 11 May 1963, Brian – godfather to John and Cynthia's new-born son,

Julian – persuaded Lennon to join him for a 12-day break in Spain. Paul McCartney's notion about the acceptance of such an invitation from a known homosexual was "John, not being stupid, saw his opportunity to impress upon Mr Epstein who was the boss of the group. He wanted Brian to know who he should listen to. There was never any indication that John was gay."

Who cares anyway? Back in 1961, Brian's first task had been to transform the four louts into what a respectable London agent or record mogul in those naive times expected a good pop group to be. As he'd been a leading light in school plays, and had once spent not quite a year as a student at the Royal Academy of Dramatic Art, Brian was only too glad to give a few pointers with regard to presentation and professional conduct.

Brian had decided from the onset that The Beatles needed a smarter, more corporate image. Despite John's forceful arguments to the contrary, he visualised them, he said, in stylish but not too way-out suits plus all the accoutrements. He'd pay for these just as he'd paid off all outstanding HP debts on their equipment.

There were shows of resistance too when he insisted that they played to a fixed programme with no patter that embraced swearing – meaning anything stronger than "bloody" or "crap", then the vilest oaths cinema censorship would permit. Neither was John to insert rude words in songs as instanced by "All my life, I've been waiting/Tonight there'll be no masturbating" in Buddy Holly's 'Oh Boy!'. Luckily, they were intending to drop that number anyway.

The Beatles had to be taught to bow when they'd finished a song, and smile in a gentlemanly way. They had to rest that smile not on individuals but on the general populace. Had they ever come across the term "back projection"?

In short, Epstein wanted to instil into them poise, and charm, not to mention clear diction during continuity. However, John Lennon wouldn't take any such tutorials seriously, and kept staring at Brian in a disconcerting and penetrating manner, full of Brooding Intensity that promised nothing but mockery.

A Professor Higgins job on Lennon proved, therefore, to be too Herculean an effort, and there was no choice in the end but to let him cuss, sneer, tell off-colour jokes, give front row scrubbers the eye, and generally be just the sort of exhibitionist yob that Brian had been brought up to despise.

Yet some of what his manager had tried to do had rubbed off after a superficial fashion – or maybe John had become so desperate to Make It that he was prepared to mellow out as required to achieve the desired end. He couldn't bring himself to be extravagant with praise, but, for all the fussing around with suits and bowing, he acknowledged how Epstein kept his cool in any kind of difficulty more effectively than Allan Williams or Mona Best might have done, even when in the midst of some tightwad of a promoter and his shirtsleeved hitmen who were shouting and swearing that the contract wasn't worth the paper it was written on, and The Beatles were in breach of it anyway. Not raising a bland voice, Brian's reasoned contentions would be riven with phrases like "If you'll pardon my correction" and "Excuse me, but five minutes ago, you said something about…" that wore them out, and made them pay the agreed fee – which was, nonetheless, still small enough for the lads to piss it away at the nearest pub within the hour.

These days, "the lads" was tending to mean just John, George and Paul, now that Pete was becoming a being apart from the other three. As a start, he had kept his quiff while the others adopted the *pilzenkopf* – "mushroom head" – hairstyle that had long been worn by Stuart since he'd paired off with Astrid.

News of Sutcliffe's sudden death in April 1962 – of "cerebral paralysis due to bleeding into the right ventricle of the brain", according to the post-mortem report – came to John directly from Astrid when he arrived in Hamburg the day before The Beatles were due to open at a new venue, the Star-Club, which was soon to be the most famous landmark in the Grosse Freiheit.

The Beatles had last seen Stuart in February during his final visit home. "Wearing your mum's suit then?" Paul had quipped when he turned up at a Cavern bash in a lapel-less outfit, buttoning up to the throat – one of Astrid's creations. Stuart laughed too – but not at himself. A lot of the lads watching The Beatles had their hair combed like the *pilzenkopfs* that John, George and Paul were now sporting. He'd bet even money that it wouldn't be too long before they'd be copying The Beatles' lapel-less, high-buttoned stage costumes too.

6 "I Don't Know – What Do You Think?"

More than half of John Lennon's life was over when The Beatles made their next escape attempt from the Merseyside–Hamburg treadmill. Acting swiftly, their new manager had laid on with a trowel NEMS's position as a major retailer in the northwest to cajole Decca recording manager Dick Rowe to try out his group on New Year's Day 1962 over the edge of the world in London.

Listening to the results today, the overall impression is that The Beatles weren't at their best when they ran through numbers predetermined by Brian to demonstrate their prowess as "all-round entertainers". Paul seems too eager to please, while John's lead vocals have about them an unnatural politeness.

Dick Rowe concluded, therefore, that, while they could find their way around their instruments, the vocals were merely competent. Outfits like theirs could be found in virtually every town in the country. Decca wasn't the only

54

company to reject The Beatles. Pye, Philips and three of EMI's four labels did on receiving a second-generation copy of the Decca tape: all John, Paul, George and Pete had to offer apart from the faded second-hand celebrity of 'My Bonnie'.

Among scapegoats for The Beatles marking time were the Bests, whose house was, nevertheless, still used as an assembly point. That Mona no longer held The Beatles in the palm of her hand was manifested in the way the others started treating Pete – whose isolation became more and more perceptible. Now and then, he'd find himself straining his ears to catch murmured intrigue when, say, Lennon and McCartney, speaking in low voices, tinkered on secretive guitars in a backstage alcove.

While John was handsome after a funfair bumper-car operator fashion, it was hardly Pete's fault that he was the darling of the ladies for his more conventional good looks as well as an unobtrusive content in posing no deliberate threat to the front line except when he was required to surrender the kit to Paul in order to sing and demonstrate Joey Dee And The Starliters' 'Peppermint Twist'. He did so with all the endearingly flustered poise of an otherwise desk-bound head of accounts dancing with some voluptuous typist at the office party. In the watching throng, he'd see his mother, her eyes shining with pride, but there was no such encouragement from George, Paul and John these days.

As well as Pete and Mona, there was no one else for John and the others to blame but painfully committed Brian for the apparent petering out of interest, apart from each other. Besides, bickering helped pass the time. Yet, thanks to their learner manager dialling his finger to a stub, The Beatles were leading what the economist would call a "full life" in a way. A list that had once signified a week's work became a day's. A lunchtime session at the Cavern might be followed by a few hours convalescent sloth until an early evening session at the same venue. Before onlookers realised that they'd left the building, The Beatles' van would be halfway down the street on a dash to a town hall over the river in Birkenhead.

As for Hamburg, the latest visit in April had found them supporting and socialising with Fats Domino, Gene Vincent, Little Richard and other visiting heroes of their school days that, unlike the Top Ten, the Star-Club could afford. Lennon, however, had made up his mind to exercise an observed disrespect towards Richard himself. Calling him "Grandad" and telling him to shut up was the least of it, but John was as diligent as everyone else in making myriad private observations of his old idol's performance for incorporation into his own.

The previous month, Epstein had negotiated Pete, George, Paul and John's first BBC radio broadcast – three numbers on *Teenagers' Turn* from Manchester's Playhouse. Even this was no indication that The Beatles were anything more than a classic local group, despite an enthusiastic response from the studio audience – with Pete Best the recipient of most of it.

However, he proved to be ostensibly the least promising member of The Beatles when George Martin, recording manager of Parlophone, summoned them to Abbey Road on Wednesday 6 June 1962. Accustomed to onstage inconsistencies of tempo caused by the mood of the hour, drummers were most prone to behind-the-scenes substitution in the studio. "The reasons were purely financial," elucidated ex-Johnny Kidd sticksman Clem Cattini, the first dyed-in-the-wool rock 'n' roller to emerge as a familiar figure on the capital's recording scene. "You were expected to finish four tracks – two singles – in three hours. A group might take a week to do two titles, not because they were incapable, but because sessions are a different mode of thinking to being on the road. You can't get away with so much. You need more discipline."

Having someone like Cattini ghost his drumming, would, therefore, have been no slight on Pete Best, but the mere suggestion that it would be necessary was sufficient to compound the doubts, justified and otherwise, that the others had about him, and precipitate his heartless sacking a few weeks later.

His replacement, Ringo Starr, once of Rory Storm's Hurricanes, wasn't the most versatile drummer in Liverpool, but he was a Pete Best for girls to adore more as a brother than dream lover, and bright enough not to ask too many questions yet. Moreover, despite his hangdog appearance, Ringo turned out to be blessed with a ready wit that was as guileless as John's was cruel. "Ringo was a star in his own right in Liverpool," asserted John. "Whatever that spark is in Ringo, we all know it, but we can't put our finger on it. Whether it's acting, singing or drumming, I don't know. There's something in him that's projectable."

The new recruit was, however, the least significant participant in September when The Beatles recorded their maiden Parlophone single, 'Love Me Do'. EMI's executive body were to be in two minds about it during their weekly scheduling conference where, before committing themselves, the more obsequious underlings tried to gauge the opinion of each label's head of A&R. Thus after the customary "I don't know – what do you think?" discussion, it was decided that 'Love Me Do' would be cast adrift on the vinyl oceans in the first week of October.

7 "Pinching Our Arrangements Down To The Last Note"

John's euphoria at this latest development had been undercut by a grave domestic complication. Pregnancy wasn't what happened to nice girls like Cynthia, but one afternoon in the summer, she'd announced that her period was a week overdue – and she'd been sick in the morning, though that might have been through stomach-knotted anxiety. That her waist measured one inch bigger may have been nothing either, but her wrists, armpits and ankles felt peculiar.

She was seeing prams and pregnant women everywhere, in the streets, in public parks and on television. In an episode of *Dr Kildare* – the *ER* of its day – there'd been an unmarried mother. Her boyfriend smiled like John. The screen couple had separated and the baby was adopted – but perhaps there'd be a delightful romantic scene with John proposing on one knee, and promising to love Cynthia forever. Gruff pragmatism ruled, however, and she may have been left with the impression that, if the lyrics to some of The Beatles' numbers – about mister moonlight and words of love – were anything to go by, John and she were being conned out of something.

John's courtship of Cynthia had been fraught much of the time, but that was when they'd been closest because, as far as John – torn between resentment and panic – was concerned, the minute they left the registry office on 23 August 1962, they were already over somehow. The heart, the essence of what they had been, was wrapped up by the time they arrived at the reception – at which Aunt Mimi was pointedly absent – in an unlicensed restaurant. Yet, while marriage wouldn't blinker his roving eye, Cynthia at least felt hopeful during that hiatus between the wedding celebrations – interrupted by a Beatles booking that evening at some ballroom in Chester – and the issue of 'Love Me Do', which was to slip into the *New Musical Express* chart at Number 21 on 8 December to hover on the edge of the Top 20 until just after Christmas. At Number One was Frank Ifield, a new pretender to Cliff Richard's crown, with an exhumation of a 1949 country-and-western million seller, 'Lovesick Blues'. He'd headlined over The Beatles earlier that month on a mismatched bill at Peterborough's Embassy Cinema.

The local paper reported that they'd "made far too much noise", adding insult to injury as 'Love Me Do' continued to lose its tenuous grasp on the British hit parade. Yet, all told, The Beatles had done well for first-timers, but who would assume that they wouldn't be back doing Liverpool–Hamburg piecework by this time next year, even as Brian Epstein negotiated their maiden national tour, low on the bill to Helen Shapiro, the country's most popular female vocalist.

However, the rip-tide of Merseybeat that was to overwhelm Helen and Frank Ifield swept closer with *Mersey Beat*'s announcement in January 1963 of the impending release of a second Beatles single, 'Please Please Me'. Hinged loosely on 'Please', a Bing Crosby ballad from the 1930s – which Frank Ifield had sung at Peterborough – it had been written mostly by John, and conceived initially in the style of Roy Orbison, an American balladeer typecast as a merchant of melancholy.

Similarly, 'Love Me Do', had been as dirge-like in embryo, presented as, recalled Lennon, "a slower number like Billy Fury's 'Halfway To Paradise', but George Martin suggested we do it faster. I'm glad we did." He was also to confess later, "We all owe a great deal of our success to George, especially for his patient guidance of our enthusiasm in the right direction."

From the beginning, Martin had involved the group in the technical side of studio methodology. He'd also been prepared to accommodate the most radical suggestions – initially, The Beatles' preference for 'Please Please Me' to the perky and "professional" non-original 'How Do You Do It', which Martin considered ideal as a follow-up to 'Love Me Do'. On the producer's instructions, nonetheless, the arrangement of 'Please Please Me' was accelerated and simplified with tight harmonies and responses behind Lennon's lead vocal. Even at this early stage, George Martin had discovered that John, immodest about other matters, was genuinely unconceited about his singing to the point of insisting, "I can't say I ever liked hearing myself." It made him wary of compliments about such contrasting items on The Beatles' first LP, *Please Please Me*, as downbeat and sensitively handled 'Anna' to 'Twist And Shout' on which he almost ruptured his throat with a surfeit of passion.

"I could never understand his attitude," sighed Martin, "as it was one of the best voices I've heard. He was a great admirer of Elvis Presley's early records, particularly the 'Heartbreak Hotel' kind of sound, and he was always saying to me, 'Do something with my voice. Put something on it. Smother it with tomato ketchup. Make it different.' He was obsessed with tape delay – a sort of very near-echo. I used to do other things to him, and as long as it wasn't his natural voice coming through, he was reasonably happy – but he'd always want his vocals to get special treatment. However, I wanted to hear its own natural quality."

The timid songbird and his new bride were living at Mendips when 'Please Please Me' was released. Children would swoop from nowhere to see John Lennon, Woolton pop star, answer the door or be collected in the van for transportation to a palais maybe six or more counties away. Wherever "the newest British group to challenge The Shadows" went nowadays, it always seemed to be one week after Cliff Bennett And The Rebel Rousers and one week ahead of Johnny Kidd And The Pirates in Chatham's Invicta, Tamworth's Assembly Rooms, the El Rio in Macclesfield and like venues played by every group that expected its run of luck to fizzle out at any minute.

Back on Merseyside, heads turned when Ringo Starr's old Ford Zodiac stopped at a zebra crossing, but no Beatle yet attracted the beginnings of a crowd, despite a quote attributed to Lennon: "Our fans like us. They know that that whenever possible, we'll meet them, talk to them and sign their autographs."

Yet while Helen Shapiro was, technically speaking, the main attraction on the current round-Britain tour, she'd be upstaged by The Beatles and, on two dates when she was indisposed, so had Danny Williams and Billie Davis – each with a backlog of hits and a current chart strike.

On the very opening night in Bradford, 'Please Please Me' had, according to the *Record Mirror* – and the *Record Retailer* trade journal – entered at Number 16 in the charts. The following week, it jumped 13 places to hold the same chart position for a further seven days before reaching its apogee of Number Two.

Furthermore, in less than a week after the Shapiro jaunt, The Beatles had supported Tommy Roe and Chris Montez on another "scream circuit" trek where these boy-next-door North Americans had been obliged to conduct themselves with studied good humour when, right from the first evening, the running order was reshuffled as crowd reaction dictated that the home-grown Beatles play last, even on the three stops where they appeared as a trio, owing to John being huddled under bedclothes at Mendips with influenza.

Yet Decca and other of EMI's rivals thought they smelt a perishable commodity. What about The Beatles and Gerry And The Pacemakers' tour in May with the long-awaited Roy Orbison – who, bar the remote Elvis, commanded the most devoted British following of any US pop star? He'd be no lamb to the slaughter like Montez and Roe. Toughened by more than a decade in the business, all he had to do was stand his ground with his black guitar and emote the nine hits he'd racked up since 1960. Indeed, at the Adelphi Cinema in Slough, the sustained and rabid cheering after his finale was such that impresario Tito Burns at the back of the hall bore witness that "after 30 minutes, we still couldn't get The Beatles on. This was the first time I'd seen a standing ovation in Slough."

Alighting on this with false hope, those with axes to grind liked to imagine that the peril from the northeast was in retreat. Nevertheless, "What's this Liverpool outfit everyone's talking about?" was a question asked with increasing frequency by elderly executives in London record company offices while office juniors discussed whether The Beatles had got into a rut what with their next A-side, 'From Me To You', having the same overall melodic and rhythmic thrust as 'Please Please Me'. Next, talent scouts from the capital came sniffing round Merseyside just in case the word about a "Liverpool Sound" carried any weight – especially as other Epstein clients such as Billy J Kramer, The Fourmost and Cilla Black, had had hits with Lennon–McCartney songs long before the dissimilar ilk of Bernard Cribbins, Ella Fitzgerald and Celine Dion dipped into the same portfolio.

Under George Martin's direction, Kramer and his backing Dakotas' debut 45 had been a crack at The Beatles' album track, 'Do You Want To Know A Secret', the work of Lennon who also supplied 'Bad To Me' – penned during the Spanish holiday with Epstein – which was the team's second hit. Seeing out 1963 in fine fashion was another Beatles-associated smash – this time by Paul McCartney – 'I'll Keep You Satisfied', as well as an instrumental Top 20 entry, 'The Cruel Sea', for the Dakotas only.

Neither Billy nor the Dakotas were able to recapture the success they enjoyed in 1963 and 1964 – and the same was true of the second string to Epstein's bow. It was almost a matter of course that, prior to Kramer, Gerry And The Pacemakers would melt into Epstein's managerial caress, even though, on a first-come-first-served basis, he did not attend to their recording career until The Beatles had left the runway with theirs. So it was that a few months after 'Love Me Do', Gerry's lot had gained an EMI contract too.

Before his 'How Do You Do It' was dragged down, Gerry had joked, "How does it feel to be Brian's number two group then?" when bumping into John at NEMS. Around the same time, joint press interviews were convened in a London hotel for Marsden and Lennon as principal spokespersons for the Merseybeat movement. Both their respective ensembles remained on terms of fluctuating equality as Gerry's second offering, 'I Like It', wrenched 'From Me To You' from the top. After The Searchers did likewise to the latest by Elvis Presley in August, they, Gerry, The Beatles and Billy J Kramer slugged it out for hit parade supremacy for, more or less, the rest of the year.

Most other Merseybeat entertainers with the faintest tang of star quality had at least a moment of glory when London got in on the act, but, according to one story – probably apocryphal – the entire personnel of one picked-to-click Liverpool group wound up stacking and loading auto parts in the same warehouse by autumn. That was when they saw a picture in *Music Echo* of some southern ponces duplicating both the sheepdog fringes and the mid-air jump against brick-strewn wasteland patented by The Beatles on the cover of July 1963's *Twist And Shout* EP. Moaning about it to *Melody Maker* in August, John Lennon had noticed that Gerry And The Pacemakers suffered "terrible copying" too, but far more groups had been formed in The Beatles' image, "pinching our arrangements and down to the last note at that."

Youth club combos in the sticks wore collarless suits and moptops that resembled spun dishmops whenever they shook their heads and went "oooooo", and there'd be continuity in tortuous "wacker" accents by either "John" or "Paul", and an unsmiling lead guitarist who, in imagination at least, played a black Rickenbacker through a Marshall amplifier, just like George Harrison, the most androgynously hirsute of the four.

Was it only last year that a Billy Fury quiff was a sure sign of a cissy? Today's pony-tailed navvy might take heed how contentious the issue of long-haired males could be. A nasty rumour filtered round provincial Britain that Mick Jagger of The Rolling Stones, whose hair was girlier than that of The Beatles, was to undergo a sex-change operation so that he could marry one of the others.

Mersey Beat reckoned that the Stones were "a London group with the Liverpool sound." Metropolitan talent scouts, see, were sparing themselves a trip to England's crowded northwest by getting pop talent from different areas to steal a march on the Merseysiders. Fanning out from the Holy City, they'd discovered that numerous other acts had been rifling the same classic rock and R&B (rhythm and blues) motherlode too. Some were also coming up with originals of similar persuasion.

Thus, as the close of 1963 loomed, Liverpool's leading pop executants – most of them as good as they'd ever be – were no longer as sure as they had been only a few months earlier that accident of geography would facilitate the procuring of a slot on ITV's *Thank Your Lucky Stars* next month that would kick off a week-by-week scramble into the Top Ten. Yet one such as Rory Storm would insist, with his hand on his heart, that he'd never harboured any desires about becoming nationally famous – although he could have been any time he liked. Nevertheless, Lee Curtis, another Liverpudlian entertainer of similar standing, "would have loved to have made it, and I think about it every day of my life."

Curtis dismayed his female following when he appeared on a *Mersey Beat* list of performers thought to be married. Heading this was John Lennon, but the image of him held by most lovestruck pubescent girls in Inverness or Penzance was born of the pages of Catherine Cookson-esque romantic chivalry and grown to man's estate as a Poor Honest Northern Lad Who'd Bettered Himself as a pop singer with an electric guitar. How many of them wondered what his penis was like (or whether he even had one)? Ignorance was bliss – and worship of an idol without vice or blemish was, I suppose, less harmful an analgesic than most to an otherwise mundane provincial existence of school, homework and youth club.

John was married, true enough, but it was to Cynthia, known then – erroneously, as events were to prove – as the shrinking violet of The Beatles' clique. The speed of events after take-off with 'Love Me Do' had not, however, overwhelmed her as she coped with marathon fan vigils outside her, John and baby Julian's Kensington bedsit, and stifled giggles from those who'd winkled out the ex-directory number. Disguises, decoy tactics and secret destinations were to be as essential as spare underwear whenever the Lennons went on holiday. On one occasion, Cynthia had to be smuggled out of a hotel in a laundry basket.

Her John had been singled out as The Beatles' "leader" in the lyrics of 'We Love The Beatles', a 1964 single by The Vernons Girls, recruited originally from employees of the Liverpool Football Pools firm. Weeks prior to all four Beatles comprising the panel in a special edition at the Liverpool Empire, he was also token member on BBC television's *Juke Box Jury*. Furthermore, the main feature of the opening edition of *Midland Beat* (a periodical modelled on *Mersey Beat*) was an interview with "John Lennon of The Beatles, but otherwise the entire content is restricted to Midlands items" – for, according to editor Dennis Detheridge, "Liverpool started the ball rolling. Now the Midlands is ready to take over."

Back in autumn 1963, however, Scouse was still the most alluring dialect in the kingdom, and from its slang, words like "fab", "gear" and "grotty" filtered through the pages of teenage comics and into the mouths of the most well-spoken young Britons, especially after The Beatles had headlined both at *Sunday Night At The London Palladium* and, before that, at a recital for the seated young toffs and their with-it headmaster at Stowe public school in Buckinghamshire.

John, Paul, George and Ringo had also been seen in May 1963 waving a cheery goodbye during the closing credits on ventriloquist dummy Lenny The Lion's show on BBC TV's

Children's Hour. Then there was a prime-time evening sketch involving the donning of boaters and a singalong of 1912's 'On Moonlight Bay' with comedy duo Morecambe and Wise. Whatever next? Would there unfold a flow-chart of pantomime, soft-shoe shuffling and charity football after they were overtaken – as they surely would be – by a newer sensation?

Offstage, The Beatles were hanging around with the likes of Alma Cogan, bubbly singing perennial of television variety. She was, nevertheless, omnipresent on the pilot series of *Ready Steady Go* in autumn 1963. Not yet the most atmospheric of British television's pop shows of the Swinging Sixties, it also featured then a besuited interlocutor in his thirties and occasional send-ups of current hits by comics of the same age. Alma developed an on-screen soft spot for near-neighbour John Lennon, once cuffing him playfully on *Ready Steady Go*, following some – possibly scripted – ad-libbing between cheeky young shaver and jovial voice-of-experience commensurate with The Beatles' apparent toeing of a winsome line of pseudo-rebellious behaviour. Well, we're all a bit wild when we're young, aren't we?

It was, however, The Beatles' spot in *The Royal Variety Show* at London's Prince of Wales Theatre that November that prompted the *Daily Express* to brief its Liverpool-born showbusiness correspondent, Derek Taylor, do a "hatchet job" about their yielding to showbusiness proper, even if Lennon raised a laugh with the larger-than-life bluntness of his "rattle yer jewellery" announcement. Taylor, however, could only praise them.

Into the bargain, thanks in large part to The Beatles, the notion of pop music as a viable means of artistic expression was being taken seriously by the likes of William S Mann – who covered classical music for *The Times*. The day after his prosy end-of-year cultural overview of 1963 was published, John Lennon – not revelling in pretend ignorance as usual – confessed truly that he had no idea what Mann meant by phrases like "Aeolian cadences", "sub-mediant key switches", "chains of pandiatonic clusters" and "melismas with altered vowels". Neither was John aware of a similarity between the chord progression in 'Not A Second Time' (from *With The Beatles*, the second LP) and those in the coda to Mahler's *Song Of The Earth* (*Das Lied Von Der Erde*). He was, nevertheless, vaguely flattered by Mann's laudation of Lennon and McCartney as "the outstanding composers of 1963".

Two days later, Richard Buckle of the *Sunday Times* had them as "the greatest composers since Schubert". Nor far off were a random Beatles B-side, 'Yes It Is', analysed in *Music And Musicians* magazine, and Fritz Spiegl's *Eine Kleine Beatlemusik*, a 1965 album of their hits arranged in the style of Mozart.

Although McCartney and Lennon would still be damned with such faint praise as "reasonable good 'amateur' composers, greatly assisted by the poverty of British composing standards" in the *Sunday Times* as late as 13

November 1966, the die had been cast, and the elevation of The Beatles from dealers in ephemera to attracting the sort who read the likes of Mann and Buckle as gospel, was about to become unstoppable.

In a world beyond *Times* subscribers and, indeed, Britain's entire population, penetration of North America by The Beatles seemed an impossible dream in 1963 – though they'd entered the US Hot 100 by proxy when, during a break in a British tour, Del Shannon, a US pop vocalist of similar kidney to Roy Orbison, booked a London studio and some session players for a cover of 'From Me To You', purely for the US market. It was issued on the Bigtop label, and had slipped in at Number 86 on 6 July, climbing nine places over the next fortnight.

Progress for Beatles records in their own right was negligible. The first four singles and the *Please Please Me* long-player (minus two tracks and retitled *Introducing The Beatles*) were not deemed worthy of release by Capitol – EMI's regular US outlet – as, declared Jay Livingstone, a senior executive, "We don't think The Beatles will do anything in this market", unmindful as he was of whatever was gripping a backwater like Britain.

8 "Kids Everywhere Go For The Same Stuff"

By the middle of 1964, news of The Beatles and everything else that was gripping young Britain had spread all over the free world. In every Australasian city, you'd come across many an outfit that had reinvented itself as an ersatz British beat group. Most spectacularly of all, Sydney's Bee Gees mutated from an updated Mills Brothers into quasi-Beatles.

In Latin America, the most renowned "answer" to the Fab Four was Los Shakers – Caio (as John), Hugo (Paul), Osvaldo (George) and Pelin (Ringo) – while The Spiders cornered Japan. This was all the more piquant in the light of government disapproval of pop – to be manifested in frenzied protest demonstrations about those Beatle *ketos* polluting the Budokan Hall, Tokyo's temple of martial arts, for three evenings in summer 1966.

In reciprocation, The Spiders undertook a tour of Europe. Los Shakers, however, chose to consolidate their standing at home. Yet their take on British beat was more melodic than a lot of the genuine articles. Moreover, the pronunciation of their all-English lyrics is so anonymously precise that they wouldn't have been out of place in the Star-Club or the Cavern, *circa* 1963.

In the USA, there were also familiar-sounding rings to Michigan's Flowers-Fruits-And-Pretty Things and The Merseybeats (of Kentucky!). Likewise, The Gants from Mississippi grew out their crew-cuts and wore vestments of visual and musical personality bespoken by The Beatles and, especially, The Dave Clark Five. Northeast to New Jersey, The Knickerbockers proved so capable of sounding like mid-1960s Beatles out-takes that they scored a national hit in 1966 with 'Lies'.

No such luck befell more hastily assembled discs by the likes of The American Beatles, The Bug Men, John And Paul, The Manchesters, The Wackers and The Beatlettes – mostly the work of session musicians who probably used to bitch during coffee breaks about this Limey unit that everyone was talking about.

Until what has passed into myth as the "British Invasion", no UK pop act, let alone native copyists, had ever made sustained headway in North America. Yet our sceptr'd isle became the sub-continent's – indeed, the world's – prime purveyor of pop after The Beatles' messianic descent on 7 February 1964 onto what had been called Idlewild Airport a few months earlier.

'I Want To Hold Your Hand' had already topped the Hot 100 – and, within months, so would repromotions of 'Love Me Do', 'Please Please Me' and 'She Loves You'. Even the B-sides of the first two made the Top 40 too.

Sages in the media imagined that The Beatles' North American walkover had been an antidote to both an unexciting Hot 100 and the depressing winter that followed the Kennedy tragedy. "Kids everywhere go for the same stuff and, seeing as we'd done it in England, there's no reason why we shouldn't do it in America too," had been John Lennon's more forthright judgement on why most of the UK's major groups – and many minor ones – made progress to varying extents in the unchartered United States and Canada. Alighting on mid-west towns, even in the graveyard hours, a British group might be greeted by hundreds of hot-eyed teenagers, a large percentage chaperoned by parents who hadn't chastised them for squandering their allowances on, say, a six dollar can of 'Beatle Breath', or 'My Boyfriend Got A Beatle Haircut' by Donna Lynn.

This first US Beatle-related 45 was not to be the last. However, as well as anthems of adoration – 'Santa Bring Me Ringo' from Christine Hunter, The Beatlettes' 'Yes You Can Hold My Hand' *ad nauseum* – there were others such as 'To Kill A Beatle', a single of unconscious presentiment by someone called Johnny Guarnier. Its lyric was from the perspective of a US teenager, insanely jealous because every other girl at school had lost her marbles over the new sensations from England.

Fascination with all things British peaked most conspicuously in that 1964 week when two-thirds of the Hot 100 was British in origin, and The Beatles occupied nine positions in the Canadian Top Ten. So insatiable was demand for anything on which any of the Fab Four had even breathed that Tony Sheridan was brought to a wider public than he may have warranted in the normal course of events after a reissued 'My Bonnie' sold a purported million in 1964.

Meanwhile, The Beatles' cast-out drummer had already milked his affinity to the group via a six-month run of sell-out dates in North America – principally in Canada – with his Pete Best Combo. For many, Pete will always remain "the Fifth Beatle", but less plausible candidates for this ludicrous honour had already included New York disc-jockey "Murray The K" (also "the Sixth Rolling Stone") – because he almost-but-not-quite blagged his way into rooming with George Harrison during that first US visit – and Cynthia Lennon after *Confidential*, Hollywood's most scurrilous showbiz gossip magazine, assured readers that she had once been considered as the group's lead singer.

This deathless claptrap apart, there was a Cynthia Lennon US Fan Club that found plenty to fill the pages of a monthly newsletter. "They wrote about what I wore to film premières, and what I said," elucidated Cynthia to me in 1996. "They were really sweet. I was only a housewife, but a very special housewife to them until divorce divorced me from The Beatles."

While our colonial cousins exhibited a fanaticism that left British Beatlemaniacs, at the starting line, the group's renown back home remained such that any direct connection with them was a handy bartering tool to rake in a bit of loot. After 18 years as the most shadowy figure in John's life, Freddie Lennon, then a kitchen porter in a Surrey hotel, had reappeared with his hands open in March 1964 on the Twickenham set of *A Hard Day's Night*, The Beatles' first movie. After a short conversation with a bemused John, he left and some money was – through John – mailed to his place of work. Freddie capitalised further by selling his life story to something-for-everybody *Titbits* magazine and then recorded a self-written single, 'That's My Life' (My Love And My Home) for Pye late in 1965.

Because of its singer's talismanic surname, 'That's My Life' received a modicum of airplay and was said to be "bubbling under" the UK Top 50. Allegedly, Brian Epstein – at John's instigation – then prodded nerves to curtail further headway. Freddie was determined to tell the boy about what must surely be some mistake, and arrived at "Kenwood", the mock-Tudor mansion in nearby Weybridge in which John, Cynthia and Julian now lived. Outside a banged front door, Freddie would be at a loss to understand his son and heir's deafness to his pleas. So began a family feud that would never quite resolve itself.

Many others who were better qualified to board The Beatles bandwagon were finding the going rough. On the evening in 1965 when The Beatles performed before nearly 60,000 people at New York's Shea Stadium, Rory Storm had been hip-swivelling in front of his Hurricanes in a Seaforth ballroom.

Possibly because Rory was such a flamboyant showman, there'd been no place for him in that same year's *Ferry Across The Mersey*, a period film starring Gerry And The Pacemakers, that was put on general release just as the Merseybeat ferryboat was grounding on a mudbank. Indeed, the belated flick's evocative title theme was Gerry's UK Top Ten farewell – and a requiem for Merseybeat's passing.

By then, The Beatles were the only Liverpool act that could still take chart placings for granted. The *Mersey Beat* newspaper was finished too, having been absorbed in March 1965 into *Music Echo* in which the Liverpool scene was confined to a solitary page commensurate with faded interest – even in the city itself – in any more quartets who shook their moptops and went "oooooo".

Whereas they had frequently graced *Mersey Beat*'s front page – and those of national music journals – The Searchers were soon to leave the UK Top 20 forever with 'Take Me For What I'm Worth'. Yet even in the spooky era after their chart adieu, The Searchers continued delivering goods that at least *sounded* like hits – and could have been if the group's very name hadn't become a millstone round their necks. "We were groping in the dark then," shrugged bass player Frank Allen, "and we'd lost the knack of picking hits."

While The Searchers floundered, The Beatles continued to flourish – by fair means or foul. Straight in at Number One in Britain during 1964's cold, wet December, 'I Feel Fine' began with a buzz like an electric shaver: mid-range feedback. The following summer, The Kinks would approximate this at the start of 'I Need You', B-side to 'Set Me Free'. At the same time, The Who were enjoying their second hit, 'Anyway Anyhow Anywhere' – and, lubricated with feedback too would be The Yardbirds' 'Shapes Of Things' and its flip-side 'You're A Better Man Than I' in 1966. Each made a most effective melodrama of what was merely implicit in the mild gimmick that had kicked off 'I Feel Fine' – a rival group's idea that The Beatles had picked up so fast that, as was often the case, the general public assumed that they'd thought of it first.

Months before 'I Feel Fine', The Yardbirds, The Kinks and The Who had all been featuring guitar feedback on the boards as a deliberate contrivance to sustain notes, reinforce harmonics and, when necessary, create severe dissonance. This strategy had been logged by Lennon when The Kinks were low on the bill to them at Bournemouth's Gaumont Cinema on 2 August 1964. In the teeth of audience chants of "We want The Beatles!", Dave Davies, The Kinks' lead guitarist, began 'You Really Got Me', their recent chart breakthrough, by turning up his amplifier to feedback level, "and the high-pitched frequency cut right through the screams of The Beatles' fans" his brother was to write in his autobiography, *X-Ray*. Ray Davies noticed too that Lennon was watching from the wings.

Come Christmas and Lennon had composed 'I Feel Fine'. "That's me completely," he was to insist. "The record with the first feedback anywhere. I defy anyone to find a record – unless it's some old blues record in 1922 – that uses feedback that way. So I claim it for The Beatles before Hendrix, before The Who, before anyone – the first feedback on any record."

Though John played the tricky *ostinato* of 'I Feel Fine' on the record, George learnt it parrot-fashion for regurgitation on stage as The Beatles travelled a world that was becoming an intrusive and frequently dangerous place; its immensity and richness lying beyond a barrier of screeching hysteria and the *woomph* of flash-bulbs – particularly during an exceptionally stressful world tour in 1966. The Coca-Cola tasted just the same, but they'd guess they might be in, say, Canada by Mounties patrolling the besieged hotel or Chicago because pizza is the city's equivalent of fish and chips.

Wherever they were, John, George, Paul and Ringo dished out a routine 30-minutes worth of unheard music through a usually inadequate sound system at what were more tribal gatherings than concerts now. Prior to each, they sometimes had to field the stock questions about haircuts and when Paul was going to marry, at press conferences where certain of the local media took umbrage that the Fab Four seemed vague about what country they were actually visiting, having long ceased to care about the glimpses they caught of the places where their blinkered lives had taken them.

The Beatles and their retinue would, however, be made to care in Manila, capital of Luzon, the largest island of the Philippine Archipelago. They'd managed two performances on 4 July 1966 at the city's Rizal Memorial Football Stadium. At the hotel, Brian Epstein received an invitation for them to be guests of honour at a party to be thrown by Imelda, wife of Philippines' autocratic President Ferdinand Marcos for the families of the totalitarian government and military junta. Not appreciating that it was less a request than an order, Epstein let the weary entourage sleep on.

The following day, Beatle fans at Manila International Airport were puzzled that they could have ventured close enough to touch their idols had it not been for a jeering, jostling wall of flesh formed of the enraged dictator's creatures, assured of official leniency and even commendation no matter how they behaved towards the departing foreigners.

Open malevolence stopped just short of naked ultra-violence as the agitated Beatles hauled their own baggage up switched-off escalators, and shuffled through a customs area pulsating with pushing, shoving and snail-paced jack-in-office unpleasantness. Sent on their way by the boos and catcalls of the mob, never had arguments – particularly from John and George – against The Beatles' continuation of touring made more sense.

Hot on the heels of The Beatles' experience of The Philippines, a battering psychological rather than physical had awaited them on the North American leg through John

Lennon's off-the-cuff comments about the increasing godlessness of our times during an interview with the London *Evening Standard*. When reprinted in the US teenage magazine *Datebook*, his opinions that The Beatles "are more popular than Jesus right now" and that "Christianity will go, it will vanish and shrink" were interpreted by a more general media as boastful "blasphemy" in a land that, until the British Invasion had been used to a pop star being relatively devoid of independent opinion, having been put in motion by his handler as a walking digest of truth, justice and the American way.

Subliminally through the medium of teen magazines and even in some of the piffle he released on disc, he would echo stolid middle-aged dictums – your parents' word was law, don't talk dirty et al – and parade an apparent dearth of private vices. With the gentlest "humor", he'd answer questions about his favorite color, preferred foodstuffs and the age at which he hoped to wed.

Lennon's nearer-the-knuckle ruminations were a particular red rag to "redneck" whites from the Deep South, caricatured as clannish, unsophisticated and anti-intellectual. Their right-wing militancy was laced with pious fear of not so much "God" as "the Lord", "the Man In The Sky", "the Boss Of The Riders" or, if one of them had swallowed a dictionary, "The Big Architect". He was entreated as the need arose as either a homespun prairie philosopher, a sort of divine pimp – or an enforcer of redneck prejudices, which included the ongoing disapproval of long hair on men as it was written in 1 Corinthians xi 14: "Doth not nature itself teach you that, if a man have long hair, it is a shame unto him?"

It was here, in the heart of the Bible Belt, that thousands of Beatles discs were being ceremonially pulverised in a tree-grinding machine to the running commentary of a local disc jockey. Other mass protests were just as demonstrative. The group's new LP, *Revolver*, was removed from 22 southern radio playlists, and hellfire sermons preached of the fire and fury that would fall from above on any communicants who attended forthcoming Beatles' concerts.

Radio blacklisting and hostile audiences, however, were trifling problems compared to the possible in-concert slaughter of Lennon by divine wrath – or someone acting on the Almighty's behalf – even if hard-nosed US promoters considered this insufficient reason for cancellations, even as 'To Kill A Beatle' was making its deserved journey to the bargain bin.

As the ripples of the "holy war" spread in August 1966, the danger was more omnipresent than ever. "The *Evening Standard* piece was by a very responsible journalist, Maureen Cleave, and the quote was put in its correct context," cried Beatles press officer Tony Barrow. "John was making a statement on the world at that moment, and the fact that a pop group seemed to be drawing more attention than God. Certainly, there were more people going to pop concerts than attending Churches. It was lifted completely out of context and, in that respect, it was a terrible thing for a PR man to have his client say."

A final attempt at damage limitation took place at a press conference hours before opening night in Chicago. There, John was trotted out to make a statement that most took as an apology. "It was the first time I had seen him really nervous at a press conference," observed Barrow, "probably because he didn't really know what to apologise for."

Lennon said as much to the assembled media, though adding "I'm sorry I opened my mouth…"

Engagements in the north passed without unanticipated incident, other than picketing by Ku Klux Klansmen outside Washington's DC Stadium. Below the Mason Dixon line, the anti-Beatles ferment was counterbalanced by "I love John" lapel badges outselling all associated merchandise. Nonetheless, a promise was made to Epstein from a pay phone that one or more Beatles would die on the boards at the Mid-South Coliseum in Memphis. Yet, though a firework that exploded on stage gave all four a horrified start, the show was delivered. The next morning, The Beatles slipped smoothly away into a temporary airborne respite from what was becoming an uneasy existence.

The Beatles played their last concert at San Francisco's Candlestick Park on 29 August 1966, and, for all their common ordeals and jubilations, the ties that bound them began to loosen. While mere sideshows to his pivotal role in The Beatles, among solo projects undertaken by John already were *In His Own Write* and *Spaniard In The Works* – two slim but best-selling volumes of verse, stories and cartoons – and he was to be seen as "Private Gripweed", a bit-part in *How I Won The War*, a movie on general release in the period between Brian Epstein's untimely death in August 1967, and December's interesting-but-boring TV spectacular, the self-produced *Magical Mystery Tour*. After that, the only direction should have been down, but Beatles discs continued to sell by the mega ton.

9 "Controlled Weirdness"

The journey to a John Lennon all but unrecognisable from
the Merseyside beat merchant of 1962 had commenced weeks
before the last date of the 1966 tour with a drug experience
beyond, say, some speed to wire him up for the show and a
"spliff" to unwind tense coils within afterwards.

Lennon had had, so he was to say, several spliffs –
marijuana cigarettes – about his person when, soberly attired,
he, Starr, McCartney and Harrison had been driven in a
black Rolls-Royce through cheering masses to Buckingham
Palace for their investiture as Members of the British Empire
on 26 October 1965. "Taking the MBE was a sell-out for
me," Lennon growled later, "one of the biggest jokes in the
history of these islands."

That the whole business was anathema to him was
reflected further when he contended that, whilst waiting to
be presented to the Queen at 11:10am, he and the other three
had retired to a palace washroom to light up and pass round

one of his spliffs. Yet Lennon's recollections may have been an attempt to beef up an image of himself as a rebel rocker – and his story was to be refuted by George Harrison, who maintained that nothing more narcotic than ordinary cigarettes were smoked. Certainly, none of the national treasures seemed noticeably under the influence of marijuana's admittedly short-lived magic when either talking to the sovereign or discussing the morning's events with the media at the Savile Theatre up the West End.

Perhaps no ordinary newshound would have noticed anyway. Not yet versed in the effects, paraphernalia and jargon of illicit drugs either, the BBC would pass The Small Faces' 'Here Comes The Nice' single – dealing with the dazzling effects of amphetamine sulphate ("speed") as it had already Bob Dylan's 'Rainy Day Women Nos 12 & 35' and its "everybody must get stoned!" chorus. 1966's 'Heroin' by The Velvet Underground, however, hadn't a hope of a solitary Light Programme spin, and the Corporation was to frown too on Beatles tracks like 'Tomorrow Never Knows', 'A Day In The Life', 'Lucy In The Sky With Diamonds' and 'I Am The Walrus' as the "us and them" divide intensified with the Fab Four among celebrities advocating the legalisation of marijuana, and assisting on 'We Love You', the Rolling Stones 45 issued in the aftershock of the famous drug bust in guitarist Keith Richards' Sussex cottage.

In 1967 too, the spoof 'LS Bumble Bee' by Peter Cook and Dudley Moore was symptomatic of a general knowledge if not use of lysergic acid diethylamide 25 – LSD. John Lennon too had come to know acid well, and was to be The Beatles' most avid consumer. It had been part of the anything-goes – some would say "nihilistic" – spirit of Swinging London for many months before John was "spiked" by one of George Harrison's passing acquaintances in January 1966. Dick Taylor, The Pretty Things' lead guitarist, recalled, "The students above me when I lived in a flat in Fulham in 1966 organised these lock-out nights – 'raves' you'd call them now – at the Marquee when LSD was legal. Personally, I was extremely wary of it."

"I had a good time on acid," parried the group's singer, Phil May, "but other people had problems." John Lennon did not include himself amongst them, and his reasons for continuing to take LSD were once much the same initially as those of Eric Burdon of The Animals: "I want to take a piece from every book. I want to learn from everything. That is why I originally took LSD. No, that's not right. I took it just to get stoned." Yet the "psychedelic" mental distortions of LSD were to transport John Lennon to untold heights of creativity – and further from 'Twist And Shout' than any Cavern dweller could have imagined.

Complementing his more celestial acid reveries were the droning ragas of Indian classical music and his and the other Beatles' reading of *The Golden Bough, Autobiography Of A Yogi* and further hardbacks of philosophic and aerie-faerie bent, purchased from the hip Indica bookshop off Piccadilly.

In correlation, pop music was being elevated from ephemera to Holy Writ, and the notion of it as an egghead activity intensified. The most lasting effect was that "bands" began demanding public attention for "concept" albums and similar epics that couldn't be crammed into a ten-minute spot on a package tour with Helen Shapiro.

Naturally, The Beatles, though no longer stage performers, were at the forefront of this new attitude towards recording, notably after George Martin declared his independence of EMI in 1965 via the formation of his Associated Independent Recording (AIR) production company, and then reaching his professional apotheosis through the making of *Sgt Pepper*.

Many – especially in the States – listened to this latest Beatles gramophone disc in the dark, at the wrong speeds, backwards and even normally. Every inch of the label and sleeve montage was scrutinised for concealed communiqués, which would turn listeners into more aware, more creative human beings, truly at one with John, Paul, George and Ringo.

Nothing would be the same, not even the past. The "come on, come on" call and response in 'Please Please Me', for example, was, estimated a member of Clayson And The Argonauts in 1977, John Lennon's vain plea to Cynthia to menstruate and thus assuage fears about an unwanted pregnancy. Such banal argument still provides hours of enjoyable time-wasting for Beatle freaks, old and new – despite, say, a lyrical error ("two foot small" instead of "two foot tall") on 1965's 'You've Got To Hide Your Love Away' that Lennon decided should be uncorrected because "The pseuds'll love it." More pointedly, his 'Glass Onion' in 1968 denied that there were ever any secret subtexts to be found anywhere in The Beatles' oeuvre in the first place, whilst inserting false clues – like "the Walrus was Paul" – and misleading self-quotations, "just to confuse everybody a bit more".

Perhaps 'Glass Onion' was a double-bluff because there's no reason for the list of "uncovered" hidden meanings to ever end, no matter how tightly an artefact like *Sgt Pepper* is tied forever to psychedelic times past – and perhaps that's the lasting "message". Listening to it decades later, a middle-aged hippy can almost smell the joss-sticks and see its fabled jacket being used as a working surface for rolling a spliff.

Technically, *Sgt Pepper* improved on its *Revolver* predecessor as close-miked vocals floated effortlessly over layers of treated sound, and gadgetry and constant retakes disguised faults, if impinging on grit. These days, a mere ten hours – the time spent recording the four's first LP – was no longer considered adequate for one Beatles track. Engineers muttered darkly but said nothing out loud when console dials went into the red during *Sgt Pepper* sessions or George Martin razored a tape of Sousa marches to pieces and ordered someone to stick it back together any old how for the instrumental interlude in John's 'Being For The Benefit Of Mr Kite!', the item that was to round off side one.

According to Martin, it was Lennon who first coined the term "flanger", which entered general technical vocabulary for an electronic strategy whereby two signals in a slightly out-of-time alignment were deployed as automatic double-tracking. It was used to enhance The Beatles' vocals – for example, John's on 'Lucy In The Sky With Diamonds' – but is more noticeable when applied to percussion, as in the effervescent drumming on The Small Faces' 'Itchycoo Park', Eric Burdon's 'Sky Pilot' and throughout 1968's *Strictly Personal* LP by Captain Beefheart.

The likes of The Small Faces, Burdon and Beefheart were, however, unable to attract the same financial outlay from their respective investors as The Beatles, whose *Sgt Pepper* vied with their most recent 45, 'All You Need Is Love', to top the Australian singles chart. Fittingly, *Sgt Pepper*'s 'A Day In The Life' epilogue was also the valedictory spin on Britain's pirate Radio London when it went off the air in August 1967.

If *Sgt Pepper* had been the station's most plugged album, the single was surely Procol Harum's 'A Whiter Shade Of Pale', which John Lennon started singing playfully as members of the group trooped into the Speakeasy one evening. He remembered Procol Harum under a less abstract appellation, The Paramounts, supporting The Beatles when they last played the Hammersmith Odeon in 1964.

The selectively amiable Lennon, however, wasn't all smiles when Pink Floyd were conducted in from the adjacent studio at Abbey Road to see the masters at work. He was the only

JOHN LENNON

Beatle not to return the call on hearing reports of the otherworldly sounds emitting from the less sophisticated four-track lair where the Floyd were recording their first LP, *Piper At The Gates Of Dawn*.

In Abbey Road, too, The Pretty Things were completing their transition from a Home Counties R&B group by *SF Sorrow*, unquestionably the first rock opera. "What we were after," elucidated Phil May, "was an album that didn't have tracks but musically was just one piece. That's why it had a story – the only way we could give it continuity. What was also relevant was that *SF Sorrow* was made on acid."

If you want my opinion, *Sgt Pepper* – on which LSD played its part too – remains a lesser work than *SF Sorrow* and *Piper At The Gates Of Dawn*. Nevertheless, The Beatles' album, rather than The Pink Floyd debut and the relatively poor-selling Pretty Things offering, had been the more manifest trigger for countless beat groups from The Rolling Stones downwards to mutate into a "band" of self-absorbed pseudo-seers, exchanging smirks across the mixing desk at one another's cleverness. Thus the Stones album, Their Satanic Majesties Request, appeared in the shops, complete with a fold-out sleeve as freighted with symbolism as *Sgt Pepper*'s. A month after 'All You Need Is Love' came 'We Love You', coupled with 'Dandelion', a piece of similar pixified scenario as 'Lucy In The Sky With Diamonds'.

When 1967's Summer of Love climaxed on 25 June with The Beatles' satellite-linked televisual broadcast of their 'All

You Need Is Love' flower-power anthem, others moved in quick. Direct from Denmark Street, 'Let's Go To San Francisco Parts 1 & 2' was spread over two sides of a single by The Flowerpot Men – who mimed it on *Top Of The Pops* and went on the road in beads, chiffony robes and like regalia, tossing chrysanthemums into the audience.

The Flowerpot Men were not among the more superficial pop newcomers who captivated John Lennon, but his taste was sufficiently broad-minded to appreciate The Monkees, four youths put together by a cabal of Californian business folk for a networked TV series based on the *Hard Day's Night*-period Beatles. Their hit records were merely part of the package of one of the most ruthless marketing strategies the entertainment business had ever known.

When The Monkees visited Britain, John was amenable enough towards them when introduced, but was to have a deep friendship – comparable to that he'd known with Stuart Sutcliffe – with one of the four's hired songwriters, Harry Nilsson, then a semi-professional who kept body and soul together as a Los Angeles bank clerk.

One of his most immediate personal characteristics was that Nilsson was prey to sudden mood shifts, commensurate with the classic "artistic temperament". A closer parallel that he had with John Lennon was that, when he was young, his parents had separated.

Finished with formal education at the age of 15 in 1956, Harry hitch-hiked from New York to Los Angeles, where he worked as a cinema usher, rising to assistant manager before being made redundant when he landed a post with the Security First National whilst writing songs and hawking the results round Hollywood. 'Groovy Little Suzy' was accepted by Little Richard, who, stunned by the young man's vocal range and mastery of "scatting", suggested that Harry might make it as a pop star in his own right, despite an ingrained dislike of singing in public ("I just wanted to be a record person"). He ticked over with television jingles and demos for music publishers, and, backed by the cream of Hollywood session musicians, released unviable singles.

Still semi-pro, he became recognised around Los Angeles studios as a reliable session vocalist and jobbing tunesmith. After he placed two of his compositions with The Ronettes, and another with The Modern Folk Quartet, a liaison with these acts' producer, Phil Spector, promised much, but three songs recorded by Harry with the "Svengali Of Sound" remained unissued for ten years. Though the Spector connection opened doors, Nilsson contemplated a withdrawal from the music business altogether on experiencing The Beatles ("As soon as I heard what they were doing, I just backed off"). Now married, and promoted to computer-department supervisor, he seemed to be on the verge of "settling down".

After The Monkees had selected his 'Cuddly Toy' for 1967's *Pisces, Aquarius, Capricorn And Jones Ltd* album, Nilsson was offered a contract by RCA and surfaced as the

toast of the London In-Crowd when Derek Taylor – now
publicist for The Byrds, The Beach Boys and other US acts –
mailed *Pandemonium Puppet Show*, Harry's debut LP, to
Brian Epstein with the testimonial that "he is the something
The Beatles are". The group itself agreed, perhaps flattered
by the spin-off 45, a medley of eleven Lennon–McCartney
songs, under the umbrella title, 'You Can't Do That', which
climbed the Australian Top 40.

Nicknaming him "The Fab Harry", John Lennon was
prompted to nominate the new cult celebrity as his "favourite
American group". John next took the initiative by
telephoning Nilsson at the bank ("Hello, this is John
Lennon." "Yeah, and I'm Uncle Sam."). Invited to drop by
when in London, Harry was to meet Lennon in 1968 – and
thus begin a lifelong amity.

Attempts to add the talented Harry to NEMS's galaxy
of stars proved futile as he had decided to take care of business
himself on resigning from work. Besides, Brian Epstein's stake
in Beatles' matters – and those of his remaining Liverpool
artists – was becoming more and more detached as the expiry
dates of his five-year contracts with them crept closer – as
did his association with them in more absolute terms.

Brian's often severely tested loyalty to his principal
charges had extended to proffering in vain his personal
fortune to compensate promoters if they consented to cancel
the final US tour in the light of real fear for John's life after
his "We're more popular than Christ" remark. Yet once-

merry rumours darkened to a certainty that, perturbed by some of the irretractable mistakes he'd made whilst learning the job, the group were at the very least to reduce Mr Epstein's cut and say in their affairs. In an interview given to *Melody Maker* on 9 August 1967, however, he'd been "certain that they would not agree to be managed by anyone else". Television chat-show appearances – frequent these days – also assured fans that he was as much The Beatles' clear-headed mentor as he'd ever been. Indeed, on their behalf, he was in the midst of setting the wheels in motion for *Yellow Submarine*, a cartoon fantasy about them as *Sgt Pepper* bandsmen.

To David Frost on ITV, however, he'd spoken less of the Fab Four than the Savile Theatre, in which he'd had a controlling interest since 1965. The current *Sundays At The Savile* pop presentations, which sometimes mitigated the poor takings for the drama and dance productions during the week, had been Brian's brainwave. However, his preoccupation with this and other projects were but analgesics, alleviations to the pangs of despair, general insularity and an essentially guilt-ridden homosexuality. These had been symptomised by Brian's interrelated and increasing apathy towards the needs of those still on his books, even Cilla Black, his main concern after The Beatles. She was so disenchanted that she'd been on the point of leaving him until moved by both a tearful plea for her to reconsider, and a consequent swift negotiation of a weekly TV series.

Cilla was among the few to whom Brian Epstein confessed his private anxieties. Another was Pattie, George Harrison's wife, who warned Brian of the dangers inherent in the over-prescribed tablets that he took to sleep, to stay awake, to calm his nerves, to lift his melancholia.

During the last month of Brian Epstein's life, another messiah had risen for The Beatles as he himself had at the Cavern eons ago in 1961. His Divine Grace the Maharishi Mahesh Yogi – "the Great Soul" – seemed at first glance as different from Brian as he could be. He was, he replied, a dealer "in wisdom, not money" when pressed about how his International Meditation Society was financed.

To Cilla Black, this meditation lark he propagated was akin to "somebody who goes to the loo with a big pile of papers and sits there and reads them all".

She could cackle but The Beatles were serious enough about meditation to undergo the Society's initiation course, conducted by his Divine Grace at a university faculty in Bangor during the Bank Holiday weekend in August 1967. Once, it might have been the last bolt-hole anyone might have expected to find them. Yet fans and the media were out in force at Euston railway station for what one tabloid named "The Mystical Special", the mid-afternoon train to the north Wales seaside town that was a short drive from Gerry Marsden's recently purchased home-from-home in Anglesey.

"I was there that weekend that made such a change to our lives," recalled Gerry, "and it didn't register that they were only a few miles away with the Maharishi – but I wasn't interested in all that."

Brian Epstein was interested but not convinced about all that – and, in the end, neither, collectively, were his principal clients. Both Epstein and The Beatles' misgivings had been reinforced as much by the satirical magazine *Private Eye* dubbing the Maharishi "Veririchi Lotsamoney Yogi Bear" as the fellow's own submission that they ought to tithe part of their income into his Swiss bank account.

Brian had, nevertheless, half-promised that he'd join his boys at Bangor. While packing, they rang others who might want to go too – and boarding what the descending press hordes had dubbed "the Mystical Express" at Euston station too would be Mick Jagger, Marianne Faithfull and Pattie's sister, Jennie. Waylaid by "What's the Maharishi like?", "Do you think you'll all be changed by next Tuesday?" and other bellowed questions, Jagger dismissed the outing straightaway as "more like a circus than the beginning of an original event". Unable to shove through the mob of reporters, photographers and fans, Cynthia Lennon missed the train – and one of the last opportunities to save her deteriorating marriage.

Neither the uproar at Euston nor the hard mattresses in the student hostels on the campus were as disconcerting as the press conference that Varma's public-relations agent had set up in the main hall, where most newsmongers appeared to regard The Beatles' preoccupation with meditation as flippantly as Cilla Black did. Hard to take seriously by those who thought they knew him was rough old John Lennon becoming a mystic.

A story of greater import reached Bangor on Sunday afternoon. Brian Epstein's lonely life had ended suddenly in London the previous night. Pattie Harrison's disquiet had been justified, because, as Westminster Coroner's Court would conclude, Brian had been killed by "incautious self-overdoses" after he'd become bored with a dinner party at his country home and chosen to drive back to his London flat. The doors to his bedroom were forced open the next morning and an ambulance called, but there was nothing the paramedics could do.

The expected rumours went the rounds before the day was out. The most common was that he'd committed suicide. There'd been a purported attempt late in 1966, followed by a spell – not the only one – in a London clinic in May 1967 to combat combined depression, stress and exhaustion. He was visited by Larry Parnes and John Lennon sent flowers and a note ("You know I love you. I really mean that"), which caused the tortured Brian to burst into tears.

Inside the college at Bangor, the Great Soul had consoled his famous devotees. Nevertheless, as twilight thickened, The Beatles brushed past the stick mics, note pads and flashbulbs as they strode from the university building into a black Rolls-Royce. For all the dicta they'd just absorbed that trivialised death, they were visibly shaken. "I knew we were in trouble then," John was to state with retrospective honesty. "I didn't really have any misconceptions about our ability to do anything other than play music, and I was scared. I thought: we've fucking had it."

So it was that The Beatles became as kites in a storm and the man-in-the-street started raising quizzical eyebrows at their increasingly wayward activities – beginning with *Magical Mystery Tour.*

Nearly two years after their second film, *Help!*, The Beatles were discussing the third one they were contractually obliged to deliver to United Artists. *Yellow Submarine*, apparently, didn't count. After they'd turned their noses up at suggestions ranging from a Western to an adaptation of *The Lord Of The Rings*, Paul McCartney came up with a plan to make something up as they went along.

Like many Beatle ideas – particularly after Epstein's death – it was more intriguing conceptually than in ill-conceived practice. Less than a fortnight after the funeral, journalists were pursuing a charabanc, which, with "Magical Mystery Tour" emblazoned on the sides, was trundling through the West Country containing, reportedly, The Beatles and a supporting cast as variegated as a disaster movie's. As well as the chaos that their very presence summoned, the 40-seater bus – now divested by a disenchanted Lennon of its too-distinctive trappings – failed to negotiate Devon's twisty country lanes, thus ruling out such potentially stimulating locations as Berry Pomeroy Castle and Widecombe Fair.

A completed *Magical Mystery Tour* was premièred on BBC1 on Boxing Day for the majority of Britons still with black-and-white TVs, and repeated in colour on BBC2 on 5 January prior to general big-screen release across the Atlantic. While it wasn't *Citizen Kane*, 35 years of celluloid extremity later *Magical Mystery Tour* is less the hybrid of turn-off and tedious cultural duty it used to be than an occasionally intriguing curate's egg. Finally, when divorced from the film, the soundtrack – 'I Am The Walrus', 'Flying' and the rest of the double-EP that all but topped the UK singles chart – is still a winner.

Yet, as 1967 mutated into 1968, apart from predictable plaudits from the underground press and the *New Musical Express* – and a less foreseeable one in *The Guardian* – *Magical Mystery Tour* as a film was almost universally panned. Though uneasy about it from the start, John Lennon hadn't said much at the time, passively attempting to quell media forebodings by not contradicting the others when they spoke of *Magical Mystery Tour* being "aimed at the widest possible audience" namely, "children, their grandparents, Beatle people, the lot".

In other matters, however, he seemed his usual plain-speaking self, cracking back at critics with faultless logic and calm sense laced with the quirky wit they expected of him. When the group and its creatures repaired to Rishikesh, the Maharishi's yoga-ashram (theological college) on the Ganges, for further study in February 1968, it was John who was to perceive that his Grace was all too human, telling him so to his face, and announcing his and Cynthia's immediate departure.

It was on John too that the truth about their post-Epstein business affairs – a truth that he and the others had refused to avow for too long – most inflicted itself. It was he who was chief advocate of calling in Allen Klein, one of the bigger apes in the US music business jungle, to sort out the mess that was the so-called "controlled weirdness" of their multi-faceted Apple Corps, a blanket term for artistic, scientific and merchandising ventures under The Beatles' self-administered aegis when the company was launched in April 1968.

While Apple Films was to produce a handful of worthy if rather specialist labours of love like *Messenger Out Of The East*, a documentary of Ravi Shankar and the land that bore him, Apple Records was the organisation's only lasting success. It was subject to a leasing deal (and Parlophone catalogue numbers) with parent company EMI, but the founding of an ostensibly independent label reduced the number of middlemen and increased The Beatles' own quality control of product.

While the record division was profitable, Lennon saw quickly that the rest of Apple was as dodgy as Rafferty's motor-car. In the kingdom of the brainless, the half-wit is king. That's how good intentions came to cradle deceit – with personality masquerading as principles, and power intrigues as crusades.

In his memoir, *As Time Goes By*, Derek Taylor, an obvious choice to organise the press department, likened his two years at Apple to being "in a bizarre royal court in a strange fairy tale". Derek's urbane, sympathetic manner won many important contacts for Apple, but John Lennon's was, ostensibly, the loudest voice of reason amid the madness. The music press had been full of how "mellow" he was in his late 20s too. "It's a groove growing older," he told them. He therefore gave the outward impression of a person completely in command of his faculties, an affluent and happily married family man in perfect health, smiling and laughing, with no worries.

Actually, he was deeply worried.

10 "The Change In Him Was Like Jekyll And Hyde"

By the end of 1968, Joe Average thought John Lennon was as mad as a hatter. In restaurants in which fame hadn't prevented The Beatles from dining, strangers on other tables would speak in low voices and glance towards him. Some insisted they could sense an aura of lunacy effusing from Lennon as others might the "evil" from the late child murderer Myra Hindley's eyes.

Previously, he had seemed to teeter on the edge of insanity – or, if you prefer, craziness – as epitomised by Merseyside polymath Adrian Henri witnessing him lying on the floor of a local pub, pretending to swim. Told by the landlady to stop, Lennon replied that he daren't because he'd be sure to drown. Some of his scrapes later in Hamburg and after he'd taken acid were on a par with this – but he seemed lucid enough in interview, and, in all respects, he appeared sane to Cynthia.

Neither of them were infatuated teenagers any more, holding hands around Liverpool. Now all such pretty fondnesses had long gone. That isn't to say he didn't care about the mother of his child – for all the confusion there had been since 1963 between Lennon the husband and father and Lennon the "available" pop star. Neither was he immune to twinges of conscience as the enormity of what he was about to do sank in – but, by mid-1968, he had no apparent option but to burn his boats as far as he was able and either instigate a new beginning or anticipate a fall from grace by destroying his former self. In the end, he did both.

To a journalist's tape recorder, he had declared his love for Yoko Ono, a Japanese–American who many still see as walking evidence of her own conjecture: "You don't need talent to be an artist." As some mug with a pocketful of money, John had been introduced to her on 9 November 1966 during a preview of her *Unfinished Paintings And Objects* display at the gallery attached to the Indica bookshop. Charmed by the bewildering exhibits, he was the anonymous sponsor of Yoko's *Half Wind Show* at another London gallery, taking a benevolent interest in her activities, past and present. Because she was doing a turn there, he was among promenading onlookers at the "Fourteen Hour Technicolor Dream", a mixed-media extravaganza – all flickering strobes and ectoplasmic light projections – at Alexandra Palace on 29 April 1967.

Yoko had captured his heart during a period when, according to Barry Miles, a vulnerable John was in the throes of a nervous breakdown, informing Miles later that "I was still in a real big depression after *Pepper*. I was going through murder." Yoko – who'd made the more non-committal statement that she was then "very fond" of John – was a most unlikely Morgan le Fay-esque figure. If it was a *Carry On* film, you'd see an ecstasy of off-camera bodice-ripping that fateful night in May 1968 when Yoko was invited by her secret admirer to Kenwood when Cynthia was away. Just before the closing credits roll, Yoko turns a furtive key on the bedroom door and winks at the camera to maybe a melodramatic flash of lightning.

If it was a romantic novel, however, there'd have been an abrupt and inexplicably tearful reconciliation with Cynthia – followed, no doubt, by nature taking its course – but things don't happen like that in books. At least, they didn't to Cynthia.

Lennon's behaviour was to puzzle and then infuriate what was left of the Cynthia Lennon Fan Club after he left her and Julian to move into a London flat with his new love – and at this point, the story becomes as much Yoko's as John's, and the enigma of their liaison has only deepened since.

"The change in him was like Jekyll and Hyde," sighed a still saddened and perplexed Cynthia in 1997. "John would have laughed at himself years before if he could have seen the future. Before he met Yoko, there was an item in *The Times* about her film, *Bottoms*" – myriad naked human buttocks in close-up – "and John said, 'Look at this mad Japanese artist. What will they print next?!' So his attitude then was she was a nutcase – and I agreed. I'm not a conceptual artist. When I look at things, I like to understand what I'm looking at."

For schoolgirl subscribers to *Beatles Monthly*, Yoko was destined to turn into pop's cross between Wallis Simpson and Beryl Formby, who watched her henpecked husband, George, the Lancashire music-hall entertainer, like a hawk, and ruled him with an "iron petticoat". However, in the world of Art – and music – Ono was already a Tracey Emin *du jour* via exhibitions that embraced, say, an all-white chess set and an apple with a £200 price tag, and an event in Liverpool's Bluecoat Chambers, where she'd had different paying customers picking up pieces of a jug she'd just smashed. Other escapades included wrapping Trafalgar Square statues in brown paper, the writing of *Grapefruit* – a self-help book of stultifying inanity – and, of course, *Bottoms* (remade as *Four Square*).

Yoko had also tried to make it as a pop singer, actually sending demos to Island, a record label that went in for oddball ethnic material. She had, however, found a niche in the distant reaches of the avant-garde through vocal gymnastics that owed much to the free choral babbling and odd tone clusters of modern "serious" composers Schoenberg and Penderecki as well as stubbornly chromatic *seitoha* (Japanese classical music).

Moreover, in the company of free jazzers, notably Ornette Coleman, she used her voice like a front-line horn – as she did at a performance on a Sunday in March 1969 at the University of Cambridge with musicians of the same kidney as Coleman. With Lennon at her feet, back to the audience, either holding an electric guitar against a speaker – causing ear-splitting spasms of feedback – or twiddling with some electronic device to create bleeps, flurries, woofings and tweetings to complement the peep-parps from Danish saxophonist John Tchikai, the clatterings of drummer John Stevens and Yoko's screeches, wails and nanny-goat jabberings.

The crazy, far-out music at Cambridge warranted a review in *Melody Maker*, but reaching a wider public was Lennon and Ono's first album together, *Unfinished Music No 1: Two Virgins*, not least for its sleeve photographs of the pair naked, back and front, that pledged John to Yoko more symbolically than a mere engagement ring ever could. After a macabre fashion, it paralleled the front picture of 1963's *The Freewheelin' Bob Dylan*, showing the artist in casual attire ambling down a wind-swept New York street, arm-in-arm and happily in love with his then-girlfriend. Lennon and Ono too demonstrated that they didn't look much different from anyone else, but the intention of *Two Virgins* was more to do with magnifying the gap between its makers and the common herd – or in their mind, "us two and you lot" – which would soon include Ringo, Paul and George as well.

When auditioning unsuccessfully to join The Texans – later, Rory Storm And The Hurricanes – in 1957, Harrison as a 14-year-old had played and sung Gene Vincent's arrangement of a song from the 1920s, 'Wedding Bells'.

Its hookline ran: "Those wedding bells are breaking up that old gang of mine."

"The old gang of mine was over the moment I met Yoko," concurred John Lennon. Forgetting about both previous *amours* and Cynthia, he continued, "It was like when you meet your first woman, and you leave the guys at the bar and you don't play football anymore and you don't go play snooker and billiards. Maybe some guys like to continue that relationship with the boys, but once I'd found *the* woman, the boys became of no interest whatsoever, other than they were like old friends – but it so happened that the boys were well known and not just the local guys at the bar."

As well as an expression of this, *Two Virgins* was also, so he and Yoko explained, an Art Statement. Joe Average was, however, too bewildered to give an Art Reply.

John Lennon's intimates had not associated penis display with one who, only three years earlier, had seethed, "You don't do that in front of the birds!" when he, Cynthia and the Harrisons had been confronted by a drunken Allen Ginsberg wearing only underpants – on his head – at a London *soirée* held on the beatnik bard's birthday.

That was before LSD entered Lennon's life. *Two Virgins* might have been rooted in too much acid triggering onsets of self-imposed humiliations. He and Yoko were also to start on heroin, now a more popular chemical handmaiden to creativity for certain songwriters than hallucinogens.

It was feasible that, as well as consumption of hard drugs, Lennon's conduct also had a connection with St Francis of Assisi, who was given to sometimes preaching the gospel in the nude as an act of self-abasing godliness. Though it was the sort of statement he might have made, it was not St Francis but Lennon who assured *Melody Maker* editor Ray Coleman, "I try to live as Christ lived. It's tough, I can tell you." Furthermore, a few months prior to the cloak-and-dagger release of *Two Virgins* – and the day before he consummated his desire for Yoko in Weybridge – it was said that Lennon had summoned McCartney, Harrison and Starr behind closed doors in an Apple board room in order to proclaim himself the Messiah. He wasn't being funny ha-ha either.

Soon, John's extreme broadness of gesture – which extended to changing his middle name by deed poll from "Winston" to "Ono" – was an embarrassment to the world outside The Beatles clique too. Perhaps the more resolute gentlefolk of the press got wind of the "Messiah" nonsense, because early in December 1969 it was reported in the *Daily Express* and then in several other newspapers that John was "considering" an offer to play the title role in a forthcoming musical, *Jesus Christ Superstar*, but only on condition that Yoko star too as "Mary Magdalene". All this was a surprise to composer Andrew Lloyd Webber and his lyricist, Tim Rice, who issued a terrified denial straightaway.

The *Express* feature was, allegedly, the first John heard of the matter too, but he didn't mind. It gilded the image of him as the coolest cat ever to walk the planet, the most messianic symbol of hipness since Bob Dylan, the most way-out star in the firmament – though not a star in the sense of sending teenage girls into paroxysms of screaming ecstasy any more. *Two Virgins* had put paid to that – as articulated in the hookline of the topical disc "John You Went Too Far This Time" by Rainbo, alias Hollywood starlet Sissy Spacek: "Since I saw that picture, my love will never be the same."

A special "Groupies" edition of *Rolling Stone* in 1969 concerned female music-lovers renowned for evading the most stringent security barriers to impose themselves on rock stars. The more free-spirited of these "groupies" (not "scrubbers" anymore) remained interested in John Lennon sexually – "It'd be a privilege for him to even notice me," said one – but others were wary of one who had mutated from object of desire to not so much a spoken-for all-father as a universal batty uncle, a Holy Fool, a sort of clown godhead of pop.

In reciprocation, a fur-coated woman had shouted, "You are a very holy man," when he and Yoko had emerged on 28 November 1968 from Marylebone Magistrates Court, where John had been fined after pleading guilty to possession of substances contrary to the provisions of the 1966 Dangerous Drugs Act, section 42.

He and a pregnant Yoko had been recipients of a Narcotics Squad pounce the previous month after they'd found a temporary refuge from self-aggravated media attention in a rented maisonette a few blocks from Regent's Park. Unacceptable to the officer in charge was John's excuse that the cannabis he and his men – and a sniffer dog – had discovered was the lost property of some earlier tenant, maybe Jimi Hendrix or novelist William Burroughs.

The first Beatle of three to be "busted", Lennon was no longer above the law, MBE or not. The rip-tide of the drama – "an offence of moral turpitude" – was to wash over his attempts in the next decade to settle permanently in the United States, but in 1968 he accepted it as part of life's small change and he didn't find the furore completely unwelcome.

He seemed so bound up in himself and Yoko that every occurrence and emotion was worth broadcasting to as wide a forum as possible, just as it happened – just as, in microcosm, Rory Storm was prone to do in the old days, ensuring that his birthday celebrations were public events, and being nabbed by a porter spray-painting "I Love Rory" on a wall at Bootle railway station.

With the means to go infinitely further, John Lennon ordered the issue on Zapple, Apple's short-lived "experimental" subsidiary label, of his second LP with Yoko, *Unfinished Music No 2: Life With The Lions*. The back cover was a *Daily Mirror* photograph of him with his arm around a distressed Yoko in the midst of policemen and morbid inquisitiveness outside the Marylebone court room. The disc's content, however, was concerned principally with Yoko's subsequent miscarriage – and included the dying foetus's heartbeat, which was offered to and rejected by *Student* magazine as a giveaway flexidisc.

Most self-obsessed of all was autumn 1969's *Wedding Album*. One side of this feast of entertainment was the two's repeated utterances of each other's name suspended over their own pounding heartbeats – though there was a blurry link, I suppose, with Marcel Duchamp's "ready-made" art and the provocation of Dada just after the Great War.

If that was the case, then *Self-Portrait* paralleled Duchamp's *Fountain*, a urinal with "R Mutt 1917" painted on it ("which is just out of this world", gasped John). *Self-Portrait*, a 42-minute movie starring Lennon's famous cock – and some fluid that dribbled from it – was screened at London's Institute of Contemporary Arts in September 1969 as one of several British premières of Warhol-esque films of similar non-events made by John and the more seasoned movie director, Yoko. Like other Ono–Lennon artistic collaborations during this period, most of them were laboured, inconsequential and generally misconstrued comedy. The chief exception was *Rape*, a disturbing hour or so of an obtrusive cameraman following an increasingly alarmed foreign student around London. *Rape* aside, however, some viewers tried to fool themselves that Yoko and John's celluloid ventures were quite absorbing in parts, even as others fidgeted in their seats.

Rape was broadcast on Austrian television on 31 March 1969, as just-married Yoko and John were completing their first "Bed-In for Peace". Now with centre-parted hair splayed halfway down his back, bearded to the cheekbones and defiantly round-spectacled, John had smoked a cigarette during a quiet, white-costumed wedding in Gibraltar on 20 March. It was followed at the Amsterdam Hilton's luxurious honeymoon suite by the Bed-In. They hoped that lying about for a week whilst entertaining the press would stop the atrocities in Vietnam and Biafra more effectively than any post-flower-power protest march or student sit-in.

Both the ceremony and the Bed-In were mentioned in 'The Ballad Of John And Yoko', The Beatles' final British Number One. That each chorus began with the interjection "Christ!" – him again – restricted airplay, and the entire narrative confirmed the Lennons' status as a Scandalous Couple on a par with Serge Gainsbourg and Jane Birkin, makers of that summer's chart-topping 'Je T'Aime…Moi Non Plus', on which an easy-listening arrangement seeped incongruously beneath their grunts, moans, whispers and half-crooned lines as prospects of imminent sexual climax increased towards the fade.

Ono and Lennon's canoodling went beyond the bounds of generally acceptable ickiness too. Moreover, to say things most people didn't want to hear or understand, they'd made their headline-hogging lives an even more open and ludicrous book with further eye-stretching pranks such as press conferences from inside kingsize white sacks; the slapdash letter to the Queen that would accompany John's renunciation of his MBE; sending acorns to world leaders; his scrawly lithographs of themselves having sex; and ordering the plastering of billboards proclaiming "War Is Over!" all over eleven city centres.

The outlines between The Beatles and Lennon's undertakings with Yoko were fast dissolving and yet widening the chasm between him and his old comrades – though Yoko was to counter with, "I don't think you could have broken up four very strong people like that. There must have been something that happened within them – not an outside force at all."

With all pretensions of The Beatles' four-man brotherhood now gone, Yoko's constant and baleful adherence to John at Abbey Road had entitled Paul McCartney to bring along Linda Eastman, soon to be Linda McCartney. There were moments of congeniality, but generally the lukewarm rapport between the chief Beatles' immovable women was one of Ringo's "little niggly things", which cropped up as the group worked through what became known as "the White Album" and then *Let It Be*: "the most miserable session on Earth", scowled John.

The idea of *Let It Be* was to tape nothing that couldn't be reproduced on stage. "It would be honest," so George Martin had understood, "no overdubbing, no editing, truly live, almost amateurish." It was, therefore, to be The Beatles pared down to just vocals, guitars, bass and drums, plus keyboards where necessary. However, after George Martin became as fed up with the project as they were, Phil Spector was drafted in to make the best of a bad job.

Of all of them, John Lennon and George Harrison had been the keenest on the record productions of this undersized if self-important New Yorker, but his fastidious doctoring did not please Paul McCartney, who was to demand – to little effect – that *Let It Be* be divested of the superimposed orchestral and choral grandiloquence that both attempted to smother ugly moments (such as Lennon's poor bass playing on 'The Long And Winding Road') and contradicted George Martin's original uncluttered production brief.

Nevertheless, Spector was out of the picture when the team – Lennon, McCartney, Harrison, Starr and Martin – rallied for the *Abbey Road* finale, which the discerning Frank Zappa regarded as "probably the best mastered, best engineered rock 'n' roll record I've heard," albeit adding, "which has nothing to do with the material on it".

When *Abbey Road* was hot off the press, John was approached to compère an open-air pop festival in Canada with a majority of olde-tyme rock 'n' rollers – Fats Domino, Little Richard, Chuck Berry, Gene Vincent and Bo Diddley – on the bill. Instead, he, Yoko and some hurriedly rehearsed Plastic Ono Bandsmen – guitarist Eric Clapton, drummer Alan White (from The Alan Price Set) and, on bass, Klaus Voorman – performed at midnight on Saturday 13 September 1969. Issued as *Live Peace In Toronto 1969*, their ragged set consisted mainly of 1950s classic rock, a nascent arrangement of 'Cold Turkey' – a forthcoming new Plastic Ono Band single – 'Give Peace A Chance' and Yoko's screech-singing.

Manning the barricades in front of the stage, the Hell's Angels stewardry called Ono and Lennon dirty names, it was enough for most of the 20,000-odd onlookers that it happened at all: John Lennon's first major concert – the first by any Beatle – since the showdown at Candlestick Park.

For all that, the album sold but moderately, ie less than a million, while 'Cold Turkey' touched a high of between 10 and 30 in most charts by Christmas. Its B-side was Yoko's 'Don't Worry Kyoko (Mummy's Only Looking For Her Hand In The Snow)' – which could have been about anything – or nothing. However, a Beatle-ologist might conjecture that it was an exaggerated commemoration of John missing a bend and rolling over a hired Austin Maxi somewhere in the Scottish highlands during a brief holiday the previous July. Only one passenger – six-year-old Julian – escaped uninjured; Yoko, John and Kyoko, Yoko's daughter by a previous marriage, needed stitches.

Lennon found 'Don't Worry Kyoko' as potent as his adolescent self had Little Richard's 'Tutti Frutti'. Indefatigable work-outs of 'Don't Worry Kyoko' and 'Cold Turkey' filled his last stage appearance in Britain – with a Plastic Ono Supergroup containing the bemused likes of George Harrison and The Who's madcap drummer, Keith Moon – at London's Lyceum ballroom in December 1969.

They'd done it for charity, even though no one was sure or not if Lennon was joking in a recent interview that he was "down to my last 50,000". If ever he'd believed that his means were infinite, a letter from The Beatles' accountants had disabused him of this. His overdraft on the corporate account was £64,988 – and those of the other three were of comparable amounts. Worse, they'd lost control of Apple, where embezzlement and more open theft – such as that of the television and fitted carpet in the room the Lennons had commandeered at Savile Row – was rife.

Matters improved with the arrival and consequent purge by Allen Klein, whose reputation as the "Robin Hood of pop" stood on his recouping of disregarded millions for his clients from seemingly irrefutable recording company percentages. When the '60s started swinging, he'd made himself useful to The Dave Clark Five, The Kinks, The Animals and Herman's Hermits. After The Rolling Stones had also bitten, Klein sought to win the biggest prize of all. He began hovering over John, Paul, George and Ringo like a vulture over a horseless cowboy with an empty canteen staggering across the burning desert.

By 1969, his prophecy that he'd one day represent The Beatles seemed to be fulfilling itself. Yet, though Lennon, Harrison and Starr yielded to Allen's contractual seduction, McCartney, once his champion, preferred to believe his lawyer brother-in-law's tales of Klein's sharp practices, high-handedness and low cunning.

McCartney, however, had to applaud the Klein purge that discontinued Apple's sinecures and unviable ventures. Even Apple Records, starkly the enterprise's only money-spinner, was to be subject to inevitable cuts as unviable releases were cancelled, contracts unrenewed, and retainers stopped. In the offices too, personnel were subject to Klein's pruning stick; a clocking-on system was installed and the fiddling curbed.

However, Allen Klein's streamlining of Apple was nothing compared to his renegotiation of a royalty rate with Capitol that amassed millions for The Beatles – albeit a Beatles that would disband within months.

11 "An Escape Valve From The Beatles"

In 1969, John Lennon won an *NME* poll in which other famous vocalists had each been asked to nominate their own three favourites. He was, debatably, as adept as he'd ever be by the late 1960s – as illustrated by the coda of the White Album's 'Happiness Is A Warm Gun' when he swerved cleanly into falsetto, having already built from muttered trepidation to strident intensity earlier in the song, tackling its surreal lyrics without affectation.

Yet self-doubt about his singing skills was to persist as an ex-Beatle who allowed Phil Spector and a later producer, Jack Douglas, to smother his vocals in what became a trademark echo, not only in the mix but even as he sang onto tape, refusing to open his mouth unless this was so. "After he left me, he did all his own distortion to his heart's content," lamented George Martin, "and I didn't like that. After all, the raw material was so good."

With vocal vehemence taking precedence throughout over nicety of intonation, the studio version of 'Cold Turkey' was issued, so Lennon put it, "as an escape valve from The Beatles", from whom he'd cast his net furthest. He was also absenting himself from press calls, business meetings and record dates. As if in prophecy, John wasn't around for what seemed to be The Beatles' final recording date on 3 January 1970. In skittish mood during this tying-up of a *Let It Be* loose end, George Harrison – whose progress as a composer was among other factors that had led to the present state of affairs – indulged in a little taped tomfoolery at John's expense: "You all will have read that Dave Dee is no longer with us, but Micky, Tich and I would like to carry on the good work that's always gone down at (Studio) Number Two."

On hearing of this, John grinned askance and told the wife – and Allen Klein, now his official manager. As fatigued as everyone else was of the fraternal animosity, Lennon had been relieved that the atmosphere during the making of *Abbey Road* was more co-operative than it had been for *Let It Be*. The subtext, of course, was a tacit agreement that *Abbey Road* was to be the last LP, and they might as well go out under a flag of truce.

Like children of parents who stay together just because neither has yet quite enough motivation to leave, Ringo and George – who'd both quit briefly already – were waiting for one of the other two to marshall his words and dare the speech everyone knew he'd been agonising over for months.

Paul had been preparing a press release that almost, but not quite, proclaimed the end of The Beatles. Behind closed doors, he'd also been setting wheels in motion for the formal dissolution of Messrs Harrison, Lennon, McCartney and Starkey as a business enterprise. Yet months before the writs were served, John had slipped a teasing "...when I was a Beatle" into an interview with *Disc*, and, feeling as little regret, had announced privately his own exit well before Paul – though this had been hushed up, mainly for fear of it cramping Allen Klein's bullying of Capitol.

Having said it at last, much of the tension of the preceding months had flowed from John Lennon. An unsettled chapter in his life had just ended. If a lot of his problems had been self-aggravated, it had been a stressful and demanding time that he wouldn't wish on anyone else. Now he could get on with the rest of his life. How could he have known then that he had only ten years left?

Moreover, having soundtracked the 1960s, he and the others wouldn't be able as solo stars and ex-Beatles to so minister to the next decade when all but the most snowblinded would understand how ordinary, even disagreeable, the mere mortals behind the myth could be. "George was the most normal and friendly of men," said Richard Reed, the architect who restored Harrison's newly purchased mansion in Henley-on-Thames. "He introduced me to John Lennon. He was shorter than I expected and not as pleasant as George. He just shook my hand and turned away."

In the wake of February 1970's echo-drenched 'Instant Karma' – recorded and mastered within a day of its composition – I discovered quite early on how yawnsome Lennon was becoming via an associated interview headlined "Shut Up And Listen!: The Thoughts Of Chairman John" in *Record Mirror*. What I could not articulate to myself then was that I was being tested by a horrified realisation of being unendurably bored by his pontifications about The Plastic Ono Band, his and Yoko's new short haircuts, his peace mission and an oscillating commitment to other worthy (or not) causes – the *Oz* trial, say, or the clearing of convicted murderer James Hanratty – he was espousing with varying degrees of pragmatism at the rate of roughly one a week.

Readers paid attention, however, because, even as 'Power To The People', his first 45 as a *bona fide* ex-Beatle, penetrated the UK Top 40 on 20 March 1971, somewhere in such discussions Lennon might fan the dull embers of The Beatles' future, which were becoming duller by the day. While clouds of litigation gathered, he and the others had been "tight, nervous, everyone watching everyone else", noticed the forgiving Cynthia, who, before her ostracism from that most innermost of 1960s in-crowds, was "at home" one afternoon for guests that included her increasingly distant Beatle pals and ex-husband.

Yet the illusion of reconciliation that was *Abbey Road* had tricked the general public into believing that The Beatles weren't over. Indeed, until well into the 1970s, not a week would pass without some twit or other asking John, George, Paul or Ringo when the four of them were going to get together again in the studio. It was seen as almost inevitable by even the most marginally hopeful outsider for whom the concept of collecting every record The Beatles ever made was not yet economically unsound. Thus an ex-Beatle was assured of at least a minor hit, even with substandard merchandise.

In 1976, when all four happened to be on the same land mass at the same time, they would be tempted to call the bluff of Lorne Michaels, producer of *Saturday Night Live* (a TV satire transmitted from New York), who said that, if they agreed to play together before his cameras for the prescribed Musicians' Union fee, he'd squeeze them onto the show. Depending on whose account you read, unfortunately – or, perhaps, not so unfortunately – Lennon and McCartney ordered a taxi, but decided they were too tired. Alternatively, Paul, Ringo and George arrived for the show, but John's chauffeur drove to the wrong studio, thereby capsizing what might have been the ultimate practical joke.

As things turned out, an eponymous *Ringo Starr* album of 1972 would be the nearest the living members would ever come to a reunion on disc, embracing as it did compositions and active participation by all four, albeit not at the same time. Lennon's main contribution, 'I'm The Greatest', came close as it featured himself, Starr and Harrison at Los Angeles' Sunset Sound Studio. McCartney had been amenable to pitching in too, but was refused a US visa owing to a recent conviction for possessing narcotics, which had been seized during a European tour with Wings, his new outfit, in which Linda fingered the keyboards.

That the Fab Four were theoretically together on the same piece of plastic was sufficient to feed fans' expectations that soon everything would be OK again, and The Beatles would regroup formally to tour and release the chart-toppers that John and Paul – all friends again – would be churning out once more.

Pressed on the subject, glam-rock overlord Gary Glitter hit the nail on the head: "They'll have to come back as a bigger creative force than before, which will be very difficult indeed." As difficult had been Muhammad Ali regaining his world heavyweight title in 1975. Possibly, The Beatles might have regained theirs, even though the world had become wiser to their individual weaknesses – and the fact that, after picking and choosing from both illustrious chums and the trendiest and most nonchalantly squeaky-clean studio musicians, none of them would ever accomplish what The Beatles, for all their casually strewn errors, had committed to tape instinctively and without complacency.

With their wealth now secure, John, Paul, George and Ringo were all above the tour-album-tour sandwiches incumbent upon poorer stars, and each could wait until he felt like going on the road again or making a new record. However, an unkempt-looking Lennon still took the trouble to plug 'Instant Karma' – a "live" vocal over a backing tape

– twice on *Top Of The Pops*, with that creepy Yoko next to him on a stool, either blindfolded and holding up her scrawled signs with "PEACE", "SMILE", "BREATHE" and other cryptadia on them, knitting a jumper, or mouthing silently into a microphone. Weird, eh?

Yet George Harrison, the former Beatle least addicted to the limelight, had been first off the starting line after sifting through a backlog of around 40 compositions for a new LP, a double, even a triple if he felt like it – which he did. This he titled *All Things Must Pass*, which was completed with more than a little help from an insufferably smug cabal of "heavy friends", "supersidemen" and Phil Spector, applying his spent "genius" to the console.

The first *All Things Must Pass* single, 'My Sweet Lord', sold millions, certainly more than 'Instant Karma', but both were reflective of a turn-of-the-decade fad for spirituality. Born-again fervour saw evangelical marches up high streets, the Bible on hip bookshelves, the Scriptures quoted at parties, and record deals for outfits like The Water-Into-Wine Band, from England's West Country, whose come-to-Jesus output was epitomised by 'Song Of The Cross', a 1971 album track that was quite moving in a *Ben Hur*-ish sort of way. On the other side of the same coin, Graham Bond led an early 1970s unit, Magick, which focused on his fascination with the occult and was as different from The Graham Bond Organisation, once the toast of London's mid-1960s in-clubs, as the Moon from the Earth.

The same comparison might be made between Lennon's first post-Beatles album and *Abbey Road*. Like its vinyl companion, *Yoko Ono/Plastic Ono Band, John Lennon/Plastic Ono Band* was the cathartic outcome of a course of Primal Scream therapy under Los Angeles psychologist Dr Arthur Janov. Its basic premise, that all neuroses stemmed from deprivation of parental love, enabled John to look up from the bottom of his 30-year-old pit and imagine that he saw a strip of blue sky with God peering over the edge. It wasn't Him but the good doctor who made a half-hearted attempt to film a sitting with the famous pop star for use, he said, in a documentary – presumably to rope in further well-heeled patients.

John would be smiled in and smiled out of such consultations, which overflowed with extravagant lamentations and, ideally, rejoicings too. All the pain John had been carrying since the departure of his father and the death of Julia was supposed to disappear like the sack of woe falling from Christian in *The Pilgrim's Progress*.

With the starkest instrumentation, and the exhilaration of the impromptu prized more than technical accuracy, the Primal Scream experience came to a head in the songs he'd written for *John Lennon/Plastic Ono Band*. There was also a point of contact with Sleepy John Estes, Lightnin' Hopkins and other black bluesmen who trafficked in individual visions of an immediate world, about which they strove to say enough without too much lingering intimacy or any of that "oh gawd!" tweeness that characterised Melanie, Nick Drake and any other precious post-Woodstock balladeer, seated singing to a guitar and beaming a small, sad smile every now and then.

John's personal exorcisms, like 'Mother' and 'Isolation', mingled with stark rejections of former heroes and ideals – notably in "God" – and 'Working Class Hero', an acoustic ballad that railed against the mysterious "they", and got itself banned from most daytime radio stations for its use of the f-word.

Ripe language and soul baring were apparent in Lennon's newspaper interviews too – as was the almost audible snigger whenever he sniped at McCartney. His old comrade was pilloried further in 'How Do You Sleep' from 1971's *Imagine*, though the two had still been on speaking terms, with John ringing Paul when the track was on point of release. By contrast, *Imagine* also contained paeans of uxorious bent (such as 'Oh Yoko!', 'Oh My Love' and the apologetic 'Jealous Guy') as well as a utopian title track, fairy-dusted with strings, that, for better or worse, was to endure as Lennon's most memorable post-Beatles opus.

'How Do You Sleep' had had George Harrison in support on lead guitar – and the month before the release of *Imagine* in September 1971, George was to invite John to participate in his "Concerts For Bangla Desh" in New York, but only on the understanding there'd be no place in the set for a number or two from Yoko as well. As the evil hour when her husband was actually going to perform without her crept closer, the humidity in New York thickened to what The Lovin' Spoonful had sung about in 'Summer In The City'. No breeze blew, and Yoko's forehead and upper lip was bestowed with pinpricks of sweat. It was weather that breeds maggots in dustbins and Ono's tantrum was so violent that, crushing his spectacles in his fist, John had slammed out of their hotel for the next flight back to Europe.

Harrison's giant step for Bangla Desh took place regardless and, in one throw, he outshone all the Lennons' more mystifying tactics to right the wrongs of mankind. Perhaps in a spirit of resentful competitiveness, John spoke briefly of a Wembley show for a worthy cause with him, Yoko and their sort of people instead of George and his crowd.

No time was better for Lennon to be charitable on such a scale. With *Imagine* soon to be at Number One in the States, no time was better either for him to make hay with a world tour too, but both ideas – if they were ever even considered seriously – had been jettisoned by the time he left his country of birth forever for the United States on 3 September 1971.

The first album – a double – from his "American period" was 1972's *Sometime In New York City*. He and Yoko were backed by Elephant's Memory, a local band fresh from a maiden Hot 100 strike. This joint venture also embraced excerpts from both the Lyceum extravaganza and a guest spot at the Fillmore East with Frank Zappa's Mothers Of Invention. Nevertheless, apart from the odd inspired moment, notably a driving revival of The Olympics' 'Well (Baby Please Don't Go)' with Zappa, the kindest critics agreed that *Sometime In New York City* was documentary rather than recreational.

The essence of it was slogan-ridden musical journalism that had less in common with 'John You Went Too Far This Time' than the likes of 'He's Gonna Step On You Again' and 'Tokoloshe Man', UK hit singles the previous year by John Kongos, a South African – and a *Wedding Album*-period John Lennon lookalike – who freighted his songs with uncompromising lyrics born of the socio-political situation back home.

The music was strong enough for Kongos to ride roughshod over the principal worry about topical ditties: what becomes of them when they are no longer topical or the topic becomes tedious? That's how it was with John and Yoko's statements about the National Guard shooting rioting convicts in an upstate "correctional facility" ('Attica State'); a bloke receiving a ten-year gaol sentence for possession of an inappreciable amount of dope ('John Sinclair'); the troubles in Northern Ireland ('Sunday Bloody Sunday', 'The Luck Of The Irish'); and further current – and, generally, very North American – events and scandals.

Lennon was the central figure of one such *cause célèbre* himself. Though respected – or at least patronised – by powerful allies, his attempts to settle on US soil were hindered by, purportedly, ceaseless official harassment provoked by anti-government sentiments on *Sometime In New York City*, and his and Yoko's active part – an acoustic set – in a concert-*cum*-political rally in Ann Arbor, Michigan, on 10 December 1971 on behalf of marijuana miscreant John Sinclair, who was freed three days later.

The following August, the Lennons hosted a bigger spectacular, *One To One*, at Madison Square Garden for a children's charity, but that didn't serve as *quid pro quo* for the quashing of John's "moral turpitude" offence back in 1968. How can we ever know whether his splendid *One To One* effort – and a personal donation of $60,000 on top of the nigh-on $2 million raised – was prompted by a simple desire to help or an ulterior motive? It was the same equation as those pop stars who pranced before the world at Live Aid in 1984.

Whatever the reason, it wouldn't wash with the US Immigration Department. This meant that John still had to keep reapplying for an extension of his visa to stay in the USA.

For all *Sometime In New York City*'s display of marital and artistic unity, the deportation notice that hung like a sword of Damocles over Lennon was among factors that were causing trouble in his marriage – so much trouble that he left Yoko in New York in 1973 for a 15-month "lost weekend" in California, where he lived with May Pang, her Chinese secretary, in a well-appointed ocean-side chalet, once owned by the Kennedys, in Santa Monica beneath the woodland sweep of the Hollywood hills. The place was open house for his circle of friends and friends of friends as well as callers like Alice Cooper, once and future Monkee Mickey Dolenz – and Paul McCartney.

Far more permanent a guest was Harry Nilsson, whose pop-star mystique had accumulated since *Aerial Ballet*, owing to out-of-focus publicity photographs and a reluctance to be interviewed. In 1971, he'd enjoyed a major international breakthrough (if mixed reviews) with *Nilsson Schmilsson*, recorded in London in June with help from famous mates. This contained three hit 45s, 'Without You', 'Coconut' and 'Jump Into The Fire'. He liked England enough to live there for a while, dwelling in the exclusive metropolitan flat where John and Yoko had holed up during the divorce from Cynthia – and where Keith Moon was to die. Some 50 old folk from a nearby Darby and Joan club would be featured as the choir on 'I'd Rather Be Dead' on *Son Of Schmilsson*, which, Nilsson's commercial tide-mark, brought another US Top 30 single, 'Spaceman'. The album was promoted in Britain via *Nilsson In Concert*, which, on the proviso that there would be no studio audience, was taped and shown on BBC2 – along with *The Point* – on New Year's Day 1972.

He failed to consolidate his success owing to an unsound decision to record *A Little Touch Of Schmilsson In The Night*, an album – possibly satirical – of orchestrated standards like 'Over The Rainbow', 'Makin' Whoopee' and 'As Time Goes By'. Produced by Derek Taylor, rejected tracks included 'Auld Lang Syne', 'I'm Always Chasing Rainbows' and 'Hey Jude'.

Nilsson also overhauled selections from his first two LPs as *Aerial Pandemonium Ballet*. I dare say it's heresy to say so to those in a 1960s repetend, but in nearly every case, it was a change for the better. Yet, however much his critical standing had, on balance, improved, Nilsson's marriage, like John Lennon's, was failing. In much the same boat, Ringo Starr also strung along with John and Harry for three-in-the-morning bar-hopping followed by late-afternoon mutual grogginess by the Santa Monica swimming pool. Joining in the fun too was Keith Moon, The Who's chief show-off, whose buffoonery would often deteriorate into a nonsensical frenzy and, eventually, it would make headlines: explosives in hotel suites, slashing his wrists at the drop of a hat, and applying a lighter to his £150 pay packet for a day's film work (in days when £150 was worth something).

After accidentally running over and killing his chauffeur in 1970, Keith began punishing up to four decanters of spirits a day. More likely to fling a bottle at a television screen as rise from the armchair to switch it off, his fee for his last UK tour with The Who would be a paltry £40 on subtracting compensation for damage he'd inflicted along the way.

The gang and its hangers-on were regular frequenters of topless bars, and were prone to gatecrashing parties and kerb-crawling. As dilettantish in their way were projects like Nilsson's slovenly *Pussycats*, which got underway simply because he, his Irish girlfriend, Lennon and May Pang "were sitting around with nothing to do, so we said, 'Let's do an album.'" With Starr, Moon and all the usual shower, he and producer John wrapped up *Pussycats* in New York after the sessions in Los Angeles had collapsed in a fog of drug abuse, which was discernible on a record that veered fitfully from long, leaden melodies to strident but oddly flat cracks at such as Dylan's 'Subterranean Homesick Blues' and a 'Rock Around The Clock', which was "speedy" in every sense of the word.

On the swift follow-up, *God's Greatest Hits* (retitled *Duit On Mon Dei* to placate the record company), Nilsson and his accomplices were also audibly half-seas over in an assortment of sub-'Without You' *Lieder* and unfunny gabblings on such as 'Good For God' and other perpetuations of an arrogance that encapsulated at its most loathsome the self-destructive disdain of the "superstar" for the record-buying public.

Further endeavours to stay the phantoms of middle age included John's excessively worshipful and inebriated audience with Jerry Lee Lewis – whose own over-indulgence, brushes with the law and extreme domestic ructions had only enhanced the legend.

More widely reported was Lennon's ejection on 12 March 1974 – two years to the day after his US visa was revoked – from west Los Angeles' Troubadour, where, whilst drinking heavily, he had been constantly interrupting a show by The Smothers Brothers with interjections that included swearing and a recurrent "I'm John Lennon!" There were also allegations that he had assaulted both the comedy duo's manager and – with a sanitary towel attached to his forehead – one of the night club's waitresses, who was to file a complaint against him to the city's district attorney. Once outside the building, Lennon instigated another scuffle with a waiting photographer.

John managed to keep a civil tongue in his head the following night, when he and May Pang attended an American Film Institute dinner in honour of James Cagney, and a few weeks later, when he got together with Paul McCartney for a chat in the light of appeals from the United Nations for them, Ringo and George to do their bit for the Vietnamese boat people. There'd also been someone with more money than sense who was ready to shell out $50 million for just one more Beatles performance, even if there was a danger that what he'd hear might not be magic, just music.

Lennon was then in the throes of producing *Pussycats* at Los Angeles' suburban Burbank Studios, whilst taping demos back at Santa Monica. "We picked songs off the top of our heads and just did them," he shrugged. This strategy was very much in force when McCartney, staying at the Beverly Hilton Hotel, looked in – with Linda – at what were becoming fiascos at Burbank on Thursday 28 March 1974. Paul helped in trying to salvage an arrangement of 'Midnight Special', which was once in The Quarry Men's skiffle repertoire, and was invited to a musical evening the following Sunday at Lennon's house.

Present too would be Nilsson, guitarist Jesse Ed Davis –
Eric Clapton's understudy at the "Concerts For Bangla Desh"
– "supersideman" saxophonist Bobby Keyes and blind singing
multi-instrumentalist Stevie Wonder, Tamla Motown's
cosseted former child star, who'd notched up his first US hit,
'Fingertips', in 1963. He'd been on the bill with Lennon for
both the John Sinclair benefit and the *One To One* concert.

As there were so many distinguished participants at Santa
Monica, it was decided to keep a tape rolling for posterity –
and the inevitable bootlegs – on equipment borrowed from
Burbank. With McCartney choosing to beat the drums, they
cranked out an interminable quasi-reggae version of Ben E
King's much-covered 'Stand By Me', a slow and raucous
'Lucille' and, with Wonder to the fore, a medley of Sam
Cooke's 'Cupid' and 'Chain Gang'.

These were punctuated by various meanderings during
which were heard the intermittent strains of Bobby Byrd's
'Little Bitty Pretty One' – revived two years earlier by The
Jackson Five – and, beneath, improvised lyrics by Paul, Santo
and Johnny's 'Sleepwalk' instrumental from 1959, as well as
blues-derived chord cycles over which Lennon, who
bellyached throughout about the low volume of his voice in
the headphones, kicked off an extrapolation that touched on
his immigration woes.

None of the sung or spoken dialogue was anywhere as
entertaining as that on the fêted "Troggs Tape" (an illicit
recording of a cross purposes studio discussion riddled with

rude words) and, musically, the clouds parting on the gods at play over in California revealed nothing more remarkable than what you might hear whenever any idle session crew warms up with loose jamming not intended for public ears.

Regardless of quality, however, it – and 'Midnight Special' at Burbank – amounted to a Lennon and McCartney reunion of sorts, though it wasn't the harbinger of any permanent amalgamation. Yet, if time hadn't healed, there lingered still memories of the struggle back in Liverpool and its unbelievable consequence. McCartney let slip that he wouldn't mind working with Lennon again on a less casual basis, while John was now saying how wrong it had been for the group to have split so decisively.

What's more, though the lines drawn over Allen Klein were among reasons for it, all the ex-Beatles were now of the same mind about one who'd overseen the solo careers of Lennon, Harrison and Starr until 1973, believing as they did now provocative tales – not all of them true – by their friends and various of Klein's incensed former clients of shifty manoeuvres and artful transfer of cash into his own account, passed off later by Keith Richards as "the price of an education".

Klein was, nevertheless, not as greedy as he might have been – on paper anyway. Compared to some of his peers, who'd made themselves entitled to over half of everything their artists earned, the Robin Hood of Pop took but a fifth of what he'd actually secured. Yet, John, George and Ringo unravelled enough supposed evidence of "excessive commissions" from Klein's mazy balance sheets to justify a court case. While administrative matters were being resolved, Lennon, McCartney, Harrison and Starr's very vacillation over a reunion in the studio and, less likely, on the boards, indicated neither destitution nor any real enthusiasm. John and Ringo went back to the woozy vortex of Santa Monica, Paul to Wings and the simple life on his Sussex farm, and George to an ill-judged North American tour.

John and George had nattered affably enough at one post-concert party. At another, however, everything turned red as hell for Harrison, and he saw himself rounding on Lennon and the flat of his hand shooting out in an arc to make glancing contact with John's spectacles. These clacked onto the ground and, while John was grubbing for them, George was loud enough to be heard in Liverpool. The subsequent tongue-lashing streamlined what had become, in Lennon's estimation, "a love-hate relationship of a younger follower and older guy. I think George still bears resentment towards me for being a daddy who left home." This time, the "hate" sprang specifically from John's procrastination over signing some papers relating to The Beatles – and that John hadn't taken up an open invitation to join George on stage one night during the troubled tour to do a turn as a surprise treat for the fans. No more the tough guy that he'd never been, Lennon "saw George going through pain – and I know what pain is – so I let him do it".

The hatchet was never quite buried, and, as the months turned into years, only infrequent postcards filtered between Harrison and Lennon. Other than that, they knew each other only via hearsay and stray paragraphs in the press – and John was to be wounded by the "glaring omissions" of him from George's pricey autobiography, *I Me Mine*.

This volume was published early in 1980 when a musical, *Beatlemania*, shattered box-office records in London's West End and a sign appeared outside Mendips – from which Aunt Mimi had long gone – reading "OFFICIAL NOTICE. PRIVATE. NO ADMISSION. MERSEYSIDE COUNTY COUNCIL" for the benefit of foreign visitors, mostly from the USA and Japan, pouring huge amounts into the English Tourist Board's coffers for conducted treks round Liverpool to such shrines.

By 1980 too, Beatles conventions had become annual fixtures in cities across the globe, complete with guest speakers, archive film and forums for fans to reveal "My Beatles Experiences" as well as trivia quizzes, "celebrity" discussion panels, showings of ancient film footage, sound-alike contests and continual community singing to acoustic guitars. Life-size displays of LP covers might enable you to "be photographed with the Boys", and a mock-up of Abbey Road studio plus 40 pre-recorded Xeroxes of Beatle backing tracks may cater for less tangible fantasies. Along a single corridor at one such extravaganza, I passed a Cynthia Lennon lookalike, a high-buttoned moptop and a *Sgt Pepper* bandsman.

All the major conventions hire groups that are, if anything, even more contrived than Los Shakers, The Beatlettes, The Monkees et al, with their big-nosed drummers, moon-faced bass players; handles like "Walrus", "Cavern", "The Blue Meanies", "Abbey Road" and "The Beetle Brothers"; and *raisons d'être* centred on impersonating the founders of the feast, note for note, word for word, mannerism for mannerism. On a global scale, the most famous are The Bootleg Beatles, formed from the cast of *Beatlemania*. Maybe the most accurate copycats anywhere, they cover every phase, from the coming of Ringo to the end of the Swinging Sixties, via cleverly co-ordinated costume changes.

While the ex-Beatles themselves have proffered saleable artefacts for charity auctions at these events, none – bar Pete Best – has ever attended one. Instead, "special guests" have been drawn from old colleagues, former employees – and, scraping the barrel, authors of Beatle biographies. A typical example is Sam Leach, an unsung hero of Merseybeat when compared to the Brian Epsteins and Bill Harrys of this world. However, as perhaps the era's most adventurous promoter – the one responsible for John, Paul, George and Pete's terrible journey to Aldershot – Sam cut a popular figure at a 1992 convention in Chicago. The Yanks couldn't get enough of him retelling anecdotes from the old days in his lush wacker dialect, and presenting well-argued theories about the Liverpool beat explosion and its aftermath, whether on the podium in the ballroom or whilst signing books and posters at his stall in a memorabilia fleamarket, which dwarfed any in Britain, even Liverpool's *Merseybeatle* weekend.

Customers covered a waterfront from babes-in-arms to pensioners, but mostly young marrieds disenfranchised by post-*Abbey Road* pop and older individuals who once might have been part of a screaming mass as amorphous as frogspawn at this or that stop on a Beatles US tour. Since then, they'd settled into jobs and parenthood – but while 'She Loves You' or 'I Feel Fine' yet spins its little life away, balding Weybridge stockbrokers and face-lifted Minneapolis hairdressers will become irresponsible Swinging Sixties teenagers again.

Nothing by The Beatles had ever been deleted, and because EMI/Capitol still owned the master tapes, it had been able to run riot with posthumous million-selling double albums like the all up-tempo *Rock 'n' Roll Music*, which, in the States, spawned a smash 45 in 'Got To Get You Into My Life', culled from *Revolver*. Meanwhile, Britain experienced the chart-swamping aftermath of 20 Beatles singles being repromoted on the same spring day in 1976, almost a quarter of a century after 'Love Me Do'. Perusing the UK Top 40, a correspondent from *Time* magazine enquired rhetorically, "Has a successor to The Beatles finally been found? Not at all – it is The Beatles themselves."

12 "Who'd Want To Be An 80-Year-Old Beatle?"

The worst aspects of Beatles idolatry are likely to be represented forever by the homicidal Mark David Chapman – but, as Bob Dylan reminds us in 'The Times They Are A-Changin'', we shouldn't criticise what we can't understand. When John, Paul, George and Ringo landed in New York in 1964, Chapman was eight and living with his parents and younger sister in Atlanta, Georgia.

He compiled the first of many scrapbooks that kept track of The Beatles' ever-unfolding career. By the time Mark's voice broke, every nook and cranny of his bedroom was crammed with Beatles' merchandise: pictures of them all over the walls, and piles of records with label variations, foreign picture sleeves and the canons of associated artists: the Word made vinyl in the comfort of his own home. His function then was to remain uninvolved directly, just to absorb the signals as they came.

For hundreds, thousands of hours, he'd file, catalogue and gloat over his acquisitions, finding much to notice, study and compare. Should you express polite interest, Mark would probably explain apologetically that nobody got to *look* at it, much less *hear* it. The Beatles wasn't about enjoyment any more, but being addicted as surely as someone else can be to heroin. Wanting to learn everything about them, no piece of information was too insignificant to be less than totally absorbing. Mark could dwell eloquently and with authority on his interest, but couldn't grasp why fellow pupils at Columbia High School were not as captivated. The ones kind enough not to look fed up regarded the pudgy youth in round John Lennon glasses as otherwise "just a real quiet, normal guy". Descriptions of him by others ranged from "slightly eccentric" to "a creeping Jesus", but Mark had taken his Beatles' fixation too far now to care any more than a chimp in the zoo does about what the people looking through the bars think.

When he graduated in 1973, the Fat Owl of Columbia High had experienced both LSD and, fleetingly, the glory and the stupidity of being in a pop group. In keeping with a mood of the early 1970s, he was now a born-again Christian. Two years later, Mark was working with Vietnamese refugees in Arkansas, pleasing his superiors with his diligence and aptitude for onerous tasks. Through the love of a good woman, he was contemplating enrolling at a theological college. No longer outwardly living his life through The Beatles, it was the nearest he'd ever come to contentment.

Mark Chapman's future victim, however, was in a bad state. Flitting between California and New York, John Lennon had grown fatter, if less publicly ridiculous. Glassy-eyed musings and vocational turbulence also slopped over onto albums such as *Pussycats* and Ringo's *Goodnight Vienna* – with a title track by John Lennon. Because both he and Ringo were enthusiastic listeners to Johnny Winter, a boss-eyed and albino Texan bluesman who had been catapulted from regional celebrity to the front page of *Rolling Stone*, Lennon contributed 'Rock 'n' Roll People' for 1974's *John Dawson Winter* album. This was a delayed reaction to a captivation with 1969's Grammy winning 'The Thrill Is Gone,' the only mainstream pop hit by BB King, one of the few surviving links between post-war blues and mid-1970s rock.

John's own *Mind Games* in 1973, however, was as so-so as *Goodnight Vienna*; yet *Walls And Bridges*, if rehashing some old ideas, still effused potent singles in ethereal 'Number Nine Dream' – which, as usual, climbed far higher in North American charts than anywhere else – and, also in 1974, the US Number One 'Whatever Gets You Thru The Night'. This was recorded with help from Elton John, a now famous singing pianist, who had first become known to Lennon when Xeroxing the hits of others for EMI's *Music For Pleasure* budget label (to which *Mind Games* was to be consigned one day) before metamorphosing into a cross between Liberace and a male Edna Everage.

Another British star omnipresent in the States then was David Bowie, no longer a glam rocker, but touring as a blue-eyed soul man, a fair indication of the direction he was to pursue on his forthcoming *Young Americans* album. It was through this that John Lennon made his most iconoclastic contribution to 1970s popular culture. As his "lost weekend" approached its Sunday evensong, he'd been invited to a Bowie session for a resuscitation of 'Across The Universe' – from *Let It Be* – in New York. There, he ended up co-writing 'Fame', *Young Americans'* infectious US chart topper, with David and an awe-struck Carlos Alomar, a highly waged guitarist of urgent precision and inventiveness. This and his apprenticeship in James Brown's employ qualified him for the house band at the trend-setting Sigma Sound complex, from which had emanated Philadelphia's feathery soul style earlier in the decade.

All three writers of 'Fame' were present at a Grammy awards ceremony at the Uris Hotel in New York on 1 March 1975. John was sporting a lapel badge that read "ELVIS" – who, back on the concert platform, displayed ardour for little but the most conservative post-Beatles pop. Moreover, in an amazing and ramblingly respectful letter to President Nixon, he had requested enrolment as a federal agent in order to fight "the Hippie Element".

Unconscious of his boyhood hero's reactionary tendencies, John Lennon – who evidently typified all that he detested – was seen at one of a dismayingly portly

Memphis Flash's grandiloquent pageants at 20,000-capacity Madison Square Garden, where the King included songs that had fuelled the ex-Beatle's adolescent imaginings – plus bursts of patriotism like 'American Trilogy' and just plain 'America'. The last that John, like most people, would ever see of him would be in the white garb of a rhinestone cowboy *sans* stetson.

As regressive in its way as seeing Presley was Lennon's growing collection of Beatles bootlegs – dating as far back as rehearsals in early 1960 with Paul, George and Stuart – and recording 1975's non-original *Rock 'n' Roll*, its content telegraphed on the sleeve by a photograph of 1961 Hamburg vintage and the artist's own sentiment: "You should have been there".

Its spin-off single – which rose to Number 20 in the States, 30 in Britain – was another stab at 'Stand By Me'. Viewers of BBC 2's *Old Grey Whistle Test* on 18 April 1975 were treated to an *in situ* film of Lennon at the microphone in New York's Record Plant, delivering both an exaggerated broad wink at the camera and 'Stand By Me' with its curiously stentorian vocal. Neither were very appealing.

Having gone full-cycle professionally with this plus other favourites that The Beatles may or may not have performed in the Hamburg era, and a greatest hits collection entitled *Shaved Fish*, Lennon chose to take a year off to master his inner chaos and take professional and personal stock. At a press conference back in 1964, he'd answered a question about retirement with a rhetorical "Who'd want to be an 80-year-old Beatle?" Well, he was nearly halfway there now.

Reunited with Yoko, John was finally granted US residential status. His and his wife's happiness was completed by the arrival of their only surviving baby, Sean, by caesarian section on John's 35th birthday. The very proud father judged this to be an appropriate moment to extend the "year off" indefinitely to become Yoko's quasi-incommunicado "house husband" in the apartments they'd purchased in New York's snooty Dakota block. This retreat was, he felt, the "karmic reaction" to the holocaust of pop, summed up by his much-quoted, "Don't bother trying to make it, because when you do there's nothing to make".

Besides, the gang had broken up long ago. Having gained no contentment from following John and Ringo to California, Mal Evans's slaughter on 5 January 1976 by gun-toting police – after a woman alleged he'd threatened her with what turned out to be an air-pistol – was said by some to have been a form of suicide.

While Mal's extinction was unexpected, few were caught unawares entirely on 7 September 1978 by Keith Moon's body's final rebellion after a lifetime of violation. As he drifted away on the tide of twice the recognised lethal intake of a potion to combat his alcoholism, his last utterance was to tell his girlfriend to get lost.

However, with remarriage and the birth of his eldest son, Harry Nilsson – as heavy a drinker as Moon – was perhaps the first of the Santa Monica clique to pull back from the abyss. He continued to grind out one album per year until the RCA contract expired. On 1980's *Flash Harry*, he was to mobilise illustrious contemporaries again, among them John Lennon – though their friendship had cooled because he was regarded by then as the proverbial "bad influence" by Yoko. Indeed, he passed much of the next decade jet-setting whilst nursing debilities not unrelated to the stimulants that had been common currency amongst the "superstar" elite in the 1970s.

A proposed 1993 album contained a revival of The Platters' 'Only You' – a rediscovered duet with Lennon, *circa* 1974 – and a huge helping of comic songs. Now dried out, Nilsson was making the most of whatever new opportunities came his way whilst looking forward to the past as a regular speaker at Beatle conventions where, before his death in 1994, he engaged in question-and-answer sessions and, surprisingly for one once well known for never singing in public, even performed a couple of numbers on stage.

Meanwhile, Lennon had elected not so much to settle cosily into middle age on the consolidated fruits of his success, but to find out what else awaited him on the other side of the Santa Monica interlude, when he'd been unable to make long-term plans. Whatever was wrong appeared to be righting itself. The intolerable adulation, the smash hits, the money down the drain could be transformed to matters of minor importance compared to the peaceful life he felt he deserved, the potential for domestic stability, and providing young Sean with the best of everything, especially more paternal attention than most – certainly far more than John ever had.

It was enough as well to be on the way to tolerable health after all the physical and mental vicissitudes his 35 unquiet years had sustained. In the title track to a 1979 album, *Rust Never Sleeps*, Neil Young, an *après*-Woodstock bedsit bard, was to whinge lines like "It's better to burn out than to fade away", which seemed to laud the banal live-fast-die-young philosophy involuntarily played out by Jimi Hendrix, Jim Morrison, Janis Joplin, Keith Moon, Sid Vicious and like unfortunates chewed upon and spat out by the pop industry. "For what?" inquired John during one of his last interviews. "So that we might rock? If Neil Young admires that sentiment so much, why doesn't he do it?"

Every day he still lived was a bonus now that John Lennon had let go, stopped trying to prove himself – though if he had abandoned the world, the world hadn't abandoned him, not while his work was kept before the public via, say, The Damned's high-velocity overhaul of 'Help!' in 1976, or a revival of 'Working Class Hero' by Marianne Faithfull in a voice grippingly bereft of any former soprano purity on 1979's *Broken English*, an album that was as much a fixture in student halls of residence in the late '70s as a poster of Che Guevara's mug had been years earlier.

A centre-page *NME* article pleaded for if not a full-time return, then Lennon's blessing on the burgeoning punk movement, but it elicited no immediate response from one no longer preoccupied with cooking up marketable food of love and sprinkling it with cheap insight. Nothing from John Lennon, not even another repackaging, would show its face in the charts from a belated appearance of 'Imagine' in the UK Top Ten in November 1975 until '(Just Like) Starting Over' in November 1980. Neither would a solitary new melody or lyric be heard commercially from him after 'Cookin' (In The Kitchen Of Love)', a self-satisfied donation to Ringo's *Rotogravure* in 1976. What right had anyone to expect more? He said as much in a brief and reluctantly granted press conference in Japan a year later.

Lennon's was almost as sweeping an exit from public life as that of the great Belgian chansonnier Jacques Brel, who chose to "stop once and for all this idiotic game" – in 1975 too – by fleeing to the last bolt-hole his fans and the media would expect to find him, namely the remote Pacific island where the painter Paul Gauguin had lived out his last years.

Brel and Lennon weren't the only ones to fling it all back in their faces. The *ultima Thule* of pop hermits is Syd Barrett, whose departure from The Pink Floyd in 1968 was on a par with John Lennon, unable to cope with being a Beatle after 'From Me To You', scurrying back to Woolton to dwell in seclusion with Aunt Mimi, or – as actually happened – Chris Curtis washing his hands of The Searchers in 1966 for the security of the civil service.

Self-deception, genuine belief and the balm of ignorance become jumbled as such a recluse's enigma deepens. A legend takes shape, bringing out the strangest yarns.

Thus it was that, in the teeth of a possibly dull truth, John Lennon continued to fascinate the English-speaking pop world as much as Brel did the Gallic one. Mention of Lennon during his so-called "house husband" years still brings out strange tales of what alleged "insiders" claim they heard and saw.

The mildest of these were that he had albums of The Goons on instant replay, and that he was also "into" new age, the only wave of essentially instrumental music to have reached a mass public since jazz rock in the mid-1970s. You hear it today in hip dental surgeries. Is it merely aural wallpaper or low-stress "music for the whole body" to ease the ravages of modern life? Do you buy it with the same discrimination as you would three pounds of spuds?

A wholesome diet figured prominently in Lennon's new life too. When filling in the *NME*'s "Lifelines" questionnaire early in 1963, George, Paul and Ringo had all chosen chicken, lamb and steak cuisine as their favourite foods while John went for non-committal "curry and jelly". He had acquired such a comparatively exotic taste via Pete Best's Indian mother and, later, in a Britain where most restaurants that served a late-night square meal were Indian or Chinese. Otherwise, during that year's travelling life of snatched and irregular meals. On the run around the world that followed, gourmet dishes with specious names – *trepang* soup, veal Hawaii, *furst puckler* – pampered stomachs yearning for the greasy comfort of cod and chips eaten with the fingers.

Nevertheless, after the decision to quit touring, Lennon was the first, apparently, to at least try a meat-free diet – though Cynthia and Julian didn't then. Later, he backslid, justifying himself in 1980 with "We're mostly macrobiotic – fish and rice and whole grains – but sometimes I bring the family out for a pizza. Intuition tells you what to eat." Nowadays, he was studying cookery books and baking bread, monitoring Sean's meals with a detail that dictated how many times each bite was to be masticated, and undergoing long fasts when only mineral water and fruit and vegetable juices entered his mouth.

A story leaked out later that he was also swallowing temazepam-like relaxants. Among the side-effects were stream-of-consciousness monologues, directed as much to himself as anyone listening, and mood swings from I'm-a-dirty-dog self-reproach to rhapsodies of peculiar exaltation. Straight up. A mate of mine told me.

By thus internalising, was John Lennon running away from himself in a place where, in his heart of hearts, he didn't want to be? What seems to be true is that, encouraged by his wife, he began spending lonely holidays progressively further afield – Bermuda, Cape Town, Hong Kong, anywhere that was the opposite of the Dakota, where life with Yoko wasn't exactly Phyllis and Corydon in Arcady.

Yoko had become quite the astute business person, ably representing John at Beatles business meetings and investing particularly wisely in properties and agriculture. What he called "work" was attempting to write a third book – "about 200 pages of *In His Own Write*-ish mad stuff" – and now and then tuning his acoustic guitar after breakfast. After strumming and picking for a while, all the fragments of music he was struggling to turn into a composition would sound flat. Then his fingers would start barré-ing the old, old chord changes from when the world was young. Languor would set in and he'd let out an involuntary sigh.

When his former songwriting partner, six-string in hand, attempted to visit the Dakota one day, Paul McCartney was sent away by a harassed John via an intercom message: "Please call before you come over. It's not 1956, and turning up at the door isn't the same any more. You know, just give me a ring." Neither could Lennon bring himself so much as to put his head round the door when McCartney, with Harrison and Starr, met Yoko in the same building to discuss further the division of the empire. Yet belying a growing legend of Lennon as "The Howard Hughes of Pop", both Mike McCartney – Paul's brother – and Gerry Marsden were able to reach him.

"I didn't see John for many years when he was in the States," reminisced Gerry, "or hear much about him other than what I read in the papers. Then once when I was appearing in New York, I called him after a gap of nearly a decade of not communicating, and it was just as if the days of the Seamen's Mission in Hamburg hadn't gone." Moreover, a chance encounter with Lennon in some Bermudan watering-hole caused one journalist to report that not only did the myth-shrouded John stand his round but that his songwriting well wasn't as dry as many imagined. This was confirmed in August 1980, when he and Ono recorded sufficient new material to fill two albums.

The first of these, *Double Fantasy* – which could almost be filed under "Easy Listening" – was issued that autumn, when, from Rip Van Winkle-esque vocational slumber, a fit-looking 40-year-old was suddenly available for interviews again with the unblinking self-assurance of old. He was even talking about a return to the stage.

Some of the faithful might have preferred John's to remain an ever-silent "no return" saga rather than him perhaps trying and failing to debunk the myth of an artistic death. However much they might have gainsaid it, they didn't want a comeback from someone who would thrive on goodwill with a side-serving of morbid inquisitiveness, a Judy Garland among Swinging Sixties pop heroes. Let's keep the memory of a jewellery-rattling 'Twist And Shout' at the Royal Command Performance and a bow-legged profile defined by an *Ed Sullivan Show* arc light. Otherwise, the sweet mystery will rest in pieces.

It appeared, however, that John Lennon meant business, and maybe, like his pal Elton John, was set to enter middle life as a fully integrated mainstay and wanted party guest of contemporary rock's ruling class. Though May Pang was to maintain that most of the "new" material had been written long before, he seemed rejuvenated as a composer too, as there were plenty of numbers left from both the two albums and stark demos of songs – like 'Free As A Bird' and 'Real Love' – which he'd taped as far back as 1975. There were, indeed, enough for him to present 'Life Begins At 40' and three more to Ringo when, in November 1980, the two ex-Beatles spoke for the last time, and parted as good friends.

John Lennon and Mark Chapman were more than good friends – at least, in Mark's mind. Something enormous if perverse had taken place, possibly as a sublimation of the depression brought on by parting with his girlfriend, an unhappy espousal on the rebound, his parents' divorce and a general psychological malaise.

With everything else in his life now stripped away, the old Beatles craving had reared up with a vengeance. This time around, however, Mark was perceiving directives from them – to the degree that he was certain that he'd been sent a telepathic message from John. "I know you and you know me," it read. "We understand each other in a secret way." They had become as one.

Chapman was, therefore, no longer someone not far removed from a rabid supporter of a football team. He had evolved too strong a need to affiliate himself to a world of fantasy from which he would never emerge unless he received regular psychiatric monitoring, even residential care – which, in a manner of speaking, he would do, albeit too late.

During the autumn preceding that eerie Christmas in 1980, Mark David decided that the chief Beatle's control of his life could not remain remote, hence, he finished his last shift as a security guard in Hawaii – signing off as "John Lennon" – and appeared in New York as if from nowhere early in December. The needle was in a big haystack, but it was the right haystack.

He was in high spirits, despite the body pressure and the chatter when being jolted from the airport by internal railway to the city centre. It was a moment of quiet joy when he stood at last outside the Dakota, looking upwards, paying muttered homage and wondering what was busying those rooms at that very minute. For hours daily, he stood on that pavement with all his soul in his eyes, totally desensitised to the stares of passers-by as he continued to gaze at what he could make out of outlines that seemed to dart across the Dakota's windows. He felt endlessly patient and vaguely enchanted that his vigil might last forever.

Then something incredible happened! Twilight was falling on Monday 8 December when John – with Yoko – strolled out of the building. Of the few pop stars Mark had ever seen close up, nearly every one had disappointed him. Bob Dylan, for example, had looked like someone who looked a bit like Bob Dylan. However, for all the sunken cheeks and expected ravages of middle age, the person who was crossing the sidewalk, with a slightly pigeon-toed gait and hair frisking in the cold breeze, was 100 per cent John Lennon. The Quarry

Bank school tie he'd taken to wearing in recent photographs wasn't in evidence, but he wasn't that much different from the way he'd appeared in "The Beatnik Horror!".

What do you say when you meet God?

Mark did not assume an instant intimacy with one who'd opened a door to his psyche, even though no one knew Lennon like he did. For a split-second, John stared at Mark, almost with dislike, as if he resented his adoration. Obviously, he was suffering from shock and could not grasp the magnitude of the encounter. Then, in one soundless moment, that adoration was extinguished like a moth in a furnace. After assuming that all he had to do was autograph another copy of *Double Fantasy* – "Is that OK? Is that what you want?" – John Lennon sort of smirked.

That was all. It came and went in the blink of an eye. Yet in that instant, Mark saw a stranger. Had they always been strangers? Had there never been anything special between them in the first place? Lord, I believe: help thou my unbelief. But that was when the being Chapman had worshipped for three decades mutated before him into just The Man Who Used To Be John Lennon.

He sauntered off, and Hell's magnet began to drag Mark David Chapman down. Before the day was done, Mark would be standing on the same spot with a smoking revolver in his hand. Yards away, The Man Who Used To Be John Lennon would be grovelling and open-mouthed with his life's blood puddling out of him.

13 "The Look Of Fated Youth"

In common with everyone else who cared, Gerry Marsden remembers the very moment he received the news. In his house on the Wirral, he was wrenched from sleep at 5am that mind-boggling Tuesday by a call from Liverpool's Radio City. With phlegmatic detachment, Gerry "went back to sleep. It wasn't the kind of information I expected to turn out to be true."

When the world woke up, John Lennon had not recovered from being dead. His slaying had sparked off suicides by mid-morning, and conspiracy theories were flying up and down when flags were still at half mast and the wireless was broadcasting the dead man's music continuously in place of listed programmes. Was it an Art Statement more surreal than anything John and Yoko did post-*Two Virgins*? Was John cursed with "the look of fated youth", as suggested in a *Daily Express* editorial?

How about a rite by which the kingdom of the "Beatle generation", now with paunches and punk children, was rejuvenated by the sacrifice of its leader – well, one of them – in his prime? It said as much in *The Golden Bough*, and it was visible on general release in *The Wicker Man*, a 1973 B-feature that Lennon – and Mark David Chapman – may well have seen, in which a far-flung Scottish island reverts to pagan ways in hope of rich harvests.

For all the mystical, arty – and political – analogies that went the rounds, most people reckoned that John Lennon had been killed simply because Chapman, who'd also been sighted sniffing around Bob Dylan, was as nutty as a fruitcake – though he was to be confined not to a mental institution but gaol after he pleaded guilty, saying in effect, "I insist on being incarcerated for at least the next 20 years."

In New York's Attica Correctional Facility – the setting of Lennon's 'Attica State' from *Sometime In New York City* – Mark served his sentence, spending most of it separated from other prisoners for the sake of his own safety, particularly when he seemed to be becoming something of a celebrity as the focal point of a video documentary and numerous magazine features.

However, eligible for parole again, an apparently remorseful and rehabilitated Chapman is, if freed, likely to become, advisedly, as reclusive as his victim was during the "house husband years". In prison, he'd refused written requests for autographs, remarking, "This tells you something is truly sick in our society. I didn't kill John to become famous, and I'm horrified by these people."

When Mark Chapman first began amassing this supposedly unlooked-for immortality, John's side of the tragedy had bequeathed unto *Double Fantasy* and its follow-up, *Milk And Honey*, an undeserved "beautiful sadness" – with particular reference to tender 'Beautiful Boy', which told five-year-old Sean Lennon of "what happens to you when you're busy making other plans", and 'Hard Times Are Over' with its line about "you and I walking together round a street corner".

Elsewhere, 'Watching The Wheels', 'Nobody Told Me' – which borrowed the tune of 'Mama Said', a Shirelles B-side – and the remaindered 'Help Me To Help Myself' were riven with an amused, grace-saving cynicism, while the first *Double Fantasy* single, '(Just Like) Starting Over', hinted at Lennon's Merseybeat genesis.

Overall, however, both *Double Fantasy* and *Milk And Honey* were bland, middle-of-the-road efforts musically – with the former's 'Woman' reminding me vaguely of Bread's slushy 1970 hit, 'Make It With You'. As for the lyrics, smug, slight statements were made by a rich, refined couple long detached from the everyday. Once, their antics had been wilder than those of any punk rocker, but with 1981 approaching, John and Yoko had been derided by punks and hippies alike as indolent, Americanised breadheads.

Be that as it may, Lennon's passing was a boom time for those with vested interest. Universal grief and an element of ghoulish Beatlemania was to reverse the fall of *Double Fantasy* and '(Just Like) Starting Over' from their respective listings as Christmas petered out, and John Lennon would score a hat-trick of British Number Ones within weeks, an achievement that matched that of his Beatles in the dear, dead Swinging Sixties. Out of sympathy too, Yoko engineered her only solo Top 40 entry – with 'Walking On Thin Ice' – in February 1981, thus lending further credence to the cruel old joke: death is a good career move.

The next time her poor husband made the charts, however, was in 1982 when 'Beatles Movie Medley' reached the Top 20 in both Britain and the States. Always it boiled down to The Beatles. Yet, in interview, George Harrison in particular underlined his boredom with the ceaseless fascination with the group – a fascination that was to escalate with the runaway success in 1994 of *Live At The BBC*, a compilation of early broadcasts.

This prefaced an official proclamation of a coming anthology of further items from the vaults. These were to be hand picked by George, Paul and Ringo themselves for issue over the period of a year on nine albums (in packs of three) as appendages to a six-hour documentary film to be spread over three weeks on ITV, and presented likewise on foreign television.

Then came talk of the Fab Three recording new material for the project. The general feeling, however, was that it wouldn't be the same without Lennon. Yet, after a fashion, a regrouping of Harrison, Starr and McCartney in the later

1990s wasn't without him. Their labours in George's and Paul's respective private studios yielded the grafting of new music onto John's voice-piano tapes of 'Free As A Bird' and 'Real Love', provided by Yoko after much negotiation.

Released as A-sides, both were hits and the *Anthology* albums shifted millions, confirming enduring interest in The Beatles that made even this abundance of out-takes, demos and other leftovers as much of a joy forever as similar produce issued around the same time by The Beach Boys, The Doors and The Zombies.

In deference to the years before the coming of Ringo, the first *Anthology* package contained tracks with Beatles who'd left the fold one way or another. Such inclusions were of no use to Stuart Sutcliffe, mouldering in a Liverpool parish cemetery for 35 years – or John Lennon.

What victory was his? "The leader of the band's arrived!" *NME* reader's letter had bawled back in the aftershock of 8 December 1980, presuming that John was being conducted to the table head in some pop Valhalla. A spiritualist *au fait* with Lennon's afterlife adventures knew of his affair with a long-departed Hollywood screen idol – intelligence that might have inflamed his widow whose *Season Of Glass* album sleeve in 1981 had depicted a pair of bloodstained spectacles – while the following year's *It's Alright (I See Rainbows)* employed trick photography whereby a spectral John stood next to her and Sean in what looks like a recreation ground.

Even before the necessarily hasty cremation, although a Coalition To Stop Gun Violence – of which Harry Nilsson was an active supporter – was inaugurated, less altruistic was the bursting of a commercial dam of such force that John Lennon's name would continue to sell almost anything. Publishers liaised with biographers that included a team who had a life of Lennon – entitled *Strawberry Fields Forever* – in the shops inside a fortnight and Albert Goldman, the US journalist whose brief was to portray Lennon as being as certifiable a lunatic as Chapman.

Needless to say, there were also individuals thick skinned enough to start work on a tribute disc within minutes of catching the first bulletin on 9 December. With a bit of luck, it'd be in the shops and on radio playlists in time for mourners to spend their Christmas record tokens on it. Totally eclipsing efforts like 'Elegy For The Walrus' and 'It Was Nice To Know You, John', George Harrison's 'All Those Years Ago' was the promotional 45 from his *Somewhere In England* album, and the reason why George by association was to end 1981 seven places behind Lennon as tenth Top Male Vocalist in Billboard's annual poll.

Regardless of this singalong canter's mediocrity, another incentive for buyers was the superimposed presence of Ringo and Paul, who, with Wings, had taken a break from another project in George Martin's Monserrat complex to add their contributions when the unmixed 'All Those Years Ago' arrived from Harrison.

It's futile to hypothesise about John's beyond-the-grave verdict on George's first big hit since 'Give Me Love (Give Me Peace On Earth)' in 1973, but I like to think that he would have preferred Roxy Music's go at 'Jealous Guy'. Lennon was, after all, an artist with whom the group's Bryan Ferry, via a *Melody Maker* article, expressed a wish to collaborate. Bryan may have told the man himself when, in 1974, he dined with John, George and Ringo in New York. Touring Germany with Roxy Music the week after the slaying, Ferry suggested closing the show with 'Jealous Guy'. A German record company executive ventured that it would be a sound choice for the next Roxy Music single, but Bryan felt it might appear tasteless. Nevertheless, after further deliberation, the outfit tried an arrangement during an exploratory studio session. With the oblique message "A Tribute" on the picture sleeve, the sole reference to its main purpose, 'Jealous Guy' scudded all the way up the UK charts, the only Roxy Music 45 to so do, by March 1981.

Sean Lennon's godfather, Elton John got no further than Number 51 with his 'Empty Garden' tribute in 1982. Though he procrastinated for even longer, Mike 'Tubular Bells' Oldfield – with sister Sally on lead vocals – slummed it on *Top Of The Pops* with 1983's 'Moonlight Shadow', which addressed itself to the horror outside the Dakota on the night it happened. Waiting a decent interval, more deserving of a chart placing was the title song of The Downliners Sect's *A Light Went Out In New York*, a 1993 album that mingled remakes of some of the reformed British R&B combo's old tracks and Beatle obscurities. Dare I suggest that the Sect actually improve upon 'I'll Keep You Satisfied', 'That Means A Lot' et al? Also, that 'A Light Went Out In New York' – composed by the Sect's own Paul Tiller – may be the most moving Lennon oblation ever released, knocking the likes of 'All Those Years Ago', 'Empty Garden' and po-faced 'Moonlight Shadow' into a cocked hat?

The principal subject of Mike Oldfield's ditty was not John but Yoko Ono, who was to sanction and partly compère 1990's televised and international concert tribute to John at Liverpool's Pier Head. Since 1980, Yoko has not retreated from public life. As recently as summer 2002, she endeavoured to re-invent herself as a disco diva with a remix of 'Open Your Box', her self-composed flip-side to 'Power To The People'. While this was still being advertised via posters in London underground stations, Ono was presented to the Queen during Her Majesty's golden jubilee visit to Liverpool's John Lennon – formerly Speke – Airport. It's likely that I've got Yoko all wrong but, to me, she gives an impression of hurrying her duties by John out of the way in as bombastic a manner as possible while simultaneously using him as leverage to further her own artistic ends: kind of "Yes, he was quite a guy, but listen…"

The ease with which Yoko's step-son secured a British Top Ten hit in 1984 might be the most renowned instance of affinity to The Beatles kick-starting a musical career. In April of the following year, Julian Lennon also played three nights in a theatre in New York. During this brief residency, he and his mother Cynthia were spotted at a dining table, sharing the proverbial joke with his half-brother and Yoko Ono. "It was after Julian's first appearance in New York," Cynthia elucidated, "and he and I, Yoko and Sean were there – so for the photographers, it was a classic coup, but though we both wed the same man and both had a child by him, we were and still are worlds apart."

A more convivial repast was eaten by Cynthia with Maureen, Ringo's late ex-wife, at Lennon's, Cynthia's short-lived Covent Garden restaurant, which bored journalists made out to be in fierce competition with ex-Rolling Stone Bill Wyman's Kensington eaterie, Sticky Fingers. The two well-dressed, "liberated" divorcees might have hardly recognised their younger Merseyside selves. "We'd remained best friends through thick, thin, births, deaths and marriages," smiled Cynthia. "I happened to be staying with Maureen when Ringo rang at dawn with the news of John's death. She was also my last link with The Beatles. I'm out of their social orbit completely now."

Though Cynthia had gained a lucrative design contract in 1984 on the strength of her Art College qualifications, her memoir, *A Twist Of Lennon*, had done brisk business when published in 1978. Another account may follow "because so much has happened since then. It would be very easy to get in a ghost writer, but, because the first one was all my own work, it'd have to be in the same vein, in the way that I saw it – not the way other people want to see it. In the film *Backbeat*, I was a simple girl who wore tweed coats and head scarves, and that all I ever wanted in life was marriage, babies and a house – which was totally untrue. I was training to be an art teacher for four years, and it was only when I became pregnant that marriage followed, and The Beatles followed after that.

"People think of The Beatles in terms of millions of dollars. I don't see those dollars. What dollars I see are from my own damned hard work since I was out on my own after the divorce. From being so protected by millions that I never saw, and having a secure family, it was desperate really."

Yoko held the purse strings of John's fortune, but, after much to-ing and fro-ing of solicitors' letters, Julian Lennon received assorted – and, according to him, long overdue – monies. There was, therefore, no love lost between him and his father's relict. While noting that she and Sean attended 88-year-old Aunt Mimi's funeral in December 1991, another of John's blood relations felt the same as Julian about Yoko Ono. "Dad bought his half-sister Julia and her family a house to live in," snarled Julian by way of example. "As soon as Dad passed away, Yoko went and took their home that had been given to them by him, and then gave it to charity with no compensation for them."

The second Mrs Lennon didn't appear to be very popular with John's former workmates either. On 27 April 1981,

Yoko had been conspicuously absent from Ringo Starr's wedding to film actress Barbara Bach. Furthermore, George Harrison was to have nothing to do with Ono's Pier Head shenanigans and, while Paul and Ringo each sent a filmed piece, they declined to show up in person.

No Merseybeat groups "who'd got drunk with him" had been invited even to warm up for Kylie Minogue, Christopher "Superman" Reeve, Roberta Flack, Hall And Oates, Cyndi Lauper and the rest of Yoko's star turns. Some, however, paid their respects that same year in a John Lennon Memorial Concert at the Philharmonic Hall. Blowing the dust off their instruments, many of those on the boards on that night of nights were belying daytime occupations as pen pushers, charge hands and captains of industry.

Old friendships and rivalries had been renewed likewise in May 1989 at the Grafton Rooms, scene of many a rough night in the early days, during the inaugural evening of Merseycats, a committee formed by Don Andrew, once of The Remo Four, to facilitate reunions of Merseybeat groups in support of KIND (Kids In Need and Distress), an organisation that provides activity holidays for seriously ill and handicapped local children.

Brian Epstein, "John Lennon of The Beatles" and "Stuart Sutcliffe of The Beatles" were pictured amongst "absent friends" in the souvenir programme. The latter two were also central to *Backbeat*, the 1994 bio-pic from the makers of *Letter To Brezhnev* – set in Liverpool – and *The Crying Game*.

The action took place against the background of the *vie bohème* of Liverpool and Hamburg and concentrated on the often volatile relationships between John, Stuart and Astrid (and, to a lesser degree, Cynthia).

Backbeat's commercial success helped Sutcliffe close the gap on John as the most popular dead Beatle – at least, until George Harrison was taken by cancer in 2001. During the early 1990s, small fortunes changed hands for both a letter to Stuart from George and a Sutcliffe oil painting, not in the murmur of a museum or art gallery committee rooms but the bustle of a pop-memorabilia auction – for, regardless of how regrettable a loss he was to the world of Fine Art, as a figure in time's fabric Sutcliffe's period as a Beatle remains crucial to most considerations of him.

Conversely, his own merits, more than their association with The Beatles, has enabled Gerry Marsden to be among the few of the old Merseybeat school who have managed to cling on to a recording career – though his *Much Missed Man*, a remarkable 2001 CD hung on a title requiem for Lennon with lyrics by Joe Flannery, once Brian Epstein's friend and business associate. Within weeks of 8 December 1980, Flannery had written 'Much Missed Man' with Marsden in mind. "I felt it was too soon for a tribute from me then," thought Gerry. "However, when the anniversary of John's 60th birthday was coming up in 2000, Joe rang and asked me to give it another listen as he felt that the time might be right for me to record it – and he was right. The words said

169

what I thought about John. People who like John will like the record." A fragment of dialogue by Lennon and an 'Imagine'-esque piano figure segued into a lush and adventurous arrangement behind a serenade that is on a heartfelt par with 'A Light Went Out In New York'.

To a greater degree than The Downliners Sect, Gerry Marsden still earns good money as an entertainer and, less often, as a guest at Beatles conventions, sometimes with others less entitled to cash in on The Beatles ticket.

Who could begrudge Lennon's ex-wife from doing so with unprecedented abundance? A 1999 exhibition of her paintings at the KDK Gallery down London's Portobello Road was only part of it. Was I attending a preview or a cocktail party? White wine, please. Red gives me heartburn. Do those canapés contain meat? Don't look now, but wasn't that fellow with the camera once in The Troggs? Is that Mick Hucknell or one of Kula Shaker? That bloke I can't quite place: I'm sure he played Lennon in some play or other?

Actually, he was Lennon. Julian was there supporting his mother and Phyllis McKenzie, friends since student days in Liverpool when they breathed the air around others occupying that wide territory between realism and abstract expressionism. Phyllis leant closer to the latter form than Cynthia – who freighted *A Twist Of Lennon* with her own illustrations. The originals were on display in KDK for most of the summer, along with further visual mementos of her life at the storm centre of 1960s pop as well as later pictures bereft of such reference.

Cynthia Lennon was not nominated for that year's Turner prize. Nevertheless, her work had a charm that begs the question: does only the surname prevent her from being an artist in her own right? Maybe, but in such matters, your opinion is as worthy as mine, and beyond both of us, the only approbation KDK, McKenzie and Lennon need really are those whose time is utilised interestingly in an experience that, through my eyes, was as much aesthetic as historical. Three years earlier, while it may not have reactivated the Cynthia Lennon Fan Club, the release of a debut single, a revival of Mary Hopkin's chart-topping 'Those Were The Days', had precipitated a more far-reaching reassessment. Produced by Isle of Man neighbour Chris Norman, formerly of Smokie, for his own Dice Music label, Cynthia's was not one of those discs that you buy for the wrong reasons – not like her former father-in-law's unmelodious 'That's My Life' in 1965.

Fifty-five-year-old Cynthia turned in a surprisingly appealing vocal – though perhaps not so surprising considering that "from the age of 10 until I was 14, I was in the Hoylake Parish Girls' Choir, and I ended up as soloist. As an adult, I had no aspirations to be a singer. I didn't even sing around the house or in the bath, but a fax came through from a German record company who wanted to get in touch with Julian. So Jim, my partner, phoned back and said sarcastically, 'Julian's not here, but you can have his mother' – a throwaway comment that they answered in all seriousness,

'We can't do anything unless we know whether she can sing.' My voice had dropped about two octaves – probably because of all the cigarettes I smoke – but I'm game for anything nowadays, so I taped a selection of songs *a cappella*. Chris asked to hear it out of curiosity and said, 'Let's give it a whirl.'

"Chris thought 'Those Were The Days' would be a good song for a person of my age, and very pertinent, looking back – though I resisted a temptation to sing, 'Once upon a time, there was a Cavern' on disc. For weeks after the session, I was on cloud nine. I was so pleased with it – and it was so creative for me. Six months earlier, if somebody had told me a record of mine was going to be on the radio, I'd have fallen about on the floor in hysterics, but – what's John's expression on *Double Fantasy*? – 'Life is what happens when you're busy making other plans.' At nearly every interview I've done, I've got one of the same two questions. 'Don't you think you're jumping on the bandwagon?' 'Won't people think you're cashing in?' I've tried for intelligent answers that don't sound aggressive, but no one other than me will ever understand. 'Cashing in' is earning a living as far as I'm concerned. Why should you feel guilty for working?"

With this in mind, Cynthia took the show on the road as novelty headliner of *With A Little Help From Their Friends*, a revue that you shouldn't have missed but probably did, judging by the half-capacity audience at any given theatre *en route* around Britain. Other "insiders" on the bill were more hardened to both poor turn-out and general stage exposure than Cynthia – notably The Merseybeats, who appeared with her ex-husband's group more times than anyone else.

Subtitled "a celebration of The Beatles by those who were part of the story", this package was not a convention-like evening of selective reminiscences, but a musical spectacular coalesced by scripted patter and short cameos like Cynthia's then-boyfriend Jim Christie scuttling on as "Brian Epstein" during a spot by the soundalike Silver Beatles, who focus on their namesake's apogee as a local attraction.

The Silver Beatles captured the required ramshackle grandeur. Other *With A Little Help From Their Friends* antics, however, appear lame or peculiar in cold print today – such as a sketch in which matronly Cynthia was embraced by The Silver Beatles' Andy Powell as youthful "John" in his high-buttoned suit – but they made sound sense in the context of proceedings in which it seemed that, the older you were, the louder you clapped and shouted, the more you waved your arms about. Everyone whose life has been soundtracked by The Beatles should have attended, but the Congress Theatre, Eastbourne, on 14 March 1996 was the last opportunity to do so as cancellation of the remaining dates was the only way to staunch the financial losses that the trek had suffered since opening in February.

At the last hurrah in Eastbourne, a palpable wave of goodwill had washed over Mrs Lennon the instant she walked centre-stage before a backdrop mock-up of the graffiti-covered

Cavern wall. From being a softly spoken outcast after the world and his wife were confronted with a John they'd never known before in 1968, Cynthia, if no Ken Dodd, proved a self-assured, likeable MC. Moreover, the former chorister also dropped sufficient reserve to open the second half with 'Those Were The Days'. Shorn of the Welsh soprano's incongruous maidenly innocence, Cynthia's pining for past times was as poignant as 'Free As A Bird'. The customers, typically English, loved Cynthia for being a survivor – and for reaching her half-century in such great shape, too.

14 "And Now, Thank Christ, It's Over"

How different could John Lennon's life have been? This is probably a senseless hypothetical exercise, but let's transfer to a parallel dimension for a few minutes.

Sean Connery has failed his screen test for *Dr No*; Cassius Clay didn't beat the count when knocked down by Henry Cooper, and, in summer 1966, Dave Dee, Dozy, Beaky, Mick And Tich top the US Hot 100, the first British act to do so since The Tornados.

Around the same time, John Lennon quits The Beatles, an also-ran beat group, opting instead for a hand-to-mouth existence as a jobbing commercial artist back in Liverpool. For a while, he's on the periphery of the Liverpool scene, a mixed-media aggregation, before a supplicatory chat with Arthur Ballard lands him a post as a technician in Ballard's department at the college.

As his marriage to Cynthia deteriorates, John becomes a fixture in Ye Cracke, still a student pub, where he often rambles on with rueful and misplaced pride about The Beatles' meagre achievements. On one maudlin evening, he brings in his photo album – "us with Tony Sheridan", "me and George with Ringo Starr in the Top Ten. Ringo was in Georgie Fame's Blue Flames later on, you know…" Most regulars find both John's reminiscences and the pictures mind-stultifyingly boring.

For beer money and a laugh, Lennon reforms The Beatles for bookings in local watering-holes. They became as peculiar to Liverpool alone as Mickey Finn, a comedian unknown nationally but guaranteed work for as long as he can stand on Merseyside. A typical engagement is providing music after Finn's entertainment at a dinner and dance at Gateacre Labour Club on 8 December 1980. The group's personnel on that night of nights consists of Pete Best, deputy manager at Garston Job Centre on drums; George Harrison, a Southport curate, on guitar; Paul McCartney, a Radio Merseyside presenter and amateur songwriter, on bass; and Lennon, his singing voice darker and attractively shorn of 1960s ingenuity, now a slightly batty art lecturer who'd wed a Japanese performance artist he'd seen at a 1967 "happening" at the college.

The four leave a dancing audience wanting more after a finale of a 1965 Oriole B-side, 'I'm A Loser', during which Lennon accommodated suitable – and often amusing – gestures and facial expressions as well as wailing an endlessly inventive harmonica. He also displayed a commendable sense of historical perspective during humorous continuity. Meanwhile, George delivered workman-like solos, and Paul sent frissons through middle-aged female nervous systems with his pretty

'Till There Was You', but a more unsung hero of the night was Pete, ministering unobtrusively to overall effect and, in his way, a virtuoso.

Brought back for an encore, The Beatles affirm their staying power once more. None of their few records ever sold much beyond Merseyside but, as an eminently danceable live act, they've outlasted most of their local rivals – and there's every reason to suppose that they'll still be around in the next millennium.

Unreal life isn't like that – at least, it wasn't for John, whose unmeasurable fame had accorded unto him a magnificently god-like certainty about everything he said and did for invisible armies of fans, old and new, whose adoration will never dwindle. As pressured denizens of the media cobbled together hasty obituaries on the morning of 9 December 1980, one of the more memorable comments any of them reported was by the recently retired Arthur Ballard: "I think his death is more significant than that of a leading politician. Like Michelangelo has never been forgotten, neither will John Lennon be."

Shall we try again with an interview with John Winston Lennon, MBE, retired musician and composer at Fort Belvedere, Sunningdale, Berkshire, on 9 December 2002...

To the click-clack of his own approaching footsteps, the former Beatle sings what sounds like "Softly, softly spreads the grunion/thinner thorn our saviour's feet..." to the tune of 'Johnny Todd', title theme to the old BBC television series Z-Cars.

"Welcome to the inner sanctuary," he begins. "Better not shake hands. I've just given the old feller a swift dekko at the scenery. My MBE's on the wall in the bog, y'know. Best place for it. I only asked the Queen for it back to cheer up my auntie during her last illness.

"Do I seem larger than life? Don't worry. That'll change as this chat progresses. I'm ordinary, modest, boring and all too human since that arsehole winged me outside the Dakota in 1980. Quite spoiled Christmas, it did – though it was that other gun-slinging get who did for Reagan in '82 that finally put the tin lid on my 'American period'.

"I miss New York sometimes, and I got pissed off recently with Berkshire County Council or whoever they are, when they turned their noses up at the plans to modernise this place. Used to belong to Edward and Mrs Simpson, don't-ye-know? All the same, I'm unlikely to live out of England ever again – especially since getting back together with Cyn and his Holiness down in Sussex, even if the old chart-busting magic isn't there any more.

"Never mind, we made our contribution to society a 100 times over in the '60s, and I reckon now that the four of us should have been put out to grass as soon as we split up the first time. But the game dragged on, didn't it? And now, thank Christ, it's over. Live Aid was a laugh, but all it *proved was that looking forward to the past isn't healthy for any bunch of musicians, let alone John, Paul, George and Pete. Anyway, I wouldn't want to be an 80-year-old Beatle…"*

Songography
By Ian Drummond

All songs composed by John Lennon, with co-writers appearing in brackets. Listed by artist/band and then in chronological order of composition. All dates refer to album and single releases unless otherwise stated.

THE BEATLES

'Cry For A Shadow' (Harrison)	*Anthology 1* (Nov 1995)
'Like Dreamers Do' (McCartney)	
'I Saw Her Standing There' (McCartney)	*Please Please Me* (Mar 1963)
'Misery' (McCartney)	
'Chains' (McCartney)	
'Ask Me Why' (McCartney)	
'Please Please Me' (McCartney)	
'Love Me Do' (McCartney)	
'PS I Love You' (McCartney)	
'Do You Want To Know A Secret?' (McCartney)	
'There's A Place' (McCartney)	
'From Me To You' (McCartney)	Single (Apr 1963)
'Thank You Girl' (McCartney)	'From Me To You' B-side (Apr 1963)

'She Loves You' (McCartney)   Single (Aug 1963)
'I'll Get You' (McCartney)   'She Loves You' B-side (Aug 1963)

'I'll Be On My Way' (McCartney)   *Live At The BBC* (Nov 1994)

'It Won't Be Long' (McCartney)   *With The Beatles* (Nov 1963)
'All I've Got To Do' (McCartney)
'All My Loving' (McCartney)
'Little Child' (McCartney)
'Hold Me Tight' (McCartney)
'I Wanna Be Your Man' (McCartney)
'Not A Second Time' (McCartney)

'I Want To Hold Your Hand' (McCartney)   Single (Nov 1963)
'This Boy' (McCartney)   'I Want To Hold Your Hand' B-side (Nov 1963)

'I Call Your Name' (McCartney))   *Long Tall Sally* EP (Jun 1964)

'A Hard Day's Night' (McCartney)   *A Hard Day's Night* (Jul 1964)
'I Should Have Known Better' (McCartney)
'If I Fell' (McCartney)
'I'm Happy Just To Dance With You' (McCartney)
'And I Love Her' (McCartney)
'Tell Me Why' (McCartney)
'Can't Buy Me Love' (McCartney)
'Any Time At All' (McCartney)
'I'll Cry Instead' (McCartney)
'Things We Said Today' (McCartney)
'When I Get Home' (McCartney)
'You Can't Do That' (McCartney)
'I'll Be Back' (McCartney)

'I Feel Fine' (McCartney)   Single (Nov 1964)
'She's A Woman' (McCartney)   'I Feel Fine' B-side (Nov 1964)

'No Reply' (McCartney)   *Beatles For Sale* (Nov 1964)

JOHN LENNON

'I'm A Loser' (McCartney)
'Baby's In Black' (McCartney)
'I'll Follow The Sun' (McCartney)
'Eight Days A Week' (McCartney)
'Every Little Thing' (McCartney)
'I Don't Want To Spoil The Party' (McCartney)
'What You're Doing' (McCartney)

'Ticket To Ride' (McCartney)   Single (Apr 1965)
'Yes It Is' (McCartney)   'Ticket To Ride' B-side (Apr 1965)

'I'm Down' (McCartney)   'Help!' B-side (Jul 1965)

'Help!' (McCartney)   *Help!* (Aug 1965)
'The Night Before' (McCartney)
'You've Got To Hide Your Love Away' (McCartney)
'Another Girl' (McCartney)
'You're Going To Lose That Girl' (McCartney)
'It's Only Love' (McCartney)
'Tell Me What You See' (McCartney)
'I've Just Seen A Face' (McCartney)
'Yesterday' (McCartney)

'That Means A Lot' (McCartney)   *Anthology 2* (Mar 1996)

'We Can Work It Out' (McCartney)   Single (Dec 1965)
'Day Tripper' (McCartney)   'We Can Work It Out' B-side (Dec 1965)

'Drive My Car' (McCartney)   *Rubber Soul* (Nov 1965)
'Norwegian Wood (This Bird Has Flown)' (McCartney)
'You Won't See Me' (McCartney)
'Nowhere Man' (McCartney)
'The Word' (McCartney)
'Michelle' (McCartney)
'What Goes On' (McCartney-Starkey)

'Girl' (McCartney)
'I'm Looking Through You' (McCartney)
'In My Life' (McCartney)
'Wait' (McCartney)
'Run For Your Life' (McCartney)

'12-Bar Original' (McCartney–Harrison–Starkey)   *Anthology 2* (Mar 1996)

'Paperback Writer' (McCartney)   Single (Jun 1966)
'Rain' (McCartney)   'Paperback Writer' B-side (Jun 1966)

'Eleanor Rigby' (McCartney)   *Revolver* (Aug 1966)
'I'm Only Sleeping' (McCartney)
'Here, There And Everywhere' (McCartney)
'Yellow Submarine' (McCartney)
'She Said She Said' (McCartney)
'Good Day Sunshine' (McCartney)
'And Your Bird Can Sing' (McCartney)
'For No One' (McCartney)
'Doctor Robert' (McCartney)
'Got To Get You Into My Life' (McCartney)
'Tomorrow Never Knows' (McCartney)

'Penny Lane' (McCartney)   Single (Feb 1967)
'Strawberry Fields Forever' (McCartney)   'Penny Lane' B-side (Feb 1967)

'Sgt Pepper's Lonely Hearts Club Band'   *Sgt Pepper's Lonely Hearts*
     (McCartney)   *Club Band* (Jun 1967)
'With A Little Help From My Friends' (McCartney)
'Lucy In The Sky With Diamonds' (McCartney)
'Getting Better' (McCartney)
'Fixing A Hole' (McCartney)
'She's Leaving Home' (McCartney)
'Being For The Benefit Of Mr Kite!' (McCartney)
'When I'm Sixty-Four' (McCartney)

'Lovely Rita' (McCartney)
'Good Morning Good Morning' (McCartney)
'Sgt Pepper's Lonely Hearts Club Band (Reprise)' (McCartney)
'A Day In The Life' (McCartney)

'All Together Now' (McCartney)   *Yellow Submarine* (Jan 1969)

'All You Need Is Love' (McCartney)   Single (Jul 1967)
'Baby You're A Rich Man' (McCartney)   'All You Need Is Love'
        B-side (Jul 1967)

'You Know My Name' (McCartney)   'Let It Be' B-side (May 1970)

'Hello Goodbye' (McCartney)   Single (Dec 1967)

'Magical Mystery Tour' (McCartney)   *Magical Mystery Tour* (Dec 1967)
'The Fool On The Hill' (McCartney)
'Flying' (McCartney-Harrison-Starkey)
'Your Mother Should Know' (McCartney)
'I Am The Walrus' (McCartney)

'Jessie's Dream'   *Magical Mystery Tour* film (Dec 1967)
    (McCartney-Harrison-Starkey)

'Christmas Time (Is Here Again)'   'Free As A Bird' B-side (Dec 1995)
    (McCartney-Harrison-Starkey)

'Lady Madonna' (McCartney)   Single (Mar 1968)

'Hey Jude' (McCartney)   Single (Aug 1968)

'Across The Universe' (McCartney)   *World Wildlife* (Dec 1969)

'Hey Bulldog' (McCartney)   *Yellow Submarine* (Jan 1969)

'Back In The USSR' (McCartney)   *The Beatles* (Nov 1968)
'Dear Prudence' (McCartney)
'Glass Onion' (McCartney)
'Ob-La-Di, Ob-La-Da' (McCartney)
'Honey Pie' (McCartney)
'The Continuing Story Of Bungalow Bill' (McCartney)
'Happiness Is A Warm Gun' (McCartney)
'Martha My Dear' (McCartney)
'I'm So Tired' (McCartney)
'Blackbird' (McCartney)
'Rocky Raccoon' (McCartney)
'Why Don't We Do It In The Road' (McCartney)
'I Will' (McCartney)
'Julia' (McCartney)
'Birthday' (McCartney)
'Yer Blues' (McCartney)
'Mother Nature's Son' (McCartney)
'Everybody's Got Something To Hide Except Me And My Monkey' (McCartney)
'Sexy Sadie' (McCartney)
'Helter Skelter' (McCartney)
'Revolution 1' (McCartney)
'Honey Pie' (McCartney)
'Cry Baby Cry' (McCartney)
'Revolution 9' (McCartney)
'Good Night' (McCartney)

'The Ballad Of John And Yoko' (McCartney)   Single (May 1969)

'Two Of Us' (McCartney)   *Let It Be* (May 1970)
'Dig A Pony' (McCartney)
'Across The Universe' (McCartney)
'Dig It' (McCartney-Harrison-Starkey)
'Let It Be' (McCartney)
'I've Got A Feeling' (McCartney)
'One After 909' (McCartney)

'The Long And Winding Road' (McCartney)
'Get Back' (McCartney)

'Don't Let Me Down' (McCartney)   'Get Back' B-side (Apr 1969)

'Come Together' (McCartney)   *Abbey Road* (Sep 1969)
'Maxwell's Silver Hammer' (McCartney)
'Oh! Darling' (McCartney)
'I Want You (She's So Heavy)' (McCartney)
'Because' (McCartney)
'You Never Give Me Your Money' (McCartney)
'Sun King' (McCartney)
'Mean Mr Mustard' (McCartney)
'Polythene Pam' (McCartney)
:She Came In Through The Bathroom Window' (McCartney)
'Golden Slumbers' (McCartney)
'Carry That Weight' (McCartney)
'The End' (McCartney)
'Her Majesty' (McCartney)

'Free As A Bird' (McCartney-Harrison-Starkey)   *Anthology 1* (Nov 1995)

'Real Love' (McCartney-Harrison-Starkey)   *Anthology 2* (Mar 1996)

'Thinking Of Linking' (McCartney)   *Anthology DVD* (Apr 2003)

JOHN LENNON
'Jock And Yono' (spoken)   *The Beatles 1968 Christmas Record* (Dec 1968)
'Onceuponapooltable' (spoken)

'Here We Go Again' (Spector)   *Menlove Ave* (Nov 1986)

'Great Wok'   *John Lennon Anthology* (Nov 1998)
'Satire 2: News Of The Day From Reuters'
'Satire 1: Lord Take This Make-Up Off Me'

'Satire 3: They Say The Best Things In Life Are Free'
'It's Real'

'(Just Like) Starting Over'	*Double Fantasy* (Nov 1980)

'Clean Up Time'
'I'm Losing You'
'Beautiful Boy (Darling Boy)'
'Watching The Wheels'
'Woman'
'Dear Yoko'

'Grow Old With Me'	*Milk And Honey* (Jan 1984)

'I Don't Wanna Face It'
'Borrowed Time'
'I'm Stepping out'
'Forgive Me (My Little Flower Princess)'
'Nobody Told Me'

'Real Love' (demo)	*Imagine John Lennon* (Oct 1988)

'Stranger's Room'	*John Lennon Anthology* (Nov 1998)

'Serve Yourself'
'My Life'
'Life Begins At 40'
'Rishi Kesh Song'
'Mr Hyde's Gone (Don't Be Afraid)'
'Dear John'

JOHN LENNON AND YOKO ONO

'Two Virgins Section 1' (Ono)	*Two Virgins* (Nov 1968)

'Together' (Ono)
'Two Virgins Section 2' (Ono)
'Two Virgins Section 3' (Ono)
'Two Virgins Section 4' (Ono)
'Two Virgins Section 5' (Ono)

'Two Virgins Section 6' (Ono)
'Hushabye Hushabye' (Ono)
'Two Virgins Section 7' (Ono)
'Two Virgins Section 8' (Ono)
'Two Virgins Section 9' (Ono)
'Two Virgins Section 10' (Ono)

'Cambridge 1969' (Ono)   *Life With The Lions* (May 1969)
'No Bed For Beatle John' (Ono)
'Baby's Heartbeat' (Ono)
'Radio Play' (Ono)

'John And Yoko' (Ono)   *Wedding Album* (Nov 1969)
    (based on 'John And Marsha' by Stan Freberg)
'Amsterdam' (Ono)

'Fortunately' (Ono)   *John Lennon Anthology* (Nov 1998)

THE PLASTIC ONO BAND
'Give Peace A Chance' (McCartney)   Single (Jul 1969)
'Cold Turkey'   Single (Oct 1969)

JOHN LENNON AND THE PLASTIC ONO BAND
'Instant Karma'   Single (Feb 1970)

'Mother'   *John Lennon/Plastic Ono Band* (Dec 1970)
'Hold On'
'I Found Out'
'Working Class Hero'
'Isolation'
'Remember'
'Love'
'Well Well Well'
'Look At Me'
'God'
'My Mummy's Dead'

'Power To The People'   Single (Mar 1971)

'Imagine'   *Imagine* (Oct 1971)
'Crippled Inside'
'Jealous Guy'
'It's So Hard'
'I Don't Wanna Be A Soldier Mama'
'Gimme Some Truth'
'Oh My Love' (Ono)
'How Do You Sleep?'
'How?'
'Oh Yoko!' (Ono)

JOHN AND YOKO/PLASTIC ONO BAND WITH THE HARLEM COMMUNITY CHOIR

'Happy Christmas (War Is Over)' (Ono)   US single (Dec 1971)

JOHN AND YOKO/PLASTIC ONO BAND WITH ELEPHANT'S MEMORY PLUS INVISIBLE STRINGS

'Woman Is The Nigger Of The World' *Sometime In New York City* (Jun 1972)
    (Ono)
'Attica State' (Ono)
'New York City'
'Sunday Bloody Sunday'
'The Luck Of The Irish' (Ono)
'John Sinclair'
'Angela' (Ono)
'We're All Water'
'Jamrag' (Ono)
'Au' (Ono)
'Scumbag' (Ono-Zappa)

JOHN LENNON WITH THE PLASTIC UF ONO BAND

'Mind Games'   *Mind Games* (Nov 1973)
'Tight As'

'Aisumasen (I'm Sorry)'
'One Day (At A Time)'
'Bring On The Lucie (Freda People)'
'Nutopian International Anthem'
'Intuition'
'Out The Blue'
'Only People'
'I Know (I Know)'
'You Are Here'
'Meat City'

JOHN LENNON WITH THE PLASTIC ONO NUCLEAR BAND
'Going Down On Love'   *Walls And Bridges* (Oct 1974)
'Whatever Gets You Thru The Night'
'Old Dirt Road' (Nilsson)
'What You Got'
'Bless You'
'Scared'
'Number Nine Dream'
'Surprise Surprise (Sweet Bird Of Paradox)'
'Steel And Glass'
'Beef Jerky'
'Nobody Loves You (When You're Down And Out)'

'Rock And Roll People'   *Menlove Ave* (Nov 1986)
'Move Over Ms L'

'Yesterday' (McCartney) (parody)   *John Lennon Anthology* (Nov 1998)

YOKO ONO/PLASTIC ONO BAND
'The South Wind'   *Yoko Ono/Plastic Ono Band* (Jul 1997)

YOKO ONO/PLASTIC ONO BAND/JOE JONES TONE DEAF MUSIC CO
'Mind Train' (Ono)   *Fly* (Dec 1971)

'Mind Holes' (Ono)
'Toilet Piece/Unknown' (Ono)
'Telephone Piece' (Ono)

BILL ELLIOTT AND THE ELASTIC OZ BAND
'God Save Us' (Ono)   Single (Jul 1971)
'Do The Oz' (Ono)   'God Save Us' B-side

DOG SOLDIER
'Incantation' (Cicala)   *Beatles Undercover* (Oct 1998)

CILLA BLACK
'Love Of The loved' (McCartney)   Single (Sep 1963)

'It's For You' (McCartney)   Single (Jul 1964)

'Step Inside Love' (McCartney)   Single (May 1968)

BLACK DYKE MILLS BAND
'Thingumybob' (McCartney)   Single (Aug 1968)

DAVID BOWIE
'Fame' (Bowie-Alomar)   *Young Americans* (Mar 1975)

THE FOURMOST
'Hello Little Girl' (McCartney)   Single (Aug 1963)

'I'm In Love' (McCartney)   Single (Nov 1963)

MARY HOPKIN
'Goodbye' (McCartney)   Single (Mar 1969)

BILLY J KRAMER AND THE DAKOTAS
'Bad To Me' (McCartney)   Single (Jul 1963)

'I'll Keep You Satisfied' (McCartney)   Single (Nov 1963)

'From A Window' (McCartney)   Single (Jul 1964)

PAUL McCARTNEY
'PS Love Me Do' (McCartney)   'Birthday' B-side (Oct 1990)

HARRY NILSSON
'Mucho Mungo/Mount Elga' (Nilsson)   *Pussycats* (Aug 1974)

PETER AND GORDON
'World Without Love' (McCartney)   Single (Feb 1964)

'Nobody I Know' (McCartney)   Single (May 1964)

'I Don't Want To See You Again' (McCartney)   Single (Sep 1964)

TOMMY QUICKLY
'Tip Of My Tongue' (McCartney)   Single (Jul 1963)

RINGO STARR
'I'm The Greatest'   *Ringo* (Nov 1973)

'Goodnight Vienna'   *Goodnight Vienna* (Nov 1974)

'Cookin' (In The Kitchen Of Love)'   *Ringo's Rotogravure* (Sep 1976)

STRANGERS WITH MIKE SHANNON
'One And One Is Two' (McCartney)   Single (May 1964)

Paul McCartney

Printed in the United Kingdom by MPG Books Ltd, Bodmin

Published by Sanctuary Publishing Limited, Sanctuary House, 45–53 Sinclair Road,
London W14 0NS, United Kingdom

www.sanctuarypublishing.com

Distributed in the US by Publishers Group West

ISBN: 1-86074-520-2

Paul McCartney

Alan Clayson

Sanctuary

Contents

1 "Que Sera Sera"

When, in the first flush of their stardom, The Beatles made their stage debut in Ireland – at Dublin's Adelphi Cinema on 7 November 1963 – Paul McCartney announced that "It's great to be home!". Liverpool, see, is known facetiously as "the capital of Ireland" – and three of the Moptopped Mersey Marvels had more than a splash of the Auld Sod in their veins.

Most of Paul's was inherited from mother Mary, whose maiden name was Mohin. Almost as a matter of course, she was devoutly Roman Catholic. Yet, while she kept the pledge required of the Catholic party in such a union to have any offspring baptised into the faith, her two sons – James Paul and Peter Michael – were not to be educated in Roman Catholic schools or to attend Roman Catholic churches, which stood in Merseyside suburbs becoming lost in an encroaching urban sprawl that had spread from central Liverpool since The Great War when 14-year-old Jim McCartney had entered the world of work on the ground floor at a dockside cotton merchant's. He'd risen to the high office of salesman there by the next global conflict when, as an infinitesimal cog provisioning the bloodshed afar, he did his bit in a local munitions factory. Then, following Hitler's suicide, Jim passed a written test for eligibility to work for Liverpool Corporation. He was introduced to Mary Mohin by one of his sisters and married her in 1941.

Just over a year later, the remarkable James Paul was born on 18 June 1942, a dry Thursday with alternate warm and cool spells, in Liverpool's Walton Hospital, the nearest maternity ward to the furnished rooms in Anfield where Jim and Mary lived in a forlorn cluster of Coronation Streets.

The "James" was both after his father and in respect of the scriptures, but, from the cradle, the boy was called by his middle name, just as his brother – who arrived two years later – was to be.

From Anfield, the family moved to the south of Liverpool, settling eventually in 20 Forthlin Road, a semi-detached on a new estate in Allerton, ten minutes dawdle from the river, and more convenient for Mrs McCartney in her capacity as health visitor and then a district midwife.

In the living room stood an upright piano. Whilst it suffered the investigative pounding of the infant Paul and Mike's plump fists, it also tinkled beneath the self-taught hands of their father who, in the 1920s, had had no qualms about performing in public, whether extrapolating often witty incidental music as silent movies flickered in city cinemas or performing at parochial entertainments on the 88s – and, for a while, trumpet – with his Jim Mac's Jazz Band.

Obliged by economic necessity to focus more exclusively on his day job, Jim cut back on the extra-curricular Charlestons, finally breaking up the band, circa 1927. Nevertheless, he continued to play for his own amusement and compose too, though the only extant Jim McCartney opus seems to be 'Walking In The Park With Eloise', an instrumental.

Sensibly, while Jim was only too willing to impart hard-won knowledge, neither he nor Mary goaded their lads to over-formalise what were assumed to be innate musical strengths. Of the two, Paul seemed keenest and, from being a fascinated listener whenever Dad was seated at the piano, progressed at his own speed on the instrument, acquiring the rudiments of harmony, and adding to a repertoire that embraced tunes from cross-legged primary school assemblies and – then quite a new idea – traditional songs from *Singing Together* and other BBC Home Service radio broadcasts to schools.

More exciting than the Home Service's dashing white sergeants, drunken sailors, Li'l Liza Janes and John Barleycorniness was the Light Programme, which interspersed the likes of Educating Archie – comic goings-on of a ventriloquist's dummy (on the radio!) – and *Workers' Playtime* with approved items from the newly established *New Musical Express* record sales "hit parade".

Like all but the most stuffy adolescents of the 1950s, Paul McCartney would be thrilled by 'Rock Around The Clock' whenever it intruded upon the Light Programme's jingle bells and winter wonderlands as 1955 drew to a close. But as he later explained, "the first time I really ever felt a tingle up my spine was when I saw Bill Haley And The Comets playing it on the telly."

Now a loose-lipped and rather chubby youth, Paul had left Joseph Williams Primary School, a "bus ride away from Forthlin Road, after passing the Eleven-Plus examination to gain a place at Liverpool Institute, which was located within the clang of bells from both the Roman Catholic and Anglican cathedrals, along with most of the city centre's other seats of learning, including the university – opened in 1978 on the site of the old lunatic asylum – and the Regional College of Art.

Thus far, Paul had proved sound enough, even very able, in most subjects. He had a particular flair and liking for creative writing because as well as submitting homework, he would tinker with fragments of verse and prose for a purpose unknown apart from articulating the inner space of some private cosmos.

It goes without saying that he shone during music lessons too. Indeed, while he'd never be able to sight-read faster than the most funeral pace, he became as well-known for his musical skills as the school bully and football captain were in their chosen spheres. However, an attempt to master a second-hand trumpet his father had given him was, let's say, an "incomplete success", put off as he was by the unpredictable harmonics, which jarred his teeth during his first shaky sessions in front of a prescribed manual. "Guitars hadn't come in yet," he'd recall. "Trumpeters were the big heroes then." Eddie Calvert, Britain's foremost trumpeter, was from Preston in the same neck of the wood as Liverpool. If well into his 30s, he'd shown what was possible by scoring a 1954 Number One in the *New Musical Express*'s chart with sentimental 'Oh Mein Papa', recorded at EMI's studio complex along Abbey Road, a stone's throw from Lord's Cricket Ground in far-away London.

Eddie's renown was to infiltrate a Giles cartoon in the *Daily Express* in which an elderly classical musician with a trumpet under his arm is mobbed for autographs by teenagers at the Edinburgh Festival. Three other members of the orchestra watch the frenzy ill-humouredly. "How does he do it?" rhetoricates a cellist. "Signs himself Eddie Calvert. That's how he does it."

How could any British musician become more famous than to be the inspiration for Carl Giles? Young Paul McCartney was impressed, "but I couldn't sing with a trumpet, and I wanted to sing." This wish was granted after a fashion because Paul's musical genesis was ecclesiastic as well as academic, and his then unbroken soprano was put to use in the choir at St Barnabas Church, off Penny Lane, common ground between the raw red council houses of Allerton and, half a class up, the mock-Tudor thoroughfares of Woolton, a suburb that regarded itself as more "county" than "city".

In cassock, ruff and surplice, Paul cantillated at three services every Sunday and, when required, at weddings and in St Cecilia's Day oratorios. Then, in 1953, with hardly a murmur, he had gone along with his father's advice to try for Liverpool's Anglican Cathedral choir. Another supplicant was John Charles Duff Lowe, a boy who was to be in the same class as Paul at the Institute. In middle life, Lowe came upon "a photograph taken when Paul and I both auditioned for the Liverpool Cathedral choir when we were ten, just before we went to the Institute. We both failed on that occasion. I got in six months later, but Paul never tried again. I think he was recorded as saying he'd tried to make his voice break because he didn't really want to do it. "

Whatever Jim's thwarted aspirations for Paul as perhaps a round-vowelled solo tenor setting the Cathedral walls a-tremble with one of Handel's biblical arias, his wife imagined Paul as either a teacher or a doctor. She was, however, never to see either of her children grown to man's estate because, during the summer of 1955, 47-year-old Mary had the removed look of a dying woman – which she was. What she may have self-diagnosed as stomach acidity and non-related chest pains turned out to be terminal cancer.

A photograph on the mantelpiece was to prompt opaque memories of life before the end came on 31 October 1956 –

though, in many respects, Mary continued to govern family behaviour patterns from the grave, especially those rooted in appreciation of the value of money, and the notion that hard work and tenacity are principal keys to achievement.

Life without a wife wasn't easy for Jim at first. For a northern male, he was obliged to become unusually attentive to household tasks, particularly cooking. With assistance from relations and neighbours, however, he ensured that his – thankfully, healthy – offspring were as comfortable and contented as his new station as a single parent would allow.

Paul and Mike helped according to their capabilities with jobs on the rotas their father would pin up in the kitchen. Yet though the situation nurtured self-reliance, Paul's childhood was shorter than it needed to be, even as he stayed on at school beyond the statutory age, raised recently to 16. He was a likeable and seemingly unassuming pupil, who walked a tightrope between teacher's pet and the source of illicit and entertaining distraction as some withered pedagogue droned like a bluebottle in a dusty classroom. "Paul was a very amusing cartoonist," laughed John Duff Lowe. "His drawings – maybe one of the master taking the lesson – would appear under your desk, and you'd pass it on."

Before entering the sixth form, Paul had been securely in the "A" stream throughout his sojourn at the Institute, even winning a school prize for an essay. As it was with future Beatle colleagues, Pete Best and Stuart Sutcliffe, distinguishing themselves likewise at Liverpool Collegiate and Prescot

Grammar respectively, teacher training college, rather than medical school, was looming larger as the summer examinations crept closer. Paul, however, wasn't keen, half-fancying the idea of being some sort of bohemian artist. One of the two GCE "A" levels he was expected to pass was actually in Art, a subject that the ordinary working man from the northwest saw as having doubtful practical value. Certainly, no artist based in Liverpool was usually able to rely solely on his work for a reasonable income.

Musicians were in the same boat. If on a business trip to Manchester, "Entertainment Capital of the North", moguls from EMI or the kingdom's other three major record companies rarely seized the chance to sound out talent in Macclesfield, Preston, Liverpool or other conurbations within easy reach. In the realm of pop, it had been necessary for Eddie Calvert to go to the capital to Make It. The same applied to chart-climbing Liverpudlian vocalists like Lita Roza, Michael Holliday – and Frankie Vaughan, who, in 1958, had become a bigger pop star than even Eddie Calvert. There were, nonetheless, perceptible signs of danger for Frankie after the coming of ITV's *Oh Boy!*, a series pitched directly at teenagers.

Oh Boy! arrived a year after Bill Haley's first European tour – the first by any US rock 'n' roller. "The ticket was 24 shillings," remembered Paul, "and I was the only one of my mates who could go as no one else had been able to save that amount – but I was single-minded about it, having got that tingle up my spine. I knew there was something going on here."

Described by *Melody Maker* as resembling a "genial butcher", Haley was an ultimate disappointment at the Liverpool Empire and virtually everywhere else, though he paved the way for more genuine articles.

Paul McCartney had been approaching his 14th birthday when he first caught Elvis Presley's 'Heartbreak Hotel' on the Light Programme. In a then-unimaginable future, he was to own the double-bass thrummed on this 78rpm single, but in 1956, he was just one of countless British youths who'd been so instantly "gone" on 'Heartbreak Hotel' that all he could think was that its maker was surely the greatest man ever to have walked the planet. Listening to this and consequent Presley hits either sent McCartney into a reverie that no one could penetrate or brought on an onset of high spirits that drew in Mike and even a bemused Jim. It was to be the same when he discovered Little Richard. In a typically succinct foreword to Richard's 1984 biography, Paul would recollect, "The first song I ever sang in public was 'Long Tall Sally' in a Butlin's holiday camp talent competition when I was 14."

So "gone" was he this time that he started buying Little Richard discs without first listening to them – as you could in those days – in the shop, thus bringing upon himself angered dismay when "I found this Little Richard album that I'd never seen before. When I played it, I found there were only two tracks by Little Richard. The rest was by Buck Ram and his Orchestra. You needed a magnifying glass to find that out from the sleeve. It's rotten, that kind of thing."

Richard was not to visit Britain until he'd shed the qualificative bulk of his artistic load, but a singing guitarist named Buddy Holly did, leaving a lasting and beneficial impression upon one who was to be his greatest champion. Visually, Holly, unlike Presley, was no romantic lead from a Hollywood flick, recast as a rock 'n' roller. To offset an underfed gawkiness, Buddy wore a huge pair of black horn-rims. Until he and his accompanying Crickets – guitar, bass and drums – played Liverpool's Philharmonic Hall on 20 March 1958, Paul McCartney had been attracted by "really good-looking performers like Elvis. Any fellow with glasses always took them off to play, but after Buddy, anyone who really needed glasses could then come out of the closet."

Yet it was still a magazine picture of a smouldering Elvis on the bedroom wall that greeted Paul when he first opened his eyes in the pallor of dawn. Presley was also hovering metaphorically in the background during Paul's maiden attempts to make romantic contact with girls who, in the years before the contraceptive pill, had been brought up to discourage completion of sexual pilgrimages until their wedding nights.

McCartney, however, was to enjoy more such conquests than most, his appeal emphasised by not infrequent paternity allegations after The Beatles left the runway. Among forums for initiating carnal adventures were coffee bars like the Jacaranda where, according to a regular customer named Rod Jones, "there used to be office girls who'd go up there to get laid because all the art students used to hang around there."

2 "That'll Be The Day"

Paul knew Rod Jones, but not as well as he did one who'd started his art college course a year earlier in 1957. How had Paul classified John Lennon during the first days of their acquaintance? Was he a friend?

To all intents and purposes, Lennon – nearly two years older than McCartney – had lived with his aunt in well-to-do Woolton from infancy. Soon to die, his mother dwelt nearby with his half-siblings and her boyfriend. After she'd gone, John was not to understand the profundity of the less absolute loss of his father until much later. The situation with his parents was a handy peg on which to hang all sorts of frustrations. Life had long ceased to make sense for a very mixed-up kid with a huge chip on his shoulder. From breakfast to bedtime, he projected himself as being hard as nails, as hard as his hardened heart.

Despite everything, Paul – like so many others – couldn't help liking John Lennon. For a start, he was hilarious. His calculated brutishness never quite overshadowed a grace-saving, if sometimes casually shocking, wit as well as a disarming absence of a sense of embarrassment, a selective affability and a fierce loyalty towards those few he'd accepted as intimates.

Something else that interested Paul about John was that he was leader of a "skiffle" group called The Quarry Men. He sang and was one of too many rudimentary guitarists. A chap named Rod Davis picked at a banjo, while the rest used instruments manufactured from household implements.

The skiffle craze had followed a hunt for an innocuous British riposte to Elvis Presley. The job had gone to Tommy Steele, a former merchant seaman, but his first chart strike, 'Rock With The Cavemen', had been shut down in 1956's autumn Top 20 by 'Dead Or Alive' from Lonnie Donegan – 'The King of Skiffle', a form born of the rent parties, speakeasies and Dust Bowl jug bands of the US Depression. Other skiffle stars included Johnny Duncan, a Tennesseean, who came to Britain with the US army, but, awaiting demobilisation, stayed on to cause Lonnie Donegan some nervous backward glances during skiffle's 1957 prime. Johnny drew from the same repertory sources as everyone else – blues, gospel, rockabilly, country et al – but, being a bona fide Yank, he had an edge over the plummy gentility of most native would-be Donegans.

Yet it was Lonnie rather than Johnny who was the dominant precursor of the 1960s beat boom, given those future stars who mastered their assorted crafts in amateur outfits that followed his example. As well as Cliff Richard, Marty Wilde, Adam Faith and others who received more immediate acclaim, Paul McCartney too had taken on skiffle after buying himself an acoustic guitar. Encouraged as he always was by his father, he'd taught himself to play after an initial setback on discovering that he needed to restring it in order to hold down chords commensurate with his left-handedness.

Paul had absorbed pop like blotting paper, and was making what he hoped was a pleasant row on his new acquisition, but Jim would remind him that perhaps it was time to cast aside adolescent follies. He might think that this rock 'n' roll was the most enthralling music ever, but he'd grow out of it. There was no reason why it should last much longer than previous short-lived fads. It just happened to be going a bit stronger than hula-hoops and the cha-cha-cha. Hadn't Paul read in *Melody Maker* that many skiffle musicians were switching their allegiance to less-than-pure traditional jazz, the next big thing, so they said? Unlike skiffle, anyone couldn't do it.

Feeling the chill of reality, Paul sat his GCE "O" levels – two a year early, the remainder during 1958's rainy June. Two months later, the results alighted on the Forthlin Road doormat. Having passed enough to enter the sixth form, he was able to keep that most noxious of human phenomena, a decision about his future, at arm's length for a while longer,

enabling the growth of an *idée fixe* that if he kept at it, he
might make a reasonable living as a musician.

He didn't know how Jim was going to take any
suggestions about a profession that tended to be treated
with amused contempt, unless you'd been born to it, but
the rising sap of puberty found Paul McCartney seeking
openings among suburban music-makers. That's how he'd
come to hear of The Quarry Men during the hiatus between
"O" and "A" levels. Prospects didn't seem all that bright
for them. Engagements beyond Liverpool were unknown,
and the line-up was mutable in state, and yet drawn from
the same pool of faces. Neither had The Quarry Men yet
received actual money for playing when McCartney saw
them for the first time at a church fête in Woolton on
Saturday, 6 July 1957.

"I noticed this fellow singing with his guitar," said Paul,
smiling at the memory, "and he was playing bum chords,
and singing 'Come Go With Me' by The Del-Vikings. I
realised he was changing the words into folk song and chain
gang words, a clever bit of ingenuity. That was Johnny [sic]
Lennon. My mate Ivan knew them, so we went backstage,
and after a couple of drinks, we were around the piano
singing songs to each other. Later, they sort of approached
me on a bike somewhere, and said, 'You want to join?'."

From his first date as a Quarry Man – reckoned to be at
a Conservative Club functions room on 18 October 1957 –
Paul rose quickly through the ranks, coming to rest as

Lennon's lieutenant, and in a position to foist revolutionary doctrines, namely the songs he'd started to write, onto the status quo. The affront to the older boy's superiority was such that Lennon contemplated starting again with new personnel before deciding to try this composing lark himself, and then joining forces with McCartney in what neither of them could even have daydreamed then was to evolve into one of the most outrageously successful songwriting partnerships of all time.

There was no indication of that in 1957. Few, if any, Lennon–McCartney efforts were dared on the boards – probably none at all during slots of three numbers at most in talent contests advertised in the *Echo*, where they'd be up against comedy impressionists, knife-throwers, Shirley Temples and "this woman who played the spoons," glared Paul. "We reckoned we were never going to beat this little old lady as she wiped the floor with us every time. That's when we decided to knock talent contests on the head."

It cost just a little ego-massaging to hire The Quarry Men to do a turn at wedding receptions, youth clubs, parties and "Teenage Shows" offered by cinema proprietors on Saturday mornings – so that Lennon (and McCartney) could enjoy fleeting moments of make-believing they were Donegan or Presley.

As well as a singing voice that was on a par with Lennon's, that McCartney had taken more trouble than the others to learn guitar properly made him one of the group's two natural focal points. Lennon got by less on orthodox ability than force of personality. Moreover, unlike everyone but Paul, he wasn't in it for the sake of his health, but as a purposeful means to make his way as a professional musician.

Not exactly the attraction of opposite as some biographers would have it, John and Paul's liaison was now based as much on amity as shared ambition. Nevertheless, they began weeding out those personnel who either regarded The Quarry Men as no more than a hobby or were just barely proficient passengers who made you flinch whenever you heard a difficult bit coming up in a given song.

Those who got by on home-made instruments were the first to go. Among replacements was John Duff Lowe, who was now a competent rock 'n' roll pianist. Even so, he was subjected to McCartney's quality control. "He asked me to play the introduction to Jerry Lee Lewis's 'Mean Woman Blues'," grinned Lowe. "I did so to his satisfaction, so he invited me to his house in Allerton to meet John Lennon. By then, the repertoire was all Gene Vincent, Buddy Holly, Chuck Berry and so on."

Lowe was present on The Day The Quarry Men Went To A Recording Studio in June 1958. They came away from this suburban Aladdin's cave of reel-to-reel tape machines, editing blocks and jack-to-jack leads with a now-legendary acetate that coupled a pointless replica of 'That'll Be The Day' by Holly's Crickets with 'In Spite Of All The Danger', an original by Paul and 15-year-old lead guitarist George

Harrison, as new a recruit as John Lowe, who affirms that McCartney was the main writer, qualifying this with "Some say that he was inspired by a favourite record of his, 'Tryin' To Get To You' by Elvis Presley, which, when Paul went to Boy Scout camp in 1957, was Number 15 in the UK charts."

The disc was in John Lowe's possession when The Quarry Men faded away sometime in 1959 – though he'd hear that "John and Paul got together again – and George was playing with other groups." As for Lowe himself, "I joined Hobo Rick and his City Slickers, a country-and-western band. I've got a feeling that George played with us on one occasion. It never occurred to me to become a professional musician – though most evenings, I'd be in either a club called the Lowlands or down the Casbah, Pete Best's mother's place."

3 "It's Now Or Never"

Apart from a smattering of offstage lines many acts later, John Duff Lowe's part in the play was over, but, as the world knows, George Harrison was there for the duration. He'd been in the year below Lowe and McCartney at the Institute, but he owned an electric guitar and amplifier, and his fretboard skills had been the most advanced of any Quarry Man – "though that isn't saying very much," qualified Paul, "as we were raw beginners ourselves." Yet, even before McCartney's sponsorship had brought Harrison to the group, the idea of an Everly Brothers-type duo with George may have crossed Paul's mind – and, before teaming up with John, a McCartney–Harrison songwriting liaison had borne half-serious fruit.

Overtures from other combos for George's services had been among factors that had led to the unnoticed dissolution of The Quarry Men, but, for reasons he couldn't articulate, Harrison was to commit himself exclusively to not so much a working group as a creative entity whose principal audience was a tape-recorder in the living room at 20 Forthlin Road.

After Paul had fiddled with microphone positioning, the valves warmed up to this or that new composition, attributed to him and John, regardless of who'd actually written it. Of these works, all that remain are mostly just titles – 'That's My Woman', 'Just Fun', 'Looking Glass', 'Winston's Walk', anyone? One that survived, Paul's 'Cayenne', was, like a lot of the others, an instrumental that took up the slack of The Shadows, very much the men of the moment in early 1960. If backing group to Cliff Richard, a more comfortable British Elvis than Tommy Steele had been, they'd just scored the first of many smashes in their own right.

Perhaps when they'd acquired a more professional veneer (and a drummer) accompanying a Cliff Richard sort was the way forward for Paul, George, John – and Stuart Sutcliffe, an art student who Lennon had stampeded into hire-purchasing an electric bass guitar for what it looked like rather than its sound. Sutcliffe's arrival in their midst had followed Lennon's proposal that Harrison switch to bass. This had had as much effect as if he'd suggested an Indian sitar. John didn't even bother sounding out McCartney for whom "bass was the instrument you got lumbered with. You didn't know a famous bass player. They were just background people."

Paul would maintain that Sutcliffe "was kind of a part-time member because he'd have to do his painting, and we'd

all hang out, and Stu would come in on the gigs." Though
he was thus a rock 'n' roller, Sutcliffe moved too in beatnik
circles, consuming specific paperback books rather than
records. Though not even a pretend beatnik himself, Paul
McCartney was caught in the general drift, but actually read
some of the literature bought merely for display by others.

Sometimes, he got stuck as his brow furrowed over Soren
Kierkegaard, the Danish mystic, and his existentialist
descendants, chiefly Jean-Paul Sartre. Because it contained
more dialogue, Paul was far keener on Kerouac and
Burroughs, foremost prose writers of the "Beat Generation"
as well as associated bards such as Corso, Ginsberg and
Ferlinghetti. Now a television scriptwriter, Johnny Byrne,
one of Merseyside's arch-beatniks, went further: "I fell in
with a group of people who, like me, were absolutely crazy
about books by the beats. We were turning out our own little
magazines. In a very short time, we were into jazz, poetry –
straight out of the beatniks – and all around us were the
incredible beginnings of the Liverpool scene."

While this was to become homogeneously Liverpudlian
in outlook, beatnik culture in general was as North American
as the pop charts. Moreover, in most cases, it was intrinsically
as shallow in the sense that it wasn't so much about being
anarchistic, free-loving and pacifist as being seen to sound
and look as if you were. With practice, you would insert
"man" into every sentence, and drop buzz-words like
"warmonger", "Zen", "Monk", "Stockhausen", "Greco",

"Bird", "Leadbelly" and "Brubeck" into conversations without too much affectation.

A further "sign of maturity" was an apparent "appreciation" of either traditional or modern jazz, but the nearest McCartney, Sutcliffe, Lennon, Harrison and the tape-recorder got to it was black, blind and heroin-mainlining Ray Charles who, as The Twisted Voice Of The Underdog, caused the likes of Kerouac and Ginsberg to get "gone" on 'Hallelujah I Love Her So', 'Don't Let The Sun Catch You Cryin' and the "heys" and "yeahs" he traded with his vocal trio, The Raelettes, during 1959's 'What'd I Say', with all the exhorter-congregation interplay of an evangelist tent meeting. Jerry Lee Lewis and Little Richard were products of the same equation, but they didn't punctuate their catalogues of vocal smashes with instrumental albums and collaborations with such as Count Basie and Milt Jackson of The Modern Jazz Quartet.

Through John and Stuart, midday assaults on the works of Charles and other favoured pop entertainers were heard in the life room at the art college. Another place to rehearse was the flat Stuart shared in Hillary Mansions along Gambier Terrace within the college's environs. For a while, John dwelt there as well before returning to Woolton. It went without saying, however, that he and his ensemble could still use Gambier Terrace, said Rod Jones, another tenant, "to make a hell of a lot of noise" to the exasperation of two middle-aged ladies on the ground floor.

It also reached the ears of Johnny Byrne, one of the organisers of poetry readings accompanied by local jazz musicians at Streate's. Further jazz-poetry fusions took place at the Crane Theatre. One presentation there was at the behest of Michael Horovitz who launched 1959's *New Departures*, a counterculture poetry magazine: "At the party afterwards, Adrian Henri, who was the host, said, 'Oh, this poetry stuff is all right, I think I'm going to start doing it.' Roger McGough had read with us in Edinburgh – and Brian Patten, who'd sat in the front row of the Crane gig trying to hide his school cap, was this marvellous boy who came up and read rather different, passionate, romantic poems."

While they weren't exactly "jazz", Lennon, Sutcliffe and their two pals from the Institute framed the declamations of Brighton's *vers libre* bard Royston Ellis in the Jacaranda's bottle-and-candle cellar. Afterwards, he introduced them and other interested parties in the Gambier Terrace fraternity to a particularly tacky way of getting "high" with the aid of a Vick nose-inhaler from the chemists. You isolated the part of it that contained a stimulant called benzadrine. This, you then ate.

While each tried not to put his foot in it with some inane remark that showed his age, Paul and George went along with this and other bohemian practices of the big boys from the college as they cut classes for not only rehearsals but simply to sit at one of the kidney-shaped tables in the Jacaranda, proudly familiar as John Lennon held court. The pair pitched in too when proprietor Allan Williams required the painting of murals in the basement.

Services rendered to Williams were in exchange for his acting in a quasi-managerial capacity for Lennon et al who now called themselves The Silver Beatles. The two most willing to picket for more bookings were Paul and Stuart. With silver-tongued guile, they'd lay on their "professionalism" with a hyperbolic trowel, either face-to-face or in letters when negotiating with this quizzical pub landlord or that disinterested social secretary. To this end, while they spurned the synchronised footwork with which The Shadows iced their presentations, The Silver Beatles were at one with an ancient *New Musical Express* dictum concerning "visual effect". "Some sort of uniform is a great help," it ran, "though ordinary casual clothes are perhaps the best as long as you all wear exactly the same."

On settling for black shirts, dark blue jeans and two-tone plimsolls – strictly off-the-peg chic – all they needed now was the drummer they'd lacked since they were Quarry Men. They secured one of uncertain allegiance in Tommy Moore, a forklift truck driver at Garston Bottle Works. Impossibly ancient at 26, he would suffice until the arrival of someone more compatible with young "arty" types like The Silver Beatles with their long words and weaving of names like Modigliani and Kierkegaard into conversations that would lapse into student vernacular. Not over-friendly, Moore preferred the no-nonsense society of Cass and his Cassanovas,

Gerry And The Pacemakers and other workmanlike semi-professionals who derided The Silver Beatles as "posers".

McCartney and Lennon's pretensions as composers caused comment when reputations were made much more easily by churning out rock 'n' roll standards and current hits. One of 1960's summer chart-toppers was 'Three Steps To Heaven' by Eddie Cochran, a US classic rock latecomer, whose long-awaited tour of Britain's "scream circuit" was freighted with an indigenous supporting programme made up mostly of clients on the books of Larry Parnes, one of Britain's most colourful pop managers.

On the bill too was Tony Sheridan, a 19-year-old singing guitarist from Norwich. After the final date in Bristol on 17 April 1960, Sheridan had been "stranded alone in the dressing room when everyone else had gone. For the first and last time in my life, I'd bought myself a bottle of whiskey, and was trying to vent my frustration at being an inferior British musician by getting sloshed. In the end, I smashed the bottle against the wall – but the next day, I was alive and well."

Cochran, however, wasn't, having perished when his taxi swerved into a lamp-post whilst tearing through a Wiltshire town in the small hours. "Sympathy sales" assisted the passage of 'Three Steps To Heaven' to Number One, just as they had 'It Doesn't Matter Any More' by Buddy Holly – snuffed out in an air crash – the previous year. Like Holly too, Cochran was more popular in Europe than on his own soil. In the same boat was one of Eddie's fellow passengers on that fatal journey, Gene Vincent, who paid respects with a heavy-hearted 'Over The Rainbow' when, on 3 May, he headlined a three-hour spectacular at a 6,000-capacity sports arena in Liverpool, supported by an assortment of Larry Parnes ciphers and some first-division Scouse groups procured by Allan Williams.

When the show was over, "Mister Parnes Shillings And Pence" had charged Williams with procuring an all-purpose backing outfit for use by certain of his singers for some imminent runs of one-nighters in Scotland. Among those who auditioned successfully the following week were a Silver Beatles that Allan agreed had much improved. He hadn't actually been there, but it had been reported that they'd worked up a wild response from a full house of 300 at the Casbah, a basement club in leafy Hayman's Green, run by a Mrs Mona Best, mother of the drummer in the house band, The Blackjacks.

Therefore, within three weeks of the Gene Vincent extravaganza, The Silver Beatles were north of the border for eight days in the employ of a vocalist with the stage alias "Johnny Gentle".

To use an expression peculiar to the north, Jim McCartney had "looked long bacon" when his son had announced that he was interrupting "A" level revision to go on the road with John Lennon's gang and this risible Gentle man. Like the younger Silver Beatles, Paul was even going to give himself a stage name too – "Paul Ramon", for heaven's sake. All that could be hoped was that the trip would flush this Silver Beatles nonsense out of him.

In the no-star hotels where The Silver Beatles would repair each night, Paul, like all the others, "wanted to be in a room with John". The week also coincided with Sutcliffe being temporarily *persona non grata* with the mercurial Lennon. Going with the flow, McCartney no longer had to contain a pent-up resentment of Stuart. Spiking it with the diplomacy that would always come naturally to him, Paul would "remember the first argument we really had. We came down to breakfast one morning, and we were all having cornflakes and sort of trying to wake up. Stu wanted to smoke a cigarette, and I think we made him sit at the next table: 'Oh bloody hell, Stu, come on, man! You know we're having cornflakes. Do us a favour.' There was a sort of a flare up, but, you know, we soon got back together. There was never anything crazy, and we got on fine."

Tommy Moore, however, had had more than enough of being a Silver Beatle. His resignation after the expedition put paid to the group next going to work with Dickie Pride, a diminutive Londoner whose trademark convulsions on stage had earned him the sub-title "The Sheik Of Shake".

Back on the trivial round of suburban dance halls, Paul volunteered to beat the skins before and after the loss of Moore's successor, a picture-framer named Norman Chapman, after only three weeks. Despite hardly ever sitting behind a kit before, McCartney was quite an adroit sticksman. He would also pound available yellow-keyed upright pianos, amplified by simply shoving a microphone through a rip in the backcloth.

While he was one rhythm guitarist too many as well, his and John's respective tenor and baritone were the voices heard most during any given evening. A hybrid of plummy ex-choirboy and nose-blocked Scouse, Paul was genuinely surprised when his singing caused some of the sillier girls beyond the footlights – if there were any – to make unladylike attempts to grab his attention. He wasn't impervious to their coltish charms, far from it, but was, nonetheless, aware of how brittle such adoration could be. Symptomatic of the new pestilence now ravaging the record-buying public, a TV series entitled *Trad Tavern* filled the 30 minutes once occupied by *Boy Meets Girls*.

A sure sign of stagnation in pop is adults liking the same music as teenagers. *Trad Tavern* appealed to both – and, while they might not have bought their records, grandmothers warmed to Ronnie Carroll, Mark Wynter, Craig Douglas and others from a mess of UK heart-throbs in the early 1960s who took their lightweight cue from the States. Some breached the Top Ten, but hovering between 20 and 40 was more their mark.

Amidst all the trad and Bobby candyfloss were the kind of big-voiced ballads and singers that had preceded 'Rock Around The Clock'. As much a culmination of all that had gone before as a starting point for what followed (as The Beatles would be), even Elvis succumbed in 1960 with 'It's Now Or Never', an adaptation of 'O Sole Mio', a schmaltzy Italian job from the 1900s – and his biggest hit thus far.

1960 also accommodated Top Ten debuts by Roy Orbison ('Only The Lonely'), Liverpool comedian Ken Dodd (in "serious" mode with 'Love Is Like A Violin') – and Matt Monro, whose 'Portrait Of My Love' had been made under the supervision of George Martin, recording manager of Parlophone, an EMI subsidiary, which usually traded in comedy and variety rather than outright pop. Monro, Ken Dodd and Roy Orbison were exceptions, but it was a sweeping adult generalisation that the common-or-garden pop singer "couldn't sing". That was the main reason why they loathed another hit parade newcomer, Adam Faith, the most singular of our brightest post-skiffle stars. Yet his verbal contortions and less contrived wobbly pitch had enough going for it to lend period charm to his 'What Do You Want' breakthrough and even 'Lonely Pup In A Christmas Shop' – "a ridiculous, stupid thing to do," he'd shrug in his 1996 life story, but still a Top Ten entry.

Such was the state of pop affairs when, shortly after the Johnny Gentle jaunt, The Silver Beatles hacked the adjective from their name, and wondered what to do next.

4 "What'd I Say?"

Trad bands were everywhere as were places they could play. With this stylistic stranglehold on many venues, it was small wonder that groups keeping the rock 'n' roll faith were open to offers from abroad – particularly West Germany where bastions of Teutonic trad (from Cologne's Storyville to Kiel's Star Palast) had converted to rock 'n' roll *bierkellers*, complete with the coin-operated sounds of Elvis, Gene, Cliff, Adam and the others.

Among difficulties encountered by the Fatherland's club owners was that of "live" entertainment. Patrons were often affronted by native bands who invested the expected duplications of US and British hits with complacent exactitude, a neo-military beat and an unnatural gravity born of singing in a foreign tongue.

Back in Britain, Cliff Richard, Marty Wilde, Dickie Pride and nearly everyone else who'd driven 'em wild on *Oh Boy!* had gone smooth as epitomised by wholesome film musicals from Cliff; Marty jubilant in his newly married state, and Dickie's 1960 album, *Pride Without Prejudice* – Tin Pan Alley chestnuts with Ted Heath's orchestra in accord with a lodged convention of British pop management that it was OK to make initial impact with rock 'n' roll or whatever the latest craze was, but then you had to ditch it quickly and get on with "quality" stuff so that your flop singles could be excused as "too good for the charts".

Yet if the average teenager was faced with a choice between Dickie Pride as third rate Sinatra's 'Bye Bye Blackbird' and Screaming Lord Sutch's 'Jack The Ripper' – "nauseating trash," sniffed *Melody Maker* – it'd be his Lordship every time. The most famous pop star who never had a hit, Sutch and his backing Savages were among few of their sort assured of plenty of work, with or without hits – or trad – and so were Johnny Kidd And The Pirates. The focal point of each was a blood-and-thunder stage act with the performances of Kidd and Sutch themselves as fervently loyal to classic rock as Lonnie Donegan was to skiffle.

The Beatles were more Johnny Kidd than Cliff Richard. Paul McCartney drew the short straw if ever they responded to a request for 'Voice In The Wilderness', 'Please Don't Tease' and other of Cliff's recent chartbusters, but Paul left a deeper wound with Kidd's 'Shakin' All Over' and party-pieces like 'What'd I Say' as a window-rattling, extrapolated finale in which he'd enhance his vocals with knee-drops, scissor kicks and general tumbling about during George's solos. Then about to form The Merseybeats in The Beatles' image, Tony Crane would recall, "McCartney had a guitar that he didn't play slung around his neck. They finished with 'What'd I Say', and he was madder than any time I've seen Mick Jagger. He danced all over the place. It was marvellous."

This was part of a transformation wrought by a 1960 season in Hamburg's cobbled Grosse Freiheit, a prominent red-light district just beyond the labyrinthian waterfront of the Elbe. As late as 1968, sending a group over for residencies in German night spots was, reckoned Jim Simpson, a noted West Midlands agent, "rather like training a 1,000m (1,100 yards) sprinter by making him run 5,000m (5,500 yards) courses." On the Grosse Freiheit, a haunt called the Kaiserkeller had struck first in June 1960 by enticing some unemployed London musicians across the North Sea to mount its ricketty stage as "The Jets". Their number included Tony Sheridan – with whom The Beatles were to begin the commercial discography.

That lay a year in a future, which Paul, John, Stuart and George couldn't imagine during an endless search for work in and around Liverpool. Then, to cut a long story short, an offer came via Allan Williams of a residency in the Indra, a companion club to the Kaiserkeller, commencing in August 1960. A stipulation about a drummer was satisfied because, at the Casbah, The Blackjacks were about to disband, and, when asked, Pete Best was quite amenable to becoming a Beatle – even if, said McCartney, "he just wasn't the same kind of black humour that we were. He was not quite as Artsy [sic] as certainly John and Stu were."

As Paul had finished his "A" levels, his father supposed it was all right for him to go gallivanting off to Germany like other sixth formers might go back-packing in Thailand. Thus he and the rest boarded Allan Williams's overloaded mini-bus outside the Jacaranda, bound for the night ferry from Harwich to the Hook of Holland.

Hot-eyed with sleeplessness, they struggled with the first armfuls of careworn equipment into an Indra, pungent still with a flat essence of yesterday's tobacco, food and alcohol intake. With a face like a bag of screwdrivers, Bruno Koschmider, the proprietor, wasn't exactly Uncle Cuddles – but if his manner was cold, he did not seem ill-disposed towards The Beatles. It wasn't in his interest to be. An antagonised group might take it out on the customers.

The Beatles did not complain of any shortage of romantic squalor – well, squalor anyway – after Herr Koschmider had conducted them to three tiny rooms adjoining a lavatory in the Art Deco Bambi-Filmkunsttheater cinema over the road from the Indra. While there weren't enough musty camp beds or frayed old sofas to go round, this was where they could sleep. Like the foul coffee served – as they were to discover – behind the facade of the local police station, it would have sickened pigs, but another Liverpool outfit, Derry and his Seniors, seemed to be making do in two similarly poky holes at the back of the Kaiserkeller.

That evening, the border of light bulbs (not all of them working) round the stage were switched on, and a tired Beatles gave their first ever performance outside the United Kingdom. To their costumes, they'd added houndstooth check jackets, and replaced the plimsolls with winkle-pickers – all except for Pete who hadn't had time to buy the right gear. His gradual isolation from the others had started before they'd even reached Harwich.

After a slow start, one or two of the glum old men waiting in vain for the usual Grosse Freiheit fare of stripteasers, allowed themselves to be jollied along. A more transient clientele of sailors, gangsters, prostitutes and inquisitive youths laughed with them and even took a chance on the dance floor as they got used to the newcomers' endearing glottal intonations and ragged dissimilarity to the contrived splendour of television pop stars.

This was all very well, but, during wakeful periods after they'd retired, the full horror of The Beatles' filthy accommodation reared up in the encircling gloom. Daylight could not pierce it after Paul was jerked from the doze that precipitates consciousness by John breaking wind before rising to shampoo his hair in a washbasin in the movie-goers' toilets.

Their dismal living conditions did not prevent them from enjoying the fun that was to be had in the Grosse Freiheit mire. When the '60s started swinging, one of Paul McCartney's paternity suits emanated from the area where the night's love life could be sorted out during the first beer break. On initiating conversations with Paul, fancy-free and affectionate females were delighted that he wasn't one to deny himself casual sexual exploits. Though he had a steady girlfriend back home – Dorothy Rhone, a bank clerk – he was perpetually on the lookout for an unsteady one. Advisedly, shadowy thighs and lewd sniggering did not leap out of the pages of Paul's letters home during four months away that saw a transfer from the Indra to the plusher Kaiserkeller, where an abiding memory of Horst Fascher, Koschmider's indomitable chief of staff, was of Sutcliffe sketching secretively in a remote corner of the club, and McCartney and Lennon composing in the bandroom where, elucidated Paul, "the only things we write down are lyrics on the backs of envelopes to save forgetting them, but the tunes, rhythms and chords we memorise."

Creative advances did not correlate with personal relationships within The Beatles. John was still prone to antagonising his best friend just to see his hackles rise, but his inner ear ignored the stark truth that Stuart's playing hadn't progressed after all these months.

Had Paul expressed a recent willingness to take over on bass before the trip, the group wouldn't have been cluttered still with an unnecessary rhythm guitarist, no matter how contrasting McCartney and Lennon's chord shapes could be. If Stuart hadn't been around, Paul wouldn't have felt so redundant, just singing and gyrating with an unplugged guitar or impersonating Little Richard at the worn-out Kaiserkeller piano, from which aggravating Sutcliffe would snip wires to replace broken bass strings.

There was no let-up in the tension-charged ugliness, visible and invisible, back in the Bambi-Filmkunsttheater, more loathsome than ever with its improvised receptacles for junk food leavings, empty liquor bottles, overflowing cigarette ash, used rubber "johnnies" and dried vomit.

Germany changed The Beatles forever – though it almost destroyed them too when they hadn't even the decency to lie to Bruno Koschmider about spending their rest periods in a more uptown rival establishment, the Top Ten. He was furious to learn that its manager intended to lure them away with better pay and conditions as soon as their extended contract with the Kaiserkeller expired in December. Rather than racketeers and ruffians, the Top Ten attracted young "Mittelstand" adults – a couple of social rungs higher than "youths" – whose liberal-minded parents might drop them off in estate cars. Most of these would be collected just before midnight, owing to the curfew that forbade those under 18 from frequenting Grosse Freiheit clubs past their bedtimes.

The German administration was conscientious too about protecting minors from temptation – though it was too often the case that *Polizei* couldn't be bothered with the paperwork after catching young aliens like George Harrison, weeks away from his 18th birthday, flaunting the law. However, an ireful Koschmider's string-pulling ensured more intense interest, and George was sent home before November was out.

The Beatles seemed quite prepared to carry on without him, but the Top Ten was obliged to replace them with Gerry And The Pacemakers (straight from the civil service and British Rail rather than art college and grammar schools) after McCartney and Best were deported too – on Bruno's trumped-up charge of arson.

Though tarred with the same brush, Stuart and John had been free to go after signing a statement in German that satisfied the *Polizei* that he knew nothing about Exhibit A: the charred rag that constituted Herr Koschmider's accusation that The Beatles had all conspired to burn down the hated Bambi-Filmkunsttheater.

Lennon followed the others back to Liverpool, but Sutcliffe stayed on, moving in with Astrid Kirchherr, a German photographer to whom he was unofficially engaged. She was a leading light of Hamburg's "existentialists" – the "Exis" – whose look anticipated the "Gothic" style prevalent in the late 1970s. Exi haircuts were *pilzen kopf* – "mushroom head". Though commonplace in Germany, a male so greaselessly coiffured in Britain would be branded a "nancy boy", even if Adam Faith was the darling of the ladies with a similar brushed-forward cut.

The Exis fell for The Beatles partly because they were tacitly bored with the "coolness" of Dave Brubeck, Stan Getz, The Modern Jazz Quartet and other "hip" music-makers whose album covers were artlessly strewn about their various "pads".

Of individual Beatles, Pete was a strong-but-silent type in contrast to winsome Paul who, so Horst Fascher would insist, was the "sunny boy" of the group as he scuttled to and from microphones or lilted 'Besame Mucho', one of those sensuous Latin-flavoured ballads that, like 'Begin The Beguine', 'Sway' and 'Perfidia', never seem to go away. Generally, only the title was sung in Spanish when 'Besame Mucho', a frequent *wunche* (request) from the ladies – transported you for a few minutes from the shimmering sea of bobbing heads in the Kaiserkeller to warm latitudes and dreamy sighs and then the squiggle of lead guitar that kicked off 'Too Much Monkey Business' would jolt you back to reality – either that or Stuart's fluffed run-down into 'It's So Easy'.

A little of Stuart's singing went a long way too, and as an instrumentalist, he was as good as he'd ever get – and that wasn't good enough. Privately, he admitted as much to Astrid, adding that he had only came along for the laugh and because he was John's friend. Whatever was left for Stuart to enjoy about playing with The Beatles was for the wrong reasons. For devilment, he'd deliberately pluck sickeningly off-key notes. If Paul – and George too – thought he was the group's biggest liability, then he'd amuse himself being it. They could get John to sack him for all he cared, even if they'd slain a fire regulation-breaking audience on the last night at the Kaiserkeller.

5 "Over The Rainbow"

Before they'd departed from Hamburg so ignominiously, Paul had evolved into an outstanding showman, possessed of that indefinable something else – the "common touch" maybe – that enabled him, via a wink and a broad grin diffused to the general populace, to make any watching individual feel – for a split-second anyway – like the only person that mattered to him and his Beatles in the entire city.

There was, nonetheless, a crouched restlessness about Paul, and, however much he might have gainsaid it, he was looking out for any signpost that pointed in the direction of fame. He was even willing, so he'd intimated already to John, to play bass, even though it was a presence rather than a sound on the vinyl that crackled on the Forthlin Road gramophone, and its executants overshadowed by the higher octaves available to lead and rhythm guitarists.

Such a sacrifice would be to The Beatles' general good because, if Lennon might be closing his ears still, McCartney and Harrison had gauged Stuart Sutcliffe's limitations and could hear what was technically askew – and always would be. On stage at the Kaiserkeller, he'd usually been miles away mentally. More than ever before, he was physically elsewhere too – so much so that it had been necessary to line up an understudy in Colin Millander, a former Jet who had stayed on as part of a duo in a nearby restaurant. Though three years Stuart's junior – when such a difference mattered – George's exasperation that "he was in the band because John conned him into buying a bass" had shown itself in desultory sabre-rattling with Sutcliffe in safe assurance that Paul would support him when John intervened.

Paul, see, was Stuart's truer enemy. Their animosity boiled over after the latter lost his temper when McCartney, seated at the piano, made some remark about Astrid. Flinging down his bass, Sutcliffe bounded across the boards, mad fury in his eyes, to knock the detested Paul off his perch. Manfully, the others kept the song going as the pair tumbled wrestling to the floor. Used to The Beatles' excesses on the boards, the audience emitted whoops of drunken encouragement and bellowed instruction as the number finished and the irresolute fight ebbed away to a slanging match and the combatants glowering at each other from opposite ends of a huffy dressing room.

Characteristically, Paul would laugh off this proclamation of an open state of warfare as a bit of a lark in retrospective: "Occasionally, we would have our set-to's, not too many really – but the major one was a fight on stage. The great thing about it was it wasn't actually a fight because neither of us were good fighters – so it was a grope! We just grappled each other, and I remember thinking, 'Well, he's littler than me. I'll easily be able to fight him.' But, of course, the strength of ten men this guy had – and we were locked. All the gangsters were laughing at us, and me and Stu are up by the bloody piano, locked in this sort of death embrace. All the gangsters were going, 'Come on! Hit him!' to either of us, and we couldn't do anything."

As events were to demonstrate, McCartney might not have been so jocular had he managed to strike a blow to Stuart's head. Indeed, he might have ended up on a charge of murder before a German judge and jury tacitly prejudiced by his nationality and hirsute appearance. The next day, however, Paul was Mr Nice Guy again, but neither he nor Stuart would forgive or forget, and, for weeks afterwards, Paul found himself casting an odd thoughtful glance at Stuart sweating over the bass when Lennon was hogging the main microphone. Who'd have thought it – Stuart sticking up for himself without John protecting him?

Yet almost all the cards were on the table when four-fifths of The Beatles reassembled back in Liverpool – "and then the thing was, 'Well, who's going to play bass?'" asked Paul. As he'd rattled the traps in the absence of Tommy Moore, so McCartney had adapted likewise to bass whenever Colin Millander or Stuart had been indisposed at the Kaiserkeller, but for their first four post-Hamburg engagements, another ex-Blackjack, Chas Newby, was roped in.

Chas was there when The Beatles were a last minute addition to a bill at Litherland Town Hall the day after Boxing Day. A lot of groups would sell their souls for a career, however it ended, that had had a night like that in it. You couldn't refute their impact on a crowd who'd been spellbound from the 'Long Tall Sally' opening until the last major sixth of the final encore. Along the way, The Beatles had stoked up the first scattered screams that had ever reverberated for them.

The Beatles were to become a fixture at the Cavern, which, for all its previous jazz dignity, was in the process of "going pop". They made their debut in February 1961 during one of the newly established lunch-time sessions. This was to be Stuart Sutcliffe's only performance at what was destined to become as famous a Liverpool landmark as the Pier Head. Its idiosyncratic reek of disinfectant, mould and cheap perfume was still on his clothes 24 hours later – as it was on those of Colin Manley, among the audience for what must have been an off-day for The Beatles who "still had Stuart with them, and they really weren't very good."

Lennon had been pleased to see Sutcliffe, but to the others their errant bass guitarist's reappearance was like that of the proverbial bad penny now that they'd experienced Chas Newby's and then Paul's – and, on one occasion, Johnny Gustafson of The Big Three's – more agile playing. Stuart was back in Hamburg by March, but an official colour was given to this by The Beatles, who were pencilled in for a four-month Top Ten season commencing on April Fools' Day. Stuart was to be on hand in negotiations between the club, the West German Immigration Office and Herr Knoop, Hamburg's chief of police. Crucially, he had to support Mona Best's badgering and Allan Williams's assurances that The Beatles were reformed characters, especially fire-bugs Pete and Paul.

While Stuart had proved useful as a mediator, "I believe to this day that he would eventually have been thrown out," said Rod Jones, expressing a commonly held view, "as soon as there was some sort of future. I'm actually surprised that he didn't go before."

Just as it was a case of when rather than if Stuart left the group, so was not replacing him, opting instead for the simpler expedient of transferring McCartney permanently to bass. Paul's low-fretted cohesion with Pete's drumming was a subliminal element of The Beatles' intensifying local popularity as word got round, and it became customary for the Cavern to fill long before they followed the trad band or whatever else was in support, to invoke a mood of a kind of committed gaiety, often with cramped onlookers assuming the dual role of accompanying choir and augmenting the rhythm section.

While The Beatles' rowdy style was now not only acceptable but demanded at the Cavern and other recurring engagements, the going was erratic elsewhere, partly because certain parochial agents had no qualms about marrying a loud R&B outfit with, say, the ubiquitous trad band, the C&W (country-and-western) of Hank Walters and his Dusty Road Ramblers, and the monologues of comedian Ken Dodd – as took place at a Sunday matinee in a cinema in Maghull, more Lancashire than Liverpool.

The Beatles would arrive too in Birkenhead, Seaforth or – for one fabled night only – Aldershot, over the edge of the world in distant Hampshire, where the cissy *pilzen kopfs* that George, Paul and John would be sporting by the end of 1961 were sometimes a red rag to those for whom an Elvis quiff was not yet a symbol of masculinity.

On the firmer turf of the Liverpool jive-hives where they were rebooked into the foreseeable future, other groups would be copying The Beatles' stagecraft and repertoire, including 'I Saw Her Standing There', an original that had dripped mostly from the pen of McCartney.

Other than that terrible journey to Aldershot, however, campaigns for UK engagements beyond Merseyside yielded next to nothing – and Paul was keenly aware that his group's present state of marking time was prodding nerves at home, especially as he was still embroiled in hire-purchase payments for his equipment, and his income from The Beatles was far less than Mike's as a hairdresser.

Not helping either was the cost of a Hofner "violin" bass that Paul had bought from a Grosse Freiheit shop. This didn't leave much change from his earnings at the Top Ten.

Among The Beatles' duties there was backing Tony Sheridan both on stage – and in the studio after he was offered a recording contract by Bert Kaempfert, a power on Polydor, a division of Deutsche Grammophon, Germany's equivalent of EMI.

As a composer, 36-year-old Bert had contributed to 'Wooden Heart', Elvis Presley's European spin-off 45 from the movie soundtrack of *GI Blues*, a fictionalisation of his military service in Germany. The King acknowledged the melodic debt 'Wooden Heart' owed to the traditional 'Muss I Denn Zum Stadtele Naus', by breaking into German for a couple of verses.

Like nearly everybody else, The Beatles inserted a token song in German into the proceedings in Hamburg. The line of least resistance in this respect was for Paul to sing 'Wooden Heart', but more erudite was his 'Falling In Love Again' from the 1943 Marlene Dietrich movie vehicle, *The Blue Angel*. McCartney excerpts from stage and film musicals also impinged on otherwise frenetic hours on the boards. 'Summertime' (from *Porgy And Bess*) and, when that was dropped, 'Till There Was You' (*The Music Man*) and 'Over The Rainbow' could silence the most rumbustious crowd like a mass bell in Madrid.

A few Lennon–McCartney efforts were unveiled publically – two in as many hours by late 1962 – but though 'I Saw Her Standing There' became something of a fixture during The Beatles' later Hamburg seasons, it hadn't the immediacy of 'Twist And Shout', another from The Isley Brothers, or 'Shimmy Shimmy' by The Orlons, and other more ardently anticipated crowd-pleasers. Where did songwriting get you anyway? No one paid attention to an home-made song, least of all Bert Kaempfert on the prowl on behalf of Polydor for a bargain-basement "Beat Gruppa" rather than the preferred orchestra for Tony Sheridan's first single.

Bert put his head round the door at the Top Ten during one of many transcendental moments that could not be recreated, that would look impossible if transcribed on manuscript paper. By today's standards, the sound *per se* was puny yet harsh and atrociously distorted as Tony and The Beatles battled with amplifiers of 30-watts maximum that were sent through speakers known to tear, explode and even catch fire because of power surges and the mismatch of British and German ohms. McCartney would recall that "If we had troubles with our overworked amplifiers – we had to plug two guitars into the same one – I'd just chuck it all in and start leaping all round the stage or rushing over to the piano and playing a few chords."

Despite off-putting technical problems, Sheridan was to remember that "Bert Kaempfert came for several nights. He was impressed by what he thought was our authenticity – which, of course, was second-hand American music infused with elements of our own that were authentic. Afterwards, we discussed with Bert what we ought to record. I'd heard Gene Vincent do 'My Bonnie' – very differently

– and later on, a Ray Charles version. Long before we'd even thought about recording it ourselves, we'd done a sort of Jerry Lee Lewis-type arrangement on stage, but without piano. The B-side was the signature tune of my Norwich skiffle group, The Saints."

Tony Sheridan's was the name on the orange Polydor label when these rocked-up versions of 'My Bonnie Lies Over The Ocean' and 'When The Saints Go Marching In' were issued as a single in October 1961. So began Paul McCartney's recording career – helping Tony, Pete, John and George make the best of a couple of so-so numbers intended purely for Germany. It looked like being the only disc on which he'd ever be heard too.

6 "Some Other Guy"

As things turned out, 'My Bonnie' wasn't to be the only disc Paul and The Beatles would make. The Tony Sheridan single sold sufficiently to warrant an album containing some other tracks with The Beatles. There was also to be an associated extended-play (EP) disc, also entitled *My Bonnie*.

Import copies were spun by Bob Wooler, one of the disc-jockeys at the Cavern, and consolidated The Beatles' regional fame within a radius of about 25km (15 miles). Now they'd rid themselves of Stuart Sutcliffe, the group epitomised the two guitars–bass–drums archetype of what would go down in cultural history as 1963's Merseybeat explosion. They also moved up a further rung or two through their acquisition just before Christmas 1961 of a manager in 27-year-old Brian Epstein, a sales manager at his grandfather's central Liverpool department store, which contained what could be deservedly advertised as "The Finest Record Selection In The North". Until then, The Beatles had made do with Mona Best, who was efficient enough, but, as she herself realised, didn't have the entrepreneurial contacts and know-how to remove The Beatles from the Liverpool–Hamburg grindstone.

With the advent of Epstein, her say in the group's affairs was diminished to the point of eventual silence, despite vainglorious efforts for it to be otherwise, especially as her handsome Pete was, Mona believed – with much justification – the most effusive fount of the group's teen appeal. Because Mrs Best was of far less use to them now, "John, Paul and George resented her interference," said Bill Harry, editor of *Mersey Beat*. Why couldn't all Beatle women be more like Paul's uncomplaining Dorothy Rhone, who supplied occasional passive glamour when he made her sit on a bar-stool in the midst of The Beatles? Yet for all her apparent acquiescence, it had still been necessary for Paul to suspend his routine philanderings when she and John's future wife, Cynthia Powell, visited Hamburg during the months at the Top Ten.

It was John and Paul, rather than John and Stuart nowadays as, with their girlfriends, they went on picnic excursions by train on hot afternoons to seaside resorts like Ostsee where they would recharge their batteries for the labours of the night. If there was no work that evening, they'd travel further to Timmendorf Strand where it was sometimes mild enough to sleep on the beach.

Serenities like this would be few and far between after McCartney and Lennon – and Harrison – could no longer venture into a public place without the pestering of fans and reporters. In unconscious preparation, they took in their stride Brian Epstein's moulding of them into entertainers destined ideally to emerge from provincial oblivion. The Germans have a word for what Brian was doing: *verharmlosen*, to render harmless.

By March 1962, the black leathers – aggressively redolent of Nazi officer trench-coats or motor-bike hoodlums – had been superseded by tweed suits of nondescript design. These, however, were a holding operation for the following year's epauletted jackets with no lapels, that buttoned up to the throat, and had no unsightly bulges in the high-waisted trousers owing to the absence of pockets around tight hips. While the basic pattern had been taken from a blue-brushed denim get-up sold in the Hamburg branch of C&A's, that The Beatles had consented to wear it was down to the fastidious Epstein assuring them that it was for the best.

Thanks to Brian's persistence via telephone and post, the group had also risen to the challenge of the ballroom circuit, becoming a reliable draw as their booking spectrum broadened intermittently to Yorkshire, Wales and as far south as Swindon. Courtesy of Epstein's dogged prodding of Polydor's UK outlet too, 'My Bonnie' by Tony Sheridan and The Beatles was released in Britain on 5 January 1962. *NME* reviewer Keith Fordyce was generous – "both sides are worth a listen for the above-average ideas" – but, unaired on either the Light Programme or Radio Luxembourg, the disc sank without trace.

In June, the same was in store for 'You Got What I Like' by Middlesex's Cliff Bennett And The Rebel Rousers, but Parlophone seemed to regard the group as a long-term investment because it was prepared to risk another six singles before reaping the harvest of its faith in X-factor Bennett, highly regarded as a bandleader, and one of few Britons who imagined that they had a black soul within a white skin, that could actually take on black pop without losing the overriding passion.

Yet chart recognition of this seemed a far-fetched afterthought to Cliff when he and his Rebel Rousers were on the wrong side of the North Sea, putting on the agony night after night at Hamburg's new Star-Club where Paul and John of The Beatles promised to give him a leg up by writing him a song if their group got famous before his did.

Both the southern and northern English factions at the Star-Club were mixing socially with Little Richard and Gene Vincent as each disturbed Tony Sheridan's reign as incumbent rock 'n' roll king of the Grosse Freiheit. Like Caesar deified by the Gallic peasants, Richard would offend none by refusing gifts pressed upon him. One such gift was one of Paul's best shirts after "I developed a specially close relationship with Paul. He would just look at me. Like he wouldn't move his eyes – and he'd say, 'Oh, Richard, you're my idol. Let me touch you.' He wanted to learn my little holler, so we sat at the piano going 'Oooooooh! Oooooooh!' until he got it."

By the middle of the decade, Richard was to have cause to be grateful to The Beatles when they revived 'Long Tall Sally' on disc. In 1962, however, while he continued to feed off a more glorious past, they could only carry the torch of classic rock – well, their take on it – back to the confines of Liverpool.

Yet more than mere Merseybeat was unravelling there now. Following a lucrative London exhibition, abrasive Arthur Dooley had become a professional Scouser, often on BBC television's early evening magazine, *Tonight*. A protégé of Pop Art pioneer Richard Hamilton, Adrian Henri had reached beyond slapping oil on canvas to performance art and, as he had promised Michael Horovitz, poetry.

Other bards and *nouvelle vague* artists of the same vintage included Roger McGough, Brian Patten, John Gorman, Alun Owen (who was to write the script of *A Hard Day's Night*, The Beatles' first feature film), Mike Evans – and Mike McCartney who, with Gorman and McGough, had formed Scaffold, an ensemble that mingled poetry and satirical sketches during the audio-visual and literary events that, walking a tightrope between near magical inspiration and pseudo-intellectual ramblings, were springing up as alternatives to doing the 'Hippy Hippy Shake' with all o' your might down the Iron Door.

The gifted Mike was to adopt the stage surname "McGear" to stay accusations of boarding his more famous brother's bandwagon though in 1962, the two were on terms of fluctuating equality in their respective spheres. Scaffold were leading what the economist would call a "full life" with regular bookings at Streate's, the Everyman and the Blue Angel, while The Beatles were to be flown, not driven, to Hamburg for a penultimate spell at the Star-Club in November.

While the previous season had been a professional triumph, it had been blighted by the cerebral haemorrhage that had killed Stuart Sutcliffe the afternoon before their arrival. An advance party of Paul, Pete and John hadn't heard the news when they'd taken off from Liverpool. In the skies, they'd been shrill with their first BBC radio broadcast (*Teenagers' Turn* from Manchester's Playhouse) the previous weekend. Raring to go as the aeroplane descended, the three came down with a bump when Astrid Kirchherr, drained of her usual sparkle, met them after their passports had been checked. Paul was at a loss for words. Anything he said or did then wouldn't ring true somehow: "It affected John the most because he'd been closest to him. John was most disturbed by it. For me, it was a distant thing. I can't remember doing or thinking anything – but the main thing for me, that I remember feeling bad about was that he died of a brain thing. It struck me as all being Van Gogh and sort of a wild artistic thing, but I think by then, I'd got a little hardened to people dying. It wasn't like Stu was with us. We'd got used to not being with Stu – but it was a shock."

That night, Paul and Pete grizzled into their beer for a boy they hadn't understood but had liked because, outside the context of all the in-fighting, he'd come to like them.

Their eyes were still sore the next day when they went with John and Astrid to greet Brian, George and Stuart's distraught mother at the airport. A few hours later, however, The Beatles were pitching into their opening number with all their customary verve.

The next to go – albeit in less absolute terms than Stuart – was Pete Best after the group and manager had netted a hard-won recording contract with Parlophone, having been turned down by virtually every other UK company that mattered. The first session took place on 6 June in the EMI complex along Abbey Road. Like every consequent visit, it was supervised by no less than the head of Parlophone himself, George Martin, who preferred to tape pop groups in cavernous Studio Two where he'd vetoed freshening up the paintwork in case it affected the acoustics that had spiced up the chart entries of such as Eddie Calvert and Shane Fenton.

Martin's only reservations about The Beatles that first day was that he'd heard no unmistakable smash hit within their cache of Lennon–McCartney originals, and that the drummer's lack of studio experience was more pronounced than that of the guitarists. A hireling would have to ghost him when The Beatles returned to record 'Love Me Do', a McCartney opus that, for want of anything better, had been picked as the first A-side.

BBC Radio Merseyside presenter and pop historian Spencer Leigh was to devote an entire book to chronicling the saga of Pete Best's subsequent sacking. One of the lengthier chapters explores divergent theories as to why he was replaced by Ringo Starr, one of Rory Storm's Hurricanes, two months after that initial trip to Abbey Road. One of these suggests that a green-eyed monster had whispered to the other three – particularly McCartney – that Best was the fairest of them all. This was exacerbated by *Mersey Beat*'s report that, during the *Teenagers' Turn* showcase, "John, Paul and George made their entrance on stage to cheers and applause, but when Pete walked on, the fans went wild. The girls screamed! In Manchester, his popularity was assured by his looks alone."

At the stage door afterwards, Pete was almost killed with kindness by over-attentive females from the 400-strong audience while Paul, John and George were allowed to board a ticking-over charabanc after signing some autographs. Jim McCartney was on the periphery of this incident, and admonished the sweat-smeared drummer: "Why did you have to attract all the attention? Why didn't you call the other lads back? I think that was very selfish of you."

Did Mr McCartney have an indirect hand in Pete's dismissal? To what extent did his unfair reprimand – and interrelated exchanges at Forthlin Road – make dark nights of the ego darker still? He rubbed salt into the wound on observing the dismissed Best in the Cavern shadows when a Beatles bash was being documented for the ITV series, *Know The North*. "Great, isn't it!" he crowed. "They're on TV!" Pete bit his tongue and left quietly.

Jim's glee had to be contained as edited footage – of Paul, John, George and the new member doing 'Slow Down' and 'Some Other Guy' – wasn't screened until it had gained historical importance, and the concept of a Beatles without Ringo had become as unthinkable to the world as one without Pete had once been in Liverpool.

"I was a better player than him," protested Starr 30 years later. "That's how I got the job. It wasn't on no personality [sic]." Nevertheless, a session drummer had been on clock-watching stand-by for the recording of 'Love Me Do', but Ringo kept his peace just as Paul did when directed by George Martin to extend the sung hook-line, radically altering the embedded arrangement of the humble little ditty that changed everything.

7 "Till There Was You"

The release of 'Love Me Do' in October 1962 meant that The Beatles could be billed as "EMI Recording Artists", and that the glory and the stupidity of being in a 1960s pop group now necessitated being shoulder-to-shoulder in a van for hours on end during a staggered procession of one-nighters that were often truly hellish in an age when England's only motorway terminated in Birmingham.

While local engagements were becoming less frequent, the single shifted plenty in loyal Liverpool, and eventually touched the national Top 20 – just. This followed on from ITV's *Tuesday Rendezvous* on 4 December 1962, which was the first we southerners at large ever saw of The Beatles.

The follow-up, 'Please Please Me', gave more cause to hold on hoping as, before slipping in mid-March, it lingered in a Top Ten in which Frankie Vaughan, Cliff Richard, Bobby Vee and Kenny Ball were also vying to topple Frank Ifield at Number One with 'The Wayward Wind'.

Two hits in a row was sufficient to justify a long-player – which The Beatles and George Martin were expected to complete in an allotted 12-hour day with Musicians Union-regulated tea and lunch breaks during conventional London office times and an evening period with a jobsworth locking-up well before midnight.

After Gerry And The Pacemakers, The Big Three, Billy J Kramer, The Searchers, The Merseybeats and The Fourmost notched up respectable chart entries too before 1963's cool, wet summer was out, what was deemed by the media to be a "Mersey Sound" or "Liverpool Beat" gave way to a more generalised group boom, the Big Beat, also spearheaded by John, Paul, George and Ringo – EMI's "Fab Four".

The Beatles' domination of an edition of *Sunday Night At The London Palladium* drew out the agony for Decca and all the other companies who'd turned them down in 1962. Worse was to follow when the group stole *The Royal Variety Show* at the Prince of Wales Theatre on 4 November 1963 when, with McCartney's pretty 'Till There Was You' oiling the wheels, the general feeling among adults and others who hadn't wanted to like them, was that John, Paul, George and Ringo were the stock Nice Lads When You Get To Know Them.

Ireland's Bachelors – more Viscounts than Beatles – were even nicer lads who, as token pop group in the next year's *Royal Variety Show*, had been quite willing to face the Royal Box for an amended opening line – "we wouldn't change you for the wurrrrld!" – of their most recent Top Ten strike.

If The Bachelors and The Beatles put themselves in the way of potentially damaging publicity – like married Bachelor Declan Clusky's amour with a well-known female vocalist or a Liverpool woman's imputation of her baby's irregular kinship to Paul McCartney – their respective managers would ensure that no nicotine-stained fingers would type out lurid coverage of it for the following Sunday's *News Of The World*. Besides, even if it was true, nothing too sordid was likely to be yet brought to public notice about The Beatles, Gerry, Billy J, The Fourmost and other ostensibly wholesome groups by a scum press who judged any besmirching of cheeky but innocent personas as untimely: save the scandal for The Rolling Stones, who, seized by Decca, were to be a closer second to The Beatles than earlier pretenders like Gerry And The Pacemakers, The Searchers and, in early 1964, The Dave Clark Five.

As anti-Beatles, the Stones cut appositely sullen figures on the front photograph of an eponymous debut long-player – though anyone awaiting seething musical outrage was disappointed because its content didn't ring many changes. Almost as weighty with R&B standards as the first LPs by The Animals, The Yardbirds, The Kinks, The Downliners Sect, Them, The Pretty Things and The Spencer Davis Group, it even contained 'Route 66', a set-work that any self-respecting R&B aficionado now heard no more than a mariner hears the sea.

The rise of such groups – principally Londoners – was

indicative of the decline of Liverpool as a pop Eldorado by the close of 1963. Too rapid turnovers of personnel within The Merseybeats and The Big Three didn't help either at a time when teenagers needed to identify clearly with a favoured group to the extent that, ideally, the drummer toiling over his kit was as much its public face as the lead singer.

Striking while the iron was lukewarm, all manner of German labels were still rushing out as much associated product as the traffic would allow. Most of it was pressed onto cheap compilations such as 1964's *Liverpool Beat*, an album featuring both Kingsize Taylor And The Dominoes and the more versatile Bobby Patrick Big Six – from Glasgow! – who were to be taken on semi-permanently to back Tony Sheridan. Some were immortalised *au naturel* at the Star-Club, while others were often hastened to a studio as soon as the final major sixth of the shift had reverberated so that their adrenalin could be pumped onto a spool of tape.

On the rebound from a night on stage, Kingsize Taylor and his boys thought nothing of banging out an entire LP in four hours from plug-in to final mix. Certainly, they came closest here to capturing the scintillatingly slipshod power forged unknowingly from the Star-Club fracas, day after day, week upon week.

As Taylor did, Cliff Bennett could have continued making a good living in Germany, but he preferred to take his chances at home where he and The Rebel Rousers aroused the interest of Brian Epstein who, encouraged by his runaway success with the cream of Liverpudlia, was eager to diversify. With this entrepreneurial muscle behind them, Cliff's seventh single, a tougher Anglicised copy of The Drifters' 'One Way Love', tore into the Top Ten in autumn 1964, but a second bite at that particular cherry wouldn't present itself for another two years.

Thus Cliff and his group weren't to secure a slot on 1965's "*NME* Pollwinners Concert" at Wembley Empire Pool on a bill that embraced what was then the very upper crust of British pop – including The Rolling Stones, The Kinks, Twinkle, The Animals, Them, The Searchers, Georgie Fame, Tom Jones, Wayne Fontana And The Mindbenders, The Moody Blues, Donovan, Herman's Hermits, Dusty Springfield, Freddie And The Dreamers, Cilla Black – and, of course, The Beatles who closed the show.

This afternoon extravaganza on 11 April 1965 encapsulated, I suppose, the beat boom at its hysterical, electric high summer. An act drowned in tidal waves of screams that, while subsiding to mere cheers for Twinkle, Dusty and Cilla, hurled rampaging girls towards crash barriers where they'd be hurled back again by flushed bouncers, shirt-sleeved in the heat, and aggravatingly nearer to Mick, Georgie, Tom, Wayne, Ray, Donovan and Paul than those who'd give their souls to be. In the boiling mêlée further back, unluckier ticket-holders burst into tears, rocked foetally, flapped programmes and scarves, hoisted inexpertly daubed placards, tore at their hair, wet themselves and fainted with the thrill of it all.

8 "Nobody I Know"

Bing Crosby, that most influential of pre-war singers of popular song, hadn't realised that The Beatles composed their own material. Until he did, he shared the view of evangelist Billy Graham – and every other right-thinkin' North American adult – that they were just "a passing trend". Crosby was to be sufficiently impressed by The Beatles to record an idiosyncratic 'Hey Jude', but wasn't so anxious to return to the charts that he was driven to sift through their albums and, if lucky, demo tapes for a potential smash.

Among the most conspicuous chart climbers for Bing's favourite singer, Matt Monro in the mid-1960s was the first ever cover of 'Yesterday', subject of over a thousand subsequent versions. As early as March 1967, it was approaching 500 as announced by Dick James, director of Lennon and McCartney's publishing company Northern Songs.

"I just fell out of bed and it was there," divulged Paul. "I have a piano by the side of my bed, and I just got up and played the chords. I thought it can't just have come to me in a dream. It's like handing things in to the police; if no one's claimed it after six weeks, I'll have it." 'Yesterday' was then launched into life with the provisional title of 'Scrambled Eggs' until the tailoring of lyrics that McCartney sang on disc accompanied by his own acoustic guitar strumming – and a string quartet, an early example of Beatles augmentation of conventional beat group instruments. Sitars, horn sections, orchestras, tape collage and other resources were yet to come.

Matt Monro's big band rendering of 'Yesterday' made the UK Top Ten in the teeth of a belated rival 'Yesterday' on Decca by Marianne Faithfull – with an accompanying choir – that was advantaged by apparent endorsement by sole composer Paul McCartney. First refusal, however, had been given to Billy J Kramer ("it was too nicey-nicey for me") before 'Yesterday' was offered to Chris Farlowe, a white Londoner who was, nevertheless, bruited as "the greatest Blues Singer in the world today". Marianne Faithfull had dithered over it too. Then Matt Monro's headlining spot on *Sunday Night At The London Palladium* settled the matter – though McCartney's blueprint on the soundtrack album of *Help!*, The Beatles' second movie, scored in the States.

It was George Harrison's task to introduce 'Yesterday' on stage, viz, "For Paul McCartney of Liverpool, opportunity knocks!". George and the others had nicknamed Paul (not always affectionately) "The Star", partly because he seemed to have the most highly developed instinct – and desire – for gliding on the winds of showbusiness protocol whilst gilding the image of loveable and slightly naive lads from back-of-beyond taken aback by their celebrity. His skill for combining necessary ruthlessness with keeping his popularity intact was freeze-framed in an episode centred on him at the window of a chartered aircraft that had just landed somewhere in the American Midwest.

A reception committee of town burghers and their hoity-toity children are waiting on the tarmac. Behind the glass, Paul is waving and smiling. From the side of his mouth, however, he is issuing instructions to Mal Evans, a principal of the road crew, to tell the assembly outside that he – Mal – had decided that, though The Beatles were delirious with joy at the thought of meeting them, they were in need of rest for that evening's show. I'm sorry you're disappointed, but, for their own good, I've had to disappoint the boys too. Thus Evans rather than Paul, John, George or Ringo was the *bête noire* via a strategy worthy of the most battle-hardened public relations officer.

Of all The Beatles too, Paul was the one most abreast with contemporary trends such as the injection of Oriental sounds into pop as originated by either The Yardbirds – or The Kinks on 1965's 'See My Friends' with its plaintive, whining vocal and droning guitars. Their lead guitarist Dave Davies would recall an encounter in a London club, the Scotch of St James, when "McCartney said, 'You bastards! How dare you! I should have made that record.'"

Above all, however, Paul listened hard to black soul music. "Paul loves Tamla Motown," Michael Jackson would observe when he and McCartney were friends. "He also loves gut music: early, early American black music like Elmore James – but if you want to see him smile, just start talking to him about 1960s Motown. He says he was a fan like everybody else – and since those years were really important to his career, his memories are very sharp, very sensitive about that time."

On the bill of the German leg of The Beatles' final world tour in 1966, Cliff Bennett And The Rebel Rousers' set contained 'Got To Get You Into My Life', presented to Cliff in a dressing room one night by Paul McCartney on guitar and vocal, and John Lennon dah-dahing a horn section. Whereas The Beatles had attempted Motown on disc with such as Barrett Strong's 'Money', 'Please Mr Postman' from The Marvellettes and The Miracles' 'You Really Got A Hold On Me' (all on 1963's *With The Beatles*) this new offering was a Lennon–McCartney original – "one of Paul's best songs," said John – in the more ebullient of Motown house styles. Produced by McCartney, this "best song I ever recorded" was to be Cliff's biggest smash, coming within an ace of Number One in Britain.

"When John and I first started writing songs," conceded Paul, "everything was a nick. Now that's a tip for budding songwriters. We pinched ideas from records all the time. There's nothing immoral or dishonest about it because the imitation's only a way of getting started. Like, you might hear 'Please Mr Postman', and be knocked out by it, and want to do something in that style – so you could start with a line like, 'Sorry, Mr Milkman...' By the time the song's finished, you've probably got rid of the first line anyway. Maybe it doesn't sound even remotely like The Marvelettes either, but it's got you going, acted as the spark. For example, in my mind, 'Hey Jude' is a nick from The Drifters. It doesn't sound like them or anything, but I know that the verse, with these two chords repeating over and over, came when I was fooling around playing 'Save The Last Dance For Me' on guitar."

The circle remained unbroken with Beatles numbers on a Supremes album, 1965's *With Love From Us To You*, and respective revivals of 'Eleanor Rigby' and 'Lady Madonna' by Ray Charles and Fats Domino. In 1967, Charles also did 'Yesterday', which, lasting a month low in the UK Top 50, couldn't have hoped to match Matt Monro's feat two years earlier.

The rainy winter that welded 1965 to 1966 had been party time too for The Overlanders with their Paul Friswell's contention that they "did Lennon and McCartney a favour" via a faithful if unsolicited reproduction of 'Michelle', McCartney's bilingual ballad from The Beatles' *Rubber Soul* album. Friswell's cheek was mitigated when it became the first Xerox of a Beatles LP track to top the UK singles chart.

The Overlanders arrived too late for what had come to be known as the "British Invasion" of North America, which may be dated from The Beatles' landing in Kennedy airport on 8 February 1964 with 'I Want To Hold Your Hand' at Number One in the Hot 100. To the chagrin of The Beach Boys and other US acts on the same label – Capitol – John, Paul, George and Ringo had been propelled by one of the most far-reaching publicity blitzes hitherto known in the record industry. While the intruders swamped the Hot 100, The Beach Boys' resident genius, Brian Wilson had felt both threatened and inspired artistically.

"I knew immediately that everything had changed, and that if The Beach Boys were going to survive, we would really have to stay on our toes," Brian Wilson wrote in 2001. "After seeing The Beatles perform, I felt there wasn't much we could do to compete on stage. What we could try to do was make better records than them. My father had always instilled a competitive spirit in me, and I guess The Beatles aroused it."

In reciprocation, *Pet Sounds*, The Beach Boys' most critically acclaimed LP, caused The Beatles' nervous backwards glances – with Paul McCartney citing Wilson as "the real contender" rather than The Rolling Stones. Yet, during one Abbey Road session in 1966, Mal Evans was sent out to purchase *Aftermath*, the new Stones album – because, formidable though Lennon and McCartney's head start was, a year after their first original Stones A-side –

1965's 'The Last Time' – their Keith Richards and Mick Jagger had penned all 14 tracks of *Aftermath*, which would net as rich a shoal of cover singles as *Rubber Soul* had done, among them one by The Searchers, who if surviving Merseybeat's collapse, were finding it hard to crack the Top 50, let alone the Top Ten, nowadays.

If nothing else, The Searchers, Gerry, The Beatles et al had put Liverpool on the map. In doing so, the city's art scene garnered more attention than it might have done in the course of a less fantastic decade. In return, Liverpool artists remembered The Beatles at least in paintings like Sam Walsh's *Mike's Brother* (ie Paul McCartney) and *Lennon* – as well as John Edkins's *We Love The Beatles* – shown in a posthumous exhibition at the Bluecoat in 1966. Less specific homage was paid in the ritual spinning of Beatles tracks during intermissions after the Cavern was refurbished that same year to host mainly poetry readings and like soirées.

Among recurrent acts now was the mixed-media aggregation known as "The Liverpool Scene", founded by Adrian Henri and – epitomising the passing of the old order – ex-members of beat groups, The Roadrunners and The Clayton Squares. Bringing satirical humour as well as pop music to an audience that was biased against one or the other, The Liverpool Scene drank from the same pool as fellow latter-day Cavern regulars, The Scaffold who, still containing Paul's Brother, were to harry the UK Top Ten via the vexing catchiness of 'Thank U Very Much' – a response, apparently, to Paul giving Mike a Nikon camera – 'Lily The Pink' and 1974's 'Liverpool Lou'.

Over in Hamburg, there was more of a *fin de siècle* tang in the air whether Kingsize Taylor on the verge of making despondent tracks back to England or the bunkroom above the Top Ten being vacated for a reunion party after a show at the city's Ernst Merke Halle on 26 June 1966 by The Beatles. This become impractical, but a disguised McCartney and Lennon dared a nostalgic amble along the Grosse Freiheit. As the age of Aquarius dawned, British beat groups still lingered there: doughty anachronisms still giving 'em 'Some Other Guy' and 'Besame Mucho', even as The Remo Four at the Star-Club and on *Smile!*, their 1967 Germany-only LP, crossed the frontiers between R&B and jazz. Not so adaptable, fellow Scousers Ian And The Zodiacs had followed Kingsize Taylor back to England to expire quietly after turning down 'Even The Bad Times Are Good', which picked up by Essex's Tremeloes, made the Top Five.

During the global aftermath of domestic Beatlemania, John, Paul, George and Ringo had slumped too – at least as concert performers. Much of it was down to the insufficiently amplified music being drowned by screams, but the malaise was also psychological. It was a typical journeyman musician's memory, but Paul, depressed by the monotony of it all, had glowered from the window of a hotel in Minneapolis and wondered if this was all there was, just like he had in Allerton before opportunities beyond a dead-end job like his Dad's had knocked. Imprisoned luxury in Minneapolis was just like imprisoned luxury in Milan. The Coca-Cola tasted exactly the same. If it's Wednesday, it must be Genoa. Box-office receipts could be astronomical, even when shows weren't always the complete sell-outs that they had been in 1964.

Yet, how could Paul be displeased with his lot? Even before embarking on this latest public journey, he could have dug his heels in and refused to go in the knowledge that he had enough put away for him and his immediate family to never need to work again. As a recent feature in the *TV Times* had stated: "You're a lucky man, Paul McCartney" and this had been a reference not just to his swelling fortune but his proud courtship of a dashing, flame-headed actress named Jane Asher.

She was the first daughter of the quasi-dynastic marriage of eminent Harley Street doctor Sir Richard Asher – and the Honourable Margaret Eliot, a professor at the Guildhall School of Music and Drama. Among her students had been Andrew King, future manager of The Pink Floyd and a young George Martin.

Six years after he was taken on by EMI, George produced 1956's 'Nellie The Elephant', a giggly Parlophone novelty and *Children's Favourites* perennial by Mandy Miller, star of *Mandy*, an Ealing melodrama about a deaf girl, It was significant too as six-year-old Jane Asher's debut on celluloid. Her mother's connections also assisted a maiden appearance in professional theatre in the title role of *Alice In Wonderland* at the Oxford Playhouse while Jane was still completing her education at Queen's College, just round the corner from the Ashers' five-storey home in Wimpole Street.

When she first caught Paul's eye – backstage at Swinging '63, an all-styles-served-here pop spectacular at the Royal Albert Hall – 17-year-old Jane was in transition between minor child star of stage and screen, and more mature parts, having just spent her first week before the cameras in the horror movie, *The Masque Of The Red Death*. By his own account, she was more attracted initially to Mike McCartney, but before the evening was over, Paul had seen her home and asked for a date.

For the first time in ages, he'd done the running. Compared to the skirt that had solicited him since he'd been famous, nicely spoken Jane was as a chained cathedral Bible to a cheap paperback novelette. She had "class", a maturity beyond her years reflected in a wasp-waisted confidence that charmed every other male she'd known since reaching puberty. Suddenly, Paul was escorting her to the ballet, the opera, the classical theatre and other worlds of culture once outside a son of a Liverpool cotton salesman's index of possibilities.

Yet he was a hit with urbanely elegant Margaret Asher, who, affirms Andrew King, "was the one who told McCartney that he ought to go and get his clothes in Savile Row rather than Carnaby Street". She also invited him to move into the top floor at Wimpole Street for as long as it took for him to find a place of his own, now that The Beatles were in the process of uprooting from Liverpool. This, however, turned out to be as much of a social coup – and more – for Jane's brother Peter as it was for Paul.

He'd formed a duo with another singing guitarist named Gordon Waller. Known as "Peter and Gordon", they were sound enough to be signed to Columbia, another EMI label in 1964. Through knowing Paul, they were tossed 'World Without Love', a number that had been around since he was a Quarry Man. Any song with "Lennon–McCartney" as the composing credits like a licence to print money then, so after 'World Without Love' had been ousted from Number One in Britain by Roy Orbison's 'It's Over', they were back with smaller chart entries – but chart entries all the same – in two more 1964 A-sides, 'Nobody I Know' and 'I Don't Want To See You Again', specially penned by Peter's sister's boyfriend.

Two years later, Paul gave them another opus, 'Woman', on the proviso that it be attributed to the fictitious "Bernard Webb" rather than "Lennon–McCartney", just to see if it would succeed on its more intrinsic merits. His works now on the supermarket muzak bulletin as well as the hit parade, Paul had leeway for such playful financial experiments.

Peter and Gordon were, nevertheless, on the wane by 1966 when the Ashers' lodger moved out to take up residence in a large but unostentatious Regency house along Cavendish Avenue, a convenient five minute stroll from Abbey Road. That same year, Paul also purchased – on Jane's recommendation – a rural bolt-hole where fans and media would have some search to find him. A 50km (30 mile) stretch of cold, grey sea separated the northeast coast of Ireland from High Park Farm near Campbeltown, the principal settlement on Strathclyde's Mull of Kintyre, a desolate peninsula that, through McCartney, was to become known to a wider public than it might have warranted.

Meanwhile, jetting back to Britain two days after the last hurrah at San Francisco's Candlestick Park on 29 August 1966, Paul wrestled with occupational as well as personal stock-taking. Composition for The Beatles and others seemed the most potentially rewarding direction for him then, and it had been a false economy not to buy himself an expensive reel-to-reel tape-recorder, once "too big and clumsy to lug around", so that he could construct serviceable demos of the ideas – not just songs – that were now streaming from him again. Blessed with an over-developed capacity to try-try again, he grappled with his muse, drawing from virtually every musical idiom he had ever absorbed; some of them further removed from The Beatles' Hamburg core than any Star-Club bopper could have imagined.

For hours on end at Cavendish Avenue, he'd attack melody, rhyme and less specific fragments of lyrics and music from all angles, and some would become more and more cohesive with each take. This escalating engrossment in recording caused him to buy a home studio. Soon, it was theoretically feasible for every note of an entire album by Paul McCartney alone to be hand-tooled in this electronic den.

9 "I'm The Urban Spaceman"

As Peter Asher had derived benefit from his affinity, so Barry Miles, editor of *International Times* (*IT*), did when the cash-strapped underground journal was bailed out with cheques from Barry's pal, Paul McCartney, who also suggested that an interview with him in an early edition would attract advertising from EMI and other record labels. Moreover, when *IT* had been sped on its way with a knees-up on a cold October night in 1966 at London's barn-like Roundhouse auditorium, Paul (dressed as a sheik) milled about among both proto-hippies and celebrities like Michelangelo *Blow Up* Antonioni (the artiest mainstream film director of the mid-1960s), Marianne Faithfull in a cross between nun's habit and buttock-revealing mini-skirt, and Yoko Ono, a Japanese-American "concept artist", who'd lately left the New York wing of something called Fluxus. Quarter-page notices of her forthcoming exhibitions surfaced like rocks in the stream in *IT*, but, grimaced *IT* associate John Hopkins, "Yoko Ono's happenings were boring. She was the most boring artist I'd ever met."

In its 1967 to 1968 prime, *IT* leaked to back-street newsagents in Dullsville as the provincial sixth-former's vista to what Swinging London was thinking and doing. This was disturbing enough for Frankie Vaughan – who, incidentally, had covered 'Wait' from *Rubber Soul* – to launch a campaign to curtail the spread of the hippy sub-culture. "Hippies are leeches on society", he declared at a public meeting, spurning a flower proffered by one such leech in the audience.

Fellow Scouser McCartney begged to differ: "The straights should welcome the underground because it stands for freedom. It's not strange. It's just new. It's not weird. It's just what's going around."

Sometimes, however, it was weird, unless, of course, you'd read the books, seen the films – and sampled the stimulants – necessary for understanding. Paul's *IT* interview, for example, was bloated with gaga truisms such as "It's difficult when you've learned that everything is just the act and everything is beautiful or ugly, or you like it or you don't. Things are backward or they're forward – and dogs are less intelligent than humans, and suddenly you realise that whilst all of this is right, it's all wrong as well. Dogs aren't less intelligent to dogs, and the ashtray's happy to be an ashtray, and the hang-up still occurs."

To a readership uncomprehending, disbelieving or shocked into laughter, he also made the commendably honest admission that "starvation in India doesn't worry me one bit – and it doesn't worry you, if you're honest. You just pose. You don't even know it exists. You've just seen the charity ads. You can't pretend to me that an ad reaches down into the depths of your soul and actually makes you feel more for these people than, for instance, you feel about getting a new car."

After a field visit to Bangladesh in 1968, born-again Cliff Richard, regarded by then as almost as "straight" as Frankie Vaughan, was to concur with an uncomfortable "I don't pretend I felt any heartache for the people in the Third World or anywhere else for that matter."

Via his management, Richard had been requested to articulate the Christian perspective in *The Process*, mouthpiece of the Church Of The Final Judgement, another publication that went the rounds of sixth-form common rooms. Cliff deigned not to reply, but, in issue number five, dedicated to "Fear", Paul McCartney "was not really afraid of people nor of the world ending or anything like that. It's just fear really, a fear of fear". In parenthesis, Jane Asher confided to the same questioner that she "used to be afraid of the world ending and all that five years ago," but has since "learned not to think about it".

Yet, of all underground periodicals, McCartney's first loyalty was to *IT*. With deceptive casualness, he'd entered the life of Barry Miles through Peter Asher. Jane's pop star brother had provided finance for Miles – who encouraged you to address him by his surname then – and John Dunbar, Marianne Faithfull's first husband, to open in January 1966 the Indica Gallery and Bookstore, dealing in merchandise of avant-garde and fashionably mystical bent. A few months later, *IT* was born in its basement office.

Barry's recollections of his first acquaintance with the Beatle whose biography he was to write 30 years later, is worth quoting at length: "Paul helped the bookshop out with some loot occasionally. He made us some wrapping paper, a nice pattern. He just produced a big pile of it one day.

"I knew nothing about rock 'n' roll. When I first met McCartney, I didn't even know which one [of The Beatles] he was. The first time I really had a long talk with him was after Indica had just moved to Southampton Row in March 1966. When we were there, we saw a lot of Paul. He was almost mobbed one day, walking down Duke Street. He came beating on the door and we had to let him in, and there was this great horde of people following him. He'd been out looking for some kind of thread for Jane, who wanted it for a dress she was making.

"I thought it would be very good for The Beatles to know about avant-garde music – so I persuaded Paul to come along to a lecture by Luciano Berio at the Italian Institute. We got there and sat down, and almost immediately the press came bursting in with flashlights and so on. That was the kind of thing that happened all the time."

Miles and McCartney became close friends to the degree of an insistence by the millionaire Beatle that he stand every round whenever they, John Dunbar, Peter Asher, John

Hopkins et al spent an evening in one of few watering holes these days where Paul wouldn't have to listen with heavy patience to any stranger's starstruck twaddle.

As one who'd mixed with fustian intellectuals in Liverpool and Hamburg, McCartney wasn't ignorant of many of the well-read Barry's points of reference, and could hold his own amid the beer-fuelled polemics. Yet, his understanding of what literature was worth reading and what was not became more acute through knowing Miles and the Indica crowd. "Miles was a great catalyst," he agreed. "He had the books. We [The Beatles] had a great interest, but we didn't have the books. Once he saw that we were interested, particularly me because I used to hang out with him, he showed us new things – and I'd had a great period of being avant-garde, going off to France in disguise, taking in a lot of movies, which I later showed to Antonioni: very bizarre, but it seemed exciting at the time."

Reports of further self-improvements would raise puffy smiles of condescension from those for whom "culture" was second nature (and "pop music" and its practitioners beneath contempt). Such snobs may have assumed that Paul was exhibiting an observed reverence for what he felt he ought to appreciate, but didn't quite know why. Magnifying the gap between themselves and the common herd, they would not believe that one such as him could glimpse infinity during, say, Stockhausen's *Mikrophonie I* and *II*. Yet McCartney's devouring of such new experiences went further than just shallow dropping of names. Indeed, some of it was to infiltrate The Beatles' post-Candlestick Park output.

However, that the group was off the road didn't mean that McCartney was metamorphosing into an emaciated ascetic. His recreational pursuits were both far from sedentary and not always to do with intellectual curiosity. He and the other Beatles were as prone to untoward nonsense involving drugs and girls as any other in an elite of pop conquistadores whose disconnection with life out in Dullsville was so complete that their only contact with it most of the time was through personal managers, gofers – and narcotics dealers.

McCartney had been the last Beatle to sample LSD. "Paul is a bit more stable than George and I," explained John. "It was a long time before he took it, and then there was the big announcement." If a latecomer, Paul was the loudest of all the group in the defence of LSD – "acid" – as a chemical handmaiden to creativity: "We only use one tenth of our brains. Just think what we could accomplish if we could tap that hidden part."

You only had to tune in to the music wafting from California where LSD's paranormal sensations were being translated on the boards and on record by Jefferson Airplane, Clear Light, The Grateful Dead and further front-runners of the flower-power sound of the Haight-Ashbury – "Hashbury" – district of San Francisco. Once the musical wellspring of little beyond a few jazz clubs, the city was about to become as vital a pop capital as Liverpool had been.

During its 15-month Summer of Love, the proffering of sex and marijuana "joints" became a gesture of free-spirited friendliness, while the mind-warping effects of the soon-to-be outlawed LSD possessed its "Cavern", the Fillmore West's cavorting berserkers, shrouded by flickering strobes, tinted incense fumes and further audio-visual aids that were part-and-parcel of simulated psychedelic experience.

London sometimes surpassed this with events like the inauguration of *IT* at the Roundhouse, and, another *IT* benefit, the Fourteen Hour Technicolor Dream at Alexandra Palace on 29 April 1967 where The Move, The Pink Floyd, Tomorrow, John Children, The Flies (who urinated over the front row), the omnipresent Yoko Ono, you name 'em, appeared one after the other before tranced hippies and other updated beatniks, either cross-legged or "idiot dancing".

During the merest prelude to becoming a serious chart contender, the most exotic darling of the London Underground around this time was Jimi Hendrix, a singing guitarist who'd been "discovered" walking an artistic tightrope without a safety net in New York's half-empty Cafe Wha?, and had been brought over to England to become almost the last major icon to come in from the outside of the British beat boom.

"The very first time I saw Jimi at the Bag O' Nails," recalled McCartney, "it wasn't who, but what is this? And it was Jimi. There weren't many people in the club, but at the next gig, me, Eric Clapton and Pete Townshend were standing in this very packed audience, all come to pay homage to the new god in town."

On Paul's recommendation, Hendrix was booked for a watershed performance at the International Pop Music Festival in Monterey – an overground "coming out" of what was occurring a few miles up the coast in San Francisco. It was here that the fated Jimi's showmanship as much as his innovative fretboard fireworks spurred a gallop to international stardom.

A contrasting surprise hit at Monterey was Ravi Shankar, the Indian sitar virtuoso, whose *West Meets East* album with the equally acclaimed violinist Yehudi Menuhin was issued just before 'Norwegian Wood' and 'Paint It Black' brought the sitar to a pop audience – though Shankar had been accused already by longtime devotees of "selling out" and of emasculating his art with Grammy-winning collaborations such as this.

Just as George Harrison had been the principal advocate of the application of Indian musical theories and instrumentation (and spiritual beliefs) to The Beatles' oeuvre, so McCartney was chiefly responsible for at least superficial use of their pioneering tonalities of Berio, Stockhausen et al as evidenced in 'Tomorrow Never Knows' in which only a repeated tom-tom rataplan and Lennon's battered lead vocal endowment on its trace of melody put it into the realms of pop at all.

On the same album, 1966's *Revolver*, McCartney shone brightest on 'Eleanor Rigby' – "Paul's baby, and I helped with the education of the child," quipped Lennon. She was, however, destined to die alone – with, seemingly, no one to welcome her through the pearly gates. That was how Eleanor had always lived until she expired in the church that was her only comfort, and was buried "along with her name" with just Father McKenzie, another lonely person, who darns his own socks, in attendance. Old maids would make further appearances in the corporate and solo canon of The Beatles – almost all through the offices of McCartney, who penned the bulk of 'Lady Madonna' and all of 1971's 'Another Day'.

'Eleanor Rigby' nestled comfortably among easy-listening standards like Stevie Wonder's 'I Was Made To Love Her', Jose Feliciano-via-The Doors's 'Light My Fire', 'Brown-Eyed Girl' by former Them vocalist Van Morrison, Fifth Dimension's 'Up Up And Away', gently reproachful 'Pleasant Valley Sunday' by The Monkees, and flower-power anthems like 'San Francisco' from Scott McKenzie.

'When I'm Sixty-Four', a recreation of a Jim Mac Jazz Band-type refrain, was the item that most fitted this brief on *Sgt Pepper's Lonely Hearts Club Band*. The most celebrated of all Beatles' long-players had sprung from late Abbey Road hours of cross-fades, stereo panning, intricately wrought funny noises and similarly fiddly console minutiae when the team were at the forefront of a trend for "concept albums" (which included "rock operas" and like *magnum opi*) – though others weren't far behind.

Mere weeks after *Sgt Pepper* reached the shops, 'Grocer Jack', a kiddie-chorused excerpt from *A Teenage Opera*, composed by Mark Wirtz, once a would-be German Elvis, was in the UK singles list. Nevertheless, while this built up anticipation for an associated album and stage show, the 'Sam' follow-up barely rippled the Top 40, and another 45rpm clip didn't even "bubble under". As a result, investors lost heart and the opera was abandoned.

Joe Average has heard even less of a concept LP that was realised by Paul McCartney late in 1965. As reported in the *Disc And Music Echo* gossip column, a few copies were pressed as Christmas presents for just the other Beatles and Jane Asher. It was said to be an in-joking send-up of a radio variety show with the irrepressible Paul as a one-man compère, singer, instrumentalist, comedian and all-purpose entertainer. If it ever existed, the roots of *Sgt Pepper* may lie in this *ultima Thule*, this unobtainable prize for collectors of Beatles artefacts.

If one ever turned up in a memorabilia auction, it might bolster McCartney's assertion that it was he who came up with the basic notion of *Sgt Pepper* on a return flight from a holiday in Kenya in November 1966 – though he was to aver that "only later in the recording did Neil Aspinall [The Beatles' personal assistant] have the idea of repeating the 'Sgt Pepper' song, and The Beatles and George Martin begin to use linking tracks and segues to pull it together."

The *Sgt Pepper* era remains the principal source of countless hours of enjoyable time-wasting for those who collate "hidden messages" in the grooves and packagings of Beatles discs. While this is a subject worthy of 1,000 university theses, we can only scratch the surface here by attending to the most enduring so-called communiqué which supported a rumour that Paul McCartney had been beheaded in a road accident on 9 November 1966 and replaced by a doppleganger. All that actually happened was that he cut his lip that day in a mishap whilst riding a moped, but surely you can hear John say "I buried Paul" in a daft voice in the last seconds of 'Strawberry Fields Forever' – and at the end of 'I'm So Tired' on 1968's 'White Album' (*The Beatles*), doesn't he mumble "Paul is dead. Bless him, bless him, bless him..."?

None of them were hits, but there was soon an impressive array of "Paul Is Dead" singles behind counters. Penetrating the crowded airwaves then were the likes of 'Brother Paul' by Billy Shears And The All-Americans, 'Saint Paul' from Terry Knight – future manager of Grand Funk Railroad – and Zacharias and his Tree People's 'We're All Paul Bearers (Parts One And Two)'. In a vocational slow moment after 'Light My Fire', Jose Feliciano issued a 'Paul' 45 too. As an ex-Beatle, Lennon's snigger was almost audible when, not content with airing grievances against McCartney in the press, he sniped at him on disc in 1971 with 'How Do You Sleep' from *Imagine*, confirming that Billy, Terry, Zacharias et al were "right when they said that you were dead".

A real death, however, *had* occurred within The Beatles "family" in 1967. In need of careers advice, Denny Laine, former mainstay of The Moody Blues, arrived on the off-chance at Brian Epstein's Belgravia doorstep during 1967's August Bank Holiday. He received no answer to his knock. Inside, Brian was expiring in a drug-induced slumber.

He was found on the Sunday afternoon. At around 4pm, eight-year-old Ruth McCartney, daughter of Jim McCartney's second wife, Angela Williams, had been visiting her step-brother and his Beatles in Bangor, a university town where the Welsh mainland nears the island of Anglesey. She and Angela had been bidding him farewell when he'd been requested to take an urgent telephone call. She was to learn its content on arrival back home in Hoylake, over the river from Liverpool, two hours later. The telephone there was ringing too. George Harrison's mum was on the line with an example of how the story had become confused. Brian, she told Angela, had shot himself.

By then, the truth The Beatles had refused to avow had inflicted itself. They could no longer not believe it. An attempt to sooth their anguish had been made by the Maharishi Mahesh Yogi, the Indian guru who'd been running the weekend course in transcendental meditation that they'd all been attending at the University of Bangor.

The appeal of a community more enclosed than the innermost pop clique was attractive enough for The Beatles to study meditation further at the Maharishi's yoga-ashram – theological college – in the Himalayas the following spring. Even prior to his association with Indica, Paul McCartney had explored Buddhism and Hinduism as well as mystical and esoteric Christianity, but had not been completely convinced by any of them. Furthermore, while he continued to practice meditation, even designating a room in his house for that specific purpose, his jet-lagged return from India was a fortnight ahead of George and John, and his most piquant memory of the visit one of a solitary session on a flat roof when "I was like a feather over a hot-air pipe. I was just suspended by this hot air, which had something to do with the meditation – and it was a very blissful thing."

Back to the day-to-day mundanities of being a Beatle, Paul was still living down *Magical Mystery Tour*, the made-for-television movie – and their first major post-Epstein project – of which he'd been both the instigator and main producer. To disaffected observers – and, indeed, to John, George and Ringo now and then, his methodology had appeared slap-dash – as if he was making it up as he went along, which he was much of the time. Concordant with the bare bones of the "plot" – summarised by the title – there was much spontaneity, improvisation and scenes that seemed a good idea at the time. Worse, though some clutter fluttered onto the cutting-room floor, direction and outcome still remained vague – but maybe that was almost the point.

The finale was a big-production number, 'Your Mother Should Know', written by Paul, and recorded the week before Brian Epstein's sudden passing. Like 'When I'm Sixty-Four', it was at one with a fad for olde tyme whimsy that had prevailed in the hit parade since 1966's chart-topping 'Winchester Cathedral' – all vicarage fête brass and posh megaphoned vocals – by The New Vaudeville Band. In its wake came such as Whistling Jack Smith's 'I Was Kaiser Bill's Batman', boutiques like 'I Was Lord Kitchener's Valet' and experiments – by The Beatles too – with dundreary side-whiskers, raffish moustaches and similar depilatory caprices that prompted a Mancunian costumier to manufacture fake ones so those without the wherewithal to sprout their own could still "Make The Scene With These Fantastic New Raves".

On the strength of their debut 45, 'My Brother Makes The Noises For The Talkies', The Bonzo Dog Doo-Dah Band ran in the same pack, but, as it turned out, they defied entirely adequate categorisation – except that, though the outfit's *raison d'être* was centred on getting laughs, they were more Scaffold than Freddie And The Dreamers in that they conveyed in pop terms that strain of fringe-derived comedy that was to culminate with Monty Python's Flying Circus.

"In 1966, we decided to expand our style," explained Neil Innes, who was, with Vivian Stanshall, the group's principal composer. "We did 1950s rock 'n' roll, flower-power, anything went – and started writing our own stuff. It only took a year to develop. If it got a laugh, it stayed in the act. On the cabaret circuit and then the colleges, and we were earning as much as any group with a record in the charts. We were liked by people like Eric Clapton as a band most of them would liked to have been in – even though we were never mega recording artists."

Their eventual modicum of Top Ten success – with an Innes opus, 'I'm The Urban Spaceman' – was testament to courage in remaining true to their strange star, but it was, however, secondary to an eye-stretching stage act, which earned them both a cameo in *Magical Mystery Tour*, and a weekly turn on the anarchic ITV children's series, *Do Not Adjust Your Set*.

"I wrote 'Urban Spaceman' in one afternoon," said Innes with quiet pride. "Our producer, Gerry Bron, was fairly strict about studio time, and Viv Stanshall complained about this to Paul McCartney, who he'd met down the Speakeasy. Paul came along to the 'Urban Spaceman' session, and his presence obliged Gerry to give us more time. Paul also had great recording ideas – like double-tracking the drums, and putting a microphone in each corner of the playing area to catch Viv's garden hose with trumpet mouthpiece as he whirled it round his head.

"I was quite keen to do a follow-up that was sort of humorous but still catchy. We selected 'Mr Apollo', which was once like that. Most of it was mine, but Viv got hold of it, and it ended up well over acceptable single length – because it wasn't until 'Hey Jude' that you could get away with it."

10 "Those Were The Days"

In Brian Epstein's final months, the same questions had come up over and over again. Plain fact was that the contract was up for renewal anyway, and, according to hearsay, his stake in Beatles affairs would have been reduced, though they wouldn't have carried on totally without him.

Therefore, though Brian might not have approved of Apple Corps, had he lived, he probably wouldn't have been able to do much to prevent it. On paper, nevertheless, it made sound sense, combining a potential means of nipping a huge tax demand in the bud and a diverting enterprise that could equal profit as well as fun. It was intended to house all manner of artistic, scientific and merchandising ventures under The Beatles' self-managed aegis. By 1970, however, this had been whittled down to Apple Records, a label whose releases were monitored by EMI.

Yet, once upon a time, Apple had been visualised as the most public expression of the underground's "alternative economy", and as much its embodiment as the free open-air rock concerts that pocked post-flower power Britain's recreational calendar. Motives, as always, were suspect. Apple, nevertheless, seemed at first to be genuinely if romantically anxious to give a leg up to those with deserving causes.

The Beatles were on such a person's side. They alone understood the difficulties of gaining recognition and finance, having had to struggle for so long themselves before George Martin lent an ear to their efforts. In addition, with Barry Miles the Aaron to his Moses in *IT*, "Paul McCartney asked me to point out that Apple exists to help, collaborate with and extend all existing organisations as well as start new ones. It is not in competition with any of the underground organisations. The concept, as outlined by Paul, is to establish an underground company above ground as big as Shell, BP or ICI, but, as there is no profit motive, The Beatles' profits go first to the combined staff and then are given away to the needy."

Apple's chief non-Beatle triumph was Mary Hopkin, whose records were produced – and, in the case of 1969's 'Goodbye', composed – by McCartney. An 18-year-old soprano, Hopkin was known already in the parallel dimension that is the Welsh pop scene. Until a winning appearance on ITV's *Opportunity Knocks*, her abilities had been directed at the Welsh-speaking market mostly via slots on BBC Wales's weekly pop showcase, *Disc A Dawn*. She began making headway east of Offa's Dyke after fashion model Twiggy brought her to McCartney's attention.

At her father's insistence, some of her B-sides were in Welsh, but her debut Apple A-side, 'Those Were The Days', was in pop's international tongue, and thus began Hopkin's three-year chart run in fine style by spending most of 1968's autumn at Number One after ending the two-week reign of seven-minute 'Hey Jude'.

John Lennon had been put in charge of another female vocalist in which Apple had been "interested". Unlike John Hopkins, he hadn't found Yoko Ono boring at all. As well as taking the place of Cynthia in his bed, Yoko also superseded Paul as a lovestruck John's artistic confrère. Through her catalytic influence, the world and his wife were confronted with a John Lennon they'd never known before, one for whom The Beatles would soon no longer count any more.

Apart from Cynthia, how could anyone begrudge Yoko and John their joy? Many did after *The News Of The World* front-paged the rear cover of *Unfinished Music No 1: Two Virgins*, the couple's first album together. It was a back view of themselves hand-in-hand – and stark naked. The front photograph was too indecent for a self-called family newspaper.

This, like the rest of John and Yoko's many funny-peculiar pranks in the name of art, didn't "give me any pleasure" wrote Paul later, but he showed cursory solidarity by accompanying John and his inseparable Yoko to an appointment with EMI chairman Sir Joseph Lockwood to discuss the distribution of *Two Virgins*. He also allowed the inclusion of a shot that almost-but-not-quite revealed all of himself too in the pull-out poster that was part of the packaging of the Beatles' 'White Album'.

It had been snapped by Paul's new girlfriend from New York, Linda Eastman. Ultimately, he'd been unlucky with Jane Asher – to whom he'd been engaged since January 1968. She'd made an unexpected entry into the Cavendish Avenue master bedroom where another young lady – a New Yorker too – clutched a hasty counterpane to herself. Paul had always been incorrigibly unfaithful; it was one of the perks of his job, but this was the first time he'd been uncovered. Nevertheless, he and Jane weren't over immediately. Indeed, they'd seemingly patched things up when they attended Mike McCartney's wedding in July, but the damage had been done, and was permanent.

A free agent again, Paul chased a few women until they caught him – albeit only fleetingly, but there was no one for the press to take seriously for several months – though it would have been quite a scoop had a tabloid editor got wind of an incident at the Bag O' Nails when McCartney attempted to chat up Rolling Stone Bill Wyman's Swedish sweetheart, Astrid.

It was in the same London night club that Linda Eastman had introduced herself to Paul in 1967 on shivering with pleasure at the smile he flashed from the other side of the room. He in turn was to be impressed by a disarming self-sufficiency that would not permit him to be bothered by the fact that she was a divorcée – and the mother of a six-year-old, Heather. In any case, it would have been hypocritical of him not to have been morally generous.

From a family of prominent showbusiness attorneys, Linda was quite accustomed to the company of professional entertainers. This was compounded by her skills as a freelance photographer, and her social intercourse with pop musicians visiting or resident in New York. She was on particularly good terms with The Animals – and the group's former bass player, Chas Chandler had been Linda's escort at the Bag O' Nails on the occasion she met Paul. Two years later, she was gripping the Beatle arm with a bright, proprietorial grin, and there was less anger than amusement from Heather's father, a geophysicist named Melvin See, when his daughter and ex-wife moved into Cavendish Avenue less than six months after the split with Jane Asher.

Beatles traditionalists did not regard this upheaval as profound an erosion of Fab Four magic as John's estrangement from Cynthia, and the entrenchment of that dreadful Yoko – with whom he was now recording chartbusting singles with an ad-hoc Beatles splinter group, The Plastic Ono Band. Her baleful presence at Abbey Road had exuded too from the needle-time on the White Album, most notably in 'Revolution 9', dismissed by most as interminable musical scribble.

As fans may have expected, Paul had been responsible for the track that mirrored *Rubber Soul*'s 'Michelle' as the biggest selling cover from the White Album, namely 'Ob-la-di Ob-la-da', inspired, so one story goes, by the Jamaican patois of Georgie Fame's percussionist, Speedy Acquaye. In March 1969, a Benny Hill television sketch centred on a disc jockey obliged to host an early morning radio show after a night on the tiles. Exacerbating his hungover queasiness was a listener's request for "any platter by Grapefruit, Cream – or Marmalade!" This gag was an illustration of the latter outfit's chart-topping success with a shrewd Yuletide copy of 'Ob-la-di Ob-la-da'. As four of this quintet were Glaswegian, they celebrated by miming it on *Top Of The Pops* in national costume: the Clydeside boys resplendent in sporrans, gorgets, clan tartans et al with their English drummer in redcoat gear as a reminder of Culloden.

Each new edition of the weekly show hammered home to Denny Laine the extent to which his fortunes had declined since he left The Moody Blues. Two solo singles had missed the charts, and Balls, a so-called "supergroup" of which he'd been a member, had bitten the dust too: "then Ginger Baker [former drummer with Blind Faith] came to my house one night and asked me to join Airforce. It was a shambles – too many players all trying to outdo one another, not enough discipline."

Baker's post-Blind Faith big band made its stage debut at Birmingham Town Hall. Most personnel stuck it out for just one more engagement – at the Royal Albert Hall – where a rambling and unrepentantly loud set was captured on tape. From this was salvaged a single, Bob Dylan's 'Man Of Constant Sorrow', sung by Laine.

Airforce was one example, but about twice a month from around the middle of 1966, the music press would report a schism in – or complete disbandment of – one group or other; either that or a key member setting himself apart from those with whom he'd been in earshot for every working day since God knows when. Manfred Mann took formal leave of Paul Jones at the Marquee; Yardbirds vocalist Keith Relf edged into the Top 50 with a solo 45, and the firing of Jeff Beck from the group wasn't far away. Another lead guitarist, Dave Davies, enjoyed two 1967 hits without his fellow Kinks, and Wayne Fontana had cast aside his backing Mindbenders. The Walker Brothers were to part after a final tour, while Brian Poole and The Tremeloes were recording separately. Alan Price had had several Top 20 entries as an ex-Animal, while Van Morrison had made a less sweeping exit from Them.

All four Beatles were uncomfortably aware that some sort of crunch was coming for them too. John's activities with Yoko and The Plastic Ono Band were bringing it closer by the day. Who could blame Paul, George and Ringo for pondering whether a relaunch as either a solo attraction or in a new group was tenable? Was it so unreasonable for Paul especially to hold in his heart that either way, The Beatles would be recalled as just the outfit in which he'd cut his teeth before going on to bigger and better things?

11 "Wedding Bells"

Weeping female fans mobbed London's Marylebone Registry Office on that dark day – 12 March 1969 – when Paul and his bride tied the knot. Next, the marriage was blessed at a Church local to Cavendish Avenue. To limit the chances of an outbreak of Beatlemania, neither George, Ringo nor John – who was to get hitched to Yoko a week later – showed up at either building, and a police raid on Harrison's Surrey home and the subsequent discovery of controlled drugs upset his plans to attend the Ritz Hotel reception.

On the BBC's *Six O'Clock News*, girls who'd witnessed the newly-weds exit from the registry office were not undismayed by the last bachelor Beatle's choice, even if most had expected it to be Jane Asher. Though their views weren't broadcast, some speculated whether or not Linda was pregnant.

She gave birth to Mary on 28 August 1969 in London, though, as it would be with half-sister Heather and two younger siblings, Mary was to look upon East Gate Farm near Rye, Sussex, as home after what would amount to eventual years of house-hunting by Paul and Linda. Cavendish Avenue, however, was to remain McCartney's principal address for at least as long as The Beatles endured – though they weren't much of a group anymore by the second half of 1969. Increasingly rare moments of congeniality occurred most frequently when not all of them were present at Abbey Road. The old brusque tenderness between Paul and John, for instance, was caught in a photograph taken during a session when, with the former on bass, piano and drums, they were the only Beatles heard on 'The Ballad Of John And Yoko'. It had been composed by Lennon as he continued painting himself into a corner with Yoko, going so far as to change his middle name by deed poll from "Winston" to "Ono" in a ceremony on the flat roof of Apple's central London office.

This was also the location of that famous traffic-stopping afternoon performance – The Beatles' last ever – with organist Billy Preston, an old pal from the Star-Club. "That idea came from the bottom of a glass," said Paul of this most captivating sequence from *Let It Be*, the *cinéma vérité* follow-up to *Help!*. Elsewhere, you could slice the atmosphere with a spade now that Paul's boisterous control of the quartet's artistic destiny had gathered barely tolerable momentum since John's unofficial abdication as de facto leader of the four.

It wasn't all smiles at business meetings either. The crux of all disagreements was that McCartney advocated his own father-in-law, Lee Eastman, to disentangle Apple and The Beatles' disordered threads, while Lennon, Harrison and Starr favoured Allen Klein, a New York accountant who Eastman – and, by implication, Paul – disliked and distrusted.

It was scarcely surprising, therefore, that each Beatle was readying himself for the end in his own fashion. Because everyone involved understood that there weren't to be any more Beatles after *Abbey Road*, a spirit of almost *Sgt Pepper*-ish co-operation pervaded. As healthy too in their way were the flare-ups that replaced the irresolute nods of *The Beatles* and *Let It Be*. Of all of them, none was so bitter as the one over Paul's 'Maxwell's Silver Hammer'. This was overruled as a spin-off single in favour of a double A-side of George's 'Something' – and 'Come Together' by John, the most vehement opponent of 'Maxwell's Silver Hammer'. It was, he thought, a glaring example of what he and George derided as "granny music".

Regardless of content, *Abbey Road* as a whole had a clearer sound than *Let It Be*'s associated album, which had been doctored by US producer Phil Spector, whose muddy bombast and heavy handed orchestration was frowned upon by McCartney, whose poor opinion was echoed by studio engineer Glyn Johns. Yet, issued out of sequence, ie after *Abbey Road*, *Let It Be* earned another gold disc for The Beatles, albeit a Beatles who couldn't care less.

12 "Love Is Strange"

"I suppose it ceased to be a working partnership months ago,"
admitted Paul to journalist Anne Nightingale in 1970, "but
the Beatles' partnership goes on for seven more years, and this
is why I want out now. The other three of them could sit down
now and write me out of the group. I would be quite happy.
I could pick up my cash and get out. I don't know how much
is involved, but I don't want Allen Klein as my manager."

Neither for now did McCartney wish to endure the
unpleasantnesses that occur when human beings congregate
in a recording studio. During the mild winter that had seen
in the new decade, how much more gratifying it had been to
tape by multiple overdub enough for an eponymous solo
album on four-track equipment in the privacy of Cavendish
Avenue and his home-from-home in the Mull of Kintyre.
Other than some backing vocals by Linda, Paul had sung and
played every note. With the help of a manual, he had now
become sufficiently schooled in the equipment's aural

possibilities to commence a day's work with nothing prepared. Without the emotional overheads of working with John, George and Ringo, he layered instrument upon instrument, sound upon sound, for hours on end, anchored by a metronome or retractable "click-track".

Following some fine-tuning in "technically good" Abbey Road and a "cosy" complex in Willesden, *McCartney* was finished to the last detail – or at least the last detail its creator had any desire to etch. "Light and loose" was how he described it in a press release – a "self-interview" – that also got off his chest a lot of feelings about Lennon, Klein ("I am not in contact with him, and he does not represent me in any way") and other issues including the "personal differences, business differences, musical differences" with The Beatles.

Some of its consumers were to find a copy within a package that, after much angered to-ing and fro-ing between Paul and the Klein conclave, reached the shops in April 1970, a fortnight before the valedictory *Let It Be*, and just after *Sentimental Journey*. Without spawning a spin-off 45, *McCartney* shifted an immediate two million in North America alone, and the general verdict at the time was that it was OK but nothing brilliant. Perhaps it wasn't supposed to be, even if The Faces, fronted by Rod Stewart, thought highly enough of 'Maybe I'm Amazed' to revive it a year later (as would McCartney himself in 1976).

Overall, the album captures a sketchy freshness, even a stark beauty at times. Certainly, it was much at odds with more intense offerings of the day, whether Led Zeppelin, Deep Purple, Man, Black Sabbath, Humble Pie and other headbangingly "heavy" outfits or the "pomp-rock" of ELP, Yes and borderline cases like Pink Floyd and The Moody Blues, castigated for preferring technique to instinct – and *McCartney* couldn't be accused of that.

While the likes of Man and ELP appealed to laddish consumers lately grown to man's estate, self-doubting bedsit diarists sailed the primarily acoustic waters of the early 1970s denomination of singer-songwriters ruled by James Taylor as surely as Acker Bilk had ruled British trad jazz. While there were elements of the same self-fixated preciousness of Taylor, Melanie, Neil Young and their sort, *McCartney* wasn't anywhere as mannered in its embrace of, say, a paeon to its maker's wife ('The Lovely Linda') – and *Let It Be* leftovers ('Teddy Boy') and, the first track ever aired in Britain (on *Pick Of The Pops* one Sunday afternoon), 'That Would Be Something', still being performed by McCartney in the 1990s.

Most of his first true solo effort had resulted from a kind of purposeful mucking about that didn't suggest that Paul McCartney was ready to soundtrack the 1970s as he had the Swinging Sixties with John Lennon, especially after the two's artistic separation was to be confirmed when The Beatles dissolved formally in the Chancery Division of the London High Court on 12 March 1971.

Inevitably, too much would be expected of Paul, John, George and, if you like, Ringo – but whether the much-

anticipated *McCartney, John Lennon: Plastic Ono Band*
and Harrison's *All Things Must Pass* had been tremendous,
lousy or, worse, ordinary wasn't the issue for the sort of
fan for whom just the opportunity to study each one's sleeve
was worth the whole price of what amounted to a new
ersatz-Beatle album. It was adequate that it just existed.
Nevertheless, like The Rolling Stones, Bob Dylan and Frank
Zappa, though McCartney, Lennon and Harrison would
rack up heftier sales and honours as individuals, the
repercussions of the records they'd made during the 1960s
would resound louder. Having gouged so deep a cultural
wound collectively, whatever any of them got up to in the
years left to him was barely relevant by comparison, no
matter how hard he tried.

Paul, in particular, acquitted himself well as a chart
contender, made nice music, but none of it made the
difference that The Beatles had. His first post-Beatles single,
'Another Day' – as melancholy as 'Eleanor Rigby' – zoomed
to a domestic Number Four on 4 March 1971, and began
a journey to one position short of this in the US Hot 100 a
week later. All that stood in his way to the very top in Britain
before the month was out was 'Hot Love' from T Rex, glam-
rock giants, whose "T Rexstasy" was as rampant among
schoolgirls as Beatlemania once was, and "Rollermania"
was to be when Edinburgh's Bay City Rollers – in their
gimmick bow-ties and half-mast tartan trousers – were hyped
as "the new Beatles". *Plus ça change.*

Lennon's extreme strategies had taken him beyond the pale as an orthodox pop star, while Harrison insisted that he "wouldn't really care if nobody ever heard of me again" after his finest hour at the forefront of the "Concerts for Bangla Desh" in August 1971. McCartney, however, wasn't so happy about someone else having a turn as the teenagers' – or any other record buyers' – fave rave. At the same age – 28 – Roy Orbison had been revered as something of a Grand Old Man of pop during the 1963 tour, but he'd had a receding chin, jug-handle ears and pouchy jowls like a ruminating hamster.

The allure of Paul's yet unwrinkled good looks, his hair remaining on his head, and his relative boyishness were belied only by the sorry-girls-he's-married tag that had so irritated the adulterous John before the coming of the second Mrs Lennon when "I really knew love for the first time".

Paul was happily married too, and, like John, intended his missus to get in on the act. Linda had endured piano lessons as a child, but had come to loathe the carping discipline of her teacher. Yet she was sufficiently self-contained to disassociate the music from the drudgery. Indeed, when the dark cloud of the lessons dissolved, she and her school friends had often harmonised *a cappella* for their own amusement in imitation of 1950s vocal group hits such as 'Earth Angel' (The Penguins), 'Chimes' (The Pelicans) and 'I Only Have Eyes For You' (The Flamingos).

Many other outfits of this vintage gave themselves ornithological appellations too – The Crows, The Orioles,

The Feathers, The Robins and so forth. The story goes that, with this in mind, Linda, heavily pregnant with a third daughter, modified Paul's original suggestion of "Wings Of Angels" to just plain "Wings" as a name for the group he planned to form for both stage and studio. That there was already a US entity called Wings with a recording contract too, was of no apparent consequence.

After recovering from the premature birth of Stella – named after both her maternal great-grandmothers – in London on 13 September 1971, Linda began her diffident tenure in Wings, vamping keyboards as well as ministering to overall effect as a singer. Unlike Yoko Lennon, she was a timid songbird, and wasn't willing initially to walk a taut artistic tightrope with her vulnerability as an instrumentalist. "I really tried to persuade Paul that I didn't want to do it," she protested. "If he hadn't said anything, I wouldn't have done it."

The other more experienced members recruited shared her doubts: "Linda was all right at picking things up, but she didn't have the ability to play freely. If we'd had her and another keyboard player as well, we would have been fine, but Linda was given too much to do. She was a professional though. She got paid like the rest of us."

Thus spake Denny Laine, who had been engaged on an album of his own when summoned to the Mull of Kintyre in August 1971. McCartney had first met his future lieutenant when the pre-Moody Blues Denny Laine And The Diplomats

PAUL McCartney

had supported The Beatles at a poorly attended booking at
Old Hill Plaza near Dudley back on 11 January 1962. Each
had since stayed in the picture about the other's activities,
and so it was that "Paul knew I could sing, write and play,
and so he called me. It knocked me sideways a little because
I wasn't used to being a sidekick, but I admired Paul. That
was the first time I'd been with a band with someone more
famous than me."

It was also the first time Laine had been in a band with
someone of the same Christian name. At the drum stool for
several months before Laine's coming was Denny Seiwell,
who McCartney had discovered in New York during a thin
time in which the versatile Seiwell had proved equally at ease
attending to "godfather of soul" James Brown's anguished
raps as the easy-listening country-rock of John Denver. By
1970, however, he was living a hand-to-mouth existence in
the Big Apple where the McCartneys, purportedly, stumbled
upon him cluttering a sidewalk along the Bronx. "We thought
we'd better not pass him by," recalled Paul-as-Good
Samaritan, "so we picked him up, put him on a drum kit,
and he was all right."

There was another more pragmatic reason for taking him
on. "The other New York session guys Paul had approached
wanted a lot of dough," elucidated Denny Laine, "and only
Denny Seiwell agreed with the amount offered".

As he was also amenable to uprooting to Britain, Seiwell
seemed to be just what McCartney needed. As well as being

110

an adaptable and proficient time-keeper, his blithe dedication to his craft was refreshing to Paul after the malcontented shiftlessness of certain Beatles in the months before the end.

With US guitarists Dave Spinozza and Hugh McCracken – as well as sections of the New York Philharmonic Orchestra – earning their coffee breaks with infallibly polished nonchalance, Seiwell's period in the former Beatle's employ had started with *Ram* an album that was to be attributed to "Paul and Linda McCartney". Neither presumed to dictate notes and nuances to sidemen with close knowledge of each other's considerable capabilities through working together on countless daily studio sessions, but ran through the basic essentials of every number.

The outcome was a no-frills precision that lent the majority of *Ram*'s 12 selections a dispiriting squeaky-cleanliness as if the hand-picked and highly waged players couldn't accomplish what Paul alone – for all his wispiness and casually strewn mistakes – had committed to tape instinctively on home-made *McCartney*.

This opinion was echoed also by contemporary critics with the *NME*'s "a mixed bag of psychedelic liquorice all-sorts" a prototypical reaction to the compositions *per se*. In what amounted to a personal attack, the now-radical *NME* also denigrated the McCartneys as a smug, bourgeois couple who had been too long and maybe guiltily detached from the everyday ennui of the ever-lengthening dole queues in 1970s Britain.

Yet a public that didn't read the music press were willing to assume that *Ram* and its spin-off singles would grow on them like most of *Sgt Pepper* had after repeated listening. Raw fact is that *Ram* topped the UK album list, though 'Back Seat Of My Car' struggled wretchedly to the edge of the Top 40. That *Ram* stalled at second place in Billboard's Hot 100 was mitigated by its US-only 45, 'Uncle Albert/Admiral Halsey' – freighted with sound effects and stiff-upper-lip vocal – going all the way, despite *Rolling Stone* dismissing the album as "the nadir of rock".

Comparisons of Paul's output with that of his former creative confrère were inevitable, and the conclusion of the record industry illuminati was that Lennon was cool and McCartney wasn't. Because of a cathartic projection of himself as 'Working Class Hero' on raw and intense *John Lennon: Plastic Ono Band*, Lennon was an executant of "rock" – which only the finest minds could appreciate – while McCartney peddled ephemeral "pop".

Matters didn't improve with the issue of *Wild Life*, Wings's maiden album, in time for 1971's Christmas sell-in. Four months earlier, engineer Tony Clarke had come to the Mull of Kintyre farmhouse to assist on tracks that were recorded as soon as they'd been routined. What struck him was how much was accomplished in one day compared to the months of remakes, jettisoned tracks and trifling mechanical intricacies that had to be endured from others. Understanding that it was the margin of error that had put teeth into *McCartney*, if not *Ram*, Paul was jaded with endless multi-track mixing, and made transparent his desire for *Wild Life* to be as belligerently "live" as possible – no arguments, no needless messing about with dials – and on to the next track.

However, for all its brisk finesse, *Wild Life* stalled on the edge of the Top Ten in both Britain and the USA – a tangible comedown by previous commercial standards. It was even less of a critical success than *Ram*, asking for trouble as it did with a capricious revival of The Everly Brothers' 'Love Is Strange' from 1965, and so-so originals that were also pounced upon as symptoms of creative bankruptcy. After a decade on the run – of snatched meals, irregular sleep, and pressure to come up with the next Number One – who could blame McCartney for resenting anyone who begrudged a back-street lad who'd climbed to the top of the heap, letting go, stopping trying to prove himself?

"I think I've got some idea of the way he feels about things," reckoned Denny Laine, "because I've been through the same stuff myself. The longer you go on, the tougher it is in lots of ways. People expect more and more of you. For Paul, having been part of the best rock 'n' roll band in history, it must be very heavy. I admire him so much, the way he handles it and doesn't let it interfere with his music."

"I just don't know how he does it," gasped Linda, but, to paraphrase Mandy Rice-Davies, she would say that wouldn't she? A disaffected listener's angle might be that

McCartney, *Ram* and *Wild Life* weren't magic, just music – though Paul seemed to have fun on them. He himself was to say of *Wild Life*, "OK, I didn't make the biggest blockbuster of all time, but I don't think you need that all the time. *Wild Life* was inspired by Dylan, because we'd heard that he just took one week to do an album. So we thought, 'Great, we'll do it a bit like that, and we'll try to get just the spontaneous stuff down and not be too careful with this one.' So it came out like that, and a few people thought we could have tried a bit harder."

In retrospect, nevertheless, *Wild Life*, if skimpy rather than grippingly slipshod, was enjoyable enough after the manner you'd expect from an album that, like Kingsize Taylor's Hamburg long-player, had taken three days to create from plug-in to final mix – and even 'Bip Bop', *Wild Life* at its most inconsequential, was to make more rock 'n' roll sense when Wings oozed rather than exploded onto the stage after a launch party at the Empire Ballroom, Leicester Square, London on 8 November 1971.

A small army of Paul's famous friends – Elton John, Keith Moon, Ronnie Wood of The Faces, all the usual shower – rallied round for the celebration. Paul's new hand-made suit hadn't been quite ready that afternoon, but he wore it anyway with the tracking stitches for all to see. Perhaps it was an art statement, like. Maybe the entire evening was. Most conspicuously, the entertainment laid on was nowhere to be found on the map of contemporary rock. Seated on the Empire podium was tuxedoed Ray McVay and his Dance Band, lifted by time machine from the pre-Presley 1950s. Their duties included accompanying a formation dance team; inserting rumbles of timpani at moments of climax during a grand prize raffle, and providing a framework for those who wished to hokey-cokey the night away or pursue romance to lushly orchestrated stardust-and-roses ballads.

Seizing the opportunity to rewind his life in another respect too, Paul had decided that Wings were to re-enter the concert arena with small, unpublicised, even impromptu engagements now that nearly all the essential elements were intact to enable Wings to tread the boards.

Largely through Denny Laine's urging, another guitarist was roped in. Born and raised in Londonderry, Henry McCullough had, in 1966, thrown in his lot with The People, a combo of psychedelic kidney from Portadown. Being enormous in Northern Ireland wasn't, however, enormous enough, and the group migrated to London where they were renamed Eire Apparent after being taken on by Chas Chandler, now devoting his energies to behind-the-scenes branches of the music business. As he also had The Jimi Hendrix Experience on his books, Chandler was in a strong position to obtain both a contract for Eire Apparent on Track, the Experience's label, and support spots to Hendrix both in Britain and the USA. Moreover, McCullough was rated as a guitarist by the discerning Jimi, who produced an Eire Apparent album.

Obliged by visa problems to return to Ireland during an Eire Apparent trek round North America in 1968, Henry passed through the ranks of Sweeney's Men, a renowned folk rock outfit who were about to thrust tentacles into the folk circuit on the other side of the Irish Sea, notably at that summer's Cambridge Folk Festival. Founder member Johnny Moynihan recalled, "Henry put funk into it. He'd just pick up on traditional tunes and they would come out in his playing. One night, we were playing in Dublin, and after the gig, Henry jumped in a car and drove like mad to catch the end of a John Mayall concert elsewhere. This told us what direction he was heading in, and when he was offered a job with Joe Cocker, he took it."

McCullough's arrival in Cocker's Grease Band coincided with Denny Cordell's production of the group's 'With A Little Help From My Friends' wrenching Mary Hopkin from Number One in November 1968. He was backing Joe still when the grizzled Yorkshireman was acclaimed by the half-million drenched Americans who'd braved Woodstock, viewed from a distance of decades as the climax of hippy culture. For Henry, any Woodstock euphoria was blunted when Cocker ditched the Grease Band to tour the States as *de jure* leader of retinue known as Mad Dogs And Englishmen.

Henry fell on his feet with Wings for all Cocker producer Denny Cordell's reservations: "When he played well, Henry was a genius, but he could only play in one certain bag, and you had to get him just right. Otherwise, he was very mercurial. He'd just fall out of it."

Paul McCartney was prepared to take a chance on Henry McCullough just as he was on Linda's hit-or-miss keyboard-playing – because, so he reasoned, "Linda is the innocence of the group. All the rest of us are seasoned musicians – and probably too seasoned. Linda has an innocent approach which I like. If you talk to an artist like Peter Blake, he'll tell you how much great artists love the naivety of aboriginal paintings. Linda's inclusion was something to do with that."

As well as pre-empting punk's more studied guilelessness, Linda McCartney was, according to Eric Burdon, lead singer of The Animals, an unwitting pioneer of female visibility in mainstream rock: "I think Linda played a part in paving the way for more female performers to join the boys' club called rock 'n' roll."

For those who prized technical expertise, she served as a bad example of this, beginning with her professional concert debut on Wednesday, 9 February 1972 at the University of Nottingham. The date and venue had been chosen arbitrarily as Wings cruised by car and caravan up the spine of England the previous morning. Turning off the M1 somewhere in the Midlands, they wound up at the university campus and volunteered their services. Room was made for them to do a turn during lunch hour the next day in the student's union auditorium.

Seven hundred paid 50p admission to stand around as Wings strutted their stuff – principally olde tyme rock 'n' roll and excerpts from *Wild Life*. Permitting himself the luxury

PAUL MCCARTNEY

of apparent self-indulgence, Paul didn't give 'em 'Yesterday', 'Let It Be' or, indeed, any of the good old good ones from The Beatles' portfolio as he took lead vocals on everything apart from reggaefied 'Seaside Woman', penned solely by Linda. A few blown riffs, flurries of bum notes, vaguely apocalyptic cadences and yelled directives – mainly at Linda – were reported, but pockets of the audience felt a compulsion to dance to Paul McCartney's first performance on a bona fide stage since Candlestick Park.

Similar casual and unannounced bashes – mostly at other colleges – filled the calendar for the next fortnight. By the final date in Oxford, Linda was solidly at the music's heart, and, for the most part, it had been an agreeable jaunt for a Paul McCartney unbothered by keening feedback bleeps, one of the sound crew blundering on to sort out a dead amplifier, a mistimed falling curtain, audience interruptions or anything else that wasn't in a slap-dash script. Either on piano or at the central microphone too, he'd been joking and swapping banter during proceedings that were epitomised by an amused cheer on the second night – in York – when Linda, crippled with nerves, forgot her cliff-hanging organ introit to *Wild Life*'s title track. Response generally was as heartening as might be expected from crowds enjoying both an unexpected diversion from customary mid-term activities and a surge into the bar afterwards, having participated, however passively in the proverbial "something to tell your grandchildren about".

13 "Mary Had A Little Lamb"

Since their manager's death, the sundering of The Beatles and the formation in 1969 of what was to become McCartney Productions and then MPL Communications, whether he made wise or foolish executive decisions, Paul alone would accept responsibility for them. However, taking care of much McCartney business were Eastman and Eastman Inc, a relationship based not so much on profit as family affinity – and friendship, particularly with brother-in-law John Eastman.

In 1972, the most immediate concern of McCartney's financiers was the mercantile possibilities of Wings's follow-up to *Wild Life*. With this in mind, stadium managers from every major territory were on the line to McCartney Productions, yelling "Klondike!" at the prospect of a round-the-world carnival of Beatles-sized magnitude.

The only snag was that the heavyweight wouldn't fight – well, not for the world championship – yet. As he had with that first low-key sweep round England with Wings, Paul not so much plunged headfirst as dipped a toe *sur le continent* with mainly 3,000 rather than 20,000 seaters over seven summer weeks that covered France to Germany, Switzerland to Finland. Wings were received with affection for what onlookers now understood they ought to expect. The set was longer and, as instanced by a projected array of rural, coastal and lunar scenes on a backcloth during the second half, more elaborate than before. Nevertheless, with the 'Long Tall Sally' encore the only nod towards The Beatles, the audiences heard much the same as their British counterparts plus sides of two recent singles and two singles yet to come.

First up had been 'Give Ireland Back To The Irish'. Perhaps not really by coincidence, John Lennon had just recorded 'Sunday Bloody Sunday', an album track which was also inspired by the bomb-blasting, bullet-firing malevolence in Northern Ireland rearing up again with the incident in Londonderry that January when 13 were shot dead by British soldiers during a civil rights demonstration. Paul's doctrinal statement about the Troubles topped the hot-blooded Irish lists, while struggling elsewhere in the teeth of radio bans and restrictions, even with an alternative instrumental version on the flip-side.

To redress the balance, Wings followed through with 'Mary Had A Little Lamb' – yes, the nursery rhyme – which, like the National Anthem, turned out to have verses other than the one everyone knew. "It wasn't a great record," confessed McCartney – and in this, he was at one with nearly all reviewers, even if, aided by four contrasting promotional shorts, it rose higher in the domestic chart than its predecessor.

"I like to keep in with the five-year-olds," he beamed, but, six months later, what did this corner of the market make of 'Hi Hi Hi', which was excluded from prudish airwaves for sexual insinuation. Yet, partly because disc-jockeys began spinning the perky, reggaefied B-side, 'C Moon', 'Hi Hi Hi' was Wings's biggest British hit thus far, going flaccid at Number Three as 1972 mutated into 1973.

The new year got underway with the UK issue of syrupy 'My Love', a taster for a forthcoming album. If sent on its way with the expected critical rubbishings, the single would be a US Number One whilst just scraping into the domestic Top Ten. Paul's status as a non-Beatle as much as that as a former Beatle was further confirmed by a *Melody Maker* journalist's random survey among schoolgirls shuffling into the Bristol Hippodrome, the first stop on Wings's first official tour of Britain that May. "What's your favourite Paul McCartney song?" "Dunno," replied one moon-faced female before pausing and adding, "Oh yeah – 'My Love'."

No longer the dream lover of old, he had emerged as a cross between admired elder brother, favourite uncle – and, for some, a character from *The Archers*, BBC Radio Four's long-running rustic soap opera. If he wasn't living the so-called "simple life" after he'd moved to East Sussex, he was living it hundreds of miles away on his farm in Scotland.

He, Linda and the girls seemed the very epitome of domestic bliss while they trod the backwards path towards the morning of the Earth.

While Rye's most renowned addressee was commuter-close to McCartney Productions, only the odd flight overhead from Gatwick airport miles away need remind him of what was over the hills in London, New York and Hollywood. It had left its mark on Paul's songwriting already – in, for example, 'Heart Of The Country' on *Ram*, and would continue to do so in the likes of the imminent 1973 B-side 'Country Dreamer' – actually taped in one of his backyards – and, most memorably of all, 1977's 'Mull Of Kintyre'.

Shrouded by meadows, greenery, exposed oak rafters, stone-flagged floors and Peace in the Valley, Paul had been all for the quietude and fresh air. Whereas they might have pressed ivory or fret, the 31-year-old musician's fingers became hardened from fencing, logging and moving bales. The most exciting daily excursion was the uncomplicated ritual of shopping for groceries as Paul and Linda became an everyday sight, hand in hand around the parish. Soon he was chatting about field drainage, nativity plays, winter farrowing and muck-spreading with the best of them – as demonstrated by him kicking up a fuss when Hibernian stag hunters presumed it was OK to cross his land, and a less justifiable one when staff at the junior school that his children attended joined a national teachers' strike in November 1986; his disapproval immortalised by one lucky amateur photographer whose back view of a McCartney stamping off in a pique across the playground, front-paged *The Times Educational Supplement*.

Nevertheless, as his home studio wasn't yet up to recording a group, he chose to fashion most of the second Wings album, *Red Rose Speedway*, in no less than five different metropolitan locations including Abbey Road. No spectator sport, the recordings themselves were only the most expensive part of a process that, before session time was even pencilled in, had started with Paul rehearsing the material with un-*Wild Life*-like exactitude, balancing ruthless efficiency with the old sweetness-and-light. Titles like 'Big Barn Red' and 'Little Lamb Dragonfly' were reflective of the maturing McCartney family's rural contentment, and a confirmation that Paul's capacity for "granny music" was bottomless. *Rolling Stone* judged *Red Rose Speedway* to be "rife with weak and sentimental drivel".

But, how could *Rolling Stone*, the *NME* and the like turn their noses up at a disc that in the USA spent a month at Number One? It may have afforded McCartney a wry grin when 'My Love' was brought down at the end of June by George Harrison's 'Give Me Love', but that lasted only a week before the latest by Billy Preston took over. Ringo's turn would come during the autumn when 'Photograph' climbed to the top of that same Hot 100. He did it again – just – in January when his "You're Sixteen" ruled pop for seven glorious days. Before the year was out, John Lennon would stick it out for a week up there too with 'Whatever Gets You Thru The Night' – and so would Wings with 'Band On The Run'.

14 "Crossroads"

The Wings show that crossed Britain in summer 1972 passed without incident other than a road manager bringing on a birthday cake for Denny Seiwell at Newcastle City Hall where the bill-toppers were joined for the encore by support act Brinsley Schwartz, harbingers of the pub-rock movement.

In the first instance, Wings too had been a reaction against the distancing of the humble pop group from its audience. Empathy with ordinary people going about their business did not extend, however, to police who had appeared backstage after a performance in Gothenberg the previous August. It had come to their ears that controlled substances, to wit 200g (7oz) of marijuana, had been discovered in a package from Britain addressed to McCartney. The tedious wheels of the Swedish legal process had been set in motion, and fines had to be paid before Wings could continue with dates in Denmark, the next country on the itinerary.

Paul passed this off as a farthing of life's small change, even hurling a metaphorical stone after his prosecutors by confiding to a journalist's cassette recorder that he intended to smoke some more of the stuff as soon as the opportunity arose. Such insolence may have provoked the unwelcome interest of the constabulary local to Campbeltown, who, visiting High Park for a routine check on the absent owner's security arrangements, recognised cannabis plants, cultivation of which was counter to the provision of the 1966 Dangerous Drugs Act, section 42.

Interrupting work on a forthcoming ITV special entitled *James Paul McCartney* to answer the summons, the McCartneys were free to go after coughing up £100. A few hours later, he was back in London, focussing his attention once again on *James Paul McCartney*. While *Melody Maker* sneered at the "overblown and silly extravaganza", it was to run a two-part feature, obsequiously headlined "Wings – Anatomy Of A Hot Band", after according the ensemble's third album, *Band On The Run*, and the single that preceded it, 'Live And Let Die', grudging praise.

Melody Maker noted too the involvement of George Martin in 'Live And Let Die', the first time he'd worked with McCartney – or any Beatle – since *Abbey Road*. The song had been commissioned as the theme for the James Bond flick of the same name and was nominated for an Oscar after almost-but-not-quite reaching Number One in the US. While 'My Love' had demonstrated that chart supremacy could give false impression of Wings's standing with the critics, 'Live And Let Die' cut the mustard, and, for the time being, most of them let McCartney in from the cold. They also listened sympathetically to *Band On The Run*, a combination of force and melody that yielded hit singles in 'Helen Wheels' (a track remaindered from the UK pressing), 'Jet' and its complex and million-selling title track.

Because Paul's favourite Studio Two at Abbey Road had been block-booked already, Wings had chosen to record the album at the only other EMI complex then available – in Lagos, Nigeria – and, even then, they were obliged to transfer to the same city's ARC Studios and endure the scowling disapproval of hired local musicians who resented what they'd perceived as non-African pop stars "plundering" the continent's musical heritage. As well as being accused unfairly of cultural burglary, the McCartneys were mugged in broad daylight by the occupants of a kerb-crawling car not long after Paul had been poleaxed by a respiratory complaint.

It never rains but it pours, and there'd been something rotten in the state of Wings before they'd so much as booked the flight from London. It had set in when Henry McCullough slumped into a glowing huff over what McCartney remembered as "something he really didn't fancy playing". This was symptomatic of a general antipathy felt by both McCullough and Denny Seiwell towards the group's music, Linda's keyboard abilities and some of the antics in *James*

Paul McCartney. Since *Wild Life*, the poisoning of Wings's reputation by pens dipped in vitriol didn't help either.

Five days after the guitarist had resigned by telephone, Seiwell threw in the towel too, mere hours before the rest left for Africa, where the troubled making of *Band On The Run* had continued with Denny Laine and, especially, Paul often finding themselves with headphones on, playing an unfamiliar instrument. Yet from the internal ructions, the tension-charged atmospheres, the drifting from pillar to post, from studio to unsatisfactory studio, surfaced the first Wings album that was both a commercial and critical triumph, back and forth at Number One at home and the Hot 100.

The release of the album and its singles hadn't been accompanied by a tour of any description, simply because Wings didn't have the personnel then. Therefore, before they could hit the road again, a search began for a replacement guitarist and drummer. An advertisement for one in the music press burst a dam on a deluge of hopefuls. To accommodate those on a short-list, Paul rented London's Albury Theatre, and hired an existing group to play four numbers with every contender while he, Denny and Linda listened in the dusty half-light beyond the footlights.

It was a long and sometimes mind-stultifying chore that led McCartney, 50 drummers later, to conclude that "I don't think auditions are much use. We won't do it again, but it was quite an experience: 50 different drummers playing 'Caravan' [a mainstream jazz standard]." Yet Paul saw it through to the bitter end, pruning the list down to five, who were to sit in with Wings. Then there were two to be each subjected to a full day – that included an interrogatory dinner – with their prospective colleagues.

There was nothing to suggest that 31-year-old Geoff Britton wasn't the *beau ideal*. He was versatile enough to have coped with stints in both rock 'n' roll revivalists, The Wild Angels and East Of Eden, one of Britain's most respected executants of jazz-rock. Geoff's black belt in karate had been a reassuring asset at the more unrefined engagements that either of these groups played.

Yet, the pop equivalent of the chorus girl thrust into a sudden starring role, Geoff turned out to be living evidence of McCartney's "I don't think auditions are much use". For a start, he was at loggerheads almost immediately with both Denny Laine and the new guitarist, Jimmy McCulloch, a Glaswegian whose *curriculum vitae* embraced stints with Thunderclap Newman – the entity responsible for anthemic 1969 UK chart-topper 'Something In The Air' – and John Mayall and Stone The Crows, fronted by Maggie Bell, a sort of Scottish Janis Joplin. The group was, however, on its last legs, and Jimmy had been one of Blue, a nice-little-band connected genealogically with Marmalade, when, on the recommendation of Denny Laine, a friend of several years standing, he was invited to play on 'Seaside Woman' (to be issued as a pseudonymous Linda McCartney single). After he gave as creditable a performance on a Mike McGear solo album at Strawberry Studios in Stockport, Jimmy became a member of Wings in June 1974.

With the group seemingly reconstituted, the McCartneys announced that dates were being pencilled in for a tour of ten countries. This, they said, was intended to last over a year, albeit with breaks lengthy enough for the making of an album to follow another one that would be out prior to the first date.

Fans from Bootle to Brisbane were on stand-by to purchase tickets, but the interval between Paul and Linda's proclamation and the opening night (at the Southampton Gaumont not quite a year later) was long enough for many to wonder if the tour was ever going to happen.

The most pressing hindrance was centred on the apparently irresolvable antagonism between Britton on the one hand and McCulloch and his less expendable pal Laine on the other. So far, Geoff had kept his fists, if not his emotions, in check, but breaking point wasn't far away. Perhaps a punch-up might have cleared the air. Nevertheless, during sessions in New Orleans's Sea Saint Studios for Wings's fourth album, *Venus And Mars*, McCartney cut the Gordian knot by finding a drummer who'd get on better with Denny and Jimmy.

The job went to Joe English, a New Yorker who had been summoned to assist on *Venus And Mars*, following Geoff Britton's crestfallen return to England. Like Denny Seiwell before him, Joe was, by his own admission, "on the bottom". This had followed six years of vocational contentment as one of Jam Factory, a unit that had criss-crossed North America, second-billed to the likes of Jimi Hendrix, The Grateful Dead and Janis Joplin. He took up the post with Wings in time for the unleashing of *Venus And Mars* and its first single, 'Listen To What The Man Said', in May 1975.

Because *Band On The Run* had been deemed a commendable effort, both were guaranteed a fair hearing by reviewers – and sufficient advance orders to slam the album straight in at Number One in every chart that mattered. 'Listen To What The Man Said' also went to the top in the States, but, true to what was becoming a precedent, fell slightly short of that in Britain. The 'Letting Go' follow-up traced a similar scent in macrocosm, nudging the US Top 40 while stopping just outside it at home. By a law of diminishing returns, however, a third A-side, 'Venus And Mars' itself, actually climbed higher than 'Letting Go' in the States while missing completely at home, becoming McCartney's first serious flop since The Beatles.

This was but a petty dampener on the overall success of an album that the majority of listeners judged to be pleasant enough, but something of a holding operation, for all its vague star-sign "concept", complete with a *Sgt Pepper*-esque reprise of the opening track, and the penultimate 'Lonely Old People' – them again – linked to a jaw-dropping version of the contrapuntal theme to *Crossroads*, the long-running ITV soap opera, set in a Midlands hotel and then broadcast during forlorn afternoon hours between the *News In Welsh* and the children's programmes – and, surmised McCartney, "just the kind of thing lonely old people watch".

It had been decided too that the two colours and two orbs that dominated the album sleeve, were to be a recurring image in both the tour merchandise and the costumes worn on a carpeted stage in the midst of scenery sufficiently minimal and plain to accommodate back-projections such as the one for 'C Moon' – a reproduction of one of the Magritte paintings Paul had been collecting since 1966. This one depicted a candle with the moon where a flame ought to be.

Between the Australian and European legs of the tour, the dramatis personnae convened at Abbey Road to get to grips with *Wings At The Speed Of Sound*, another good rather than great album, on which Paul's delegation of artistic responsibility extended as far as featuring Joe English as lead singer on 'Must Do Something About It' – while Linda's soprano was to the fore on 'Cook Of The House'. As on *Venus And Mars*, Denny and Jimmy were permitted one each. Paul, nevertheless, was loud and clear on the attendant hits, 'Let 'Em In' – and the rather self-justifying 'Silly Love Songs', which, like the album, shot to the top in the USA, Number Two in Britain.

During this and other lay-offs during the tour, the man that *Melody Maker* had front-paged lately as "Just An Ordinary Superstar" made time to attend to MPL, now the largest independent music publisher in the world with 'Happy Birthday To You', 'Chopsticks' – the most recognised (and irritating) piano solo ever composed – and key Broadway musicals amongst its litter of lucrative copyrights.

Of more personal import, however, were the US rights to Buddy Holly's best-known songs. The 40th anniversary of the bespectacled Texan's birth was marked by the first of McCartney's yearly Buddy Holly Weeks in London. Beginning on 7 September 1976 – midway between two months in the USA and the tour ending as it had begun in Britain – it climaxed with a showbiz luncheon at which guest of honour Norman Petty, Holly's studio mentor, presented a startled Paul with the cuff-links that, so he told the watching throng, had been fastening Buddy's shirt when his corpse was carried from the wreckage of the crashed aircraft.

Later celebrations – in other cities too – would embrace concerts by what was left of The Crickets; rock 'n' roll dance exhibitions; Buddy Holly painting, poetry and songwriting competitions; the opening of a West End musical about him; a "rock 'n' roll Brain Of Britain" tournament – and song contests, although the 1996 winners (a trio with a jungle-techno crack at 'Not Fade Away') at the finals in London's Texas Embassy Cantina had some of their thunder stolen by an "impromptu" jam fronted by Gary Glitter, Dave Dee, Allan Clarke of The Hollies, Dave Berry and – you guessed it – Paul McCartney.

Back in 1976, however, McCartney's primary Holly-associated concern was supervising *Holly Days* on which Denny Laine paid his respects over an entire album. But nothing from *Holly Days* was trotted out when the tour resumed or on in-concert *Wings Over America*, said to have shut down George Harrison's *All Things Must Pass* and his

Concerts For Bangla Desh as the biggest-selling triple-album of all time. Moreover, in among its reminders of Wings and the solo McCartney's chart strikes were ambles as far down memory lane as 'Yesterday', 'Lady Madonna', the White Album's 'Blackbird', and, restored to its raw pre-Spector state, 'The Long And Winding Road' off *Let It Be*. Paul seemed, therefore, to be coming to terms with both his past and present situation as he conducted Wings with nods and eye contact while never sacrificing impassioned content for technical virtuosity. As codas died away or as someone wrapped up a particularly bravura solo, he'd direct the adulation of the hordes towards others under the spotlight, and beam as salvos of clapping recognition undercut, say, the opening chords of Denny's 'Go Now'.

Ultimately, Paul McCartney had ensured that his Wings gave the people what they seemed to want – and the consensus in North America was that he'd put forward a better show than George Harrison, whose trek round the sub-continent late the previous autumn had also contained a quota of Beatles numbers among the solo favourites. John Lennon had attended a couple of George's troubled concerts, trooping backstage afterwards to say hello and ask if George had heard this rumour that at least three out of four ex-Beatles were caving in to overtures to do it all again for either a charity or some individual with more money than sense.

"God, it's like asking Liz Taylor when she's going to get together with Eddie Fisher again," Linda cracked back at another broken-record enquiry on the subject – because neither wild horses nor net temptations that worked out at hundreds of thousands of dollars per minute each for just one little concert could drag the old comrades-in-arms together again. Nevertheless, McCartney had telephoned Lennon and caught himself asking if John wanted to lend a hand on *Venus And Mars*. John didn't materialise, but Paul did for an evening of coded hilarity and nostalgic bonhomie at the open house that was a well-appointed beach villa in Santa Monica where John was living during a 15-month separation from Yoko.

Lennon and McCartney, however, finished on a sour note on Sunday 25 April 1976 when Paul returned unexpectedly, guitar in hand, to a harassed John's New York apartment after spending the previous evening there. "That was a period when Paul just kept turning up at our door. I would let him in, but finally I said to him, 'Please call before you come over. It's not 1956 [sic] anymore. You know, just give me a ring.' That upset him, but I didn't mean it badly."

Without formal goodbyes, the two friends went their separate ways, and were never to speak face-to-face again. How could either have guessed that John had less than five years left?

Wings would be over too by then. Indeed, Jimmy McCulloch and Joe English hadn't stuck around long enough to be heard on the most memorable British hit by a group, that, by autumn 1977, was pared down to just the McCartneys and Denny Laine.

15 "Japanese Tears"

In the mid-1970s, Paul McCartney's public – in Britain anyway – was comparable to that of a recurring ITV advertisement. There he was with Linda in a comedy sketch on *The Mike Yarwood Show*; grinning and facing the lens in an after-hours cluster of small-talking luminaries at a Rod Stewart concert at London's Olympia, and sharing a joke with Mick Jagger when the Stones appeared at 1976's Knebworth Festival. The McCartneys' pre-recorded personal greetings punctuated the in-person funny stories from the past when Liverpool boxing champion John Conteh – pictured with Kenny Lynch, Christopher Lee and other worthies on the front cover of *Band On The Run* – was subject of an edition of *This Is Your Life*.

More pragmatically, Paul seemed to be omnipresent on *Top Of The Pops*. As well as miming this or that latest single in an official capacity, there were on-camera sightings of him and his wife jigging about amongst the studio audience. Amused by the memory, presenter Simon Bates would reconjure "one occasion when I was on, and, of all people, Paul McCartney strolled on to the stage. Now this is totally live, and he said, 'Hi, Simon. I'm here to plug my new record.' It was the first time in a long time that a Beatle [sic] had appeared live on the show."

Maybe Paul only seemed to put in an appearance every time you switched on prime-time television, simply because there were so many sit-coms at the time with central characters that looked just like him: John Alderton in *Please Sir*, acrylically garbed Richard O' Sullivan (in *Man About The House* and *Robin's Nest*), the late Richard "Godber" Beckinsale in *Porridge*. Muddling through a weekly half-hour in, perhaps, a classroom, shared flat or, in Beckinsale's case, prison, all sported the neat, dark-haired mop-top, clean-shaven face and aspects of the chirpy persona that was the public image of "Fab Macca", who was, he declared to a waiting press corps, "over the moon" about the birth of his and Linda's first son – James – on 12 September 1977.

Elsewhere, however, it was far from fond smiles and baby-talk. Jimmy McCulloch resigned from Wings in September 1977, just prior to their knuckling down to a new album, *London Town,* while Joe English, tiring of "months and months sitting in recording studios", waiting his turn to drum, weighed up his self-picture as a musician and the cash benefits of being the last among unequals – behind Paul, Denny and one he considered a poor vocalist and keyboard player – in a group infinite numbers of rungs higher than Jam Factory had ever been.

Joe's decision to slip his cable during sessions for *London Town* seemed justified in the aftershock of *Rolling Stone*'s condemnation of the finished product as "fake rock, pallid pop and unbelievable homilies that's barely listenable next to Wings's best work," and no less an authority than Gerry Marsden shrugging off the single that followed, 'Mull Of Kintyre', with "I've never heard such a load of crap in my life." Taking to heart less reactions like this than someone's conjecture that most North Americans wouldn't know what this "mull of kintyre" meant, let alone be able find it on a map, McCartney promoted its coupling, 'Girls' School', as the A-side in the States, where it crawled to a modest Number 33.

Yet, as much co-writer Denny Laine's baby, this eulogy to Paul's Hebridean abode was a howling domestic success, replete as it was with the pentatonic skirling of a Scottish pipe band to stoke up a seasonal flavour in keeping with its release in time for 1977's December sell-in. Milkmen from Dover to Donegal whistled it, and there was no finer rendition of 'Mull Of Kintyre' than by a nine-year-old schoolboy named Matthew who, at a fête I attended in a south Oxfordshire village the following spring, clambered onto the makeshift stage, lowered the microphone and delivered it *a cappella* in an impromptu but pitch-perfect treble.

A man's gotta do what a man's gotta do. For Wings themselves, such as they were, plugging 'Mull Of Kintyre' via both a promotional film on location in – you guessed it – and slots on Yuletide TV variety and chat shows, was all in a day's work until well into January. Yet while Paul was thus mutating into as much of a British showbiz evergreen as Max Bygraves, he was to be the only ex-Beatle to figure still in *Melody Maker*'s yearly poll.

London Town also fared better commercially than contemporaneous offerings by both George Harrison and Ringo Starr. As for John Lennon, he had, to all intents and purposes, thrown in the towel since the birth of his and Yoko's only surviving child in 1975, seemingly rounding off his post-Beatles career that October with a self-explanatory "best of" retrospective, *Shaved Fish (Collectable Lennon)*.

Paul succumbed too with 1978's *Wings Greatest*, a compilation containing his smashes as a non-Beatle up to and including 'Mull Of Kintyre'. By its very nature, it showed up *London Town*, still only a few months old, in an even poorer light, despite the second of its singles, 'With A Little Luck' tramping a well-trodden path to the top in the Hot 100 and slipping quietly in and out of the Top Ten at home.

It had been preceded by 'Goodnight Tonight', a hit 45 that, like 'Mull Of Kintyre', had nothing to do with either *London Town* or the work-in-progress on the next album, *Back To The Egg*. It was also among the first Wings tracks to feature two new full-time members.

Both were more steeped in all things Beatles than anyone who had gone before. Laurence Juber had started to learn the guitar seriously only after hearing 'I Want To Hold Your Hand', while the first LP that drummer Steve Holly bought was *Sgt Pepper's Lonely Hearts Club Band*. The enthusiasm of these tractable young men was matched by skills acquired mostly on the London studio circuit where they'd crossed paths with Denny Laine. Consequently, each had been procured in summer 1978 by Denny for executive approval by Paul.

Neither minded being indiscernibly audible on the *Back To The Egg* session for 'Rockestra Theme' and 'So Glad To See You Here', preserved on celluloid because of arrangements that Cecil B de Mille might have approved had he been a late 1970s record producer with the run of Abbey Road and with the biggest names in British rock only a telephone call away. Led Zeppelin's John Bonham alone sent the console's decibel metre into the red, but he was but one-sixth of a percussion battalion that also included Speedy Acquaye and, from The Small Faces, Kenney Jones. Fingering unison riffs on electric guitars were Denny, Laurence, Pete Townshend, Hank B Marvin and Pink Floyd's Dave Gilmour while even Bonham's Led Zeppelin cohort, John Paul Jones, one of no less than three bass players, fought to be heard amid the massed guitars, drums, keyboards and horns.

While they made outmoded monophonic Dansette record-players shudder, the two items weren't the flat-out blasts you may have imagined on top-of-the-range stereo. They held their own, however, on *Back To The Egg*, but that isn't saying much as the album for all its diversity was subjected to a critical mauling as vicious as that for *London Town*. If none of them, in their heart-of-hearts, expected it to be astounding, the faithful bought enough copies of lacklustre *Back To The Egg* to push it into Top 20's, home and abroad, but the singles, 'Old Siam Sir' and the double A-side, 'Getting Closer' and 'Baby's Request' snatched but the slightest chart honours.

Yet mean-minded critics, flop singles, the turnovers of personnel, the eternities in the studio, none of that mattered when Wings forthcoming tour of Britain had sold out. Up there on stage at this Gaumont or that Odeon was Paul's reward for working so hard: the acclamation of the great British public. That was better than any filthy lucre or rotten review.

As the artificial show cascaded during 'Wonderful Christmastime', the latest single, he was in his element. The here and now was too important – and magical – to worry about what the *NME* had printed about *Back To The Egg*. He had the people eating out of his palm in the way he'd imagined when in a brown study during physics at the Institute.

He didn't need Wings anymore – but perhaps he never had in the first place. No time was better for letting go of the group than after the cancellation of dates in Japan early in 1980, owing to Paul's extradition after nine days as Prisoner No 22 in a Tokyo jail after customs officials at Narita airport had instructed him to open his suitcase.

Sure enough, a polythene bag of marijuana leaped out and the culprit was handcuffed and hustled by uniformed men into custody. "PAUL IN CHAINS!" screamed a headline on breakfast tables back home while the subject of the report beneath it sank into an uneasy slumber in the detention centre where the local prosecutor had demanded he be sent.

As he had after the Maharishi's tutorials in 1967, Paul insisted that he was never going to touch narcotics again, whilst either continuing or resuming his habit – as demonstrated by two related if minor run-ins with the law in 1984 when he and Linda were reprimanded and made to pay fines as inappreciable as the amounts of dope with which they'd been caught. Yet while the nasty experience in Tokyo was yet to fade, McCartney may have had every intention of staying out of trouble. "I'll never smoke pot again," he assured one British tabloid the afternoon after his inglorious farewell to the Land of the Rising Sun.

That Denny Laine – and the two new boys – had left Japan nearly a week earlier may have struck Paul as disloyal. While his glorious leader's freedom was hanging in the balance, Laine had been preoccupied with another solo album – which was to contain a single, 'Japanese Tears', an attempt to come to terms with topical events close to his heart. Issued in May, its sentiments were worthy enough, and the old conviviality between Denny, Linda and Paul hadn't dissipated immediately. Nevertheless, the seeds of Denny's departure and the subsequent demise of Wings had been sown.

16 "(Just Like) Starting Over"

As far as I'm concerned, Paul McCartney's most important contribution to society has been his very pragmatic support of animal rights. Any argument that his celebrity and wealth created the opportunity to do so is irrelevant. Others of his kind were sufficiently hip to understand that, like, cruelty to animals is wrong, and were active after a detached, sweeping, pop-starrish fashion in verbally supporting vegetarianism, anti-vivisection et al. Sometimes – because it was trendy – they'd attempted not eating meat for maybe a few weeks before the smell of frying bacon triggered a backsliding. Then they'd be noticed once again in a motorway service station, autographing a table napkin whilst masticating a pork pie or indulging in new and often disgusting passions for huntin', fishin' and shootin' with monied neighbours for whom blood sports had been second nature from childhood.

Though as much a member of the rock squirearchy as anyone else, Paul stuck at vegetarianism, following a road-to-

Damascus moment one Sunday lunchtime in the Mull of Kintyre. He was settling down to a main course of roast someone-or-other with the family whilst gazing out at an idyllic rural scene of lambs gambolling round their mothers in a meadow. After at least three decades since he pushed away his plate that day, he's still tucking into non-meat dishes exclusively, preaching the gospel of animal welfare, sinking hard cash into all manner of associated organisations, and generally keeping up the good work started by him and his first wife.

The eventual founder of a multi-national vegetarian food company, Linda's picture remains the emblem of the still-expanding, constantly improving and award-winning Linda McCartney range of products stocked in a supermarket near you. Moreover, *Linda McCartney's Home Cooking* is still the world's biggest selling recipe book of its kind.

By the final months of Wings, the catering on the road was, at Paul's insistence, entirely meat-free – though, after the lamentable incident in Tokyo, he wasn't to tour again for years, no matter how hard his various investors pleaded. Among these was CBS, who had joined the queue of major US labels supplicating him for his services as soon as executive washroom whisperings filtered through that he was about to leave Capitol. One of the hottest properties in the industry, Paul was in a position to call shots about marketing procedure. If there was the slightest deviation from the ascribed riders, wild horses wouldn't drag him out to utter one solitary syllable or sing a single note on an album's behalf.

It was a tall order, but CBS was most prepared to obey, and had also proffered the unprecedented enticement of rights to *Guys And Dolls*, *The Most Happy Fella* and further musicals containing all manner of showbiz standards by the late Frank Loesser. Thus Paul McCartney melted into CBS's caress for the next five years.

Immediately, he bounced back to Number One in the States with 'Coming Up', aided by a promotional video featuring him in various guises as every member of a band. This was an apt taster for the maiden CBS album, *McCartney II*, which returned to his solo debut's homespun and virtual one-man-band ethos.

It swept straight to the top on both sides of the Atlantic, and John Lennon grinned at his own vexation when hearing himself humming 'Coming Up' when turning a thoughtful steering wheel. Next, a personal assistant was ordered to bring him a copy of *McCartney II*. That it was such a vast improvement on the "garbage" of *Back To The Egg*, reawoke in John the old striving for one-upmanship, and was among factors that spurred a return to the studio to make his first album since reuniting with Yoko in 1975 and becoming her reclusive "househusband".

The resulting husband-and-wife effort, *Double Fantasy*, could almost be filed under "Easy Listening", but its '(Just Like) Starting Over' sold well, and, of more personal import, Paul liked 'Beautiful Boy (Darling Boy)' – track seven, side one – enough to include it among his eight choices when a "castaway" on BBC Radio Four's *Desert Island Discs* in 1982.

This lullaby to the Lennons' only child – and the album from whence it came – had been bequeathed with a "beautiful sadness" because, on 8 December 1980, two months after his 40th birthday, John Lennon had been shot dead on a New York pavement by a "fan" who was Beatle-crazy in the most clinical sense.

Accosted by a television camera crew and a stick-mike thrust at his mouth, Paul, almost at a loss for words, had uttered "It's a drag" and mentioned that he intended to carry on as intended with a day's work at a studio desk. On the printed page the next day, it seemed too blithely fatalistic, but McCartney was a shaken and downcast man, feeling his anguish all the more sharply for assuming that there'd always be another chance to talk, face each other with guitars in an arena of armchairs, and continue to bridge the self-created abyss that, in recent years, they had become more and more willing to cross. What with Wings in abeyance and John back in circulation again, the notion of Lennon–McCartney – as opposed to Lennon and McCartney – hadn't been completely out of the question.

An element of posthumous Beatlemania helped to propel 'All Those Years Ago', a vinyl salaam to Lennon by George Harrison, high up international Top 20's. A further incentive for buyers was the superimposed presence of McCartney and Wings, such as they were, who'd added their bits when the unmixed tape arrived from George's Oxfordshire mansion.

For three months, on and off, Paul and the others had been at George Martin's studio complex on Montserrat, in the distant Carribean, working on *Tug Of War*, an album that turned out to be the follow-up to *McCartney II* rather than the now-disintegrating Wings's *Back To The Egg*.

Steve Holly and Laurence Juber had had nothing to do as Paul called on more renowned if disparate helpmates such as Eric Stewart of 10cc, rockabilly legend Carl Perkins and drummer Dave Mattacks, in and out of Fairport Convention since 1969. The sessions were notable too for an artistic reunion with not only George Martin as producer, but also Ringo Starr, fresh from *Stop And Smell The Roses*, an LP with a more pronounced "famous cast of thousands" approach.

To this, Paul had donated the title track and catchy 'Attention', but had decided to cling onto another composition, 'Take It Away'. Instead, it was opening track and the fourth of no less than six singles from *Tug Of War* – which went the chartbusting way of *McCartney II*, when released in April 1982. Among other highlights were 'Here Today' – a more piquant tribute to Lennon than singalong 'All Those Years Ago' – and 1982's 'Ebony And Ivory', a duet with Stevie Wonder, which, issued on 45, was another double-first in Britain and North America.

Whereas this liaison had been instigated by Paul, he himself had been solicited by Michael Jackson who, like Wonder, was a former Tamla-Motown child star. Now chronologically adult, he had been in the throes of recording the celebrated *Thriller* in Los Angeles. Paul was among the well-known guest musicians, and 'The Girl Is Mine', his cameo as jovial voice-of-experience to Michael's cheeky young shaver, was one of its hit 45s.

McCartney was paid in kind when Jackson pitched in on 'Say Say Say' from 1983's *Pipes Of Peace*, Paul's third post-Wings album. It also contained a title track that would be its maker's commercial apotheosis in Britain during the 1980s as 'Mull Of Kintyre' had been in the previous decade. A Yuletide Number One that lingered in the Top 50 for three months, it was helped on its way by a video that re-enacted the mythical and sociable seasonal encounter in No Man's Land between British and German soldiers in World War I.

The previous month, the critics had crucified the album. Surely *Melody Maker* had mistaken *Pipes Of Peace* for *Double Fantasy*, calling it "congratulatory self-righteous" and "slushy" – while the *NME* weighed in with "a tired, dull and empty collection of quasi-funk and gooey rock arrangements". In retrospect, some of the tracks were rather in-one-ear-and-out-the-other, but, on the whole, it was pleasant enough, even if the stand-out numbers were its two singles.

The first of these, 'Say Say Say', Michael Jackson returning of the *Thriller* favour, had suffered poor reviews too, but the public thought otherwise, and it shifted millions. It helped that Jackson was still basking in the afterglow of *Thriller* to the degree that even a video about the making of the Grammy-winning album precipitated stampedes into the megastores the minute their glass doors opened.

George Harrison judged *The Making Of Michael Jackson's Thriller* "the squarest thing I've ever seen," adding, "It was a bit off the way Michael bought up our old catalogue when he knew Paul was also bidding. He was supposed to be Paul's mate."

The Beatles portfolio was to become Jackson's property for a down payment of nearly £31 million, more than McCartney could afford, when ATV, its previous publishers, were open to offers for this and other bodies of work in 1986. Neither was McCartney pleased about how 1984's self-financed and feature-length *Give My Regards To Broad Street* film was received. The initial shard of inspiration for this "musical fantasy drama" had cut him more than two years earlier during an otherwise tedious stop-start drive into rush-hour London. With a screenplay by Paul himself, the interlocking theme was a world-class pop star's search for missing master tapes for an album. There were also musical interludes of which the majority were refashionings of Beatles and Wings favourites – though 'No More Lonely Nights', an opus fresh off the assembly-line, was the attendant hit single.

Throughout the six months of shooting, Andros Eraminondas guided and tempered his endlessly inventive paymaster's designations that, to outsiders, seemed as rash as a good half of *Magical Mystery Tour* had been. Nevertheless, throughout the interminable running of each celluloid mile, McCartney had been impressive for his learned recommendations about rhythm and pacing. Yet *Variety*, the *Bible* and *Yellow Pages* of the latest cinema releases, shoved aside *Give My Regards To Broad Street* as "characterless, bloodless and pointless". As they always were, journals local to the towns where it was distributed were kinder, albeit while homing in less on the story-line than the spectacular visual effects, some of which were seen too in subsequent videos for singles such as 'Only Love Remains', the principal ballad on his next album, *Press To Play*, which was centred on two elderly actors playing some dingy couple still in love after maybe half a century of wedlock: Darby and Joan who used to be Jack and Jill.

Three years before, McCartney had addressed himself to Jack, Jill and other infant video-watchers with *Rupert And The Frog Song*, 25 minutes dominated by one of the *Daily Express* cartoon character's adventures with voiceovers by sit-com shellbacks Windsor Davis and June Whitfield plus Paul himself, who'd owned the film rights to the checked-trousered bruin since 1970. It was to defy all comers when it appeared among BAFTA nominees as 1985's "Best Animated Short Film". Proving what traditionalists toddlers are, it also topped the video charts the previous Christmas. Into the bargain, the soundtrack's principal composition, 'We All Stand Together', sung by the animated frogs, had been high in the UK Top Ten.

Was there no end to this man's talent? He popped up again at Wembley Stadium that summer, emoting a gremlin-ridden 'Let It Be' to his own piano as satellite-linked Live Aid approached its climax. Then he joined the assembled cast for a finale in which he and Pete Townshend bore organiser Bob Geldof on their shoulders.

Geldof was to be knighted for his charitable efforts. Another milestone along rock's road to respectability was the heir to the throne's Prince's Trust Tenth Birthday Gala in June 1986. Paul gave 'em 'I Saw Her Standing There' and 'Long Tall Sally' prior to closing the show by leading an omnes fortissimo 'Get Back'. A handshake from Prince Charles afterwards had less personal significance to McCartney than the fact that he'd just completed his first formal appearance in an indoor venue since Wings's last flap at Hammersmith Odeon in 1979.

If his main spot had been as nostalgic in its way as Gerry And The Pacemakers on the chicken-in-a-basket trail, in terms of audience response, he'd held his own amid Me-generation entertainers like Bryan Adams, Paul Young and, with their whizz-kid singing bass player, Level 42, not to mention Tina Turner, Eric Clapton, the ubiquitous Elton John and all the other old stagers. Like them, he couldn't take Top 40 exploits for granted anymore, but *Press To Play* hovered round the middle of most international Top 30s, and the singles made token showings in some charts, even drippy 'Only Love Remains' after it filled Paul's entire slot on 1986's *Royal Variety Command Performance*.

He had better luck both critically and commercially – in Britain certainly – with 1987's *All The Best*, his second reassemblage of selected Wings and solo. This triumph of repackaging was to be gilded months later by *Sgt Pepper Knew*

My Father on which several new acts depped for the Lonely Hearts Club Band – with Billy Bragg's 'She's Leaving Home' and Wet Wet Wet's 'With A Little Help From My Friends' as its chart-topping double A-side.

There'd be more fleeting *Top Of The Pops* visitations – either on video or in the chicken-necked flesh – with their latest releases by such young hopefuls as Cliff Richard, The Rolling Stones, The Kinks and, a week before his sudden death in 1989, Roy Orbison. As the millennium crept closer, Paul McCartney would also score to a diminishing degree, not so much with songs he could have written in his sleep, but through a combination of pulling unexpected strokes, stubbornly treading steep and rugged pathways, and otherwise maintaining a lingering hip sensibility, often justifying the words of John McNally of The Searchers: "You don't have to be young to make good records."

Even on "Sounds Of The Sixties" nights in the most dismal working men's club, The Searchers, The Troggs, Dave Berry and those of corresponding vintage would lure a strikingly young crowd by counterpoising contemporary offerings with the old showstoppers. After disappearing for years, neither was it laughable for others who'd travelled an unquiet journey to middle life to embark on sell-out trans-continental tours as did Paul Simon, Fleetwood Mac, The Grateful Dead, Leonard Cohen – and, after a decade away, Paul McCartney.

17 "Ain't That A Shame"

Present on guitar and backing vocals in *Tug Of War* and *Pipes Of Peace*, Eric Stewart had also been evident in *Give My Regards To Broad Street*. He was also on hand to sling in rhymes, chord changes and twists to the plot as McCartney pieced together possibilities for what became *Press To Play*. Musically, this album had been proficient but not adventurous.

However, many of the lodged conventions of songwriting methodology since the beat boom were thrust aside when McCartney next bonded with Elvis Costello, one of the most successful post-pub rock ambassadors to get anywhere in North America.

That 33-year-old Costello had finished his formal education in Liverpool – and spent many previous school holidays with relations there – may have been a plus point for Paul. Offering hip credibility too, Costello was just what unfashionable McCartney needed, and, after initial slight misgivings, the two buckled down to "writing a

"AIN'T THAT A SHAME"

bunch of really good songs," smiled Elvis. "It was great working with him. I was thrilled."

Five hours a day in a room above Paul's studio in Sussex resulted in items for both Paul's *Flowers In The Dirt* and Declan's *Spike*. The general thrust of the McCartney–McManus output was the tempering of an abrasive edge with attractive tunes. 'My Brave Face' – a man's bitter freedom from his woman – just about reached the UK Top 20 for Paul with follow-up 'This One' touching exactly the same apogee (Number 18) but barely troubling the Hot 100 where 'My Brave Face' had got a look in at Number 25.

These so-so market volleys were incidental to *Flowers In The Dirt* returning McCartney to the top of all manner of album lists, and the ten months of the global tour earning an award from a US financial journal as the highest grossing such excursion of 1990 – with a stop in Rio de Janeiro breaking the world attendance record for a pop concert with a paying audience.

Spanning nearly every familiar trackway of Paul's career from 'Twenty Flight Rock' of Quarry Men vintage to 'My Brave Face', he was backed by quite a motley crew consisting of Linda, guitarist Robbie McIntosh (who'd quit The Pretenders during sessions for a 1986 album), keyboard player and former PE teacher Paul Wickens, drummer Chris Whitten (who'd been with Wickens in a group led by self-styled "pagan rock 'n' roller" Julian Cope) and general factotum Hamish Stuart, founder member of the Average White Band.

153

Stuart picked guitar very prettily on quasi-traditional 'All My Trials', an in-concert single captured in Milan. As well as filling one side of a single, it, utilised time on *Tripping The Light Fantastic*, a triple-album that was the quaint vinyl souvenir of the round-the-world expedition. Another by-product was the limited-edition *Unplugged: The Official Bootleg,* an acoustic recital after the ticket-holders shuffled in from the February chill to the relatively downhome ambience of Limehouse Studios amid London's dockland wharfs. Some would see themselves in a consequent *MTV* broadcast, the first one to be issued on a record.

The loudest ovations throughout these latest rounds of public displays would always be for the many unrevised Beatles selections. Audiences also clapped hard for Paul's olde tyme rock 'n' roll excursions. Both Eddie Cochran's 'Twenty Flight Rock' and Fats Domino's 'Ain't That A Shame' had just been recorded by Paul among items of similar vintage for *Choba B CCCP* (translated as "Back In The USSR") a Russia-only album of favourite non-originals dating from between Hitler's invasion of the Soviet Republic in 1941 and The Beatles' final season at the Star-Club in his defeated Germany.

Choba B CCCP came out just before the Berlin Wall came down in 1989. With the establishment of a Macdonald's fast-food outlet off Red Square not far away, it seemed an expedient exercise to fire a commercial broadside directly at consumers hitherto deprived of music from the very morning of post-war pop. Just as The Beatles' versions of

'Twist And Shout', 'Long Tall Sally', 'Money' et al were the only versions for anyone whose entrée to pop had been 'Please Please Me', so McCartney's would be of 13 set-works from the annals of classic rock for Russian record-buyers until they came upon the originals – and, in the late 1980s, there seemed fat chance of that for a while. Besides, as David Bowie, Bryan Ferry, The Hollies – and John Lennon – were a handful of the many who'd indulged in entire albums of oldies already, why shouldn't Paul?

His walks down memory lane also extended to disguised ambles round Liverpool. How delightful it was to mingle anonymously among shoppers in a Wavertree precinct; in a pub garden on the Cheshire plain, or browsing in a second-hand book shop up Parliament Street. He noticed that *a* Cavern had been reconstructed down Mathew Street next to Cavern Walks shopping mall. On the now-busy thoroughfare's opposite side stood the John Lennon pub and, halfway up a wall, an Arthur Dooley statue of a madonna-like figure – "Mother Liverpool" – with a plaque beneath reading "Four Lads Who Shook The World", and one of them, like, flying away with wings. Get it?

Civic pride in The Beatles had been emphasised further in 1982 by naming four streets on a housing estate after each of the four most famous members – Paul McCartney Way, Ringo Starr Drive and so forth – in spite of one disgruntled burgher's opposition "in the light of what went on in Hamburg and their use of filthy language."

While *Backbeat* – a silver screen perspective on John, Paul, George and Pete in Hamburg – loomed on the horizon, "Beatle conventions" had been fixtures in cities throughout the world for years. Frequent attractions – especially when each August's Merseybeatle festival was on – at both the new Cavern in Mathew Street and the more authentic one in the Beatles museum on Albert Dock were groups whose *raison d'être* was re-enacting some phase of The Beatles' career from the enlistment of Ringo to the end of the Swinging Sixties. Others of their ilk paid homage to solely one Beatle as did Band On The Run, Hari Georgeson, Starrtime and the short-lived Working Class Heroes. By the mid-1990s, there'd be nigh on 200 such tribute bands in Britain alone, virtually all of them encumbered with a right-handed "Paul".

While it was said that he procured one of the "Pauls" as a stand-in for a video shoot, McCartney was to raise an objection that, in *Backbeat*, "John" rather than his character sang 'Long Tall Sally', and seemed bemused generally that anyone should make a living impersonating The Beatles.

18 "Come Together"

Paul's next album, *Off The Ground* was the product of a satisfied mind. Polished and mostly unobjectionable, it was never expected to be astounding – by marginal McCartney enthusiasts anyway – but it sufficed because skillful arrangements and technological advances can help conceal mediocre songs in need of editing. It nudged the Top 20 in the USA where Beatlemania was always more virulent than anywhere else, and those afflicted bought Paul's records out of habit to complete the set like Buffalo Bill annuals. Over here, too many didn't want to like *Off The Ground*, but, as it had been in 1989, the press could slag off Paul's records; latter-day punks could denigrate him as one more bourgeois liberal with inert conservative tendencies, and hippies disregard him as a 'breadhead', but there he was again, running through his best-loved songs for the people who loved them – and him – best of all in Melbourne Cricket Ground, Louisiana Superdome, Munich's Olympiahalle and further packed-out stadia designed originally for championship sport.

As always, the mood was light, friendly, but what would have happened had the main set ended with politely brief clapping instead of the foot-stomping and howling approval that brought Paul back on for the encores of 'Band On The Run', 'I Saw Her Standing There' and, finally, everyone blasting up chorus after da-da chorus of 'Hey Jude'?

Yet, however slickly predictable his stage show was becoming, he would prove to have much in common in his way with David Bowie, Jeff Beck, Van Morrison and other advocates of the artistic virtues of sweating over something new while Elton John, Phil Collins, Stevie Wonder and like Swinging Sixties contemporaries continued cranking out increasingly more ordinary albums.

Paul got into the swing of keeping you guessing what he'll be up to next by paying close attention to what made his now-teenage children and their friends groove nowadays, and making his first and foremost essay as an exponent of the Modern Dance. He managed it in collaboration with genre producer Martin "Youth" Glover – though perhaps just in case they looked back in anger at it, McCartney and Glover hid themselves beneath a pseudonym – The Fireman – for the fusion of "downtempo house" and a vague strata of dub-reggae heard on 1993's *Strawberries Oceans Ships Forest* as well the more freeform and slow-moving ambient-techno of *Rushes* four years later.

Good old-fashioned guitars reared up among the

synthesizers and samples in *Rushes*, and the overall effect
was considered tame and old-fashioned by Modern Dance
connoisseurs. Nevertheless, it demonstrated that Fab Macca
dug the latest sounds – just as *Liverpool Oratorio* had his
appreciation of classical music. As Martin Glover was to be
the catalyst for The Fireman business, so Paul had leant on
Carl Davis, known chiefly as the classically trained composer
of television incidental music and film scores, for this maiden
venture into what he'd been brought up to regard as highbrow
nonsense: "When symphonies came on the radio, my family
just went, 'Oh bloody hell!' and switched the station."

After the job had been done, there was a hiccup when
Paul insisted that it be officially titled *Paul McCartney's
Liverpool Oratorio*, but Carl, if initially affronted, caved in,
and continued kneading the work into shape for the première
at Liverpool's Anglican cathedral on 28 June 1991.

BBC Music magazine opined that even its most melodic
excerpts "fell short of the standards set in his finest pop
tunes," and suggested that McCartney had "yet to find a
distinct 'classical' voice." Nonetheless, while reaching a lowly
177 in Billboard's pop chart, the album displaced Italian tenor
Luciano Pavarotti from the top of the classical list, performing
similarly in Britain.

Although McCartney didn't thus reinvent himself as a
sort of nuclear age Sir Arthur Sullivan by juggling milkman-
friendly catchiness and Handel-like choral works, *Liverpool
Oratorio* was instrumental in narrowing the gap between

highbrow and lowbrow, "real" singing and "pop" caterwauling, 'La Donna E Mobile' and 'Long Tall Sally'. Pertinent to this discussion too, the University of Liverpool opened Britain's first Institute of Popular Music – with Mike McCartney among those in its working party. Was it not entirely fitting that a self-contained faculty to centralise existing work should have originated in the birthplace of The Beatles?

The same could be said of the Liverpool Institute of Performing Arts – LIPA – a notion that had come to Paul McCartney shortly before his old secondary school closed in the mid-1980s, and "this wonderful building, which was built in 1825, was becoming derelict. Various people suggested to me that I could help by taking the kids off the streets in some way. Four years ago, I announced the plan to build LIPA, and we started fund-raising. I put in some money to get it going, and we got a lot of help from different people."

It was to be, he said, "like the school in the TV series, *Fame*" in that talented youngsters could be primed for greener pastures via courses that included an artistic conditioning process that, time permitting, might involve songwriting tutorials by none other than the very founder himself – "but I won't be telling the kids how to do it because I think that it is part of my skill that I don't know exactly how to write a song, and the minute I do know how to do it, I'm finished. So I would want to explain that I don't agree that there is an accepted method of writing a song."

The Institute was to enroll its first students for 1996's spring term in between the preceding media hoo-hah that always went with the McCartney territory and the official unveiling of its plaque by the Queen – who'd been among those who'd dipped into her purse for LIPA – in June.

George Harrison's loyalty to the old grey stones was strong enough for him to reach for his cheque book on LIPA's behalf too. He had also been amenable to joining with Paul and Ringo in 1994 for the compilation of *Anthology*, a vast Beatles retrospective that would embrace eventually nine albums (in sets of three), a lengthy television documentary – later available on video and DVD – and a group autobiography in the form of edited transcripts of taped reminiscences. "There were one or two bits of tension," smiled Paul, "I had one or two ideas George didn't like." One of these was the project's working title, *The Long And Winding Road*, because it was after one of McCartney's songs. Ringo too blew hot and cold with Paul: "It's a good month and a bad month, just like a family."

Since John's passing, there'd been no successor to him as self-appointed paterfamilias, but Yoko had remained to The Beatles roughly what the embarrassing "Fergie", the Duchess of York, is to the Windsors. Yet she and Paul had shared a conciliatory hug at a Rock 'N' Roll Hall Of Fame award ceremony, and before the weather vane of rapprochement lurched back to the old thinly veiled antagonism, Yoko donated stark voice-piano tapes of Lennon compositions for

161

McCartney, Harrison and Starr to use as they thought fit.

Two of them, 'Free As A Bird' and 'Real Love' were transformed into successive Beatles A-sides to go with the *Anthology* merchandise. Events since have demonstrated that it was far from the last word on the group. Not a month passes without another few books adding to the millions of words chronicling and analysing some aspect or other of their history. Bootlegs have continued unabated too with their manufacturers intrigued most recently by the emergence in Holland of further hitherto-unissued unforgiving minutes from the *Let It Be* era.

Thus The Beatles endure after the apparent levelling out of Britpop from its mid-1990s apogee. While it was going strongest, as he had with the Modern Dance, Paul McCartney, well into his 50s, masticated a chunk of Britpop too by combining with 37-year old Paul Weller and, more to the point, Noel Gallagher, leader of Oasis, on an Abbey Road reworking of 'Come Together' for *Help!* a 1995 "various artists" album to raise funds to alleviate the war in Bosnia's aftermath of homelessness, lack of sanitation, disease and starvation. Symbolising three generations of pop aristocracy, the trio – naming themselves The Smokin' Mojo Filters – were *Help!*'s star turn, and, almost as a matter of course, 'Come Together' was its loss-leader of a single.

19 "Lonesome Tears"

Classical composer Sir William had been responsible too for *Fanfare For Brass* for EMI's celebration of its first 50 years in business, but for the label's centenary in 1997, Paul McCartney came up with *Standing Stone*, a symphonic poem that the sniffy *Music* periodical reckoned "represented a significant leap forward in style and substance, the persuasive outcome of almost four years labour."

His mood was one of quiet confidence when settling into a seat at the Royal Albert Hall for the London Symphony Orchestra and Chorus's première of *Standing Stone* at the Royal Albert Hall on 14 October 1997. Pockets of the audience behaved as if it was a rock concert, though they remained silent and not visibly fidgeting during the grandiloquent music that finished with "love is the oldest secret of the universe" from the choir, prefacing some ticket-holders' exclaimed "yeah!" that set off a standing ovation.

Overnight, the press gathered its thoughts. The reviews

weren't scathing, but *Standing Stone* wasn't an especially palpable hit either now that the novelty of Paul McCartney, classical composer, had faded. Nevertheless, it was received more favourably at New York's Carnegie Hall the following month in a performance that was broadcast to nigh on 400 radio stations across the whole sub-continent. Of later recitals, the most far-reaching was that on British television one Christmas morning when the nation was midway between the children's pre-dawn ripping open of the presents and the Queen's Speech.

The morning after 14 October 1997, however, the critics had tended to overlook the McCartney pieces that had prefaced the main event at the Albert Hall. These were the seven movements of 'A Leaf' and another orchestrated piece 'Spiral' – for piano – as well as 'Stately Horn' for a horn ensemble, and 'Inebriation' from The Brodsky Quartet.

Now that he'd acquired a taste for it, Paul would be knocking out more of the same, most recently *Ecce Cor Meum* – "behold my heart" – an oratorio dedicated to Linda, that was the centrepiece of the first concert given at Magdalen College, Oxford's new chapel in November 2001.

Listening to that of McCartney's classical output issued thus far on disc – which includes the 'Andante' from *Standing Stone* as a single – adjectives like "restrained", "shimmering", "caressing" and "atmospheric" occurred to me, and a lot of it has, indeed, a reposeful daintiness that's just, well, nice.

The same adjective might be applied to 1995's *Oobu*

Joobu, a radio series commissioned by the same US company that had networked the self-explanatory *Lost Lennon Tapes*. Here, Paul presided over harmless family fun with records, jingles, funny stories, celebrity interviews, comedy sketches, previously unbroadcasted Beatles and Wings tapes, you get the drift. There were also what might have been categorised in a more sexist age, "women's features" – mainly recipes – by Linda. The children, however, made only incidental contributions at most. Advisedly, they'd been so removed from direct public gaze that, as teenagers, they were able to walk around Rye and Campbeltown not unnoticed exactly, but without inviting too much comment.

Domestically, the mid-1990s would be remembered by Paul not only for what happened at the end, but also for the contentment that had preceded it. Nothing was ever the same afterwards.

Lightning struck slowly. In December 1995, Linda recovered from an ostensibly successful operation to remove a lump from her breast. Yet within weeks, she had every appearance of being seriously ill, and was prescribed chemotherapy. That held the spread of what was obviously cancer at arm's length, but X-rays were to reveal malignant cells forming a shadow on her liver.

The ghastly secret became known to a media that noted Linda's absence when Paul was driven to Buckingham Palace on 11 March 1997. As Prime Minister John Major had done on the apparent behalf of Eric Clapton MBE, Van

Morrison OBE and Sir Cliff so his more with-it successor, Tony Blair, a self-styled 'guy' had advised the Queen to invest the showbusiness legend as responsible for 'I Saw Her Standing There' as *Liverpool Oratorio* with a knighthood – for "services to music". Sir Paul McCartney then sealed his status as pillar of the Establishment by paying £3,500 for a coat of arms. Among its symbols were a guitar and two circles representing records to signify what was still his principal source of income.

To that end, *Flaming Pie*, his first non-concert album for nearly half a decade, materialised two months after the visit to the Queen. Unlike, say, *Ecce Cor Meum*, it wasn't meant to be taken especially seriously. "I called up a bunch of friends and family and we just got on and did it," he chortled. "And we had fun. Hopefully, you'll hear that in the songs."

Those that did bought *Flaming Pie* in sufficient quantity to ease it up to Number One and to Number Two in the Hot 100. This flew in the face of dejecting critiques for an album that conveyed a likeably downhome, sofa-ed ambience.

Nowhere in its lyrics was any intimation that Linda was dying by inches. More a hospital orderly than passionate inamorato now, Paul tried to blow sparks of optimism but resigned himself with wearied amazement that she was still clinging on as he helped attend to her day-long needs.

The flame was low on the evening of Thursday 16 April 1998, and 56-year-old Linda Louise McCartney was gone by the grey of morning.

20 "She Said Yeah"

Predictably, there were rumours of a lady friend within months of Linda's funeral, but there was no evidence to substantiate a new romance until late in 1999 when Paul was seen in public with a blonde from Tyne-and-Wear named Heather Mills, whose artificial leg was of no more account than an earring or a headband. On 8 August 1993, she had been knocked down by a police motorcycle, and hastened to the nearest hospital where surgeons were obliged to amputate. With extraordinary resilience, Heather Mills conquered desolation by anchoring herself to the notion that, one way or another, she'd emerge, if not entirely intact, then with hardened mettle. At least she could afford – especially with the out-of-court settlement by Scotland Yard – the thousands of pounds required for a shapely silicone limb with a flexible foot.

She also inaugurated the Heather Mills Trust, a charity for those who had become limbless in global theatres of war. Her tireless fund-raising involved a 1999 Heather Mills single entitled 'Voice' – with a lyric about a disabled girl – and spell-binding slots on chat-shows where she provoked shocked laughter by rolling up her trousers and even removing her false leg. Up in the control room, where the producer barked excited instructions to the camera operators, it was fantastic television.

It also had the desired effect of drawing attention to a campaign that was to earn Heather a Nobel Peace Prize nomination and further recognitions for her work. Famous enough to warrant a frank-and-unashamed autobiography, she was a host at one such ceremony at London's plush Dorchester Hotel. Her future husband was there too, clutching the Linda McCartney Award For Animal Welfare he was to give to the founder of Viva, an associated movement.

Taking a benevolent interest in Heather's activities, Paul McCartney was to write out a huge cheque for the trust, and contribute plucked guitar and backing vocals to 'Voice'. Then one thing led to another, and the 59-year-old widower seemed as fondly in love as he could be with a beautiful girlfriend a quarter of a century his junior.

He went public in other matters too. Three years after a Paul McCartney art exhibition opened at the Kunstforum Lyz Gallery in Hamburg on 30 April 1999, he risked a display at the Walker in Liverpool – which was also curating some Turners in an adjacent gallery. This was perhaps unfortunate in its inviting of comparisons between the distinguished Victorian "colour poet" and one who wouldn't be there if not for the Fab Four's long shadow.

While one expert deemed Paul's efforts to be "more interesting than I thought" and another in the same newspaper reckoned they had "promise", a third critic turned his nose up at "wholly talentless daubs. Perhaps endless adulation has made McCartney deaf to the voice of criticism."

Maybe the Beatles' fairy-tale had rendered this particular scribe as deaf to the voice of approbation. Either way, McCartney was in a no-win situation – unless he'd exhibited his art pseudonymously. Yet little intimates that because Paul McCartney was so fully occupied with his musical career, he was a regrettable loss to the world of fine art. As a figure in time's fabric, his period as a Beatle will remain central to most considerations of him.

He'd harked back to the years prior to the 'Love Me Do' countdown with 1999's *Run Devil Run*, a quasi-*Choba B CCCP* album, but with three originals in the same vein. Anyone with the confidence to slot these in without jarring the stylistic flow of such as 'All Shook Up', 'Brown-Eyed Handsome Man', 'She Said Yeah', and 'Blue Jean Bop' deserved attention. The most significant plug for *Run Devil Run* was an end-of-the-century bash at the replica Cavern along Mathew Street to a capacity raffle-winning crowd but with a webcast audience of over three million.

His fans loved it, but they weren't so sure about an album taped after Martin "Youth" Glover reared up again as producer of Super Furry Animals, formed in Cardiff in the mid-1990s as an amalgam of the Modern Dance, Britpop and olde tyme progressive rock. At an *NME* awards evening in February 2000, they and McCartney chatted amiably enough, and through the agency of Glover, they were to collaborate on *Liverpool Sound Collage*, which was to be up for a Grammy as 2001's "Best Alternative Musical Album". It had been intended in the first instance as an aural backdrop to "About Collage", an exhibition at the Tate Liverpool by Peter Blake, whose pop-associated pursuits had not ended with his montage for the *Sgt Pepper* front cover.

Neither had Paul's non-pop dabblings with the Walker exhibition, though he was on firmer ground with 2001's *Blackbird Singing*, a collection of over 100 poems interspersed with lyrics from some of his songs.

Over an album's worth of new compositions were dashed off in a fortnight with a guitar–keyboards–drums trio of Los Angeles session players whose keeping of expensive pace with him was leavened by technical precision deferring to spontaneity. "We didn't fuss about it," he shrugged. "I'd show them a song, and we'd start doing it." These included 'From A Lover To A Friend', the only A-side. It lasted a fortnight in the domestic Top 50, and proceeds were donated to the families of New York's fire service who perished in the aftershock of the terrorist attacks on the World Trade Center.

Paul had been present when the hijacked aeroplanes tore into the heart of the Big Apple, and had organised an all-star benefit concert at Madison Square Garden with no political agenda other than raising money for the firefighters and other victims, and to show solidarity against terrorism. Naturally, he wrote a song about it.

As a raw composition, 'Freedom' was convoluted and over-declamatory, but that didn't matter in the context of the euphoric atmosphere on that October Saturday six weeks after "nine-eleven". Nonetheless, he wasn't to perform it when he commenced what he was to call his "Back In The World" tour. Prior to setting off, however, there was something McCartney had to do that was as special in its way as the New York spectacular. In November 2001, George Harrison had died of cancer. A memorial concert took place at the Empire on what would have been his 59th birthday on 24 February 2002. Paul shared a few yarns with the audience and, at the very end, gave 'em a spirited 'Yesterday'.

He paid homage to George again on more glittering events at the Albert Hall – and on 3 June 2002 at Elizabeth II's "Jubilee Concert" in the grounds of Buckingham Palace, which reached a climax of sorts in a duet with Eric Clapton of George's 'While My Guitar Gently Weeps' from the White Album.

Not seen in the televisual coverage was the final number, 'I Saw Her Standing There'. As its coda yet reverberated, Paul was thinking ahead to the following Monday when he was to marry Heather Mills – for whom he'd penned an eponymous song on *Driving Rain* – at a castle hired for that very purpose in the Irish republic. Theirs was the fuss wedding of the year after the elderly laird, unused to press encroachment, gave the game away.

Back from the honeymoon, the groom embarked on the second leg of what was now a wartime tour. Wherever he could (on programmes or the spin-off "live" album), he ensured that composing credits read "McCartney–Lennon" like they had fleetingly before Parlophone and everyone else had made it the more alphabetically correct "Lennon–McCartney", even on the *Anthology*. Paul's attempt then to have it otherwise had been vetoed by John's volatile relict, and reawoke a dispute that hasn't yet been resolved. You can understand Paul's attitude. On the basis of mostly song-by-song breakdowns by Lennon during one of his last interviews, BBC Radio Merseyside presenter Spencer Leigh figured out that, statistically, McCartney was responsible for approximately two-thirds of The Beatles' output of originals, including 'Yesterday' and 'Hey Jude'. In a weighty press statement, Paul fulminated too that "Late one night, I was in an empty bar, flicking through the pianist's music book when I came across '"Hey Jude" written by John Lennon'. At one point, Yoko earned more from 'Yesterday' than I did."

On his 50th birthday in 1992, however, there'd been no anger but a certain melancholy as Paul mused that "despite the successful songs I've written like 'Yesterday', 'Let It Be' and 'Hey Jude', I feel I just want to write one really good song. I still have a little bee in my bonnet telling me, 'The best could be yet to come.' That keeps me going."

Songography

By Ian Drummond

All songs composed by Paul McCartney, with co-writers appearing in brackets. Listed by artist/band and then in chronological order of composition. All dates refer to album and single releases unless otherwise stated.

THE BEATLES

'In Spite Of All The Danger' (Harrison)	*Anthology 1* (Nov 1995)
'Cayenne'	
'Like Dreamers Do' (Lennon)	
'I Saw Her Standing There' (Lennon)	*Please Please Me* (Mar 1963)
'Misery' (Lennon)	
'Chains' (Lennon)	
'Ask Me Why' (Lennon)	
'Please Please Me' (Lennon)	
'Love Me Do' (Lennon)	
'PS I Love You' (Lennon)	
'Do You Want To Know A Secret?' (Lennon)	
'There's A Place' (Lennon)	
'From Me To You' (Lennon)	Single (Apr 1963)
'Thank You Girl' (Lennon)	'From Me To You' B-side (Apr 1963)

PAUL McCartney

'She Loves You' (Lennon)   Single (Aug 1963)
'I'll Get You' (Lennon)   'She Loves You' B-side (Aug 1963)

'I'll Be On My Way' (Lennon)   *Live At The BBC* (Nov 1994)

'It Won't Be Long' (Lennon)   *With The Beatles* (Nov 1963)
'All I've Got To Do' (Lennon)
'All My Loving' (Lennon)
'Little Child' (Lennon)
'Hold Me Tight' (Lennon)
'I Wanna Be Your Man' (Lennon)
'Not A Second Time' (Lennon)

'I Want To Hold Your Hand' (Lennon)   Single (Nov 1963)
'This Boy' (Lennon)   'I Want To Hold Your Hand' B-side (Nov 1963)

'I Call Your Name' (Lennon)   *Long Tall Sally* EP (Jun 1964)

'A Hard Day's Night' (Lennon)   *A Hard Day's Night* (Jul 1964)
'I Should Have Known Better' (Lennon)
'If I Fell' (Lennon)
'I'm Happy Just To Dance With You' (Lennon)
'And I Love Her' (Lennon)
'Tell Me Why' (Lennon)
'Can't Buy Me Love' (Lennon)
'Any Time At All' (Lennon)
'I'll Cry Instead' (Lennon)
'Things We Said Today' (Lennon)
'When I Get Home' (Lennon)
'You Can't Do That' (Lennon)
'I'll Be Back' (Lennon)

'I Feel Fine' (Lennon)   Single (Nov 1964)
'She's A Woman' (Lennon)   'I Feel Fine' B-side (Nov 1964)

'No Reply' (Lennon)   *Beatles For Sale* (Nov 1964)
'I'm A Loser' (Lennon)
'Baby's In Black' (Lennon)
'I'll Follow The Sun' (Lennon)
'Eight Days A Week' (Lennon)
'Every Little Thing' (Lennon)

'I Don't Want To Spoil The Party' (Lennon)
'What You're Doing' (Lennon)

'Ticket To Ride' (Lennon)   Single (Apr 1965)
'Yes It Is' (Lennon)   'Ticket To Ride' B-side (Apr 1965)

'I'm Down' (Lennon)   'Help!' B-side (Jul 1965)

'Help!' (Lennon)   *Help!* (Aug 1965)
'The Night Before' (Lennon)
'You've Got To Hide Your Love Away' (Lennon)
'Another Girl' (Lennon)
'You're Going To Lose That Girl' (Lennon)
'It's Only Love' (Lennon)
'Tell Me What You See' (Lennon)
'I've Just Seen A Face' (Lennon)
'Yesterday' (Lennon)

'That Means A Lot' (Lennon)   *Anthology 2* (Mar 1996)

'We Can Work It Out' (Lennon)   Single (Dec 1965)
'Day Tripper' (Lennon)   'We Can Work It Out' B-side (Dec 1965)

'Drive My Car' (Lennon)   *Rubber Soul* (Nov 1965)
'Norwegian Wood (This Bird Has Flown)' (Lennon)
'You Won't See Me' (Lennon)
'Nowhere Man' (Lennon)
'The Word' (Lennon)
'Michelle' (Lennon)
'What Goes On' (Lennon-Starkey)
'Girl' (Lennon)
'I'm Looking Through You' (Lennon)
'In My Life' (Lennon)
'Wait' (Lennon)
'Run For Your Life' (Lennon)

'12-Bar Original' (Lennon-Harrison-Starkey)   *Anthology 2* (Mar 1996)

'Paperback Writer' (Lennon)   Single (Jun 1966)
'Rain' (Lennon)   'Paperback Writer' B-side (Jun 1966)

'Eleanor Rigby' (Lennon)	*Revolver* (Aug 1966)
'I'm Only Sleeping' (Lennon)	
'Here, There And Everywhere' (Lennon)	
'Yellow Submarine' (Lennon)	
'She Said She Said' (Lennon)	
'Good Day Sunshine' (Lennon)	
'And Your Bird Can Sing' (Lennon)	
'For No One' (Lennon)	
'Doctor Robert' (Lennon)	
'Got To Get You Into My Life' (Lennon)	
'Tomorrow Never Knows' (Lennon)	

'Penny Lane' (Lennon)	Single (Feb 1967)
'Strawberry Fields Forever' (Lennon)	'Penny Lane' B-side (Feb 1967)

'Sgt Pepper's Lonely Hearts Club Band' (Lennon)	*Sgt Pepper's Lonely Hearts Club Band* (Jun 1967)
'With A Little Help From My Friends' (Lennon)	
'Lucy In The Sky With Diamonds' (Lennon)	
'Getting Better' (Lennon)	
'Fixing A Hole' (Lennon)	
'She's Leaving Home' (Lennon)	
'Being For The Benefit Of Mr Kite!' (Lennon)	
'When I'm Sixty-Four' (Lennon)	
'Lovely Rita' (Lennon)	
'Good Morning Good Morning' (Lennon)	
'Sgt Pepper's Lonely Hearts Club Band (Reprise)' (Lennon)	
'A Day In The Life' (Lennon)	

'All Together Now' (Lennon)	*Yellow Submarine* (Jan 1969)

'All You Need Is Love' (Lennon)	Single (Jul 1967)
'Baby You're A Rich Man' (Lennon)	'All You Need Is Love' B-side (Jul 1967)

'You Know My Name' (Lennon)	'Let It Be' B-side (May 1970)

'Hello Goodbye' (Lennon)	Single (Dec 1967)

'Magical Mystery Tour' (Lennon)	*Magical Mystery Tour* (Dec 1967)
'The Fool On The Hill' (Lennon)	

'Flying' (Lennon-Harrison-Starkey)
'Your Mother Should Know' (Lennon)
'I Am The Walrus' (Lennon)

'Jessie's Dream'   *Magical Mystery Tour* film (Dec 1967)
    (Lennon-Harrison-Starkey)

'Christmas Time (Is Here Again)'   'Free As A Bird' B-side (Dec 1995)
    (Lennon-Harrison-Starkey)

'Lady Madonna' (Lennon)   Single (Mar 1968)

'Hey Jude' (Lennon)   Single (Aug 1968)

'Across The Universe' (Lennon)   *World Wildlife* (Dec 1969)

'Hey Bulldog' (Lennon)   *Yellow Submarine* (Jan 1969)

'Back In The USSR' (Lennon)   *The Beatles* (Nov 1968)
'Dear Prudence' (Lennon)
'Glass Onion' (Lennon)
'Ob-La-Di, Ob-La-Da' (Lennon)
'Honey Pie' (Lennon)
'The Continuing Story Of Bungalow Bill' (Lennon)
'Happiness Is A Warm Gun' (Lennon)
'Martha My Dear' (Lennon)
'I'm So Tired' (Lennon)
'Blackbird' (Lennon)
'Rocky Raccoon' (Lennon)
'Why Don't We Do It In The Road' (Lennon)
'I Will' (Lennon)
'Julia' (Lennon)
'Birthday' (Lennon)
'Yer Blues' (Lennon)
'Mother Nature's Son' (Lennon)
'Everybody's Got Something To Hide Except Me And My Monkey' (Lennon)
'Sexy Sadie' (Lennon)
'Helter Skelter' (Lennon)
'Revolution 1' (Lennon)
'Honey Pie' (Lennon)

'Cry Baby Cry' (Lennon)
'Revolution 9' (Lennon)
'Good Night' (Lennon)

'The Ballad Of John And Yoko' (Lennon)   Single (May 1969)

'Two Of Us' (Lennon)   *Let It Be* (May 1970)
'Dig A Pony' (Lennon)
'Across The Universe' (Lennon)
'I Me Mine' (Harrison [-McCartney?])
'Dig It' (Lennon-Harrison-Starkey)
'Let It Be' (Lennon)
'I've Got A Feeling' (Lennon)
'One After 909' (Lennon)
'The Long And Winding Road' (Lennon)
'Get Back' (Lennon)

'Don't Let Me Down' (Lennon)   'Get Back' B-side (Apr 1969)

'Come Together' (Lennon)   *Abbey Road* (Sep 1969)
'Maxwell's Silver Hammer' (Lennon)
'Oh! Darling' (Lennon)
'I Want You (She's So Heavy)' (Lennon)
'Because' (Lennon)
'You Never Give Me Your Money' (Lennon)
'Sun King' (Lennon)
'Mean Mr Mustard' (Lennon)
'Polythene Pam' (Lennon)
'She Came In Through The Bathroom Window' (Lennon)
'Golden Slumbers' (Lennon)
'Carry That Weight' (Lennon)
'The End' (Lennon)
'Her Majesty' (Lennon)

'Free As A Bird' (Lennon-Harrison-Starkey)   *Anthology 1* (Nov 1995)
'Real Love' (Lennon-Harrison-Starkey)   *Anthology 2* (Mar 1996)

'Thinking Of Linking' (Lennon)   *Anthology DVD* (Apr 2003)

PAUL McCARTNEY

'Family Way' (original soundtrack)	*Family Way* (Feb 1967)
'The Lovely Linda'	*McCartney* (Apr 1970)
'That Would Be Something'	
'Valentine Day'	
'Every Night'	
'Hot As Sun'	
'Glasses'	
'Suicide'	
'Junk'	
'Man We Was Lonely'	
'Oo You'	
'Momma Miss America'	
'Teddy Boy'	
'Maybe I'm Amazed'	
'Kreen Akrore'	
'Another Day' (L McCartney)	Single (Feb 1971)
'Oh Woman, Oh Why'	'Another Day' B-side (Feb 1971)
'Wonderful Christmastime'	Single (Nov 1979)
'Same Time Next Year'	'Put It There' B-side (Feb 1990)
'Coming Up'	*McCartney II* (May 1980)
'Temporary Secretary'	
'On The Way'	
'Waterfalls'	
'Nobody Knows'	
'Front Parlour'	
'Summer's Day Song'	
'Frozen Jap'	
'Bogey Music'	
'Darkroom'	
'One Of These Days'	
'Check My Machine'	'Waterfalls' B-side (Jun 1980)
'Secret Friend'	'Temporary Secretary' B-side (Sep 1980)

'Tug Of War'   *Tug Of War* (Apr 1982)
'Take It Away'
'Always Somebody Who Cares'
'What's That You're Doing' (Wonder)
'Here Today'
'Ballroom Dancing'
'The Pound Is Sinking'
'Wanderlust'
'Get It'
'Be What You See'
'Dress Me Up As A Robber'
'Ebony And Ivory'

'Rainclouds'   'Ebony And Ivory' B-side (Mar 1982)

'I'll Give You A Ring'   'Take It Away' B-side (Jun 1982)

'Pipes Of Peace'   *Pipes Of Peace* (Oct 1983)
'Say Say Say' (Jackson)
'The Other Me'
'Keep Under Cover'
'So Bad'
'The Man' (Jackson)
'Sweetest Little Show'
'Average Person'
'Hey Hey' (Clarke)
'Tug Of Peace'
'Through Our Love'

'Twice In A Lifetime'   *Pipes Of Peace* (Re-released Aug 1993)

'Ode To A Koala Bear'   'Say Say Say' B-side (Oct 1983)

'No More Lonely Nights'   *Give My Regards To Broad Street* (Oct 1984)
'Corridor Music'
'Not Such A Bad Boy'
'No Values'
'Eleanor's Dream'
'Goodnight Princess'

'Stranglehold' (Stewart)   *Press To Play* (Sep 1986)
'Good Times Coming'
'Talk More Talk'
'Footprints' (Stewart)
'Only Love Remains'
'Press'
'Pretty Little Head' (Stewart)
'Move Over Busker' (Stewart)
'Angry' (Stewart)
'However Absurd' (Stewart)
'Write Away' (Stewart)
'It's Not True'
'Tough On A Tightrope' (Stewart)
'Feel The Sun'

'Hanglide' (Stewart)   'Press' B-side (Jul 1986)

'Simple As That'   *It's A Live-In World* (Nov 1986)

'Spies Like Us'   Single (Nov 1986)

'Love Mix' (Ramone)   'Beautiful Night' B-side (Jul 1997)
'Love Come Tumbling Down'   'Beautiful Night' B-side (Jul 1997)
'Same Love'   'Beautiful Night' B-side (Jul 1997)

'Once Upon A Long Ago'   Single (Nov 1987)
'Back On My Feet' (McManus) 'Once Upon A Long Ago' B-side (Nov 1987)

'Flying To My Home'   'My Brave Face' B-side (May 1989)

'My Brave Face' (McManus)   *Flowers In The Dirt* (Jun 1989)
'Rough Ride'
'You Want Her Too' (McManus)
'Distractions'
'We Got Married'
'Put It There'
'Figure Of Eight'
'This One' (McManus)
'Don't Be Careless Love' (McManus)
'That Day Is Done' (McManus)

'How Many People?'
'Motor Of Love'
'Où Est Le Soleil?'

'I Wanna Cry'	'This One' B-side (Jul 1989)
'The First Stone' (Stewart)	'This One' B-side (Jul 1989)
'Good Sign'	'This One' B-side (Jul 1989)

'Loveliest Thing'   'Figure Of Eight' B-side (Nov 1989)

'Inner City Madness'   *Tripping The Live Fantastic* (Nov 1990)
    (L McCartney-McIntosh-Wickens-Stuart-Whitten)
'Together' (L McCartney-McIntosh-Wickens-Stuart-Whitten)

'All My Trials' (Traditional arr McCartney)   Single (Nov 1990)

'PS Love Me Do' (Lennon)   'Birthday' B-side (Oct 1990)

'I Lost My Little Girl'   *Unplugged* (May 1991)

'War'   *Liverpool Oratorio* (Oct 1991)
'School'
'Crypt'
'Father'
'Wedding'
'Work'
'Crises'
'Peace'

'Off The Ground'   *Off The Ground* (Feb 1993)
'Biker Like An Icon'
'Peace In The Neighbourhood'
'Looking For Changes'
'Hope Of Deliverance'
'Mistress And Maid' (McManus)
'I Owe It All To You'
'Golden Earth Girl'
'The Lovers That Never Were' (McManus)
'Get Out Of My Way'
'Winedark Open Sea'

'C'mon People'
'Cosmically Conscious'

'Style Style'   *Off The Ground* (US release, Apr 1993)
'Sweet Sweet Memories'
'Soggy Noodle'

'Long Leather Coat' (L McCartney) 'Hope Of Deliverance' B-side (Dec 1992)
'Big Boys Bickering'   'Hope Of Deliverance' B-side (Dec 1992)
'Kicked Around No More'   'Hope Of Deliverance' B-side (Dec 1992)

'I Can't Imagine'   'C'mon People' B-side (Feb 1993)
'Keep Coming Back To Love' (Stuart)   'C'mon People' B-side (Feb 1993)
'Down To The River'   'C'mon People' B-side (Feb 1993)

'Hotel In Benidorm'   *Paul Is Live* (Nov 1993)
'A Fine Day'

'Fire/Rain'   *Standing Stone* (Sep 1997)
'Cell Growth'
'Human' Theme
'Meditation'
'Crystal Ship'
'Sea Voyage'
'Lost At Sea'
'Release'
'Safe Haven/Standing Stone'
'Peaceful Moment'
'Messenger'
'Lament'
'Trance'
'Eclipse'
'Glory Tales'
'Fugal Celebration'
'Rustic Dance'
'Love Duet'
'Celebration'

'The Song We Were Singing'   *Flaming Pie* (May 1997)
'The World Tonight'

PAUL MCCARTNEY

'If You Wanna'
'Somedays'
'Young Boy'
'Calico Skies'
'Flaming Pie'
'Heaven On A Sunday'
'Used To Be Bad' (Miller)
'Souvenir'
'Little Willow'
'Really Love You' (Starkey)
'Beautiful Night'
'Great Day'

'Oobu Joobu'	'Young Boy' B-side (Apr 1997)
'Broomstick'	'Young Boy' B-side (Apr 1997)
'Atlantic Ocean'	'Young Boy' B-side (Apr 1997)
'I Love This House'	'Young Boy' B-side (Apr 1997)

'Squid'   'The World Tonight' B-side (Jul 1997)

'Run Devil Run'   *Run Devil Run* (Aug 1999)
'Try Not To Cry'
'What It Is'

'A Leaf'   *Working Classical* (Oct 1999)
'Haymakers'
'Midwife'
'Spiral'
'Tuesday'

'From A Lover To A Friend'   *Driving Rain* (Nov 2001)
'Freedom'
'Lonely Road'
'Heather'
'She's Given Up Talking'
'Driving Rain'
'I Do'
'Tiny Bubble'
'Magic'
'Your Way'

'Spinning On An Axis' (J McCartney)
'About You'
'Back In The Sunshine Again' (J McCartney)
'Your Loving Flame'
'Riding Into Jaipur'
'Rinse The Raindrops'

'Vanilla Sky'   *Vanilla Sky* soundtrack (Nov 2001)

PAUL AND LINDA McCARTNEY
'Too Many People'   *Ram* (May 1971)
'Three Legs'
'Ram On'
'Dear Boy' (L McCartney)
'Uncle Albert/Admiral Halsey' (L McCartney)
'Smile Away'
'Heart Of The Country' (L McCartney)
'Monkberry Moon Delight' (L McCartney)
'Eat At Home' (L McCartney)
'Long Haired Lady' (L McCartney)
'Back Seat Of My Car'

PAUL McCARTNEY AND WINGS
'The Mess' (L McCartney)   'My Love' B-side (Mar 1973)

'Big Barn Bed' (L McCartney)   *Red Rose Speedway* (May 1973)
'My Love' (L McCartney)
'Get On The Right Thing' (L McCartney)
'One More Kiss' (L McCartney)
'Little Lamb Dragonfly' (L McCartney)
'Single Pigeon' (L McCartney)
'When The Night' (L McCartney)
'Loup (1st Indian On The Moon)' (L McCartney)
Medley: 'Hold Me Tight/Lazy Dynamite/Hands Of Love/Power Cut'
     (L McCartney)

'Helen Wheels'   Single (Oct 1973)
'Country Dreamer'   'Helen Wheels' B-side (Oct 1973)

'Band On The Run'   *Band On The Run* (Nov 1973)

'Jet'
'Bluebird'
'Mrs Vanderbilt'
'Let Me Roll It'
'Mamunia'
'No Words' (Laine)
'Picasso's Last Words (Drink To Me)'
'1985'

'Zoo Gang'	'Band On The Run' B-side (Jun 1974)
'Junior's Farm'	Single (Oct 1974)
'Sally G'	'Junior's Farm' B-side (Oct 1974)

WINGS

'Mumbo' (L McCartney)	*Wild Life* (Dec 1971)

'Bip Bop' (L McCartney)
'Wild Life' (L McCartney)
'Some People Never Know' (L McCartney)
'I Am Your Singer' (L McCartney)
'Tomorrow' (L McCartney)
'Dear Friend' (L McCartney)

'Give Ireland Back To The Irish' (L McCartney)	Single (Feb 1972)
'Mama's Little Girl'	'Put It There' B-side (Feb 1990)
'Mary Had A Little Lamb' (L McCartney)	Single (May 1972)
'Little Woman Love' (L McCartney)	'Mary Had A Little Lamb' B-side (May 1972)
'C Moon' (L McCartney)	Single (Dec 1972)
'Hi Hi Hi' (L McCartney)	'C Moon' B-side (Dec 1972)
'Live And Let Die' (L McCartney)	Single (Jun 1973)
'I Lie Around' (L McCartney)	'Live And Let Die' B-side (Jun 1973)
'Venus And Mars'	*Venus And Mars* (May 1975)

'Rock Show'
'Love In Song'

'You Gave Me The Answer'
'Magneto And Titanium Man'
'Letting Go'
'Venus And Mars (reprise)'
'Spirits Of Ancient Egypt'
'Call Me Back Again'
'Listen To What The Man Said'
'Treat Her Gently'
'Lonely Old People'

'My Carnival'   *Venus And Mars* (Re-released Oct 1987)

'Lunch Box/Odd Sox'   'Coming Up' B-side (Apr 1980)

'Let 'Em In'   *Wings At The Speed Of Sound* (Mar 1976)
'The Note You Never Wrote'
'She's My Baby'
'Beware My Love'
'Silly Love Songs'
'Cook Of The House' (L McCartney)
'Must Do Something About It'
'San Ferry Anne'
'Warm And Beautiful'

'Soily'   *Wings Over America* (Dec 1976)

'Mull Of Kintyre' (Laine)   Single (Nov 1977)

'Girls' School'   'Mull Of Kintyre' B-side (Nov 1977)

'London Town' (Laine)   *London Town* (Mar 1978)
'Cafe On The Left Bank'
'I'm Carrying'
'Backwards Traveller'
'Cuff Link'
'Children Children' (Laine)
'Girlfriend'
'I've Had Enough'
'With A Little Luck'
'Famous Groupies'

'Deliver Your Children' (Laine)
'Name And Address'
'Don't Let It Bring You Down' (Laine)
'Morse Moose And The Grey Goose' (Laine)
'Waterspout' (bootleg only)

'Daytime Nightime Suffering'   'Goodnight Tonight' B-side (Mar 1979)

'Reception'   *Back To The Egg* (Jun 1979)
'Getting Closer'
'We're Open Tonight'
'Spin It On'
'Old Siam Sir'
'Arrow Through Me'
'Rockestra Theme'
'To You'
'After The Ball/Million Miles'
'Winter Rose/Love Awake'
'The Broadcast'
'So Glad To See You Here'
'Baby's Request'

PAUL McCARTNEY AND THE FROG CHORUS
'We All Stand Together'   Single (Nov 1984)

PAUL McCARTNEY/SUPER FURRY ANIMALS
'Plastic Beetle'   *Liverpool Sound Collage* (Oct 2000)
'Peter Blake 2000'
'Real Gone Dub Made In Manifest In The Vortex Of The Eternal Now'
'Made Up'
'Free Now'

THE FIREMAN
'Transpiritual Stomp' (Youth)   *Strawberries Oceans Ships Forest* (Nov 1993)
'Trans Lunar Rising' (Youth)
'Transcrystaline' (Youth)
'Pure Trance' (Youth)
'Arizona Light' (Youth)
'Celtic Stomp' (Youth)
'Strawberries Oceans Ships Forest' (Youth)

'4 4 4' (Youth)
'Sunrise Mix' (Youth)

'Watercolour Guitars'   *Rushes* (Oct 1998)
'Palo Verde'
'Auraveda'
'Fluid'
'Appletree Cinnabar Amber'
'Bison'
'7am'
'Watercolour Rush'

THE COUNTRY HAMS
'Bridge Over The River Suite' (L McCartney)   Single (Oct 1974)

SUZIE AND THE RED STRIPES
'B-Side To Seaside' (L McCartney)   'Seaside Woman' B-side (Aug 1979)

CHRIS BARBER BAND
'Catcall'   Single (Oct 1967)

CILLA BLACK
'Love Of The loved' (Lennon)   Single (Sep 1963)

'It's For You' (Lennon)   Single (Jul 1964)

'Step Inside Love' (Lennon)   Single (May 1968)

BLACK DYKE MILLS BAND
'Thingumybob' (Lennon)   Single (Aug 1968)

JOHNNY CASH
'New Moon Over Jamaica' (Cash-Hall)   *Water From The Wells*
                                           Of Home (Nov 1988)

JOHN CHRISTIE
'Fourth Of July' (L McCartney)   Single (Jul 1974)

ELVIS COSTELLO
'Pads, Paws And Claws' (McManus)   *Spike* (Feb 1989)
'Veronica' (McManus)

'Playboy To A Man' (McManus)   *Mighty Like A Rose* (May 1991)
'So Like Candy' (McManus)

'Shallow Grave' (McManus)   *All This Useless Beauty* (May 1996)

ROGER DALTREY
'Giddy'   *One Of The Boys* (May 1977)

JOHNNY DEVLIN AND THE DEVILS
'Won't You Be My Baby?' (Devlin)   Aus Single (Feb 1965)

THE EVERLY BROTHERS
'On The Wings Of A Nightingale'   Single (Oct 1984)

THE FOURMOST
'Hello Little Girl' (Lennon)   Single (Aug 1963)

'I'm In Love' (Lennon)   Single (Nov 1963)

ALLEN GINSBERG
'Ballad Of The Skeletons' (Ginsberg-Glass)   Single (Oct 1996)

MARY HOPKIN
'Goodbye' (Lennon)   Single (Mar 1969)

BILLY J KRAMER AND THE DAKOTAS
'Bad To Me' (Lennon)   Single (Jul 1963)

'I'll Keep You Satisfied' (Lennon)   Single (Nov 1963)

'From A Window' (Lennon)   Single (Jul 1964)

DENNY LAINE
'Send Me The Heart' (Laine)   *Japanese Tears* (Dec 1980)

PEGGY LEE
'Let's Love'   *Let's Love* (Oct 1974)

LINDA McCARTNEY
'I Got Up' (L McCartney)   *Wide Prairie* (Oct 1998)
'White Coated Man' (L McCartney-Lane)
'Cow' (L McCartney-Lane)

'Appaloosa' (L McCartney)
'The Light Comes From Within' (L McCartney)

MIKE McGEAR
'Bored As Butterscotch' (McGear-McGough)   *Woman* (Apr 1972)

'What Do We Really Know?'   *McGear* (Oct 1974)
'Norton' (McGear)
'Leave It'
'Have You Got Problems?' (McGear)
'The Casket' (McGough)
'Sweet Baby' (McGear)
'Rainbow Lady' (McGear)
'Simply Love You' (McGear)
'Giving Grease A Ride' (McGear)
'The Man Who Found God On The Moon' (McGear)

'Dance The Do' (McGear)   Single (Jul 1975)

CARLOS MENDES
'Penina'   Single (Jul 1969)

ADRIAN MITCHELL
'Hot Pursuit'   Unreleased
     (L McCartney-Cunningham-McIntosh-Wickens-Stuart)
'Song In Space'   Unreleased
     (L McCartney-Cunningham-McIntosh-Wickens-Stuart)

PETER AND GORDON
'World Without Love' (Lennon)   Single (Feb 1964)

'Nobody I Know' (Lennon)   Single (May 1964)

'I Don't Want To See You Again' (Lennon)   Single (Sep 1964)

'Woman'   Single (Feb 1966)

THE PLASTIC ONO BAND
'Give Peace A Chance' (Lennon)   Single (Jul 1969)

PAUL McCARTNEY

TOMMY QUICKLY
'Tip Of My Tongue' (Lennon)   Single (Jul 1963)

THE SCAFFOLD
'Ten Years After On Strawberry Jam' (L McCartney)   Single (May 1974)

RINGO STARR
'Six O'Clock' (L McCartney)   *Ringo* (Nov 1973)

'Pure Gold'   *Ringo's Rotogravure* (Sep 1976)

'Private Property'   *Stop And Smell The Roses* (Nov 1981)
'Attention'

'Angel In Disguise' (Starkey)   Unreleased

ROD STEWART
'Mine For Me'   *Smiler* (Sep 1974)

STRANGERS WITH MIKE SHANNON
'One And One Is Two' (Lennon)   Single (May 1964)

10CC
'Code Of Silence' (Stewart)   *Mirror Mirror* (Jun 1985)
'Yvonne's The One' (Stewart)

'Don't Break The Promises' (Stewart-Gouldman)   *Meanwhile* (May 1992)

JOHN WILLIAMS
Theme from *The Honorary Consul*   Single (Dec 1983)

Ringo Starr

Printed in the United Kingdom by MPG Books Ltd, Bodmin

Published by Sanctuary Publishing Limited, Sanctuary House, 45-53 Sinclair Road,
London W14 0NS, United Kingdom

www.sanctuarypublishing.com

Distributed in the US by Publishers Group West

ISBN: 1-86074-518-0

Ringo Starr

Alan Clayson
Sanctuary

Contents

1 "I Was Just One Of Those Loony Teddy Boys"

In 1962, the plug was pulled and Richard Starkey was sucked into a vortex of events, places and situations that hadn't belonged even to speculation when, on 7 July 1940 he was born in the front bedroom of 9 Madryn Street, a three-up/three-down terrace in a district of Liverpool known as the Dingle. As it had been with most of his immediate forebears, unless tempted by the Merchant Navy or compelled by the government to fight foreign foes, nothing suggested that Richard too would not dwell until the grave around this Merseyside suburb that backed onto docklands carved from a plateau of sandstone and granite on the trudging river's final bend before it swept into the Irish Sea.

For the brief time they were together, he and his father were known parochially as Big Richie and Little Richie. Elsie Gleave and Big Richie's eyes had first locked among the cakes and tarts of the bakery where they both worked. Little Richie was the only issue of an unhappy seven-year espousal that ended in divorce in 1943, when Elsie was 29. Little·if any explanation could be offered the boy for why his daddy left, but his opinion of the shadowy figure that he was to see only infrequently was jaundiced to the degree that, on some of the occasions they met, "I wouldn't speak to him. I suppose my mother filled me up with all the things about him."

"Things were pretty tough for Elsie, as I've always called my mother," Richie would recollect. "She tried to bring me up decently. We were poor, but never in rags. I was lucky. I was her only child. She could spend more time with me." Her husband's rancorous departure might have hardened Mrs Starkey's resolve to ensure that Richie was as comfortable and contented as her deprived station would allow. If rather worn, his clothes were always clean, and she'd tuck in his shirt, shine his shoes and brush his hair prior to delivering him to whatever nearby relation or friend was scheduled to mind him while she was busy with diverse menial jobs, such as pulling pints behind the bar of the narrow Empress pub, a promontory but a few convenient yards from both 9 Madryn Street and 10 Admiral Grove, where, for its cheaper rent, she and Richie were obliged to move in 1944.

His formal education began at St Silas' Church of England Primary School, a five-minute dawdle from Admiral Grove, but he didn't endure it because of the first serious manifestation of the digestive maladies that were to blight his life. Possibly this delicateness was hereditary, for, like Big

Richie, he would always be nauseated by any dish with the vaguest tang of onion or garlic. One afternoon, when he was six, "I felt an awful stab of pain. I remember sweating and being frightened for a while," when, to the agitated clang of an ambulance bell and clutching his abdomen, he was hastened to the Royal Children's Infirmary on the junction of Myrtle Street, beneath the shadow of the Roman Catholic cathedral, where most of the city's chief medical, penal and higher-educational establishments were clotted.

What was diagnosed initially as a ruptured appendix led to an inflamed peritoneum. In the thick of the inserted tubes and drips after the first operation, there seemed almost no hope of survival as Richie subsided into a coma in the intensive-care cubicle. However, he surfaced as a persistently poorly old-young creature whose surroundings seemed to fill him with melancholy reflections. Inwardly, however, "I didn't mind too much. I made a lot of friends. Too bad they always got better and left me alone."

On his seventh birthday, and with discharge in sight, Richie was playing with a bright-red toy bus "and drove it 'round and 'round my huge, high bed. When he left, the boy in the next bed looked so sad and lonely, I thought it would be nice to give him my red bus to cheer him up." Leaning over, Richie tumbled to awake from concussed oblivion with burst stitches and the prospect of the rest of 1947 in hospital…

Back in time to enter St Silas' junior department, he was still virtually illiterate and would suffer the eventual indignity

of being taught with children a year his junior. Without the
usual companionships nurtured during an uninterrupted
school regime, he grew pensive and rather solitary. His
appearance suited him – shortish and hangdog, with flexible
thick lips, crooked nose, droopy Pagliacci eyes and grey
streaks in his brown hair and right eyebrow. Verbally, he
was comparable to Dr William Spooner, in that he didn't
have to try to be funny. People amused themselves by getting
him to talk.

At St Silas' and, next, Dingle Vale Secondary Modern,
Richie was judged in termly reports as "a quiet, thoughtful
type, although working rather slowly. Academic work will
no doubt improve in time, as he is trying to do his best."
Positioned academically around the middle of the lowest
stream, he was poor at music, while at drama he "takes a
real interest and has done very well". He was also discovered
to possess an aptitude for mechanics, so much so that later
he'd have no qualms about dismantling a car engine and
putting it back together again.

In one 1952 term, Richard was absent on 34 occasions,
not all of which were through illness. His "A" standard for
conduct implies that teachers were ignorant of his bouts of
truancy. A legacy of these delinquent days was the smoking
that he'd never have the will to stop. He'd already promoted
his first alcoholic black-out "when I was nine. I was on my
knees, crawling drunk. A friend of mine's dad had the booze
ready for Christmas, so we decided to try all of it out. I don't

remember too much." An appalled Elsie would always remember, but she never knew then that he sometimes spent his dinner-money on "a few pennyworth of chips and a hunk of bread and save the rest for the fairground or the pictures".

Elsie and Richie's domestic conditions had improved after she was able to give up work on marrying – with her son's approval – a painter and decorator from Romford. Of mild disposition and steady character, Harry Graves came to be accepted by a community not that removed from what he'd known back in the Cockney end of Essex.

During a half-term holiday in 1953, the new "stepladder" – so Richie in his gobbledegook dubbed Harry – took his wife and stepson over the edge of the world for a few days with his parents in Romford, where the obstinate 13-year-old refused to don a raincoat when caught in a thunderstorm of Wagnerian intensity. A simple sniff chilled to chronic pleurisy and another spell in Myrtle Street before lung complications necessitated Richie's transfer to the cleaner air of Heswall Children's Hospital in the rural Wirral.

Again, his schooling suffered, and it was officially over by 1955, when he'd regained sufficient strength to go home. All that remained was the formality of returning to Dingle Vale "to get the certificate to prove I'd left. You needed that to get a job. They didn't even remember I'd been there." More humbling was an interview at the Youth Employment Office, where there was a vacancy for a delivery boy with British Rail.

Whatever the secrets behind doors marked "Private" on every main platform, little intrigued Starkey after a week or so of errands that a child could run. Vanity demanded a uniform to be worn with negligent importance, but, in order to signify that here was a man engaged in man's work, he was given a mere *kepi*, as "you had to do 20 years to get the rest. Anyway, I failed their medical and left after a couple of months."

In the regulation-issue, two-tone jacket of a barman/waiter, his next job was on a passenger steamer pottering along the Mersey. He bumped up his wages with tips picked up mostly during peak hours, when he had hardly a second to himself, dashing from table to table with a trayful of drinks.

His pastimes outside work included brief membership of an accordion band that practised in the drill hall opposite St Silas Church. During the skiffle craze, he also attempted to teach himself to strum a guitar. Such a knack was, however, incidental to his self-image as "just one of those loony Teddy Boys standing on the corner".

Undersized, homely and of depressed circumstance, he was ripe to "run about with gangs in the Dingle as a tearaway with a Tony Curtis haircut, crêpe shoes and drape with a velvet collar". Richie tried to look the part with a belt studded with washers stolen from work. "But I wasn't a fighter," he reflected. "More of a dancer, really, though that could be dangerous if you danced with someone else's bird." Yet it wasn't in a ballroom where he paired off with a bird of his own, Patricia Davies, who was three years younger, fair and sufficiently petite not to tower over him. At the same secondary school – St Anthony of Padua's in Mossley Hill – she'd become friendly with red-head Priscilla White when both cherished ambitions to be hairdressers. "The soul of patience", Elsie Graves was a Wednesday-evening guinea pig for the giggling would-be stylists as, after cooking them a tea, she allowed Pat and Cilla to "bleach her hair and do terrible things to it".

When Pat was superseded by another local spinster called Geraldine, she may have consoled herself with the submission that, if you were after a man for his money, Elsie's lad wasn't much of a catch, especially after he was sacked from the ferry when, on clocking in direct from an all-night party, he was emboldened enough by booze to impart pent-up home truths to his supervisor. However, Harry was able to persuade Henry Hunt & Sons, an engineering firm specialising in gymnasium and swimming pool equipment, to take on his stepson as a trainee joiner and Richie was glad, as it had a youth he knew named Eddie Miles.

Richie's overalled apprenticeship began badly when he bruised his thumb with a hammer on the very first day and vertigo stranded him tremulous with terror on a high diving board during an installment job in faraway Cardiff Public Baths. But he wasn't as infinitesimal a human cog at Hunt's as he'd been with the railway. By doggedly cranking and riveting from 8am until 5.30pm day upon day for the next seven years, the road to self-advancement would be clearer.

2 "Well, I Thought I Was The Best Drummer There Was"

For beer money and a laugh, Richard Starkey and Eddie Miles started The Eddie Clayton Skiffle Group in early 1957. Augmented by three of Hunt's other, the Group moved from canteen concerts at work to a debut at Peel Street Labour Club in Toxteth and entering a skiffle contest at St Luke's Hall. Although they weren't placed, the lads weren't that dismayed because they, like most amateur skifflers, saw the group as a vocational blind alley. No one took it seriously.

From the onset, it was decided that Richie should play drums, "because it was the only thing I could do". So it was that Harry Graves bought a second-hand drum kit for his stepson. He wondered how much gratitude he could expect from Richie, who – so the tale goes – had been furious when Elsie, with the best of intentions, had arranged for him to attend an exploratory rehearsal on hearing that someone in the next street was in a "proper" band. "You can imagine

15

how I felt," he snorted, "when this turned out to be a silver band playing old Sousa marches and all that in a local park."

Richie was, however, delighted with Harry's gift. Initially, he attacked his new kit with gusto, showing no signs of ever stopping, but soon developed his hand-and-foot co-ordination, accurate time-keeping and even the beginnings of a naïve personal style by trial and error. However, "because of the noise", which irritated the entire terrace, his mother allowed him only 30 minutes of crashing about per evening upstairs in number 10's small back room "and I got really bored just sitting there banging because you can't play any tunes".

In the kitchen, when he'd finished, Elsie would object to him smiting the furniture with his sticks to music from the wireless, "and that was it for me, practising. Drumming's simple. I've always believed the drummer is not there to interrupt the song." Later, he'd liken it to "painting. I am the foundation, and then I put a bit of glow here and there, but it must have solid substance for me. If there's a gap, I want to be good enough to fill it. I like holes to come in."

Starkey would speak with quiet pride of getting by without ever being able to read a note of standard music script, let alone a drum stave. Neither could he ever manage a clean roll faster than moderato: "I know I'm no good on the technical things but I'm good with all the motions, swinging my head, like. That's because I love to dance, but you can't do that on the drums." With self-tuition impractical when he began, the only advice he'd be qualified to offer other budding drummers would be, "Get in a group as fast as you can. You'll learn more in one day than you can hope to in six months stuck in a little room. Make your mistakes on a stage in front of an audience. You'll realise them more quickly."

With the Clayton outfit often a player or two short, his errors hung in the air more flagrantly. Moreover, as he couldn't carry heavy objects far and had to rely on buses to reach Garston's Wilson Hall and like palais on the outer marches of the group's booking circuit, he'd sometimes arrive with only half his equipment. Nevertheless, the unit was a comparative rarity in that it had a sticksman with a full kit for all to see during what amounted to a residency at Boys' Club meetings in the Dingle's Florence Institute, a Victorian monstrosity near enough for the drums to be walked there.

Recitals elsewhere were infrequent, and Starkey's fealty to Clayton was tried by Miles's imminent departure to the marriage bed and its resultant casting aside of adolescent follies. Nonetheless, there came overtures from other skiffle groups for him to join them, especially since he'd bought a brand-new black Premier kit. On the basis of owning such a kit, rather than how he played it, he recalled, "Well, I thought I was the best drummer there was, better than all the other drummers. Maybe I was just convincing myself."

Contacted via Admiral Grove's corner newsagent's telephone, Richie sat in non-committally with other outfits, once drumming for three in the course of one shattering evening. A kindly conductor on the number 61 bus route to central Liverpool had eased considerably his transport problems by arranging for him to store the kit overnight at the Ribble bus depot whenever he needed, as he did in March 1959 at the Mardi Gras, a stone's throw from Myrtle Street hospital, on the occasion of his first engagement with The Raving Texans – who were to rename themselves Rory Storm And The Hurricanes in 1959.

With Richie at the kit, they came second to Kingsize Taylor And The Dominoes out of more than 100 groups during the previous month's heat of a "Search For Stars" tournament at the Empire, organised by ITV's Canadian starmaker Carroll Levis to counter the rival channel's *Bid For Fame*. In the final round, at Manchester's Hippodrome, although neither Dominoes nor Hurricanes were able to seize the prize of exposure on Levis' television series, each emerged with a more promising date schedule in which a list that had once signified a month's work became a week's. It might not have been sufficient for Richie to think seriously of resigning from Hunt's, but The Hurricanes would next appear in Liverpool in uniform black-and-white winkle-pickers (gold for Storm) and starched white handkerchiefs protruding smartly from the top pockets of bright-red stage suits for the group (light pink for Rory). Bespoken by a city-centre tailor, this sharp corporate persona was assumed because the unit's turnover of personnel had abated with Storm and second-in-command Johnny Guitar's recruitment of Starkey, lead guitarist Ty Brien and, on bass, Lou Walters.

Storm's singing voice might have been so-so, but his nickname of "Mr Showmanship" was no overstatement. A man of extreme strategy, he outraged heterosexual chauvinists with his gigolo wardrobe – which, from mere pink nylon, would stretch to costumes of gold lamé and sequins – and peacock antics. To illustrate Carl Perkins' 'Lend Me Your Comb', he'd sweep an outsized one through a precarious pompadour that kept falling over his eyes, but this was nothing to what he did when the group played venues attached to swimming baths, where, in the middle of a song, he was likely to push through the crowd, clamber to the top board, strip to scarlet swimming trunks and dive in.

The Hurricanes didn't skulk to the rear, exchanging nervous glances. A rowdy bunch with impressive self-confidence, The Hurricanes would sometimes swap instruments for comic relief in which notes chased haphazardly up and down fretboards amid feedback lament and free-form percussion. Both to restore order and to let Rory take a breather, Richie was bullied into a drum solo, which necessitated his commanding the stage virtually alone under his own voodoo spell for minutes on end – and he had to admit that "the audience love it. If there's a drum solo, they go mad."

Like many other Liverpool groups, Rory Storm and the Hurricanes had "featured singers" who specialised in areas not thought unsuitable for the chief show-off. Walters was the balladeer, while Starkey was in charge of less demanding material. By *bel canto* standards, he had a horrible voice, devoid of plummy enunciation and nicety of intonation. Instead, you got slurred diction and gravelly ranting as he got through a number any old how, frequently straining his disjointed range past its limits. In context, the effect of spontaneity over expertise was not unattractive, even gruffly charming, because "I'm more of a personality. It's a fun-loving attitude to life that comes across. I have a good time."

The group's usual opening number was Vince Taylor's spirited 'Brand New Cadillac' and the core of the set was drawn likewise from the Valhalla of classic rock. During Ray Charles's 'What'd I Say', Rory would, ideally, trade "heys" and "yeahs" with participating onlookers, take it down easy, build the tension to the verge of panic and, to round it off, flounce into the wings, leaving 'em wanting more.

Perhaps the Rory Storm And The Hurricanes story should have ended there, because arguably they were as good as they were ever going to get. Routining new numbers speedily and incompletely before ennui set it, Storm was averse to formal rehearsals, and so they'd venture but rarely beyond the boundaries of their stylistic definition. The consolidation rather than development of this was to be their downfall.

This, however, lay three years ahead. The first business of any pop group is simply to be liked, and none could deny that Rory and his Hurricanes were in the top division of

Merseyside popularity. As a measure of their wide appeal, their fan club was situated at an address in faraway Anfield, where its secretary, Julie Farrelly, would answer letters of undying love for Rory, for whom female screams were already reverberating.

3 "I Took A Chance And I Think I've Been Lucky"

In May 1960, Rory Storm And The Hurricanes gained a residency at a Butlin's holiday camp in Pwllheli. On resigning from Hunt's in order to go, Richie "took a chance and I think I've been lucky". He also accepted a colourful stage name bestowed upon him by Storm. It was inspired by Starkey's lingering Teddy Boy habit of adorning each hand with three or four increasingly splendid rings. When "Ringo" was juxtaposed with his run-of-the-mill last name, it sounded "a bit funny. 'Starr' was a natural. It made sense to me and I liked it. It stuck."

Backing the competitors in the camp's pop-singing and jiving contests as well as delivering the music night after night in the Rock and Calypso Ballroom, Ringo would claim later to have been "educated at Butlin's". What had once been casual was now stylised, and when they returned to the trivial round of Merseyside engagements Storm And The Hurricanes

22

"couldn't have had better practice for a stage career. Those [Pwllheli] audiences really used to heckle us, and when they wanted requests it was usually for some square song that we'd hardly heard of before, so it was up to us to keep things going. We simply had to ad lib and try not to take any notice of the remarks they slung at us. And, even more important, we had to play without any sort of arrangement, most of the time."

When their time at Pwllheli was up, the group moved further beyond the local orbit of engagements when working split –shifts with another Liverpool outfit, The Beatles, in the Kaiserkeller, a night club in Hamburg. It was but one such establishment around the Reeperbahn, neon starting point of innumerable languid evenings of perfumed wantonness, living tableaux of flesh and late-evening temptation by doorstep pimps. I am prohibited by inbred propriety from entering into distressing detail, except to state that, an erotic Butlins since the days of three-mast clippers, the Reeperbahn's brothels and strip-tease palaces were eye-openers to anyone who assumed that humans could be sexually gratified without mechanical complexity and only with other humans.

The first British rock 'n' roll act to play there had been The Jets, conspicuous for a singing guitarist of unusual flair named Tony Sheridan. As they had guided Hamburg's first musical Merseysiders around the district's diversions, so the information was passed on to Rory Storm And The Hurricanes by The Beatles. According to Pete Best, then their drummer, "That's where their friendship with Ringo began."

On the boards at the Kaiserkeller, Starr's teen appeal wasn't obvious, but his harmless jocularity, saucer eyes and air of bewildered wistfulness incited a protective instinct from a fair cross-section of frauleins. After ogling the drummer all evening, one girl's bottled-up emotions bubbled over and she had to be forcibly dragged from the club, shrieking, "Ringo! Ringo!", even as she was pushed into the street.

Sending palpitations through more feminine nervous systems were The Beatles, particularly Pete, but Ringo for one would remember a time less than a year before when they'd been far outside the league of Liverpool's leading groups, who had known them by sight just as riff-raff who frequented a coffee bar called the Jacaranda. Only on noticing Harrison in its basement teaching another Beatle, Stuart Sutcliffe, the stock rock 'n' roll root notes on a new bass guitar had Starr understood that they were an actual group. A pop fan of Cilla White's discernment complained that she "couldn't bear them. I thought they were scruffy and untidy. Their dress was horrible. They wore these terrible motorbike-type jackets. I didn't want to know."

Nevertheless, much of the Beatle attitude rubbed off on Rory Storm And The Hurricanes during the two outfits' shared workload of alternating 30- to 90-minute sets from dusk until the grey of morning. Soon, they too would see nothing amiss in cigarettes dangling from their lower lips whilst on stage, nor in serially consuming a gratis nightly allowance of beer and salad between numbers. Like Pete Best,

Ringo began hitting solidly and defiantly behind the beat by a fraction both to invest material with stronger definition and to increase tension. It would not be too presumptuous to say that the subtleties of Best and Starr's rhythmic developments while in the Kaiserkeller were to alter pop drumming procedures forever.

Back in Liverpool, a now more workmanlike Storm and The Hurricanes reached a rapid zenith, exemplified by their being accosted in the street to sign autographs. Part of the attraction was The Hurricanes' implied bloke-ish camaraderie of all boys together, and – with Starr in mind – the notion that you didn't have to be Charles Atlas to be in a group. With the alibi of a stage act, a mousy boy had an excuse to make himself look other-worldly as Starr did now with his rings, boots, shiny turquoise suit and gold lamé shirt.

Their name would not be synonymous with any particular club or palais, as The Swinging Blue Jeans were to their manager's Downbeat, The Undertakers to Orrell Park Ballroom – or The Beatles to the Cavern. To Cilla White, they were "just as scruffy as ever. They were sort of clean and scruffy, if you know what I mean. Then I started listening to their sound. They were better than I thought."

Cilla had become one of a handful of freelance female vocalists who performed with several different Merseybeat groups. Among these were The Big Three, Kingsize Taylor And The Dominoes – and Rory Storm And The Hurricanes. As Rory was keen on bringing Cilla with them when next they played in Hamburg, Ringo was dispatched to sound her out. She'd have to ask her dad, she said, and, perhaps predictably, Mr White, as self-appointed guardian of his daughter's job (and innocence), wouldn't hear of it.

From the family home along grimy Scotland Road, Cilla's dad would walk to work down Boundary Road, which ran directly to the docks. At number 56d, a council flat, Maureen Cox, Richie's "steady", lived with her mother, Mary, while her father, Joe, was at sea much of the time as a ship's steward. With the candour of middle age, Maureen – "Mo" – would describe herself as being "thick as two short planks" when she left school at the minimum age of 15 to begin as a junior hairdressing assistant.

En route to one of her hairstyling lessons, she'd seen Ringo emerge from the old Ford Zodiac that he drove unqualified and asked for an autograph. From the perspective of a club stage, Mo was at first no different from any of the other pale-faced "Judies" in suede, leather or fishnet who chattered excitedly until the group was announced. On one evening, however, Ringo and Mo got better acquainted to the extent of public tendernesses, like his lighting two cigarettes at once and passing one to her.

Richie, Mo and intimates like Cilla, would hold court most frequently in a parochial watering hole called the Zodiac where a jam session by personnel from The Hurricanes, Gerry And The Pacemakers, The Beatles and The Big Three was still dinning long after milk floats had braved the cold of sunrise. On another night, the door was bolted hastily when a drunken rabble converged outside. With no telephone inside, staff and members – including Maureen and Ringo – quaked to the noise of gleeful ramming and savage oaths as the mob tried to break in, only tiring of their sport hours later.

During more tranquil booze-ups in the Zodiac, the Cabin, the Blue Angel and similar musicians' hang-outs, groups would brag of imminent tours of outlandish countries and even record releases; but, while yet to deteriorate into a cauldron of back-stabbing, underhandedness and favouritism, Merseybeat's *ésprit de corps* was such that it wasn't uncommon for, say, Gerry to vault onstage for a couple of numbers with The Dominoes or Rory Storm to stand in for a laryngitic John Lennon. Although Ringo wouldn't feel that he knew The Beatles well enough to invite them to his uproarious coming-of-age party at Admiral Grove, he deputised likewise for Pete Best when the latter was poleaxed with bronchitis and on later occasions. The Beatles had lately signed with a *bona fide* manager. As well as prodding his contacts in the business on The Beatles' behalf, Brian Epstein was sinking hard cash into them and, if nought else, getting them off the Liverpool-Hamburg treadmill with a booking schedule that reached as far south as Swindon.

Rory Storm was still in much the same rut, marking time with Butlin's and Germany. However, during a second stint at Pwllheli, the atmosphere seemed more frenzied, the laughter shriller, the eyes brighter. Some nights, security officers would have to rescue Rory as he lost tufts of hair to clawing females while The Hurricanes made their escapes with mere autographs, Richie scribbling, "Best wishes from the sensational Ringo Starr."

4 "I Had To Join Them As People, As Well As A Drummer"

If second-billed now to Gerry, The Beatles and other acts that had once supported them, Rory And The Hurricanes made up for long absences in Germany and Butlin's by packing in as many local engagements as the traffic would allow before they had to vanish again. A feather in their cap, however, was that 1962's Butlin's foray would be at bracing Skegness, the Lincolnshire camp that was the oldest and largest in the network.

That January, however, Ringo Starr threw in his lot with Tony Sheridan at the Top Ten in Hamburg for a wage of £30 a week – huge for the time – and use of a flat and car. Nevertheless, the Top Ten would soon be losing trade irrecoverably to the newer Star-Club after it secured The Beatles – and Sheridan – to open the place in April. Ringo, however, would not be drumming before its stage backdrop of skyscrapers when Sheridan and The Beatles supported and proudly socialised with visiting US idols – including Ray Charles, Little Richard, Pat Boone and Gene Vincent. While Charles might have thought, "That boy [Sheridan] sings with a lot of soul," Ringo had become disenchanted with Tony, who, on closer acquaintance, was given to provoking arguments, sulking and impetuously launching into songs not in the *modus operandi*, unhelpfully leaving his accompanists to busk behind him. Like, what key's this one in, man? Like, Z minus, man.

With more than his fill of both Hamburg and Sheridan, Starr had gone home to his mother and Rory Storm And The Hurricanes. It was accepted without question that Ringo, like the equally perfidious Lou Walters, would return to the fold. Although neither could be trusted not to stray again, it was outwardly as if nothing had happened, as they got into trim for Skegness – but , as Ringo's parents often reminded him, it wasn't too late for him to resume his Hunt's apprenticeship. While taking exasperated stock, he contemplated wedding Maureen and uprooting altogether for the less humdrum USA, even going as far as writing to the Chamber of Commerce in Houston, simply because it was the nearest city to Centerville, birthplace of Lightnin' Hopkins, a post-war blues artist to whose grippingly personal style an enthralled Ringo had been introduced by Tony Sheridan one Hamburg afternoon around a record player.

Houston's reply was quite heartening, but the thickness and aggressive intimacy of the application forms for emigration were too off-putting. Hunt's seemed to be beckoning still; but, while removed from parental pressures about a "proper" job, Richie in Skegness received a letter from Kingsize Taylor promising £20 per week for him to fill the drum stool in the Dominoes. As Taylor was a bandleader of steadier stamp than Sheridan or Storm, Ringo gave tentative assent to join as soon as he was free. However, after John Lennon and Paul McCartney had driven through a windy August night to offer a fiver more per week than Kingsize Taylor, Ringo immediately joined The Beatles.

Pete Best's days with the group had been numbered after a maiden recording session for Parlophone, a subsidiary of EMI. Producer George Martin had decided that when The Beatles came back to the studio along London's Abbey Road to tape their first single, Lennon and McCartney's 'Love Me Do', the drumming was to be ghosted by someone more technically accomplished than Best. Some would recall Martin denying that there was anything fundamentally wrong with Pete as a musician, and then contradicting himself a couple of years later. Locally, Best was rated highly by no less than Johnny Hutchinson of The Big Three, who had been advocated by Brian Epstein as Pete's successor during the horrid conspiracy. However, he consented only to step in temporarily when Pete Best, for some reason, wouldn't fulfil two Beatles bookings that couldn't be postponed in the interregnum between his sacking and Ringo's arrival for two hours' rehearsal before his debut as an official Beatle in front of an audience of 500 at a Horticultural Society dance in Birkenhead on Saturday 18 August 1962.

This was the quiet before the storm. At the Cavern on the following evening, there'd be a near riot when The Beatles entered with their new member. "They loved Pete," lamented the self-effacing Starr, "Why get an ugly-looking cat when you can get a good-looking one?" To be fair, Ringo had shaved off his scrappy beard and had had his hair resculpted in a heavy fringe that, after a decade of quiffing, wouldn't cascade naturally into a Beatle moptop for nearly a year. His mother might have liked his neater, shorter style, but it took a while for the group's fans to become accustomed to this changeling in The Beatles, a frog where there'd been a prince. His supplanting of Best had been represented as the amicable if sudden consequence of scarcely more than a mild disagreement between the parties, but the hostility at the Cavern demonstrated that the truth was known in the street.

Yet, after an uncomfortable few minutes when the set opened at the Cavern – especially when George publicly welcomed Ringo – the four were cheered by the seething crowd. Other than turn from The Beatles altogether, there was nothing for it but to accept the new situation, and by November onlookers were yelling to the now-unchallenged front line to let the underdog behind them sing a number. In short, he was a Pete Best without good looks, a Beatle for girls to love more as a brother than a demon lover.

Musically, Ringo's coming made no pronounced difference. An up-and-coming Liverpool vocalist, Billy Kramer didn't "think The Beatles were any better with Ringo. I never doubted his ability as a drummer, but I thought they were a lot more raw and raucous with Pete." Often inclined to close his eyes while playing, Ringo was hardly less reticent than Best on stage. So began the typecasting of him as the one who'd "play it smoggo. I don't mind talking or smiling. It's just that I don't do it very much. I haven't got a smiling face or a talking mouth."

In the new situation, Ringo felt most at ease with the selectively amiable Harrison, who, although a better guitarist than either, had been made to feel intellectually as well as chronologically inferior to the other two, whose songwriting alliance was a fount of emotional confusion for him. Unable to penetrate McCartney and Lennon's caste within a caste, George hero-worshipped the heedless John, to whom he was "like a bloody kid, hanging around all the time". To a lesser extent, Ringo would also be caught up in Harrison's wonderment at Lennon, who was a pretty raw guitarist but a driving rock 'n' roll vocalist. He was also a scribbler of surreal stories and nonsense verse, which Starr, in his earliest sentences to the national music press, described as "the weirdest you ever saw, but it stops him going mental". Ringo also giggled politely when John outlined his invention of the group's name: "We thought of crawly things and then added the beat."

However, for Johnny Hutchinson, the crawliest thing in The Beatles was McCartney, whom he vilified as "a grade-A creep" – while the more diplomatic would judge Paul "pleasantly insincere". He had, however, a certain right to be, as he, of all The Beatles, was blessed with the most innate musical talent, and he was also the most prolific in his and John's songwriting partnership – of which 'Love Me Do' was but the tip of the iceberg. As well as inserting more of their own material into the stage set, John and Paul had started canvassing others to perform songs that they felt were unsuitable for the group. Their 'Love Of The Loved' was to be the debut A-side by Cilla White, who'd become Cilla Black when she and other Liverpool performers – including Gerry And The Pacemakers and The Big Three – were signed to Brian Epstein's NEMS Enterprises management company.

However profitable these acts became, The Beatles would forever be Brian's administrative and personal priority. They hadn't been in complete agreement about his fastidious transformation of them into smoother pop entertainers, but outbreaks of mutiny had lessened after he'd set the ball rolling for George Martin to contract them for two singles with an option on further releases if these gave cause for hope.

As Martin's humble beginnings in a north London back street were not detectable in his refined elocution, so only the most discerning could spot the Scouser in Brian Epstein as he'd endured the rigours of several expensive boarding schools at which undercurrents of anti-Semitism and homoeroticism would help to make him what he was. So, too, would a curtailed term of national service and a more constructive year at the Royal Academy of Dramatic Art.

Although Ringo wasn't a full Beatle yet, Brian still took it upon himself to call on Elsie and Harry – as he'd done on the guardians of John, Paul, George and Pete – to allay any reservations that they might harbour about their son's continued showbusiness career. The Graves were still wringing their hands about Hunt's but were reassured that The Beatles had at their helm such an orderly, nicely spoken gent like Mr Epstein.

His feelings about the new Beatle might have been lukewarm, but Brian had assimilated that Starr was unlikely to rock the boat for Lennon and McCartney, who began treating him as a mascot, and sometimes a metaphorical whipping boy. "If anything goes wrong," sniggered Lennon, "we can all blame Ringo. That's what he's here for." Acquiescent and exploitable, he didn't at first express indignation at John's sarcasm and Paul's condescension. Indeed, he'd tell how lucky he was "to be on their wavelength. I had to be, or I wouldn't have lasted. I had to join them as people as well as a drummer."

When their second 45 crept past the 'Love Me Do' high of Number 17 in the hit parade, many fears that he'd go the way of Pete Best were dispelled and he'd hear himself uttering crisp rejoinders to Paul and John's jibes. Less self-consciously, too, he'd enter into the spirit of the little comedy playlets that provided diversion during squalid time-killing in van and bandroom. By then, The Beatles had introduced their own one-song "Starr Time", which would be written-up as "one of the most popular spots of the evening". For him to take on Best's sensual 'Wild In The Country', one of Elvis Presley's ballads, might have invited ridicule, but The Shirelles' 'Boys', with its joyous verve, and – later – jaunty 'Honey Don't' from Carl Perkins, would more than do.

On a first-come-first-served basis, Epstein would not attend to the recording careers of his other charges until The Beatles had got off the ground with theirs. He ensured that *Mersey Beat* knew that they'd been genuinely and importantly airborne when they went from Speke Airport to London to tape their single. As Andy White, the hired session drummer, assembled his kit, Starr bit back on dismay – though as George Martin was to explain later, "I simply didn't know what Ringo was like and I wasn't prepared to take any risks."

Martin was actually one of the least dogmatic of British producers, and at some point during the recording of 'Love Me Do' he waved in the dejected Ringo not to the drums yet but to a tambourine to be struck every third beat in the bar, but on several later takes of 'Love Me Do' it was Ringo and not White behind the kit as the team edged nearer a satisfactory result.

As Starr had acquitted himself adequately enough then, he was trusted to execute the "intricate drumming effects" that were in Martin's recipe for 'Please Please Me', the next single. Moreover, Martin also decided that Ringo could be allowed one lead vocal on the hasty album EMI wanted from The Beatles to cash in on 'Please Please Me', after it topped the charts in March 1963. The drummer had "a voice I was uncertain about" but, beefed up with double-tracking and hyperactive reverberation, 'Boys' – if not the most euphonious – was, along with Paul's 'I Saw Her Standing There' and John's 'Twist And Shout', the LP's most exultant encapsulation of The Beatles' early glory.

5 "I'm Happy To Go On And Play Drums – And That's All"

The rest, as they often say, is history. 1963 alone brought the conquest of Britain via hit-parade Merseybeat, Beatlemania and *The Royal Variety Show*. The year ended with seven Beatles records in the singles Top 50 – including three on more expensive extended plays (EPs) – and the top two positions in the LP list. Although Ringo would confess that "we didn't understand what all this stuff about Aeolian cadences was about" a prosy *Sunday Times* article lauded John and Paul as "the outstanding composers of 1963".

Even middle-class fathers disparaging them in breakfast rooms knew the individual names, none better than that of Ringo, the only Beatle to adopt a *nom du théâtre*. "It's had a lot to do with my success and acceptance," he'd admit. "It might sound mad, but people remember it." Cornered by some foreign Beatles fans later in Cannes, Lennon dryly signed himself "Ringo Starr" and they went away quietly.

Lennon taught Ringo 'I Wanna Be Your Man' as the drummer's lead vocal on the second album, *With The Beatles*. Sometimes he'd be overlooked, but a token Starr song towards the close of the first side on every LP came to be as anticipated by Beatle traditionalists as the group came to be Number One every Christmas. "We weren't going to give him anything great," guffawed John, and often Lennon and McCartney gave him nothing at all beyond accompaniment on an unrevised 12-bar rocker of yore. Of 1964 vintage were Ringo's 'Honey Don't' for *Beatles For Sale*, and 'Matchbox', another Carl Perkins opus, on the *Long Tall Sally* EP.

"While the others created musical works of art," contended NEMS publicist Tony Barrow, "he was left in the cold and merely brought in when they wanted some percussion." Ringo himself was aware that he was just a link in the chain but that it was to his advantage to stay malleable, as he "let the others do all the worrying. I'm happy to go on up there and play drums and that's all" – though, perhaps to imprint his uncertain importance to the group, he'd put forward a song he'd made up for consideration as an LP track, originally for Paul to sing. Called 'Don't Pass Me By', the lyrics were his own but the tune was an unconscious plagiarism, so he was informed, of a Jerry Lee Lewis B-side.

While his attempt at composing for them – and his infrequent huffs and objections – remained ineffectual, Ringo felt less vulnerable a Beatle now that he was receiving as much fan mail as the rest. As such, he would chuckle along to hearty twitting about his hospitalisations, slum background and scholastic deficiencies. "We're never serious," grinned Paul, indicating Ringo. "Just look at him. How could we be serious?" On one hilariously ad-libbed radio show, Starr himself would decline to read a cue-card because he was "the one who doesn't say anything". And besides, he laughed, "I can't read."

A tendency for Lennon and McCartney to butt in when Starr was about to answer an interviewer's question was often as misunderstood as their witticisms at his expense. Nowadays, they and George seemed to be forming a protective cordon around Elsie's only child, as if remorseful about earlier indifference and the ignoble reason for which their eyes had alighted on him in August 1962. More often than not, he'd pair off with Paul for joint holidays and when the group had to double up in hotel suites, but "no matter which one I'm with, it's like being with your best friend. We're like brothers. Me and whoever I'm with are really dead close."

After The Beatles had found it a false economy to remain a Liverpool-based organization, Starr and Harrison shared an apartment below Brian Epstein's in Knightsbridge. Initially, Ringo could "move about in London like an ordinary bloke. If you behave sensibly and plan where you go, you can be OK. When we first made it, I lived in night clubs for three years. It used to be a non-stop party." In a discotheque's deafening dark, Ringo would lend truth to reports in teenage journals that "he can do all the rave dances, including a few that haven't been invented yet". Partnered by a black girl attached to a US vocal group that had just come from *Ready, Steady, Go!*, he held his own as the star dance-floor attraction when necks craned to watch him do the Banana, the Monkey and other dances that no Briton was supposed to have mastered yet.

While Maureen Cox would visit him as often as work would permit, she was not the only girl in Ringo's life, according to "friends" and press gossip, but, in his own eyes, he was faithful to Mo, in that his casual romantic adventures did not adulterate his emotional allegiance to one who "knows the moment I face her what's wrong and what to do about it, and I'm happy again in a minute". There were times, however, when the wretchedness of Mo's devotion cut keenly. In an age when a pop star would lose fans if he wasn't a bachelor and, therefore, "available", he'd been instructed "to pretend I didn't know Maureen and wasn't in love. Can you imagine what it must have been like for her reading in the papers that I didn't know anyone called Maureen Cox?" That too many jealous Liverpudlian girls did had already forced his full-time girlfriend to quit her hairdressing job, what with customers levelling none-too-pleasant stares and even physical threats at her.

Unnerving though such incidents were, Mo did not yet escape to London, suspecting as she did what her parents' reactions would be to the very idea of a daughter of theirs living in sin. If pressed about Richie, she and he were the stock "very good friends". For a change, she might say that she was his "private secretary", because the highlight of many a dull day without him was arriving at Admiral Grove to ease Mrs Graves' writer's cramp as she ploughed through sackfuls of correspondence that, as well as ordinary letters, might as easily include a life-sized sketch of Richie or – because he'd said somewhere that he liked science fiction – another tea chest of paperbacks.

Often, admirers would call personally and *en masse*, a brigade of 200 once needed much convincing that Ringo wasn't inside before leaving his stepfather suddenly alone on the doorstep. Nevertheless, pestering from journalists and fans was not so uncontainable that the Graves could not still be "perfectly happy living in Admiral Grove", even now that Richie had the means to grant them a dotage rich in more substantial material comforts.

Suffering now for his own and his relations' future luxuries and sinecures, Ringo had vomited with nerves just before The Beatles topped the bill of ITV's *Sunday Night At The London Palladium*, the central height of British showbusiness. To Ringo, it had all happened with the spooky deliberation of a dream, but he wasn't so dazzled as to think that pop stars – contrary to definition – were immortal, or that he'd never have to wonder about Hunt's again: "A couple of Number Ones and then out 18 months later won't make you rich. You'll be back on the buses."

Like any poor boy who'd never signed a cheque or called hotel room service from a bedside telephone before, his consumption was more conspicuous than those born into wealth: "When the money first began to pour in, I'd go and buy ten suits, a dozen shirts and three cars. I spent money like it had just been invented." Coveting another drummer's blue-grey pearloid kit (made by Ludwig, a US firm), Ringo shelled out for a brown one. In doing so, he inflicted untold injury on home trade as every other stick-wielder, from schoolboys to chart-riding professionals, started beating a Ludwig too. Because it travelled with The Beatles, the Ludwig became the standard group drum set for most of the 1960s. Nevertheless, some, such as the leader of The Dave Clark Five, favoured Trixon equipment from Germany.

Dave Clark would finish 1964 as the second-most famous drummer in the world. The first, of course, was Ringo Starr.

6 "Over In The States
I Know I Went Over Well"

The Beatles' subjugation of the rest of the world was a large-scale re-run of the hysteria they'd long known at home. The four were swamping foreign Top Tens five or six singles at a time, and *A Hard Day's Night*, their first film, went to Warsaw. Back home, Ringo had been proposed as president of several higher-education establishments and had been house guest at Woburn Abbey at the invitation of the Duke of Bedford's swingin' son, Rudolph. While he'd still been able to do so without too much fuss, Starr had visited Dingle Vale Secondary one open day, "and they were charging people to look at my desk" – or, at least, one that might have once been his.

"Our appeal," ruminated Starr, "is that we're ordinary lads", which, as it had in Britain, did the corrective trick in North America where The Beatles arrived fully mobilised in February 1964 for *The Ed Sullivan Show*, the sub-continent's

Sunday Night At The London Palladium. Surely nothing should have topped the *Palladium*, but, after Sullivan and their US concert debut at the Washington Coliseum, "they could have ripped me apart," raved Starr, "and I couldn't have cared less." Even after they flew out, 'I Want To Hold Your Hand' remained at Number One, while hurtling up were all their singles that in the previous year had been aired to negligible listener reaction by the more lurid disc jockeys such as Wolfman Jack and New York's Murray the K ("the fastest talker I've ever met," said Ringo). Beatles chewing gum alone netted millions of dollars within months.

As is their wont, the Americans, convinced of the incredible, exhibited an enthusiasm for it that left more reserved British Beatlemaniacs swallowing dust. Our colonial cousins were devouring the grass on which the group had trodden and the retrieved jelly-beans that had rained as votive offerings onto the stage on which the idols had played. "I enjoy it at the back," said Ringo, "and when they start throwing things, it's a good place to be." Girls would faint on fingering the guitar autographed by all four and owned by some pensioner in a moptop wig who'd declared himself "the oldest Beatles fan". The whingeing of their children would cause well-off parents to interrupt European holidays for a flight to Liverpool where back copies of *Mersey Beat* would fetch hugely inflated prices and the chair on which Ringo had always perched when in the Cavern band room would be kissed like the Blarney Stone.

Just the title of Lorne Green's 'Ringo', although an entirely unconnected dramatic monologue of the fictitious Old West pistolero, was sufficient to elevate it onto radio playlists and all the way up the Hot 100. There was, however, no doubt about who the man was in 'Ringo For President' by Australia's Rolf Harris and aimed at the States; 'Bingo Ringo' in the Deep South drawl of Huckleberry Hound; and even Beatle-Christmas crossovers in The Four Sisters' platonic 'I Want Ringo For Christmas' and 'Santa Bring Me Ringo' from Christine Hunter.

"I Love Ringo" lapel badges outsold all associated merchandise, but Starr was not thus hallowed solely because he was easily identifiable. He had also stolen the show from the others in a society that was later to concede to the adoption of Cabbage Patch dolls. Promoted in like fashion, The Beatles had in Ringo something as lovably affecting, a little boy lost, a snare-drum Cinderella, the diminutive sad sack toiling on his lonely pedestal and engaging boundless sympathy for being the most inconspicuous one. As if the audience had all sat on tin-tacks, the volume of screams would climb to its loudest when Lennon moved his microphone over to the kit for Starr Time. A wave of groaned pity would filter across cinema rows during the *Hard Day's Night* scene in which Ringo received but one fan letter against the others' thick wads, with a delighted cheer issuing when a whole mailbag is belatedly produced for him alone.

In Britain, the level of applause had not risen at the Royal Command Performance when, delayed by his descent from the drum riser, Ringo had taken his curtain call a few seconds after the guitarists, "but over in the States I know I went over well. It knocked me out to see and hear the kids waving for me. I'd made it as a personality. Who wouldn't be flattered?" As a consequence, he overcame many earlier inhibitions and grew more verbally self-assured as nicotine-stained digits scribbled down quotable Beatle repartee.

The equal of the others now, he was as instant a pundit as they, cracking back as snappily and impudently to banal, ill-informed questions. "Do you like being Beatles?" "Yes, or we'd be Rolling Stones." When are you going to retire?" "In about ten minutes." "Have you any brothers?" "My brother was an only child." "Did The Beatles come to America to get revenge for the Revolution?" "No, we just came for the money." "What would you be if you weren't a Beatle?" "The Beatles' manager." In cold print, Ringo's remarks often seemed inane and pedestrian, but it was the poker-faced, what-are-you-laughing-at way he said 'em. In *A Hard Day's Night*, a stylised celluloid account of The Beatles' eventful preparation for a television showcase, Starr also seized critical attention for non-speaking sequences that brought to light what Brian Epstein called "the little man's quaintness". Less Harpo Marx than Charlie Drake, he exuded elements of that lip-trembling, doe-eyed pathos that some find endearing.

During the filming of *A Hard Day's Night*, "the height of luxury" for Victor Spinetti (who played a neurotic television director) was to repair to their apartment "and have bread and butter and chips and watch television". Outside, the marathon vigils held by tatty girls with laddered tights and someone else's love bites was tiresome, and even boys were trying to kiss the Knightsbridge Beatles as they came and went, but it was a burglary of the flat on 19 April – while the group were recording a *Jack Good* TV special – that had been the last straw for George and Ringo, who decided to evacuate to dwellings less exposed to public attention.

City lights had not lost their allure for Ringo, who installed himself on the opposite side of Hyde Park in a leased one-bedroom. He'd suffer muffled giggling from fans who'd winkled out his ex-directory telephone number but this and worse inconveniences went with the job, and he couldn't crab about its perks. The most tangible of these was the easy money that had facilitated the purchase of a Mercedes for which he'd have a chauffeur on call "because if you haven't you can't park anywhere or go out and get drunk". However, it was somehow soothing to sit behind the wheel himself. "If things got me down, I'd just get out the car and drive away into the night. It sort of got me out of myself."

Now that he was of world renown, the past was never far away. When his father re-appeared, Starkey *père et fils* had been "strange together", partly because Ringo would not risk discomforting his mother by being chummy with her long-lost ex-husband, especially as she was so overtly enjoying her second-hand celebrity. From the Cavern, she'd joined other Beatle relatives in a costly telephone link-up with Radio WROD in Florida, to be transmitted throughout the USA the next day. "I'd love to go to America. I believe it is a lovely place you have there," she'd enthused, as if it were the Isle of Wight.

Hardly the scoop of the century, either, was Elsie's refuting that Richie had a steady girlfriend. However, matters between him and Mo came to a head when he was re-admitted to University College Hospital for the extraction of tonsils that had become so troublesome that no Starr lead vocal would be heard on some dates of their subsequent US tour. While he lay on the operating table, there was media speculation about the future of the gruesome excisions. In a *Daily Express* cartoon, a girl that was off to keep watch outside the infirmary was commanded, "You're not bringing 'em back here!" by her father.

Her patience might have been rewarded if she'd been there when George and Paul visited, bearing grapes and sympathy to their drummer's bedside. They were sent on their way with screams, but Maureen passed to and fro unnoticed by most star-struck loiterers. Legend has it that Ringo proposed matrimony during the sweet nothings of one of her visits.

7 "I've Been Thinking And Wondering Where It's All Going"

After he'd asked Mr Cox formally for his daughter's hand, Richie and 18-year-old year old Maureen tied the knot on 11 February 1965. The most depth that reportage on the event contained was speculation as to whether it would affect the popularity of the group in general and Ringo in particular. Lennon alone knew that "there might be a shuffling of fans from one Beatle to another – at least, that's what happened when news that I was married was 'revealed'." George would be the next to go, but, although his Pattie had also been a salon assistant, she was used to the trappings of inherent wealth and wasn't a poor-honest-girl-from-back-home like Mo or, I suppose, Cynthia Lennon. Like Jane Asher, Pattie combined care of a Beatle with a separate career and income, and so could not be regarded with the same affectionate approval as the other wives or be the subject of a US novelty single in the vein of The Chicklettes' 'Treat Him Tender, Maureen'.

This plea was taken to heart by the new Mrs Starkey, who was still a very northern woman and Richie a northern man. "I don't think women like to be equal," he confided, "They like to be protected and, in turn, they like looking after men." By Christmas 1966, Maureen would have a bigger house to mind when she and Ringo moved to "Sunny Heights", a mansion in the same Weybridge stockbroker estate as the Lennons.

Interestingly, while no vestige of a drum kit could be found anywhere, in nooks and crannies all over the place were light machines, tape recorders, stereo record players and – even in the toilet – televisions, on which the BBC's new second channel could be seen. Screened on either of two projectors were feature films and home movies, like 20 coloured minutes centred on close-ups of Maureen's eye and another shot from the swing that had been bought for the use of children.

The Starkeys' eldest boy was born on 13 September 1965. There were still ripples of sanctimonious opprobrium when Ringo announced that the baby was to be launched into life with the name Zak. Having always dreaded the abridgement of his own to Dick, Zak was, parried Ringo, "a nice strong name, and it can't be shortened. That was something I didn't want at all." In obsequious support, a few young parents in the States also gave their sons this "mad cowboy name that had been spinning 'round in my brain at the time".

Zak would rue "being described as my kid" when Starr's prediction that, "by the time he's grown-up, I won't be playing rock 'n' roll drums" proved false. Nevertheless, he'd received more paternal attention than most, for – heeding Elsie's advice, for once – Ringo made the most of his offspring's cradle days, although he'd attended personally to only one nappy change before engaging a matronly nanny until The Beatles elected to cease public engagements in 1966.

As well as freeing him from the more nauseating aspects of child-rearing, this appointment also enabled the Starrs to accept with an easier conscience evening social engagements in London. If Sunny Heights was more restful than the incessant background churn of traffic around Hyde Park, the Starkeys, city dwellers by instinct, understood that Weybridge wasn't forever. Despite Ringo's developing fascination and expertise in film, no cinema room had been constructed or even a proper screen unfurled when a bare wall would suffice.

With The Beatles thinking aloud already about not touring any more, Ringo's income would depend more and more on record sales, though he seemed to shaping up a credible actor as evidenced in The Beatles's second movie, *Help!* For me, Starr's big moment in *Help!* was his flat "hello" when George uncovers him rolled in a blanket in a car's boot. This deed also earned Harrison one vote against Ringo winning with 60 a *Melody Maker* reader's poll asking "Which Beatles wins the honours in *Help!*?".

Nevertheless, it was Lennon who'd been the first Beatle to appear on a cinema screen without the others - as "Private Gripweed" in *How I Won The War*, a curate's egg of a World War II satire. On location in Spain, John told a visiting Ringo how swiftly his enthusiasm for this acting lark had evaporated, but Ringo wasn't as sympathetic as he might have been. He'd have jumped at the chance to play Private Gripweed.

Yet, bound by common ordeal and jubilation, The Beatles, their aides and most of their relations "were one big happy family", Cynthia Lennon would remember, "because we were thrown together because of circumstances but luckily enough we all got on very well together". While an allegation that Ringo had had to ask the group's permission to marry was the brainchild of a bored journalist, Starr liked the notion "that I would do that because of our close ties." After Ringo had led the way by regrowing his beard, Paul, George and John – and the road crew – each experimented with dundreary whiskers, pointed Imperials and similar depilatory caprices.

No one, however, had been in complete agreement over the controversial issue of their investiture by the Queen as Members of the British Empire. To John, their acceptance of it was absurd, but Paul was delighted with his MBE. Not knowing what to think, Ringo smiled and waved like he was supposed to as The Beatles were driven through cheering crowds to Buckingham Palace on 26 October 1965. His strongest motive for going through with it was that the medal would be something big to show his parents, but he didn't propose ever to wear it.

For a laugh, he'd affix "MBE" after his name on a 1973 album sleeve. The only other use he made of it was when The Beatles and Epstein were among those celebrities who signed a petition calling for the legalisation of marijuana. He'd been slightly put out about learning from an interviewer of the others' intentions, but had been perfectly willing to be on the list, because "even in hospitals now they can't get into it, as they're not allowed to have it for research, which is silly".

Ringo had first experienced LSD in the Hollywood villa that was the nerve-centre of 1965's US tour. Stimulating though it was, "acid" was not all it was cracked up to be for Ringo and made no appreciable difference to him beyond hallucinations and surreal sensations that lasted only until he came down. While the others spoke openly about their psychedelic escapades, he hadn't much to add. After a few more trips, he decided that he'd had enough.

Sharpening paranoia as they did, drugs – always obtainable from local narcotics dealers – did not make touring any more bearable. On the boards, even Paul was forcing his customary exuberance, while John roared purgative off-mic obscenities into the constant bedlam. Afterwards, withdrawn George would inscribe autographs with bad grace or refuse altogether while Ringo would carry on with his game of patience.

In the final dinning weeks of The Beatles' most public adventure, he'd been as a fish beneath stormy waves. While bemoaning the group "not playing properly but nobody hears anyway". The group performed for three evenings in the Nippon Budokan Hall with the disquieting knowledge that, outside, there were frenzied demonstrations of protest about pop-singing occidentals polluting this temple of martial arts. However, this was nothing to the naked malevolence at Manila International Airport, where, in official retaliation for unwittingly snubbing the Philippine president's wife, The Beatles entourage underwent an ordeal of red tape in the customs area and, reportedly, the pushing and shoving of a jeering mob. Assured of leniency or even a commendation, however, they behaved in "the roughest reception we've ever had", recalled Starr, who purportedly weathered the brunt of their aggression: "They really had it in for us."

In North America, where sections of the media had sensationalised a story of how Lennon had "boasted" that his Beatles were more popular than Christ, the possible in-concert slaughter of the artists by divine wrath – or someone acting on the Almighty's behalf – improved attendances but did not forestall public bonfires of Beatle records, picketing of shows by Ku Klux Klansmen or attempted peltings of the Fab Four with decayed fruit and more odious projectiles.

The Beatles downed tools as a working band at San Francisco's Candlestick Park on 29 August 1966. Starr was "convinced we gave up touring at the right time. Four years of Beatlemania was enough for anyone." Now the antics of fans frightened him as, in straits of emotional blackmail, they'd dangle from ledges, gulp down poison and slash wrists to simply be noticed by a Beatle dashing past those close enough to maul him. Actor Leo McKern would never forget the terror that chased across Ringo's countenance when a simpering, Bermuda-shorted tourist, garlanded with cameras, had waddled towards them for autographs while they were routining a *Help!* scene amid sand dunes: "At a moment of apparent security, deep in the work in hand, he'd experienced an unexpected and unlooked-for assault."

Pondering an uncertain future, Ringo imagined that such intrusions would tail off "when the records start slipping, as they're bound to one day. I suppose the best thing to do is roll along and say 'Well, let it happen as it does,' but I've been thinking and wondering where it's all going."

8 "They'd More Or Less Direct Me In The Style I Can Play"

Released just before The Beatles quit the stage, the latest album, *Revolver*, had contained 'Yellow Submarine', the only British Number One with Ringo as lead singer. This had been contrived by Paul and John as an ideal children's song for Starr, which also captured a flavour of nautical Liverpool. The time spent recording it was longer than that spent on the group's first LP. "We're quite big with EMI at the moment," understated Ringo. "They don't argue if we take the time we want." A brass band inserted for two bars and sea-faring sound were among mere touch-ups on this *kitsch meisterwerk*.

Jog-along 'With A Little Help From My Friends' was the Starr Time on the next album, *Sgt Pepper's Lonely Hearts Club Band*. A segue from the title track, it had a sung introduction announcing Ringo in his Lonely Hearts Bandsman alter ego, "Billy Shears", because, as he explained at length, "the original concept of *Sgt Pepper* was that it was going to be a stage show – you know, we start with the clapping and people shouting and then I come on – and we were going to do it like in a theatre; we'd do it in the studio and simulate it. We didn't in the end. We did it for the first couple of tracks and then it faded into an album, but it still made it a whole concept. It was as if we did a few tracks and suddenly there was a fire and everyone ran out of the building but we carried on playing."

In 1987, Ringo declined to appear in the celebratory *It Was Twenty Years Ago Today*, Granada Television's two-hour invocation of psychedelic times past that *Sgt Pepper* had unquestionably inspired. For him, it "wasn't our best album. That was the peak for everyone else, but for me it was a bit like being a session musician. They'd more or less direct me in the style I can play." However, he had been permitted creative input, in a piecemeal manner. Praise indeed had been George Martin's acknowledgement that, in *Sgt Pepper*'s fragmented finale, 'A Day In The Life', the distinctive scuffed drum section was entirely Ringo's idea.

Like John, Paul and George, Starr had become a determined self-improver. He'd thumbed through hardbacks of mystical, religious and aerie-faerie nature – *Autobiography Of A Yogi*, *The Golden Bough*, Tolkein, *et al*, but his clear expositions during interviews of karma, the transmigration of souls and the world of illusion was evidence of more than cursory poring over these tomes, which looked as well on Sunny Heights' shelves as did the fresh lick of emulsion on its walls.

Along with bouts of highbrow reading and getting the house repainted, the Starkeys' undertaking of numerous hobbies of late was symptomatic of the triumph of sedate Surrey domesticity over nightclubbing, since the arrival of Zak's brother at London's Queen Charlotte's hospital on 19 August. Maureen named him Jason, thereby thwarting her husband's desire "to give him initials – JR or something like that."

During many a curtained evening at Sunny Heights, the Starkeys might have been any commuting executive's family at leisure, and in a sense Ringo would become just such a person during the group's period of self-management after their manager's unexpected death, on 27 August 1967, precipitated "a strange time for us, when it's someone you've relied on in the business, where we never got involved".

Otherwise all of Starr's problems seemed to be little ones. As well as children, there were the mental debates before the shaving mirror over whether the dagger beard he'd been cultivating to go with his moustache gave him a touch of the corsair or was just plain silly. He was also developing and printing his own films in a newly created darkroom at Sunny Heights. Here, at least, was an area in which he was an authority, as far as McCartney, Harrison and Lennon could see, "and I had all these funny lenses". Billed as its Director of Photography, he showed what these and the rest of his equipment could do in a lot of the television film, *Magical Mystery Tour*, such as "a scene with George where I put him in my living room and projected slides on him. It's nothing new – it was done back in 1926 or so – but I happened to be a camera buff, and I think it came out fine."

Second to Paul, Ringo was the Beatle most active in *Magical Mystery Tour*'s editing process in a cramped Soho cutting room while tossing morsels to a slavering press. In *Magical Mystery Tour*, he informed them, he was the badgered nephew of a fat lady who joined a variegated cast of holidaymakers on a charabanc to undertake a journey of no known destination or outcome. It had been Paul's idea to make it up as they went along. Who needed a screenplay, especially one like they'd had in *Help!*? Who wanted a tenth-rate Marx Brothers? The only guide that they'd devised for this film was "one sheet of paper with a circle on it, and it was marked like a clock, only there was one o'clock, five o'clock, nine o'clock and eleven – something like that. The rest we had to fill in."

He'd quell forebodings about formless eccentricity with phrases such as "aimed at the widest possible audience", and "interesting things to look at, interesting things to hear". Nevertheless, shown on 1967's Boxing Day, the laboured surrealism of the film wasn't quite the ticket for a nation in the hiatus between a cold-turkey teatime and mid-evening insobriety. "It just freaked everybody out," groaned Starr years later, "which was a pity. If it came out today, it would be more accepted. I always loved Magical."

"We all did" was his loyal addendum, knowing full well how uncomfortable John and George had been about it from the beginning. He was as defensive about the benefits of meditation when, on the very weekend of Brian Epstein's passing, he and the other Beatles had been attending the International Meditation Society's initiation course at a university faculty in the Welsh seaside town of Bangor. "That's how it used to be," Starr would reminisce. "If someone wanted to do something, all we'd do was follow them." Maureen was still recovering from Jason's birth, but Ringo would relay to her the enlightening nectar from the lips of the robed and ascetic Maharishi Mahesh Yogi, who had founded the British branch of the society in 1959.

Nonetheless, The Beatles had curtailed their indoctrination in Bangor so that they could assimilate Brian's death in the privacy of their own homes. A few days later, Ringo would be beside John's sombre swimming pool where his considered response to the tragedy was chronicled by a correspondent from *Disc* magazine. The Maharishi had "told us we mustn't let it get us down, [because] Brian would be able to feel our feelings in his spiritual state. If we try to spread happiness, then Brian will be happy too, but the thing is not to get too selfish about it. If you get depressed about it, it is a form of self-pity, because you are only sympathising with your own loss."

Mr Epstein hadn't been sure that he wholly approved of this Maharishi, and in the end Ringo "couldn't believe 100 per cent in the Maharishi. He's a very high man, but he wasn't the one for me." However, the Indian spiritual leader's advent was at a juncture when Starr might well have been ripe for religion, "at a point," as he himself construed, "where I wondered what I was and what it all was." In 1966, his flippant reaction to God in a *Melody Maker* word-association column, had been, "Somebody must like Him." In the following year, the Starkeys' approach to Him appeared too insolently sudden to those who would assume that, in February 1968, they'd accompanied the other Beatle couples to the Maharishi's yoga-ashram ("theological college") in the Himalayas simply because they hadn't wanted to be excluded from another new activity. This scepticism was supported by the pair's return to Weybridge after less than a fortnight of study.

"Of course, there were lectures and things all the time, but it was very much like a holiday," summarised Ringo, who also found the place "a bit like Butlin's".

Back at Sunny Heights, the Starkeys decided to sidestep the inevitable barrage of press attention by escaping with the boys for a couple of days at a location deep in the home-counties countryside. "At the moment, I meditate every day," Ringo would assure waiting interrogators. "Well, I might skip the odd day if I get up late or arrive in town late or something." No one doubted him for a second.

9 "I Suppose I Seem Fairly Straight"

If Mr and Mrs Average had been alienated by *Magical Mystery Tour*, the Maharishi and some of The Beatles' marijuana-smoking music, Ringo surfaced as the group's anchor of normality during the eye-stretching aeon before the group's disbandment in 1971. More relaxed and articulate than before, he was weaning himself off booze with coffee and chain-smoked American Larks. The zenith of depravity nowadays was "the odd bet on a horse, but no bookie will ever get rich on my bets".

Although extravagant in other matters, his wife was as circumspect about the children's "few bob pocket money each week". Said Ringo, "Once it's spent, that'll be that, though I guess I'll be like most dads, buying them something when they ask for it, then getting a row from Mum." His contentment with the sedate domesticity of Brookfields, the new family home outside Elstead, a village where Surrey bleeds into Hampshire, was epitomized by "Why should we be lonely?", Ringo's rhetorical demand of the final edition of *Rave* magazine,

"We have each other, and we never knew anyone in Weybridge. In the short months when rural quiet and isolation from the capital were refreshing, he swore, "We couldn't live in town again – too much noise and too much going on. I suppose I get bored just like anybody else, but instead of having three hours at night I have all day to get bored in."

His butterfly concentration now embraced all manner of soon-exhausted hobbies involving "thousands of pounds' worth of equipment. I call them my toys, because that's what they are." When winter gloom descended, he warded off ennui with more familiar pastimes such as "a week when I'll just play records. Then I might spend a day just playing with my tape recordings." Excitedly, he'd sometimes drop everything to develop some flash of musical inspiration but it would become too much like hard work. Maybe he'd have another go tomorrow. His songwriting methodology is worth quoting at length: "I usually get a first verse and then I find it impossible to get anywhere else with the song. I can't say, 'Now I'm going to write.' I just have to be around a guitar or piano and it just comes. Usually, what I do if I'm in the mood is put the tape on, if I've got a tune, and then I play the same tune like a hundred times with different words. Then I take the tape off and get it all typed out and then I pick the lines out that I'll put together."

For one incomplete 1968 ditty, 'It Don't Come Easy', he sought help with arrangement from George, who was more malcontented a victim of The Beatles' ruling composers' frequently disheartening indifference to the efforts of colleagues.

However, on BBC1 on 6 February 1968, he became the first Beatle to sing without the others on another artist's show as unseen millions watched the inauguration of Ringo Starr's solo career. In this edition of Cilla Black's weekly TV series, negotiated before Brian Epstein's death, he sported a period trilby for their duet of coy 'Do You Like Me Just A Little Bit?'. Then, donning a baggy black suit, he gave 'em a solo rendition of 'Act Naturally' before he proceeded to do just that as a "ventriloquist" – with Cilla as the dummy – in a brief sketch.

Since proving himself as instant a hit in *A Hard Day's Night*, Starr had been courted by movie moguls on the look-out for new talent – or was it with cynical expediency that "they sort of stuck on me as Ringo the Film Star because I don't write or anything"? After Lennon had tested the water with *How I Won The War*, Starr had also accepted a modest part – and his first screen kiss – in a non-Beatle film, *Candy*, an advisedly X-certificate Italian-French production with echoes of Voltaire's *Candide*. He dominated the screen for a few minutes as Emmanuel, a Mexican gardener preparing for holy orders but unsuccessfully sublimating his very worldly lust. He was perceived by Starr as "a very nervous sort of fellow. I was nervous, too, as it happened, and that's how I played the part."

Most press notices mentioned Starr only in passing. Neither did Starr then "see myself more as a film star than as a Beatle, or vice versa". The follow-up to *Help!* had not yet passed beyond someone's brainwave of trying Tolkein's

The Lord Of The Rings, but this was scotched by its originator's disapproval and Ringo's argument that "it will take 18 months to mount and, by that time, we will all go off the idea. What we must do is to start something on the spur of the moment, otherwise we will never get it done. We are always into other things."

Among these "other things" was Apple Corps, a name registered in 1963 as an eventual umbrella term for maverick artistic and scientific ventures. "We saw it [Apple] housing all our ideas, and we believed it would all go well," groaned Ringo when it didn't. "But we weren't businessmen, and we aren't now." Impetuous cash was flung at such as a so-called "electronics wizard"; two unprofitable shops; a troupe of grasping Dutch designers trading misleadingly as "The Fool"; film-makers who wouldn't make films; poets who didn't write poems and, remembered Ringo, a tent for "another guy to do a Punch and Judy show on a beach. They'd take the money and say, 'Well, maybe next week.'"

Out of his depth, Starr saw the organisation as another expensive toy to be disregarded, if not jettisoned altogether, when he grew tired of it: "we had, like, a thousand people that weren't needed, but they all enjoyed it. They're all getting paid for sitting around. We had a guy there just to read the tarot cards, the I Ching. It was craziness."

Apple Records was the only department that "didn't let us down. Within it, Ringo had founded on 16 July 1968 his Startling Music publishing concern, initially to gather royalties should any of his pedantically wrought compositions ever warrant release. Eclipsed by the other Beatles' more tangible activities, he was, nonetheless, happy to rattle the traps for Paul and George's production clients – and, after he'd got used to her, for Yoko Ono, who had now replaced McCartney as John's artistic collaborator as she had Cynthia in his bed.

Yoko had once sniffed around Ringo for his patronage for her "concept art", but he was unmoved by her wrapping Trafalgar Square statues in brown paper, her inane *Grapefruit* book, her film of people's bottoms and anything else she considered necessary to win his sponsorship. His bemusement with Yoko contrasted with John's jealous imaginings, after he brazened it out by escorting her to a London theatre presentation. A perturbed *Beatles Monthly* passed her off as his "guest of honour", but nothing could cover up the genital display on the sleeve of *Two Virgins*, the first of a trilogy of Ono-Lennon albums filled with sounds not generally thought of as pop entertainment. Although he didn't "dig their records", Ringo of all the other Beatles swooped most unquestioningly to Lennon's defence. Of the unclothed 'Two Virgins', he commented, "It's just John being John. It's very clean." Yoko became "incredible". No one else doubted it, either. "We'll be pleased when people realise that she's doing something [and] that she's not trying to be the fifth Beatle."

Waiting to console Yoko just before Lennon's cremation 12 years later, Starr's muttered "it was her who started all this" indicated an adjustment of his stated opinion, in as late as 1971, that her and John's amour had not taken priority over group commitments.

When The Beatles next convened at Abbey Road, Yoko's constant and baleful adherence to John in both control room and playing area was one of Ringo's "little niggly things that cropped up" while he sat on the fence as the group muddled through a double album that, in its prosaic name alone, justified George Martin's observation that *The Beatles* was "sort of businesslike", as engineers grew accustomed to two or even three Beatles missing at any given session. Conversely, more catalytic familiars and guest players than ever were assembled to add icing to the cake. Yoko was loud and clear on 'The Continuing Story Of Bungalow Bill' – as guitarist Eric Clapton was on 'While My Guitar Gently Weeps'. Jack Fallon – a Canadian emigrant who'd promoted Beatles bookings in the West Country during the Pete Best era – was hired to scrape country-and-western violin on 'Don't Pass Me By', the exhumation of which – although a personal triumph for Starr – illustrated the depth to which standards had fallen.

Ringo would not look back on *The Beatles* with much affection, although there'd been no discernible animosity at first. However, since the advent of Yoko, and Lennon's co-related passiveness, McCartney's attempts to motivate the other personnel had backfired, his boisterous purpose translated as barely tolerable bossiness.

An irksome lecture from *bête noir* Paul about a fluffed tom-tom fill had been the delayed-action spark that had fired

Ringo to stalk out of Abbey Road mid-session. That their weary drummer's resignation was more than a registered protest or one of his infrequent fits of pique became clear with his verbal notice to John and then Paul. Yet neither they nor George dared credit this extreme strategy by the standard-bearer of group stability. The matter was hushed up and they were endeavouring to carry on as if nothing was wrong when the prodigal returned after a fortnight in the Mediterranean. Out of The Beatles' reach, he'd calmed down enough to jot down the basic structure of a new Starr original, 'Octopus's Garden', following the vessel's chef's fascinating discourse one lunchtime about life on the ocean floor. Tight coils within had unwound and, for all that had driven him from the group, it abruptly made sense to ring up and report for duty again. Half expecting a row, he was greeted with a drum-kit festooned with remorseful flowers and "welcome back" banners.

No matter which journal still canvassed its readers on the most popular Beatle – Paul in *Jackie*, John in *Disc* – Ringo was invariably second. Seeming a beer-and-skittles sort who rejoiced in his married state, "I suppose I seem fairly straight and a family type, so people do associate more with me than, say, John." At a cousin's wedding, distant teenage kin jockeying to exchange self-conscious familiarities with their famous relation were often discountenanced at how like their fathers – and even grandfathers – he was. He was, nevertheless, *au fait* with recent "rock" developments across the Atlantic, but he preferred mainstream, musicianly artists like Canned Heat; Blood, Sweat And Tears and bottleneck guitar exponent Ry Cooder, whose sticksman, Jim Keltner, "really pleases me more than some incredible jazz drummer who can flit 'round them like a jet plane". The furthest-out limit of Starr's taste appeared to be the cartoon voodoo of Doctor John The Night Tripper – alias Los Angeles session player Mac Rebennack – with its zombie wails and throbbing murk. That Rebennack's image was not entirely contrived became evident when, on meeting him, Ringo was charmed by his "weird language, which is half English, half cajun and half rhyming madness".

When asked about Vietnam and other inflammable topics, Ringo was sufficiently hip to understand that killing people is wrong. He wouldn't join together – as Mick Jagger did – with militant anti-Vietnam War protesters outside the US Embassy, nor come up with even an irresolute anthem like Lennon's 'Revolution', but he was as active – in a detached, sweeping, pop-starrish fashion – in verbally supporting pacifism, although, "Just at the moment, we can say what we feel, but it doesn't really change anything. I can't trust politicians. They're all liars, you know. And when the younger generation get the vote, it will be very interesting to see what they decide to allow and exactly what they don't. The young people all want peace, and they'll get it if they just wait, because they're going to outlive them all."

The Starkeys' own offsprings' upbringing was undramatic and as free of major traumas as the restrictions of the paterfamilias' fame would permit: "I don't want people interested in them just because they are my children." Nonetheless, Zak and Jason could not help but become aware of their indulgent dad's wealth and the celebrity that he would always enjoy. Four-year-old Zak's daub of a beetle-like creature would grace the cover of 1969's Christmas flexidisc for the fan club. "Like any kid," grinned Ringo, "he wants to play with his own toys and mine as well." As his father had scorned drumming lessons, Zak was restricted to just one tutorial. "Then he just told me to listen to records and play along with them." Given a free choice, Zak was more likely to thunder along to The Who than The Beatles.

He'd also begun to learn recorder at the local state primary. Ringo was then reluctant to send his boys to a fee-paying boarding school. "Not unless they tell me they definitely want to go. If I can only see them as much as one hour a day, then I want that hour." When he progressed from his bit part in *Candy* to co-starring with Peter Sellers in *The Magic Christian* in early 1969, he risked bringing the family to his place of work. "But this can prove to be tricky, because the kids get bored and start fiddling about with all the equipment. It can also be very embarrassing if one of them shouts out, 'Daddy!' whilst we're doing a take."

Ringo's infants were not to be in evidence on the long-awaited third Beatles film, *Let It Be* in which they rehearsed, recorded, jammed and gave an unpublicised performance under a leaden sky on Apple's flat roof, clothed against the biting wind. Public-address speakers aimed at the street below provoked the downing of measuring tapes in neighbourhood outfitters, a swelling crowd to clog the pavement and police from the station nearly half a mile away to curb the breach of the peace, MBEs or not. The most repeated off-camera joke was Ringo saying, "For the first time in years, we give a live show. Is it our fault only 500 people turn up?"

Ringo blew hot and cold about The Beatles' further availability for bookings. He would never be against performing *per se*, "but it's the whole operation of getting there that's the drag". Also, he was afraid that, after tax and other deductions, "[we'd] be left with a fiver and a packet of ciggies each.

Nonetheless, he'd elect as usual to go along with whatever the majority – by implication, John and George nowadays – decided. His proposition of a format "where you'd have one camera, just step in and do your bit, like the Grand Ole Opry" went unheeded as the fly-on-the-wall wheeze took root. As Lennon, McCartney and, especially, Harrison had new songs to squeeze onto the album, the new Starr composition, 'Octopus's Garden' fell by the wayside, although George and then John chucked in some amused ideas when he plonked it out on piano.

This condescending levity and episodes such as an affectedly surreal exchange between John and Ringo – the film's "only true individualists", wrote *The Morning Star* – were oases of borderline comedy during the frayed celluloid miles of Paul's prodding of nerves, testy George's walk-out, masked bickering and all of the subtle discords discernible to anyone who has ever suffered being in a pop group, particularly one on its last legs. Like Andy Warhol's interesting-but-boring *Flesh*, with its improvised dialogue and frowsy scenarios, the tedium was nearly the idea.

Although heard merely toiling behind his drums, Starr's musical appetite was the least ruined by the harrowing *Let It Be* sessions. Therefore, it was he who'd sit at the mixing desk most often beside Phil Spector, drafted in to edit, spruce up and mix the "new-phase Beatles album" (as it would say on the *Let It Be* package). In the first instance, the fastidious New York producer's doctoring – overseen by Starr – satisfied McCartney, who, over the phone to Ringo, "didn't put it down, and then suddenly he didn't want it to go out. It was two weeks after that he wanted to cancel it."

Spector had been recommended to The Beatles by US accountant Allen Klein, whose prophecy that he'd one day represent the group seemed to be fulfilling itself. To Ringo, Allen came across as "a powerful man, and also, no matter what anyone says, he's fair". Despite warnings from some of his previous clients and associates, John and George were also yielding to the self-styled "Robin Hood of pop's" contractual sweet-talk that he illustrated with flattering quotes from their lyrics. However, once his champion, Paul preferred to believe his lawyer father-in-law's tittle-tattle of Klein's sharp practices, high handedness and low cunning. *L'affaire Let It Be* was a handy bone of contention.

The Beatles' dissolution became more than foreseeable when John announced that he'd be leaving soon and yet agreed that it should not be public knowledge yet, for fear that it would unman Klein's bellicose negotiation of a more advantageous royalty deal with Capitol. Nonetheless, a hint of what lay ahead could be fathomed by journalists in Lennon's reported crack that "the circus has left town but we still own the site".

"John is crazy like that," chuckled Ringo. "He will say one thing one day [and] the opposite the next." Only a handful of fans outside Abbey Road caught Ringo's sally as he ambled across Abbey Road car park for a session on 26 August 1969: "I'm going back to the circus."

10 "I Couldn't Believe It Was Happening"

Of each Beatle's preparations for the end, Ringo's were the most pragmatic. Before *Let It Be* nestled uneasily in the album lists – among *Led Zeppelin II*, Andy Williams' *Greatest Hits*, Black Sabbath and the latest from Crosby, Stills, Nash And Young, The Who and Simon And Garfunkel – he'd struck out on his own again with *The Magic Christian*, technically his second non-Beatle film. Terry Southern's short novel did not contain anyone called "Youngman Grand", but this superficial main character was inserted into the script for the screen version of *The Magic Christian* at the first hint of publicity-gaining Beatle involvement. While accepting that he was being "used for the name", Ringo had sought the part as an admirer of both Southern and the flick's co-star, Peter Sellers, and as a further opportunity to discover more about what seemed one reliable indicator of future direction, even if "I've had no special tuition but I've learned a lot from watching other people."

Today, *The Magic Christian* surfaces as one of Sellers' lesser comedies, with Starr serving mostly as witness to his appropriation of the funniest lines as the much-altered original plot dissolves into a series of themed sketches – about folk who'll do anything for money – with predictable outcomes. To Ringo, in his lead as a Liverpudlian vagrant adopted by "Grand" (Sellers), "they were just saying, 'Be yourself'" by permitting the occasional sub-*Hard Day's Night* flat truism. "To keep my ears warm" was his reply to "Why are you wearing a deerstalker?" during a scene for which he'd been kitted out in ridiculous Victorian hunting tweeds.

The general critical conjecture – with the artist in agreement – was that Ringo had coped well enough with an undemanding role. Yet the bond between Starr and Sellers tightened through hedonistic joint ventures like booking a celebrity party that, in keeping with the film, climaxed with hundreds of dollar bills fluttering from the ceiling. In the build-up to its London première, both were forever on television talk programmes.

During BBC1's *David Frost Show*, the two sang a number from *Abbey Road*, The Beatles' latest LP. Unconvincing in embryo during *Let It Be*, 'Octopus's Garden' had passed muster when the group convened for what was tacitly assumed to be the vinyl finale. A simpler companion reverie to 'Yellow Submarine' and with a country-and-western tinge, 'Octopus's Garden' stood as tall as most of McCartney's *Abbey Road* offerings and was easier on the ear than, say,

Lennon's stark 'I Want You (She's So Heavy)'. It wasn't, however, a masterpiece of song. Nevertheless, the requisite breezy, infantine effect was fully realised via Paul and George's emollient backing harmonies and Ringo's sound-effect idea of a blowing through a straw into a close-miked tumbler of water.

More indicative of John, George and Paul's disinclination than their producer's artistic regard for the budding Schubert was Ringo's good-natured appearance as token Beatle on *With A Little Help From My Friends*, a Christmas Eve tribute to George Martin on ITV. Obeying Musicians' Union dictates, he re-recorded the lead vocal to mime 'Octopus's Garden', gripping a trident with a few children at his feet.

Ringo's reputation as the straightest Beatle had been further strengthened by recent family events as "normal" as susceptible fans might have imagined them. At Queen Charlotte's as usual, Maureen's third pregnancy had on 17 November produced Lee, the daughter that she and Richie had so desired. Home for the baby was a six-bedroom spread along leafy Compton Avenue in Highgate, rather than rural Elstead, which was "too far away" for her father to commute to Apple in his new Mercedes.

Among those who saw the New Year in at Ringo's housewarming included next door neighbour Maurice Gibb of The Bee Gees. Sharing the same profession, it would have been odd if Gibb and Starr hadn't collaborated informally in the privacy of their respective home studios. One evening,

Maurice "sang" on 'Modulating Maurice', a track from an album's worth of woofing and tweeting that Ringo had concocted on one of these new-fangled synthesisers. "They take control of you, those machines," he confessed, "We found this riff and I was playing with it, and [Gibb] started humming words and read the dials, like [the] modulator and envelope shaper, things like that." Starr's more calculated twiddles were earmarked for consumption by a dwindling public still uncritical of any goods branded "Beatle", until "I got involved with John Tavener, who was doing *The Whale*, which was more far out."

Tavener was to be a behemoth of what Ringo called "underground classical music" after the Beatle listened to a cassette of *The Whale*, the tall, long-haired composer's first major work. Only vaguely aware of The Beatles' stature, he was invited by an enthusiastic Ringo to a meeting with Ron Kass, manager of Apple Records, with the intention of discussing a record deal.

Sales of *The Whale*, its creator's "serious" credibility and guaranteed Radio 3 exposure were just enough to make a second Tavener album, *Celtic Requiem (Requiem For Jenny Jones)* a worthwhile exercise. Its commercial failure, however, was less to do with the music than with Apple press officer Derek Taylor's retrospective confession, "We didn't promote it. We really couldn't."

At just over £30,000, Ringo's was but the smallest individual Beatle overdraft now harrying the company ledgers.

Overnight, glib unconcern deferred to pointed questions –
"as business men, not Beatles," verified Ringo – such as,
Which typist phones Canberra every afternoon? Why had
so-and-so given himself a rise of £60 a week? Why is he seen
only on pay day?

To steer the ship back on course, Ringo and George had
been persuaded by John to support the official appointment
of Allen Klein as manager. As old retainers were cast adrift,
sinecures discontinued and a clocking-in system installed, Starr
concurred with Klein: "We used to keep everyone on until
our new business manager came along and showed us the real
facts of what they were all doing. A lot of them got sacked
because they weren't doing their jobs, and that's fair. They
would usually hate you for it, but that doesn't bother me."

Even the enterprise's only true money-spinner, Apple
Records, was subject to cuts as unviable releases were
cancelled and contracts unrenewed. "If you have a big tree
with a thousand million roses," pontificated Ringo, "prune
it down and you'll get maybe ten fantastic roses. That's
what's happening." Starr, a component of the most fantastic
rose of all, teased both journalists and himself with talk of
a follow-up to *Abbey Road*: "There's nothing wrong with
The Beatles," he chirped as late as March 1970. "When
we've got something to do, we'll do it. We're all in touch."
Ere 1969 was out, however, he hedged his bets with a
planned solo LP of pre-rock 'n' roll standards to be titled
Sentimental Journey.

"I really dug all that old music," Ringo explained, "because that was the first I ever heard, and I thought, 'My mum'll be pleased if I sing all those songs.'" Their immaculate scoring was exemplified by the few bars of fluid saxophone busking that leaped from the horn riffing on 'Night And Day', the glissando swoops of violins in 'I'm A Fool To Care' and the witty leitmotifs of 'Have I Told You Lately That I Love You?'.

"He sings better than you'd expect him to," wrote a particularly snowblinded reviewer. Nonetheless, the hoisting of *Sentimental Journey* high up Top 40s throughout the world testified less to this virtue than to the value of showing the title clip on such as *The Ed Sullivan Show* and a media jaunt made by Ringo in the flesh. "The great thing was that it got me moving," said the artiste, "not very fast, but just moving. It was like the first shovel of coal in the furnace that makes the train inch forward."

The following June, he struck while the furnace was lukewarm with a country-and-western album, *Beaucoups Of Blues*. The job of producing it went eventually to Pete Drake, a 39-year-old steel guitar virtuoso equally at ease improvising the orthodox "Nashville sound" for entertainers as diverse as Elvis, Perry Como, The Monkees – and George Harrison, who'd had him flown to London's Trident Studios for *All Things Must Pass*, his first album as an ex-Beatle.

Drake advocated Nashville's Music City complex as the most fitting setting to cut the kinda tunes folk like a-tappin' their shoe leather to. They could begin the next week. Starr had started an opus, 'Band Of Steel', which namechecked Hank Williams and lesser country legends in much the same manner as Cowboy Copas' 'Hillbilly Heaven'. It was not, however, among those selected from more than a hundred new copyrights grubbed from demo tapes in offices clotted round 16th Avenue, the Tin Pan Alley of Nashville. To be published by Startling Music, those shortlisted were mostly lachrymose ballads, often just a few degrees from schmaltz, with titles such as 'Silent Homecoming', 'Loser's Lounge' and 'Love Don't Last Long'.

With brisk finesse, 20 tracks – for trimming down to a strong but soothing single album – were ready within three days, although for much of the first morning Ringo "was really nervous, and Pete would say through the glass, 'Hoss, if you don't get loose, I'm going to come in there and stomp on your toes.'" The mood, nevertheless, relaxed sufficiently to bring forth a record that deserved more than a wretched struggle to Number 65 in the States and no chart placing whatsoever at home.

What else could he do? Ringo "was not interested in being in a new band. I was bigger than any band I could have joined." In the wake of *Sentimental Journey*, he had already been approached to entertain diners as a solo headliner for a season in Las Vegas. His deep thought before declining – "I wouldn't mind, but it would mean putting an act together" – demonstrated the allure of mainstream showbusiness. After all, Cilla Black, was starring in the extravaganza *Way Out In Piccadilly* with Frankie Howerd. Up in the West End, too, Starr and Lennon had been there on the night that Gerry – now minus his Pacemakers – had gladly taken over the male lead in *Charlie Girl*, which ran and ran.

After a fashion, Paul McCartney, with his irrepressible spirit when in the limelight, awaited a destiny as a showbiz evergreen. By late 1970, he'd set irreversible wheels in motion for the official dissolution of The Beatles. "Suddenly your brain gets twisted and you do strange things," lamented Ringo. "I just kept thinking, 'What's he doing it to me for?', but then I realised he's got to do it to get what he wants, so I don't put him down for that. [But] you'd get lawyers coming 'round day and night, millions of affidavits, too many problems that I didn't want to do because I just wanted to play. We got a bit catcalling, which really wasn't right, but we had to go through it."

While clouds of litigation gathered, all four parties were "tight, nervous, everyone watching everyone else", noticed the forgiving Cynthia Lennon, who, with her new spouse, was "at home" one day for well-wishers that included her increasingly distant Beatle pals and ex-husband. "Everyone was wondering," recalled Ringo, "and I was the one who wondered longest."

11 "I Love It When They Let Me Go Off On My Own"

Ringo's first solo hit single was 'It Don't Come Easy', arguably his greatest work as a commercial songwriter. He'd been at so desperate a loss after *Abbey Road* that, after his own six-string tinkering on the B-side, 'Early 1970', he'd wondered whether Paul, John and George were still going to "play with me". However, million-selling 'It Don't Come Easy' and its afterglow of instant self-esteem was buoyed with the inauguration of the first fan club devoted to Starr alone and his placing as Top Drummer in *NME*'s 1971 popularity poll, in which The Beatles had been superseded as Top Group by Creedence Clearwater Revival.

On 1 August that year, the *NME*'s Top Drummer had belied previous insistences that "personally, I don't want to play in public again" by smacking the skins in George Harrison's New York spectacular in aid of Bangladesh, prostrated as it was by disease and famine in the wake of a cyclone and an invading Moslem army. With two sold-out houses to entertain, as well as consumers of the event's movie and triple-album spin-offs, Harrison knocked together a disciplined presentation embracing nothing that hadn't been a smash for someone in the all-star band he'd put together or sufficiently well known for a spatter of clapping to swell and subside over its unannounced introduction.

Ringo was loved for a distracted, breathless 'It Don't Come Easy'. He also rattled an apprehensive tambourine for Bob Dylan, whom George had talked into a 20-minute spot before the big finish. As Dylan had been in hibernation since the Isle of Wight, George spoke for everyone when he said, "It was great to have him in it at all."

Overlooked in the next morning's newspapers was the fact that it had also been Ringo Starr's first true stage show since Candlestick Park. Nevertheless, the barrage of cheering, stamping and whistling after 'It Don't Come Easy' had dissipated lingering twinges of disappointment about The Beatles' break-up. From the purposeless time-killing that followed *Beaucoups Of Blues*, he had made an indelible mark as a non-Beatle – as opposed to ex-Beatle – and now there were even handsomer dividends inherent in the work put his way these days.

That "it gave Ringo an opportunity" had been one incentive for Allen Klein's underwriting of *Blindman*, an Italian-made spaghetti western that xeroxed the salient points of those that had recently hoisted Clint Eastwood,

Lee Van Cleef and Charles Bronson to international acclaim. Indeed, like Eastwood's *A Fistful Of Dollars*, its plot was an Occidental rewrite of a Japanese picture. Two a-penny then, cowboy films were also much in vogue for pop stars wishing to extend themselves. Bob Dylan's economic acting abilities, for example, would be realised in Sam Peckinpah's *Pat Garrett And Billy The Kid*. Ringo, too, had donned spurs, "because it was so far from anything I'd ever done".

Resplendent in sombrero and dyed jet-black beard, he was proudly "evil from start to finish" as the psychotic brother of a chief bandido who kidnaps the intended brides of 50 Texan miners from a wagon train guided by The Good Guy. Ringo had decided to "start every scene fairly straight and end up as an out-and-out madman". His dementia might have verged on genuine at times, for he'd grown heartily fed up – and saddle-sore – with riding a horse so herculean that aid was required each time he mounted. Into the bargain, the main title song he'd written had been turned down. Instead of booming from the silver screen, it would eventually B-side 'Back Off Boogaloo', tardy successor to 'It Don't Come Easy'.

Supposedly a put-down of Paul McCartney, 'Back Off Boogaloo' was no profound insight into the human condition. On one Sunday, Starr had woken up with the melody in his head as he hunched over a guitar downstairs. "It just all came out, all the verses part, and then I was watching the football on the telly in the afternoon and [commentator] Jimmy Hill said, 'That was a tasty goal' about someone, and I said, 'Tasty! What a nice word!' and rushed over again, and that's how I got the middle."

Quasi-military drum tattoos that punctuated its arrangement were also a feature of 'Amazing Grace' by the Scottish regimental band that kept 'Back Off Boogaloo' from topping the UK charts in spring 1972, just as T Rex's 'Hot Love' had with McCartney's 'Another Day' a year before. Both of T Rex's next two Number Ones – 'Get It On' and 'Telegram Sam' – and 'Back Off Boogaloo' were characterised by a hard rock chug and pseudo-cryptic lyrics, so much so that T Rex devotees – and the group's self-glorifying leader, Marc Bolan – would make waspish and spurious allegations that Bolan had ghosted 'Back Off Boogaloo' for Ringo. An admirer of Marc's stagecraft – "he knows how to sway the atmosphere and that's a great skill" – Ringo telephoned his Kensington flat with "this idea. See what you think, yes or no."

The ensuing meeting between the down-to-earth Scouser and foppish Marc was one of these Momentous Encounters when, reported Bolan, "It's always the people I least expect to get close to that I end up friends with." Before Marc's magnificent certainty about everything he said and did grated, Ringo was presented with a splendid Les Paul electric guitar from one to whom he became "almost a father. He has been through it all before, and there's so much he has taught me."

As well as his unlikely counsellor snapping Bolan for the sleeve of T Rex's *The Slider* album, another concrete cause for gratitude emanated from Starr's desire to venture beyond merely acting in films, as "the easiest thing is being in them. It's harder when you start producing and getting them together." His first – and most abiding – essay as a director was to be *Born To Boogie*, a full-colour cinema picture about T Rex, financed by Apple. An artist of Marc Bolan's calibre deserved nothing less.

Its centrepiece was a T Rex bash on "the day pop came back", 18 March 1972, when tidal waves of screams hurled rampaging girls towards the stage at the Empire Pool, Wembley. There in 1966, with the cadence of the last number yet reverberating, Ringo had had to bolt pell-mell to a ticking limousine that fans, quick off the mark, had chased as far as Harrow Road. Six years on, he was in the orchestra pit presiding over operations, oblivious to the commotion. It must have been a strange sensation to be completely ignored by crazed females to whom he was just some bloke nearer than they were to darling Marc. Afterwards, the mêlée outside was so uncontrolled that a camera was demolished and one of the road crew had to heave Bolan bodily to a getaway car.

At least one lens had been focused constantly on the crowd during the show. In the cold light of a Twickenham Studios' cutting room, an intrigued Starr found that, rather than just screaming, "everyone in that audience was getting something different. That's why we used all those close-ups. There's one guy and his chick and they're just sitting very still watching it. Then there's the chicks who are going completely insane."

On further examination, "I wanted to do some more. You see, my theory about filming concerts is that you can't create the atmosphere that's in the hall. We got [Bolan] to write a few things and set up a couple more days' shooting." Set mostly at a small airfield and Tittenhurst Park – the Lennons' vacated 80-acre estate in Berkshire – the additional footage was reminiscent of *Magical Mystery Tour*, with contrasting scenes threaded together with a deadpan catchphrase – Ringo's suggestion – taken from Wanda Jackson's energetic 'Let's Have A Party' from 1958. Just as arbitrary was the random casting, which included Ringo himself (as the Dormouse to Bolan's Mad Hatter in one sequence), a bearded nun, a dwarf that gnaws offside mirrors from cars and Elton John, who, prior to his chart debut in 1971, had been Reg Dwight, pub pianist and jobbing tunesmith.

Ben Hur it wasn't, but Starr had cause to be elated by critical compliments – even back-handed ones, like the sniffy *Morning Star*'s "directed(?) by Ringo, this is the best teeny-bopper entertainment since The Beatles succumbed to insecticide". Yet, Ringo's passion for film direction cooled, not because of its creative labour but through the mind-stultifying legal and budgetary mechanics of post-production clearance and distribution. Like a gymkhana pony refusing a fence, he now balked at the project that he'd first put to Marc of a TV series documenting the day-to-day lives of famed personalities.

Always stimulated by the celebrity of others, Starr had banked on the co-operation of such as footballer George Best, Marc, Cilla and Elizabeth Taylor, for whose 40th birthday the Starkeys had jetted to Budapest – the location of her current movie, *Bluebeard* – to celebrate. As well as Liz's knees-up, vibrantly gregarious Ringo would be photographed sharing a joke with Barbra Streisand, Princess Grace of Monaco – you name 'em – at Cote D'Azur launches of new record companies, gala award ceremonies and on/off shindigs like David Bowie's lavish "retirement" do at the Café Royal in July 1973.

A soulmate – and drinking partner – during these roisterings was The Who's madcap drummer Keith Moon, Zak's hero and another *Born To Boogie* starlet. Starr tended to laugh at Moon's larks rather than be drawn into them. Although only a bit-part was provided for him in *That'll Be The Day* – a film in which Ringo had a major role – Keith made a disproportionate impression off the set by hiring a helicopter to touch down on the roof of the Isle of Wight hotel allocated to the cast so that he could emerge from this conveyance in full Red Baron flying rig. "It's the only way to travel, man."

Before the cameras, Ringo had been given *carte blanche* "to ramble on all I wanted, because people write lines for you that you'd never say. So I did my own dialogue. I love it when they let me go off on my own." This may invoke howls of derision, but I think that Ringo's second lead in this poignant evocation of provincial England in the late 1950s stands as his most powerful artistic statement. Through improvising around his own character and personal history, his role as Mike Menarry blew away like dust his previous and future efforts in records and films. Any argument that *A Hard Day's Night*, 'It Don't Come Easy' *et al* created the opportunity to do so is irrelevant.

The promotional spiel that it was "a strong dramatic part laced with humour" was justified. As Sinatra had begged for his Oscar-winning part in *From Here To Eternity*, because he "might have been" Joe di Maggio, so Ringo Starr *was* Mike Menarry – or, at least, aspects of him were. "My part as Mike is total flashback," he observed, "since he's very much me as I was in the late 1950s." A Liverpudlian Ted, Ringo/Mike dons "my own actual velvet-collared jacket. Everyone reeled back from the smell of mothballs when I put it on. I wear a pair of socks I used to wear in those days, too."

12 "I Can't Wait To Go, Half The Time"

Even with excellent notices for *That'll Be The Day*, Starr never got around to acting in another movie halfway as appealing, sticking instead to mainly minor roles that required little preparation. Furthermore, as well as his finding memorising lines and the demanding schedules with their early mornings onerous, "There's all the steps they have to take after you agree to do it. I have said yes to a few things, but they're still out there looking for the money I find it very hard to make the sort of commitment you need in movies. It's such a long-time situation."

Just prior to *That'll Be The Day*, Ringo's marking time between more challenging projects had been typified by his part in *200 Motels*, the only major film by Frank Zappa, leader of The Mothers Of Invention. As well as playing a character called "Larry the Dwarf", Ringo – in straggly black wig and dagger beard – doubled as an ill-at-ease Zappa, who composed songs around his recorded eavesdropping on the discord and intrigues that make pop groups what they are. As the fragile storyline was lost to in-jokes, cartoon sequences and Frank's ructions with his co-director, it hardly mattered that Ringo made no effort "to other be" as either Zappa or Larry. Too much for the common movie-goer, *200 Motels* faded swiftly from general circulation to be shown occasionally in film clubs and "alternative" cinemas, where it was watched by those who'd wished for time to stop in the late 1960s.

By 1973, whatever was left of hippy conviviality at Apple had contracted into a unity of darting suspicion when – uncool though it was – turgid examination of Allen Klein's handling of Messrs Harrison, Lennon and Starr's divergent affairs could not be postponed, especially with the expiry date of the contract approaching. The mustering of legal forces to compile evidence of an increasingly distant manager's transgressions was hindered by the counter-suing Klein, who, nonetheless, lost the case and Apple's complex finances were unfrozen. With its original ideal of bucking the bourgeois system long forgotten, "All Apple does is collecting," said Ringo. "We have no artists. We have nothing to push, but it looks after the films. It owns The Beatles' name, so, in fact, collects The Beatles' royalties." These would now pour along defined streams towards the deltas of each separate ex-Beatle's business executor – that is, John's Yoko, George's Denis O'Brien and Paul's Eastmans.

Ringo's counterpart was Hilary Gerrard, a former Apple executive who'd also act as personal retainer on the mighty rough road that lay ahead. To those outsiders who twigged that he was Ringo's manager and not merely some companion, Gerrard's name would for years be as synonymous with that of his flamboyant charge as Colonel Parker's with Elvis.

Missing the team activities and glamour of The Beatles, Gerrard's man was still making the most of his fresh lease of life since 'It Don't Come Easy' by seldom turning down a worthwhile opportunity to promote himself. After acting and directing, Starr had had a stab at producing, too, when it was agreed that he should be head of Apple Films, as he was the only ex-Beatle then to make strides in that direction. In this office, he completed *Son Of Dracula*, which he described as "like a non-musical, non-horror, non-comedy comedy," quipped Starr, "or it's a horror-horror, musical-musical, comedy-comedy."

Too early for the gothic craze that afflicted a faction among post-punk British adolescents, Ringo's effort was seen only in the States where it was relegated swiftly to "all the little villages because, if we put it on in a town, it got slated". The soundtrack, too, could not be rescued from deletion by wringing monetary drops from the presence within its grooves of Ringo, George Harrison and guitarist Peter Frampton from Humble Pie, whose album *Wind Of Change* – with Billy Preston and Starr on some tracks – was the small beginning to solo success in North America later in the decade.

Frampton and Starr had also been present on *Son Of Schmilsson* by Harry Nilsson, a pop star friend of Ringo's since 1968. This LP, like its bigger-selling predecessor, *Nilsson Schmilsson*, was overseen by Richard Perry, who had emerged as the most fashionable record producer of the mid-1970s. In truth, although grandiloquent in style, Perry was nowhere as inventive as George Martin or even Phil Spector, but he'd become sufficiently self-confident to offer Starr his console favours, if or when he was ready to commence another album.

When Ringo commissioned Perry to go ahead, the eponymous result was the artist's best-selling solo album. It also marked the closest that The Beatles would ever come to an artistic reunion before the 'Free As A Bird' single in 1995. On the five items that were dispatched during the initial studio sojourn, some were propelled by guitar sections too singular to have been played by anyone else but George Harrison. After John Lennon lent an ear to these, he was prompted to submit a song himself. 'I'm The Greatest' was made to measure for Starr, mentioning specifically his birthplace, his part in "the greatest show on Earth", his age and his "kids". 'I'm The Greatest' had been lacking only a middle eight, which Ringo, Lennon and Perry were puzzling out on the studio's concert grand when Harrison telephoned to invite himself along. "You could really tell that they were excited!" gushed Perry. "There was such a fantastic energy coming out of the room!! It was really sensational!!!"

Not sending him into quite the same verbal paroxysms as this coup were other instances of ex-Beatle creativity during the *Ringo* sessions, but these were enough to entitle Starr on a closing monologue that thanked everyone who'd taken part, to juxtapose the words "John", "Lennon", "Paul" and "McCartney", although neither had played on the same tracks. From England, Paul had sent a backing track for 'Six O'Clock' to be edited as necessary by Perry.

It could have been penned by McCartney in his sleep, but its intrinsic value mattered less than its use in a campaign that would colour *Ringo* as an ersatz Beatles collection, supplemented too by a *Sgt Pepper*-ish lithograph on its sleeve and the teasing insertion of the odd Lennon-McCartney song title into its lyrics. Whether they conjured up magic or mere music wasn't the issue; that the Fab Four were theoretically together on the same lump of plastic was sufficient to feed hope that soon everything would be OK again, just like it was before John went funny in 1968, and that The Beatles would regroup officially to tour and record the chart-toppers that John and Paul – all friends now – would be churning out once more.

In 1973, whether these four mortals as individuals sold records or not did not yet depend upon commercial viability. As Paul demonstrated, an ex-Beatle was guaranteed at least a minor hit, even with sub-standard produce. In the States, both he and George had clambered as far as Number One, and, after the climb of the *Ringo* spin-off, 'Photograph', up the same Hot 100 that autumn, Starr's turn came too.

Although 'Photograph' was half Harrison's, this single represented Starr's peak as a composer in hard financial terms, but just as savoury an ingredient in *Ringo* was his songwriting liaison with Vini Poncia, once mainstay of US one-hit-wonders The Trade Winds. Ranking, I suppose, as Perry's lieutenant, Poncia was fumbling one evening for a key to suit Starr's larynx for one number "and I had lots of bits of songs and I played some to him, and then he had a few bits and we found we could write together. That's how we got together, and we've been together ever since."

The first harvest of the Poncia-Starkey team reaped the catchy 'Oh My My', with a fake party atmosphere infectious enough to warrant its release as a US-only Ringo 45 and a hit to boot. So was "You're Sixteen" which, with 'Photograph' still in the Top Ten, likewise lasted seven days at Number One. While 'You're Sixteen' was not a Starkey original, only one other former Beatle – McCartney – had also hit that particular jackpot twice. To Lennon, who hadn't managed it at all, it appeared that the one least likely was "doing better than any of us". However, if signs were not yet perceptible, Ringo was about to fritter it away to all but the very dregs.

He'd anticipated the profits from *Ringo* and its offshoots by purchasing Tittenhurst Park within a fortnight of the Lennons putting it on the market in September 1973. A compromise between remote Elstead and metropolitan Highgate, this Tudor mansion and some of the outhouses were buildings of historical importance that he was obliged by law to maintain and to permit National Trust inspectors "reasonable access".

As the family settled into the new home, a strange question occurred to Maureen: would she lose the place if she and Richie split up? If in the midst of even more material comforts now, their partnership – of two old friends who used to be lovers – was not proportionally blissful.

A man suddenly preoccupied with success is likely to be an inattentive husband, but the road to the Starkeys' divorce could not be ascribed to such a tidy cause. Prior to *Ringo*, each had holidayed separately, with Ringo seizing the chance to get foxed without disgusted reprimands from her. Roaring drunk *en route* to the Bahamas, he and Marc Bolan had guffawed so hysterically and often at the in-flight comedy film that an irate fellow passenger batted their heads with his paperback and summoned the chief steward. The ensuing altercation had turned into a real-life farce.

Back at Tittenhurst Park, not so funny was George Harrison's after-dinner outburst before other guests that he was deeply in love with Mrs Starkey. Although Ringo's immediate reaction had been token anger, this tense evening had not concluded with any showdown, and he was astonished at how easily he could make light of it the next day and, worse, how slightly his pride smarted at the thought of Maureen reciprocating George's affection.

Any bad blood between Harrison and himself was soon diluted, and he'd always play on George's records whenever he was asked and was available – and vice-versa. However, George's pressured preparations for a US tour in 1974 meant that he wasn't able to pluck one note on Starr's *Goodnight Vienna*, the album calculated to snap at the heels of *Ringo*. Paul was fresh out of songs for Starr too.

The commercial inconvenience of George and Paul's desertions was cushioned by John, whose attendance on the *Goodnight Vienna* sessions in Los Angeles would be more insidious than it had been on Ringo. He had time to spare, because he'd left Yoko to hurl himself into a 15-month "lost weekend" in California in the company of Keith Moon and Harry Nilsson, hard drinkers each suffering from a premature male menopause, marital difficulties or both. With his own marriage floating into a choppy sea, Starr flopped onto the next stool for three-in-the-morning bar-hopping and late-afternoon mutual grogginess by the pool.

It wasn't uncommon for any one of them to stir with a hangover in a strange bed, unable to recollect the circumstances that led him there. If futile and public, their escapades were mostly harmless and stories of what they got up to have been improved with age. Revelling in his wickedness, Ringo was photographed with a cigarette inserted up his nose in Sunset Strip's Playboy Club, but that was nothing to his jumping three red traffic lights and a subsequent court order to attend a two-nights-a-week course on the US highway code. Then there was Lennon's ejection – with a sanitary towel fixed to his forehead – from west Los Angeles' Troubadour, where he and Nilsson had been heckling The Smothers Brothers. For John's birthday celebration, Ringo secured Cherry Vanilla – a singing actress much given to exposing her bust – to recite Shakespeare in her New York whine, while on 7 July 1974 Moon had splashed out on a skywritten "Happy Birthday, Ringo!" across Tinseltown's rind of smog. A more practical gift to the Starkeys was the $7,000 drum set Keith had no clear memory of buying a visiting Zak, for whom Moon was the god of percussion, "the very best in the world". If prompted, he'd concede, "My old man's a good timekeeper, but I've never thought of him as a great drummer."

The Grim Reaper was coming for Keith Moon, and many who knew "the Madman" – as best friend Starr knew him – were not entirely surprised at his body's final rebellion in 1978, after a lifetime of violation. Ringo didn't attend the funeral as "I totally believe your soul has gone by the time you get in the limo". Not as enigmatic as it might have been was his dejected aside, "I can't wait to go, half the time."

Mastering his inner chaos, albeit temporarily, Starr pulled back from the abyss. As the madness subsided, he'd realised, "I just got caught up in that strange belief that, if you're creative, you've got to be brain-damaged." Thus he attempted to steer through the recording of *Goodnight Vienna* using *Ringo* as his map. A spliced-up medley of Lennon's title song and its reprise was a minor US Top 40 entry as a single. An overhaul of the evergreen 'Only You' was less of a US hit, but a hit all the same. Wisely, he did not try to compete with the soaringly lovesick lead tenor on The Platters' original.

Instead, Ringo's inability to attack higher registers without sounding querulous was supposed to convey the impression that his devotion was too intense for satisfactory melodic articulation. It was a joke, all the same.

Highlights like 'Occapella' and 'Goodnight Vienna' itself balanced 'Call Me', 'Only You' and other *faux pas* on an album that was as likeable, after its fashion, as *Ringo*. Its crawl to a *Billboard* Number Eight, while abiding just a week in the UK Top 30, signified less a deterioration in quality than its dimmer "Beatle reunion" aura, plus a generally smaller quota of famous guests. Furthermore, Richard Perry's star was on the wane, as his much-touted 1974 LP for Martha Reeves – a former Tamla-Motown grande dame – failed to live up to market expectations.

Goodnight Vienna might have fared better if Starr had realised that a few half-page adverts in the music press and a round of interviews in the same were no longer sufficient to incite readers to consume his latest record. You had to howl it a bit louder in apocryphal 1974, when the "high-energy" entertainments of roving minstrels like Led Zeppelin, Peter Frampton and Grand Funk Railroad packed out US stadiums and European outdoor festivals. Despite its potential value in stabilising Starr's wobbling winning streak, "Touring right now is not my cup of tea. I just don't need it right now." After doing his minimal duty by the new album, he couldn't wait to "get back to the drinking and partying".

13 "Wherever I Go, It's A Swinging Place, Man"

After *Goodnight Vienna* and 'Only You' slipped from modest apogees in their respective charts, Ringo never had another solo hit in Britain. Any ex-Beatle's television slots were always special, but home viewers began to care less about them as personalities. More intriguing nowadays was the flowchart of titbits – true and untrue – that splattered vivid and often scandalous hues onto their private lives.

What was a minor sales territory like the United Kingdom to Ringo, now that Mammon had spirited him away to the New World? If on an irreversible slide elsewhere as a mere pop star, he was lionised almost as if he was an Artist in the States, with its "different atmosphere to anywhere else in the world. And I love television over there." His sojourn in Santa Monica had caked his speech with words like "gotten", "sidewalk", "candy" (for "sweets"), "pants" (for "trousers") and "elevator", and it became his habit to celebrate Thanksgiving – for the secession of the American colonies from his native land.

US tax laws were slightly less harsh than Britain's, but more of a magnet for Starr was its scope for playing the field. To one of many "friends" who sold his story to the paparazzi, Ringo "had been labelled for so long the least significant member of The Beatles that he was desperate to assert himself, if only by pulling beautiful girls". His infidelities in California climaxed when a romance with Nancy Andrews – a Hollywood maid-of-all-work – took a serious turn. Since graduating, she'd travailed on the periphery of showbusiness as a model, publicity agent and pursuant of other occupations that relied similarly on keeping up appearances and creating a favourable impression.

She would put her talents – some of them previously unrealised – at Ringo's disposal during her six years, on and off, as his "constant companion". Whilst proving no stranger to many of the commercial and economic machinations of his calling, Nancy's photographs were published on his album sleeves and press hand-outs, and the Andrews-Starr composition 'Las Brisas' was recorded on *Ringo's Rotogravure*, the album that appeared after *Goodnight Vienna*.

Maureen may have feigned aloofness to retain composure, but her frank nature could not allow her to stay silent about stray mutterings that she'd read in gossip columns. Recalling his cheery promiscuity as a London bachelor in 1963, she wasn't so naïve to presume that her "sodding great Andy Capp" of a husband hadn't been tempted into a fling or two while in another hemisphere for all those months. More quizzical than angry, the eclipsed Mo implored him to help her grasp what it all meant, so he "gave me the names of two or three solicitors". He'd admit adultery, and she could name Nancy as co-respondent if she so wished.

With pale, drawn cheeks and clasped hands, Maureen gave evidence on a comfortless summer morning in the London Divorce Court. The outcome was that she would not have face the prospect of earning a crust again, as long as she wasn't too frivolous with a generous award of a yearly lump sum, with increments and a side-serving of assorted sinecures and life policies. On top was Starr's continued support of her parents and Maureen's custody of the children, who would move to the mansion he'd bought her in London's Little Venice, overlooking the canal.

For a while, Ringo was unable to fully exercise his right of access *"pour des raisons fiscales"*, as *Paris-Match* had it, which permitted tax exiles only 90 days per annum in the United Kingdom. However, it was the loosening of family ties as much as his desire to shield those monies not annexed by Maureen that unleashed the gypsy in Ringo's soul, and he "went wandering". With Nancy, he roamed the Côte D'Azur and around Los Angeles from hotel to rootless hotel, where he'd be conducted to the best seat in the restaurant and the switchboard or room service would relay complimentary tickets and social invitations, offering flattery without friendship to one whose every workshy action was worth half a page in *The Sun* or *The Los Angeles Times*.

"You wonder about getting up," he sighed, "and there is nothing special to do, so you delay it. Finally, you do get out of bed, and you just try to fill the day." Fleeing from boredom, if he wasn't on an aeroplane he'd be in the departure lounge waiting for the next one. With the ease of a daily commuter on the 8.23 to Waterloo, he'd jet from Monaco to Amsterdam for dinner with Rod Steiger; from Amsterdam to Johannesburg to watch some tennis match; from Johannesburg to New York just to buy shoes from Ebony; from New York to Las Vegas for a calamitous evening of blackjack or roulette; from Vegas to London for Wimbledon's tennis and from Heathrow back to Monaco for some rich gadfly's wedding. There he'd queue for the buffet with such as Rudolf Nureyev, Christina Onassis and the principality's own Princess Caroline. When he described himself as "a jet-setter – wherever I go, it's a swinging place, man", it was a statement rather than a boast.

The most swinging place of all was Monte Carlo. With London less than two hours along the air corridor, he began to regard the resort as a base when, putting a brake on a life of suitcases, he purchased a penthouse suite. A pampered but empty semi-retirement led him to sometimes shun the sun, the beautiful people and evening meals in restaurants frequented by expatriate gentlefolk nearing middle age. Instead, he'd have a quiet night in, wallowing in episode after episode of *Coronation Street* and other videoed and soapy links with all that he'd left behind.

Bathed in tedium, he might put down his schooner of white wine, apple cider or brandy – depending on the hour – to mess about on piano or guitar and maybe sort out a chanson for the next album. More often than not, days would trudge by without a glimmer of a tune or lyric, or else everything that he attempted would sound the same. Nancy would think so, too, and intimate that a change of scene might make a world of difference – or half a world, anyway, if it took her to his bungalow, rented from Nilsson, high in the hills above Los Angeles. At an address that included the rather iconoclastic street name Haslem Terrace, Richie and Nancy would extend a gladder welcome to callers whose drawling ebullience was more comfortable than the stilted "Franglais" of the Monaco socialites they hardly knew.

Although the Starkey children would spend school holidays there, it was also open house for "all the old faces. Once the bars close, they'll all drive up here," to be greeted with Starr's expansive "'Hi, man! Yeah, come on in!' If I'm really wrecked, I say, 'You know where everything is. I'm off.' You can actually leave your guests and they don't mind if you're there or not. So that's LA for you. It is a great town, because of the passing strangers." In a playroom, their host had assembled a drum kit for anyone who fancied flailing around.

He would have no need ever again to rattle the traps – or sing, for that matter – because, by 1976, his nine-year EMI/Capitol contract would have run its course. The easiest option was to do as Lennon would and take "a year off, with no obligations to anybody. He's his own man for twelve months, and he's never been that." Nevertheless, the company submitted to Ringo – via Hilary Gerrard – a tantalising bid for Starr to re-sign, as he was still hottish property in the States, even if only as good as his latest record elsewhere.

In 1976, he was teetered on the edge of the *Billboard* Top 30 with 'A Dose Of Rock 'n' Roll', harbinger of his new album *Ringo's Rotogravure*, having pledged himself not to EMI/Capitol but Atlantic Records in the USA, and Polydor for the rest of the world. As its snatch of The Rolling Stones when they fled Decca in 1971 attested, Atlantic – and its Stax subsidiary – had long been a receptacle, as Ringo knew well, for "a lot of good acts", from The Coasters and The Drifters back in the 1950s to a bevy of chart-busting black soul singers, among them Wilson Pickett, with whom Starr had a fast friendship.

Starr's new label was a little nonplussed by statements from him like "I never work on anything. Dedication is such a weird word, after Albert Schweitzer and people like that. No one dedicates themselves to anything now." Tony Barrow, once a NEMS publicist but now working for Polydor, would complain, "Ringo just seemed content to let the producer lay down some backing tracks for him and then he would pop in from Monte Carlo and just stick on his vocals."

He liked "a party atmosphere if we're working well. We all sit around and drink and really have a good time." There might, therefore, have been plenty of scope for squiffy errors within the small army of famous friends that had rallied around to – hopefully – recreate that *Ringo* miracle, for "there isn't a player I know or have heard of who I don't feel I could call and they'd come and play for me".

Like Eric Clapton, John Lennon flew to California to join in the fun. His self-satisfied donation, 'Cookin' (In The Kitchen Of Love)', was premonitory, as he was to extend considerably his "year off". Indeed, not a note would be heard commercially from John for the next four years.

That all of the album's single A-sides were "foreign" tracks confirmed much of Tony Barrow's assessment of Starr, as well as the present aridity of the ex-Beatle's songwriting well. As always, the record industry was voracious for new faces to exploit and discard for a fickle public, and the danger of Ringo being left behind in this soul-rotting race was perceptible even in the States, now, where *Rotogravure* clawed to Number 28, a true comedown by previous standards.

To achieve even this, he had hired Los Angeles publicity firm Brains Unlimited to organise his most intense media expedition since The Beatles, covering the USA, Japan and Europe. Patiently sipping Mumm Cordon Rouge – he knew better than to mix drinks – Ringo would give unblinking copy, but his handlers would exchange frequent fretful glances at his commendably frank appraisal of his singing ("the range of a fly, but a large fly") and how he approached it ("you try it drunk, you go back sober and do it for real – some takes you use when you're drunk"). Mention at the Paris stop of Cliff Richard's contemporaneous LP, *I'm Nearly Famous*, drew the self-denigrating remark, "I used to be."

14 "If I Don't Get You, The Next One Will"

Glam-rock latecomers Queen began 1976 with 'Bohemian Rhapsody' at a domestic Number One and EMI International's dazzling party in their honour at London's Cunard Hotel. Petals from the very flower of UK pop in the 1970s were there – David Bowie, Rod Stewart, Bryan Ferry – sipping posed cocktails that looked like melted crayons, when a buzz filtered through the 300-odd guests that Ringo Starr had arrived. This wasn't television or a picture in the newspaper; that impossible yardstick of teenage escapism and aspiration – a Beatle – was actually within, asserting his old power in abundance in his involuntary lure for the younger conquistadors and their acolytes who buzzed around him like bees around a jam jar.

Ignored at his side was Lynsey de Paul, to whom he had given a fishing rod, because she was always angling for compliments. Some of these were deserved, for, although her five-year chart run was about to end with a *British Song For Europe* entry, singing in public was secondary to Lynsey's songwriting skills. 1972 had been her red-letter year, with a Top Five debut ('Sugar Me') and The Fortunes showing class in the US Hot 100 with her 'Storm In A Teacup'.

Her confidence boosted by this syndication, Lynsey crossed to Los Angeles to better ply her wares before more prestigious customers than this lucky Birmingham combo. A tangent of this expedition was her romance with actor James Coburn, and it was on her return to London after breaking with him that she embarked on a more light-hearted affair with Ringo, but when Starr's 90 days in the UK were up, so, more or less, was their amour, Lynsey penning 'If I Don't Get You (The Next One Will)' as its requiem.

Over in California, Nancy Andrews might have supposed that the main purpose of her fiancé's 90 days a year in England was to make a fuss of his children. She was, therefore, taken aback by reports of his supposed satyric exploits in UK tabloids and reported airy comments such as "there are girls in my life because I still have all the normal urges". Nevertheless, although there were frank exchanges in their Los Angeles bungalow, she held onto the belief that her ex-Beatle was worth keeping and that his intentions remained honourable. She tried, therefore, not to hear any more of his other attachments and clung onto her dignity as his official lover by devoting herself, as always, to the enhancement of his neglected career.

It may have pleased her to think that it was the ante-start agonies of the sensitive artist that impeded his knuckling down to another album. He seemed to be holding it at arm's length by accepting more record dates for friends: nothing too strenuous – "a couple of days, only three or four tracks, because I don't want to get stuck in to do the whole album, because I don't even want to do my own album."

When he got round to it, *Ringo The Fourth* fared worse than even *Beaucoups Of Blues*. Significantly, this was also his first effort since the sundering of The Beatles that was bereft of any aid from John, Paul or George – although, even without this omission, I doubt very much that *Ringo The Fourth* could have risen much higher than its dismal Number 162 in the States.

Artistically, however, *Ringo The Fourth* was Starr's most courageous musical statement, in the sense that the bulk of its ten tracks were from the Starkey-Poncia songbook. However, other than 'Gypsies In Flight' as the country-and-western weepie, most were gorged with an over-generous helping of a moderato soul style – smoother than Stax or Motown – that was then just ceasing to waft from trend-setting Philadelphia.

Yet, however much he attempted to hack it as a fervid blue-eyed soulman without affectation, Ringo was no Cliff Bennett or Steve Winwood. Although he tried hard, the voice was raucous rather than passionate when he extemporised. While it might have been enchantingly ludicrous for, say,

111

Sentimental Journey, Ringo's ingrained Scouse pronunciation – "I love you so mooch", "our uffur [affair] is over" – was often just ludicrous on *Ringo The Fourth*.

More than anyone, his mother understood, nonetheless, that "he doesn't want to be thought of as a clown anymore. He's more serious than most people realise, and he can be forceful when he needs to be. More than anything, he wants to become successful as an actor." Yet the route to any role as strong as that of Mike Menarry was fraught with potholes such as the *New Musical Express*'s not entirely justified jibe that, other than his records, Starr had spent most of the years since 1970 in "duff movies and heavy-duty ligging".

He couldn't resist the proverbial "something to tell his grandchildren about" of a not especially ample part in ageing sexpot Mae West's final movie, *Sextette*, no matter how disappointing the reviews that caused its fade with indecent haste from general circulation.

More certain an indicator of future direction for Ringo than *Sextette* was his effortless lead in *Scouse The Mouse*, a concept album of a children's story by distinguished old stager Donald Pleasence, under the musical direction of Roger Brown. As a poor consolation to Starr's UK following, chagrined at so much US-only product, its soon-deleted affiliated album was exclusive to Britain and the Commonwealth. Within Ringo's lion's share of eight numbers, 'Scouse's Dream', 'I Know A Place' (a duet with Polly Pleasence) and the hootenanny 'Running Free' stuck out, but the ace in the pack – although it's not saying much – was the nautical lament, 'SOS'. Far less objectionable than *Ringo The Fourth*, this album for infants was a suitable vehicle for Starr's unforced urbanity, always a handy resort when the going got rough, which it would with growing frequency.

Adapted from 'A Mouse Like Me', the *Scouse The Mouse* finale, 'A Man Like Me' concluded *Bad Boy*, Starr's seventh solo LP. As he couldn't get a hit to save his life now, Atlantic had let him go to Portrait, a CBS tributary. It was, therefore, a matter of pride for Ringo and Portrait to ensure that *Bad Boy* left more of a wound in the US charts than *Ringo The Fourth* had.

Bad Boy certainly clambered fractionally higher in *Billboard*'s tabulation than its predecessor, thanks largely to a leg-up from a US television special, chat-show spots and – for the inventive Beatle rumour-monger – the enigmatic and pseudonymous listing of auxiliary musicians on its sleeve. Balancing these manoeuvres were the paucity of critics who went ape over *Bad Boy* and, crucially, that mighty watchdog of pop propriety *Rolling Stone*, kicking Starr when he was down with "not even passable cocktail music. Ringo isn't likeable any more, and that truly is depressing."

A sense of simply going through the motions once more was evident in Ringo's strained and often uninvolved singing on merely workmanlike overhauls of such as Manhattan Transfer-via-The Supremes' 'Where Did Our Love Go?' and the 1957 title track by The Jive Bombers, covered lately by

both Mink De Ville and Sha Na Na. Now that he was free
from the constraints of sustaining a chain of chart entries,
Ringo would be sating himself with many more too-
premeditated reconstructions of the ancient hits of others
after *Bad Boy*. Although he'd never succumb to drum
machines, with their robotic exactitudes, the latest studio
gimmick would intrude upon guts and – especially if the
original versions of the likes of 'Where Did Our Love Go?'
had emotional significance for the listener – leave an
odd aftertaste.

So, too, would *Ringo* , the TV tie-in, which was a vehicle
for him to mime to pre-recordings of his best-loved songs
with and without The Beatles and – implying by association
that they were just as eternal – excerpts from *Bad Boy*. These
were hung on an approximation of Mark Twain's *The Prince
And The Pauper*. Set in Hollywood rather than Tudor London,
it begins with George Harrison's cameo explanation about
two identical babies born at the same moment. One grows
up as Ringo Starr, idol of a world shortly to watch him
perform in a satellite-linked concert. He swaps places with
his *doppelgänger*, "Ognir Rats" (get it?), a pitiable sandwich-
boarded pedlar of sightseers' maps of Beverly Hills. Seen
along the way as both changelings get into various scrapes
are such as Vincent Price, Angie Dickinson and *Star Wars*'
Carrie Fisher (as Ognir's girlfriend). Nonetheless – you
guessed it – all ends well in the nick of time, with Rats taken
on as highly waged road manager to the proper Ringo, who

wows 'em – as evidenced by heavily overdubbed screams – in the bounced broadcast.

Despite this element of wishful thinking, *Ringo* was a splendid if dear means of publicising *Bad Boy* and Starr's back-catalogue, and – with Ringo playing both himself and Rats – as an elaborate general audition for any suitable film roles going, because "no one is going to offer Ringo Starr a top role these days just because I used to be in The Beatles. I've got to be able to do the job. That's much more demanding, but much better, too. I could end up with egg on my face but, succeed or fail, it's all down to me standing on my own two feet as an actor." It could have been *Ringo* that brought him his first solo top billing in a family movie in preparation since 1977 called *Caveman*. "When you need a small, suave, funny, awkward, unprepossessing leading man," elucidated its director, Carl Gottlieb, "there aren't a lot to choose from: Dustin Hoffman, Dudley Moore, Robin Williams – and who else is there who's also a star? There's Ringo."

Quietly confident, he was preparing for the part when, as it had been when he was six, "Everything twisted up inside me." Rushed to a Monte Carlo hospital, he underwent laser surgery to remove five feet of blocked intestine. However, though he'd told the convalescing Ringo that "another minute or two and it would have been curtains", a surgeon was able to inform a press corps itching to relay obituaries that the patient was "a courageous man and responded well to treatment. A lot of sick people tend to be miserable after an operation, but Mr Starkey was very cheerful and able to swap jokes and banter with the nurses. The doctors are very pleased, but work is out of the question for the time being."

Although still green about the gills, Ringo was sufficiently recovered to pass a medical examination for the insurers of the postponed *Caveman*. The initial shoot was scheduled for February 1980 in the rocky sierra surrounding Puerta Vallarta, near Durango. He was to play "Atouk", chief of a rebel tribe, in this prehistoric comedy with no highbrow pretensions. Neither were there qualms about authenticity as Atouk tames dinosaurs who were extinct aeons before humankind commenced its deplorable sovereignty of the planet. While *Caveman* swiped gently at 1966's *One Million Years BC* in the Raquel Welch coquettishness of shapely Barbara Bach (as "Lana"), it was closer in spirit to earlier stabs by Buster Keaton, Charlie Chaplin and Laurel and Hardy at the Neanderthal sub-genre of film in its slapstick simplicity and jokes about dung. Apart from a 15-word language created by the community's Chinese wise man (ca-ca for "excrement", zug-zug for "copulation" – you get the drift?), the dialogue consisted mostly of grunts and moans accompanied by much gesticulation, body talk and face-pulling. It definitely beat having to learn lines. As a sop for Beatle freaks, the tale begins in one zillion BC on 9 October, John Lennon's birthday.

For the first few reels, Ringo appeared in the same guise he had striven to hurl aside since *Help!*, as a Chaplin-esque underdog, but he was in no mood to care about that. In his eagerness, he'd have cheerfully dusted off his *A Hard Day's Night* character. *The Washington Post* might have turned its nose up with "going 'round pointing and saying 'ca-ca' is not what one would have expected from a legendary Beatle", but to sweeter-natured reviewers he was "better here than he's been in anything since The Beatles' films", "a delight" and – possibly a double-edged accolade – "as puppy-dog charming as ever".

With all of the attributes of a box-office smash but none that actually grabbed the public, *Caveman* was soon booming out in half-empty Midwestern drive-ins, and on its second night in London's West End it drew all of six customers in one cinema. Some even stuck it out to the National Anthem.

However its shortcomings affected Starr professionally, his participation in *Caveman* was also one of far-reaching private import – at least, as private as one whose every waking hour was chronicled was allowed. Tongues wagged about Ringo and leading lady Shelley Long in the teeth of his stock assurance that they were "very good friends but that's as far as it goes", but of infinitely more substance were rumours about him and Barbara Bach, which provoked "confirmed reports" that they were to wed as soon as her divorce to Italian industrialist Augusto Gregorini was finalised. There was no reason not to believe that this "B-Movie Queen Might Turn A Beatle Into Prince Charming", as, holding hands, they seemed never to be off US television throughout the spring of 1981 while plugging *Caveman*.

"It wasn't love at first sight," reflected Barbara; "it began to grow within days of meeting each other." In Durango, she'd been touched when he chose to sport with local children between takes, and he'd admired her stoicism as she was hurled time and again into the Maguey River when one scene had to be re-shot until Gottlieb was satisfied.

Underneath a brash outer shell, Ringo came across as "so interesting, a very nice guy". His wooing of her was consummated "when Ringo invited me to his home in Monte Carlo to watch the Monaco Grand Prix. I didn't hesitate [for] a second. It seemed totally natural." On his part, Starr was as besotted as a middle-aged man could be with a stunning starlet eleven years his junior: "I haven't been this happy in years. I'm ecstatic."

All of this was mortifying for Barbara's boyfriend, cinematographer Roberto Quezada, who gallantly withdrew. Nancy Andrews, however, was not prepared to be so acquiescent. Via the US legal system, Richie would pay. Although his alien status was among pleas for the quashing of her case against him (a kind of updated breach of promise), a precedent had been set by showbusiness attorney Marvin Mitchelson, whose eloquence had established the right in California for unmarried partners to sue for property division. Securing Mitchelson to speak for her, Nancy sought "palimony" of several million. Nonetheless, bar the shouting, she was reduced to just a memory in Ringo's mind, as he only had eyes for his new love, now.

15 "I Knew I'd Had This Problem For Years"

Although films seemed a rosier basis for optimism nowadays, "I do want to make one rock 'n' roll album a year," insisted Ringo, "Once a rock 'n' roller, always a rock 'n' roller."

If 1978's *Bad Boy* was classified thus, Ringo was rather behind schedule when, on 15 September 1980, he spent Thanksgiving with the Lennons in New York's Plaza and picked John's brains for feasible numbers for a new LP because "he knows me better than anybody else in the world, better than the other two, so he really becomes involved – playing, singing, doing everything he can".

As well as tossing his former drummer demos of four new songs, and promising to be there when recording began in January, John sounded out Ringo about Portrait's efficiency as distributors, as he himself was now making records again. Starr seemed rather disgruntled with Portrait then. With *Bad Boy* a disheartening speculation, the label had insinuated

119

that he'd be better off with someone else. Furious, too, that CBS had denied him both adequate funding and use of the company jet for promotion of the record, Ringo had been hawking his talents around other labels before coming to roost on Boardwalk in the States and RCA for other territories. His maiden album under the new regime would bear the title *Stop And Smell The Roses*, having exhausted several others such as *Stop!*, *Ringostein*, *Can't Fight Lightning* and *Private Property*. The latter was also the name of one of two McCartney contributions, as Ringo had fallen back on his "famous-cast-of-thousands" approach.

Paul also produced 'Can't Fight Lightning' – left off the album in the eleventh hour – and a countrified Starr treatment of Carl Perkins's 'Sure To Fall'. He was also loud and clear, now, in the vocal unison sections – and in his backchat with double-tracked Ringo over a steel-guitar solo.

The album would touch on Western swing, too, in George Harrison's supervision in Paris of a vicariously delightful version of Jo Stafford's 'You Belong To Me', a 1952 million-seller that Starr sang more or less straight. He also made a credible job of George's solemn gambol 'Wrack My Brain', deservedly the LP's only single. Another Harrison piece for *Stop And Smell The Roses* had been 'All Those Years Ago', but Starr couldn't pitch its higher notes. When a hit 45 for George in 1981, it had been re-invented as a requiem to John Lennon, who hadn't been able to manage the subsequently cancelled January sessions after all.

"John who?" Pete Best had spluttered from his shaving mirror when his wife had shouted the news from the wireless that creepy December morning on Merseyside. Meanwhile, the drummer that Lennon had rescued from having to get up to go to work was far from Liverpool when he was told. He knew which John had just been gunned down on a New York pavement by a former hospital security guard – henceforth referred to by Ringo as "the arsehole" – who was mad about The Beatles in the most clinical sense.

On the Sunday after the shooting, Ringo, George and Paul behaved much the same as any outsider who kept, at Yoko's request, the worldwide ten-minute silence for her husband. Ringo "just stayed at home and I thought, 'John's dead.' That was probably the best way to pay my respects: by keeping quiet." To this day, he has forbidden himself to record the songs that Lennon had given him at the Plaza and from any media comment far beyond suppositions as uninformative of deeper feelings as any in the rash of "tribute" discs that were being composed while the corpse was still warm. According to Starr, Lennon had transcended to some meritocratic pop heaven "up there with Jimi Hendrix and Elvis and all the rest of them". For years, eyes would stretch when he began interviews by addressing an unseen Lennon, before assuring others present that "he's watching over us, you know".

Without premeditation, Starr's own death had already come close at dusk one spring evening in 1980 when he and

Barbara were motoring to a Surrey party. At 60 miles an hour, Ringo swerved to avoid a collision with a lorry on a bypass made slippery by a downpour. After ramming two lamp-posts while riding out a somersaulting skid, he ignored a leg injury and pulled his passenger clear before calmly limping back to the upside-down Mercedes for his cigarettes. As he tended to a shaken Barbara, curtains were drawn back in nearby windows and someone dialled for the police and an ambulance. His "We had a crash; it's cool" was the most-quoted remark, after he and Barbara were taken to hospital where they were discharged before the rest of the world woke up. Their resolve to stay together had hardened *en route* to the casualty ward and, three weeks later, Barbara announced to her father that she intended to marry the boy.

They plighted their troth at Marylebone Registry Office on 27 April 1981. The ceremony itself was less interesting to *The Daily Express* than "The Reunion" that it splashed across its front page the next day. The three surviving Beatles had been photographed together in public for the first time since John's passing. The second set of faces that drew the viewer were those of their North American wives, especially the new Mrs Starkey, who, mixing metaphors, "had always believed in Prince Charming if ever he came riding up on his charger".

The happy couple left in a white Rolls for a decoy honeymoon "in California". Actually, it was spent in London, the last place any prying reporter would expect to find them.

Ringo's first "American period" had terminated effectively with Lennon's murder. For several years, there'd be but flying visits on business, for TV promotions and social duties such as a pal's New York wedding in 1962. With an attempt on President Reagan's life by another "arsehole" that year, "What chance do other people have? I always loved living in England."

He would regain little lost native popularity and he'd miss the Californian sunshine, but the weeks arranging the wedding had made him understand how homesick he'd become during his six years of globe-trotting. Back at Tittenhurst Park, the fellow was never seen to do a stroke of work. As in the "happy ending" of a Victorian novel with all the villains bested and the inheritance claimed, he'd settled down to a prosperous lassitude in which nothing much was guaranteed to happen, year in, year out.

As an artiste, his wilderness years were by no means over, but *Stop And Smell The Roses* had sidled to the outskirts of the US Hot 100 on the back of 'Wrack My Brain' – his first Top 40 entry since 1976 – and the associated aftershock of Lennon, despite one influential North American journal voting *Stop And Smell The Roses* the "worst record of 1981".

Apart from a short article about Ringo's return to recording in the *NME*, his album was all but ignored in Britain. Not reaching a particularly wide audience, either, were its promotional films, *Wrack My Brain* and *The Cooler*, a musical psycho-drama that was screened in the Short Subject category of 1982's Cannes Festival.

Wrack My Brain was shown and the LP plugged on some of the US television chat-shows that Starr's handlers had been able to negotiate in spite of his "taking less and less interest in recording or promoting them". Worse, on *The John Davidson Show*, it was clear that he'd had too much to drink beforehand as he repeated his perplexed and then outraged host's questions as well as his own answers and fiddled around with a Polaroid on his lap. Starr's usual mannerisms were exaggerated as he raised his voice almost to a shout and then dropped it to near inaudibility. It was necessary to splice together two segments of the pre-recorded programme as Davidson stormed off and, recalled a contrite Ringo, "They had to convince him to come back – but I was in the dressing room, having a few more cognacs."

To Tony Barrow, Starr's alcoholism – once a private matter – had intensified because he felt himself to be "a second-class Beatle". Whatever the cause, he confessed, "I knew I'd had this problem for years". Soon, he would be resigned to a self-imposed house arrest, as going anywhere else "meant I'd have to be in the car for 40 minutes without being able to have a single drink".

Ringo made no long-term plans. From Nilsson to Elizabeth Taylor – pictured portly and plastered on the cover of Kenneth Anger's *Hollywood Babylon* exposé – Ringo kept the company of only those united by a taste for liquor. "If you were straight, I wouldn't have you in my house."

16 "Please, God, I Have To Stop Living This Way"

After Zak – now a professional drummer – married in 1985, Ringo became the first Beatle grandfather after daughter-in-law Sarah gave birth to Tatia Jayne in Ascot's Heatherwood Hospital, near enough for twice-daily visits by one whom the baby would be taught to call "Grandad".

Of all his children, the most wayward journey to adulthood was endured by Jason, who rounded it off by falling foul of the law for possessing cannabis. If Ringo dared lecture his second son on any aspect of this misdemeanour, apart from the stupidity of getting caught, he had as brittle a leg to stand on as his boozing was getting out of control, and the only ace up his sleeve was his narration for US radio of a heroin caution for "today's kids", which excused his past psychedelic escapades with "but that was then" and invoked 'Yellow Submarine', 'Blue Meanies' ("more of them than ever before") and Lennon, who'd known the drug well.

His views on the subject were further clarified when he gave John Cleese, Bill Oddie and Michael Palin – radical balusters of British comedy – percussive assistance and the run of his home studio to produce the satirical 'Naughty Atom Bomb' for the *It's A Live-In World* LP, which – with such as Paul McCartney, Paul's cousin Kate Robbins, The Thompson Twins and Zak lending a hand, too – would benefit London's Phoenix House drug rehabilitation centre.

From the starting line of *The Concerts For Bangla Desh*, pop by the 1980s pop had cranked into top gear while hurtling along the road to respectability and, after Live Aid gained The Boomtown Rats' Bob Geldof a knighthood, Ringo – who'd received an MBE for less – was seen, like everyone else of late, to be involved in quite a few good causes. These ranged from passive attendance at a Fashion Aid event at the Albert Hall to tagging onto a queue of the famous at London's Sarm Studio, where he sang one line over a craftily sampled backing collage of jungle noises in one of the more scintillating charity singles of the 1980s, 'Spirit Of The Rain Forest', proceeds of which went towards protecting the forests.

Closer to home, he dipped into his purse and, with Cilla Black, recorded a comforting message on *The Sun*'s prompt emergency hotline "to help those families try to rebuild their lives" after the Hillsborough stadium disaster in which soccer fans were crushed to death during a Liverpool XI away-match.

It was Cilla who tipped off a "very angry" Ringo when their names – and photographic images – were taken in vain in an ingenious advertising campaign by Security Omega Express, the crux of which was the correlation between success and Richard Starkey, Priscilla White and other entertainers' rechristenings. "He personally and The Beatles," gritted a Starr aide, "are always getting ripped off."

Sometimes it appeared that the ex-Beatles were being cheated by each other, too, during the perpetual unscrambling of Apple lucre. This was demonstrated by Starr and Harrison's – and Mrs Lennon's – lawsuit against McCartney over a deal whereby the last six albums he'd delivered to Capitol had rewarded him with what was interpreted as an increased royalty increment for Beatles output.

As George and Ringo were each sorrowfully aware, it was no longer so easy for new albums by old heroes to be passed without comment by record-label quality controllers. Neither ex-Beatle was sufficiently "current" in either output or "attitude" for this to happen, and Ringo was even expressing doubts about the advent of compact discs, which were "a bit too clean for me. I'm from the old school. I like a bit of dirt on the record."

George had employed a drum machine to toughen his 1982 album *Gone Troppo*, but at heart he too was "from the old school", so much so that, sickened, he told the whole fair-weather music business to get knotted by announcing – wrongly, as it happened – that *Gone Troppo* was to be his vinyl farewell. Ringo, however, was not prepared to make such unrepining calculations.

Into the bargain, Boardwalk harkened to Joe Walsh of The Eagles' hunch that Ringo still had "a good rock 'n' roll album in him". Brought in to draw it out of him, Walsh "beefed up" an album Starr was taping at Startling Studios with his over-amplified guitar clichés, developing likely fragments of song computed in Ringo's's oft-sozzled mind and persuading him to invest in harder drumheads, which certainly lent the kit a tarter drive – but, with the project's very title – *Old Wave* – indicating how seemingly out of touch Starr was, Boardwalk might have feared a tarring with the same brush.

Boardwalk's dumping of Ringo Starr – the only ex-Beatle to be thus cast adrift – was an extremity that was validated when he was then unable to kindle any worthwhile interest in *Old Wave* from any other British or US companies, who all seemed to have too vivid a recollection of the unfavourable reaction to *Stop And Smell The Roses*. He was, therefore, at more of a loose end than usual when his name cropped up as Paul McCartney planned *Give My Regards To Broad Street*, his first feature-length film since *Let It Be*.

A romantic undercurrent of this much-criticised and egocentric caper was Ringo – drummer in Paul's band – and "this gorgeous girl reporter from a music paper" (Barbara) who "get friendlier and friendlier as the movie progresses. Falling in love with your own wife isn't as easy as it looks." Although (or because) it was "more like family than work", Ringo insisted on pauses, however inconvenient, so that he wouldn't miss the goings-on in *Coronation Street*. He was also pernickety about what songs he'd drum on when Paul got to grips with the soundtrack, with a large helping of refashioned Beatles items, on which Starr would not let himself be accommodated.

He wasn't averse, however, to revisiting his Beatles past onstage. With a renewed if fleeting taste for the roar of the crowd, George Harrison had plunged into the limelight before 12,000 for each of two evenings at Wembley Arena in a two night package show for one of Prince Charles' charities. For many, Elton John's proclamation that Harrison "and Ringo Starr!" were about to play a short set rode roughshod over Level 42, Go West and all the rest of the synchronised frenzy that had gone before.

Although he merely backed George's nervous 'While My Guitar Gently Weeps' and was thwacking indistinguishably between Phil Collins and Big Country's drummer during the finale on the first night, Ringo brought the house down the next evening when, stepping down from his rostrum, he clasped the central microphone to trigger the audience and assembled cast's responses and choruses as, with voice in finer – and deeper – fettle than imagined, he prodded the right festive nerve with a rough-and-ready 'With A Little Help From My Friends', going the distance with workmanlike pitching shorn of any sticky extemporisation. To the relief of those wincing as the coda's perilous high C – "friiieeends" – approached, he was steered out of danger by both the

participatory unison and an almost palpable wave of goodwill
that continued to wash over him on the play-out when he
rattled a tambourine while shuffling off with a jaw-dropping
flicker of Billy Preston-like dancing. At 47, who'd have
thought that the old boy still had it in him?

No US or British record company did, but Hilary
Gerrard's dogged country-by-country pursuit of contracts
yielded pressings of *Old Wave* in Canada, Brazil and – most
lucrative of all – West Germany, where its wing of Boardwalk
was sufficiently enthused to risk a promotional 45 with 'In
My Car', though more effective was a competent if pointless
copy – bar contrived Dixieland interludes – of The Sir Douglas
Quintet's wondrously dim 'She's About A Mover'. 'Picture
Show Life' – describing flashes of Hollywood demi-monde
– was, nevertheless, the album's strongest opus, although
against the challengers that's no great accolade.

Ringo himself vetoed the release of a follow-up to *Old
Wave* that had been born of a Christmas holiday in the
Bahamas, where he bumped into "Chips" Moman, a
proficient rather than brilliant US producer with a fast mouth.
For Starr, a point in Moman's favour was his reputation for
reactivating waning stars such as Tommy Roe, Paul Revere
And The Raiders and The Boxtops.

Theoretically, he was just what Ringo needed and, after
initial misgivings "because we didn't understand each other's
accents", the two spoke eagerly of cutting no fewer than three
albums together. The first of these got under way in the Three

Alarm complex in Memphis in early 1987. Because "it might be an historic moment", Ringo had requested that specific sessions be videoed, especially the ones where Eric Clapton, Carl Perkins and, purportedly, Bob Dylan had dropped by. Two Perkins numbers were reported to be in the can, as were Starr treatments of Billy Swan's 'I Can Help' smash from 1974, as well as two items shortlisted from proffered demos: 'Shoobedoo' and 'Whiskey And Soda'.

For all of Moman's later claims that no session was tainted with alcohol, there is small cause to doubt Ringo's allegations that "certain nights we were all under the influence" of wine, tequila "or whatever else we felt like drinking".

After only one of the three mooted albums, Ringo had had his bellyful of Chips, with whom he "ceased to communicate" on returning to England. Two years on, he was still umming and ahing about the LP, which, in the harsh light of day, "I began to think that maybe it was not my best shot. Maybe we could find some better songs." With his ambivalence justified when only one major company – MCA – came close to taking it on, he was game enough to want to try again at London's Mayfair Studios, with Elton John in the chair, but the four-week block-booking in August 1987 had to be reallocated when Starr acknowledged finally that he was no more a serious pop recording artist.

Come 1988, the only album of his that most retailers considered worth stocking was *Starrstruck*, a "best of" compilation by Californian reissue specialists Rhino Records, who had rejected his suggestion that it include the unreleased 'Can't Fight Lightning' as a bonus track for Beatle completists.

If his career as a hit-parade entrant was spent, Ringo still had tinier fish to fry. With *Scouse The Mouse* a dry run, he addressed himself more to youngsters by succeeding the more expressive Johnny Morris in 1984 as narrator of the adventures of moveable models known to infant ITV watchers as *Thomas The Tank Engine And Friends*. From a misconception that children's hour was "all *Star Wars* and high technology" it occurred to him what little traditionalists toddlers are when Thomas became Tatia Jayne's favourite programme, "more because she's into the action than because it's her grandad's voice on screen". To Ringo, "It's just mind-blowing that Thomas is so big in this day and age. It used to be 'Look! There's Ringo' in the street. Now it's 'Look! There's Thomas.' Would you believe there's hordes of screaming three-year-olds outside the house?"

Unlike a campaigning politician recoiling inwardly at kissing babies, Ringo genuinely enjoyed the company of children, "because I used to be one". Therefore, as well as attending to more orthodox *Thomas* promotional duties, he gladly responded to a request by *Dreams Come True* – a benevolence sponsored by ITV – to brighten a day out for two seriously ill nippers – to whom he was the *Thomas* man rather than a pop singer – by conducting them around the Bluebell railway in Sussex. With his own desolations on hold, "Ringo was smashing – a really nice guy," beamed the charity's co-ordinator, Margaret Hayles. "When little Theresa had a relapse, he sent her flowers." He charmed Margaret as he had Barbara in Durango, when "he played with the children and teased them all the time".

The New York Post pronounced him "the most likeable children's TV host since Captain Kangaroo" when *Thomas* was attuned in 1988 for the US market as *Shining Time Station*, seen by many reviewers as on a par of quality with internationally popular Sesame Street.

Regarding his public activities nowadays, he admitted that, other than *Thomas'* US equivalent, "Lately, I haven't been doing much at all." He and Barbara were merely famous now for being famous, wanted and ever-present guests at every high-society shindig, club opening, after-dinner laudation, *et al*.

For profit as well as fun, Ringo warbled 'When You Wish Upon A Star' – eerie in a *Sentimental Journey*-esque way – amid other reinterpretations of Walt Disney film songs by such odd bedfellows as Sun Ra and Sinéad O'Connor on *Stay Awake*, an album masterminded by New Yorker Hal Willner, on the rebound from a preceding artistic knock-out with *Lost In The Stars*, a similar salute to Kurt Weill.

Ringo also banked a huge cheque for five days in the Bahamas for a Sun County wine commercial, the first and last he'd ever undertake for an inebriating beverage. While denying that their alcoholism was critical, Barbara would "try to straighten us out every couple of months, but then we'd fall straight back into the trap. I knew I should be doing something to get help, but I just never got around to it." Friends would suggest that they "sort of cooled it a bit" and, waking up thick-tongued and red-eyed after another bender, they'd swear not to touch another drop; but, sinking three fingers of hair-of-the-dog spirits within half an hour of getting dressed, "You're powerless to do anything about it. You get to the point where there's no choice left. You're at the point where you say, 'Please, God, I have to stop living this way.'"

In October 1988, he and Barbara checked into an exclusive rehabilitation centre 20 miles across rugged Arizona crags from the nearest town. During a five-week limbo, the couple – sleeping apart – confronted and wrestled with their inner and unknowable conflicts. Jerked from slumber, dawn would seem a year away. Nevertheless, help was but the press of a buzzer…

As well as counselling – much of it from recovered sufferers – treatment included detoxification, compulsory exercise, group therapy, confinement to the premises and no sex. In cold print, it reads like prison, but Starr interacted well within the orderliness of the regime: "You get so safe in the clinic. I didn't want to leave."

Their ways changed, Barbara and Ringo re-encountered the outside world. Evangelical in their new sobriety, they would quit parties at godly hours except ones they held themselves. At a celebration in Cannes of their first year on the wagon, they were toasted in fruit juice. They'd always be alcoholics, but, affirmed Ringo, "My intention is never to drink again."

Inactivity was his worst enemy with regard to this laudable resolve, but it was more the example of other still-stagestruck 1960s contemporaries that prompted him to think aloud about hitting the road again: "I didn't want to front a band. I wanted to have fun. I wanted to be with good players, and I wanted to be with friends." No one who listened was sure whether to believe him or not.

17 "Now I Just Stay Nervous"

With *Thomas The Tank Engine*, Ringo had shown that there was more to him than trying and failing to recapture chart glory. Having broken into the children's world without any trouble, why shouldn't he also provide entertainment as harmless for their elders now that he was compos mentis again after an age of having "your brain all twisted in some way". Nowadays, with hands no more a-tremble or nose enpurpled, he was eating regular meals, quaffing Adam's Ale and keeping daylight hours, even acquiring a tan. He was also accepting studio sessions again, mostly in Los Angeles, where, for instance, he drummed for blues singer Taj Mahal on an album that emerged in 1991 on Private Stock, an independent company best known for its New Age portfolio.

Happily persevering with teetotalism, Ringo was not, however, as voluble about its merits as Barbara had eschewed showbusiness herself, except when it provided a platform on which she could emphasise the horrors of alcoholism and appeal for cash to establish a Self-Help Addiction Recovery Programme (SHARP) centre in Britain offering the Minnesota Method. Her persistence paid off in the 1991 opening of such a clinic in London and hopes that treatment might be made available on the National Health one day. Against her former career, her commendable efforts in this direction had "more meaning – and, in the future, I'll probably do some counselling".

He wasn't Maureen's "sodding great Andy Capp" anymore, but Ringo's rise from his pit became most perceptible in 1989, when, no longer represented by Hilary Gerrard, he delegated day-to-day administrative responsibilities so that he could set about the clear-minded organisation of a show with a hand-picked "All-Starr Band", as the wheels for an autumn tour creaked into motion. It took in the States, Canada and, lastly, Japan, embracing a concert at Tokyo's precious Nippon Budokan without any of the external antagonism that had blighted The Beatles' show there.

"The honest truth," as he perceived it, "is that I would not have been able to manage the rehearsals, let alone the tour, if I was still drinking." Enforcers of their own order, bandleaders like John Mayall and avant-garde jazzer Annette Peacock would not tolerate boozing by their employees, and God help you if they caught you with drugs. Although by no means such a killjoy, it was Ringo's wish that his All-Starrs behave themselves offstage: "I explained to the band that I'd just come out of a clinic, and I'd like the hotel rooms to be left as we found them; but, after the show, if some of the members liked to drink, I couldn't be in charge of that – and you could always spot the ones who'd had a night out, when we got up the next morning for the plane."

Casting about pop's old boy network, he'd been seeking not so much an abstemious backing group than a merger something like a less heavy-handed Bangladesh band, in which all participants were capable of either handling a lead vocal or otherwise being cynosure of the spotlight while the rest took a back seat. Joe Walsh was a likely candidate. On the cards, too, were Peter Frampton, former Traffic guitarist Dave Mason and, at tour co-ordinator David Fishoff's suggestion, bass player Jack Bruce, once of Cream. McCartney and Harrison were both sent Starr's itinerary, but this long-shot would result in only Paul – or someone who looked like him – hovering in the backstage disarray at one stop.

Beatle diehards, nevertheless, still clapped hard after a drum roll heralding the main attraction's "long-lost daughter", Lee, who took a bow one night – and she'd be viewed dancing around the front row in the domestic laser disc video, edited mainly from two shows at Los Angeles' Greek Theater, where the US tour wound down. On both of these evenings, Zak Starkey sat in with his father's methuselahs.

The Band's Garth Hudson was at the Greek Theater too, in a set that had been flexible enough to allow for other guest appearances *en route* by such as Bruce Springsteen, who flashed smiles, plucked at his guitar, wrinkled his nose, clenched his teeth and mouthed the words others sang before monopolising the central microphone himself for a busked 'Long Tall Sally'.

While presiding over these comings and goings, the ultimately all-American All-Starrs' cordiality was such that any upstaging during working hours provoked no friction. At California's Pacific Auditorium, the outfit interrupted the proceedings for the community singing of 'Happy Birthday To You' for a damp-eyed Billy Preston, whose 'That's The Way God Planned It' was cut after the second show in favour of 'Get Back'.

An anti-climax, therefore, was Joe Walsh's 'Desperado' from The Eagles' songbook, if an intriguing choice as it pre-dated his period with them. Ringo had been lucky to procure Joe, who, contacted in New Zealand, was waiting for confirmation of a support spot on The Who's journey across the USA. After Starr's more enticing offer, however, he wriggled out of all prior commitments. So, too, did Mac Rebennack – announced by Ringo as "the only doctor in the house" – who had rather diluted his Night Tripper dread through compromising assistance in diverse TV commercials, from milk to American Express cards. Nonetheless, he lugged his feathered, beaded headdress and the rest of his old Dr John stage costume from its mothballs and reminded himself of the words of 'Iko Iko' – the nearest he ever came to a hit – and Johnnie Ray's intense 'Such A Night'. He wouldn't let Ringo down, and in 30 cities he'd pound his Yamaha grand, beat auxiliary drums in 'Back Off and, for his ordained time in the limelight, belt out the old magic, even if nobody was getting any younger.

If The All-Starrs' *de jure* leader, Starr had had the least recent experience of the road. During weeks of rehearsals with all the most advanced cordless radar equipment on a Los Angeles soundstage and in the Park Central Amphitheater near Dallas, scene of the opening night, "the great discovery was that I could still play at all. I rediscovered the dream I'd had when I was 13 and which, in a haze of alcohol, I'd gradually forgotten. The others had to be very patient with me, because I had to learn all my songs again. I'd sung a tune like 'Yellow Submarine' on the record, but I'd never played it live."

Ringo's lion's share of The All-Starrs' lead vocals boiled down to about ten "songs you know and love", as he'd tell those who would nearly – but not quite – swamp his tutored singing, after his cry of "all together now!" brought in the choruses. He'd lean down to direct his microphone at the lips of those congregated around the apron of the stage for responses, like John's nautical quips in 'Yellow Submarine'. Although its *Abbey Road* counterpart, 'Octopus's Garden', was missing as well as 'Don't Pass Me By', Starr did not renege on other set works that he'd recorded "a long time ago with those other chaps" by fracturing the emotional intent of, say, 'With A Little Help From My Friends' with any revision bar a brief Walsh solo. Minus its banks of strings, 'Photograph' came over more forcefully, too. Other minor changes littered the remaining mixture of Beatles items peculiar to himself and a smaller amount of his 1970s smashes, but most were improvements when heard in arenas that were also designed for sport.

Pollstar, a US trade magazine, estimated Ringo's average ticket sale at 7,000 to 8,000 per venue, with over 20,000 at New York's Jones Beach mitigating losses at half-empty stadiums in Buffalo and Sacramento. The total gross was reckoned to be in excess of $5 million. If modest compared to the dough amassed by the Stones, The Who and McCartney, $5 million was still impressive, as was the care taken to ensure customer satisfaction. For this "Tour For All Generations", children under seven were allowed in to minimise babysitting costs and facilitate a family atmosphere of picnics and deckchairs, weather permitting – which it didn't at a lot of engagements. Thanks to soundchecks lasting hours and two gigantic video screens on either side of every stage, never had Ringo or any of the others – not to mention the local heroes who'd cornered the 30-minute second billings – been heard or seen so well by so many in the given setting.

Both on- and offstage, he'd refer to his new-found sobriety. Correspondents admitted to his inner sanctums would not be offered as much as a shandy. "I used to drink when I got nervous," he told them. "Now I just stay nervous." Savouring every unclouded moment, he was quite tickled by the standing ovations that were his before he'd sung a crotchet. Prancing on, he'd wave good-humouredly while advancing stage centre. When he hit the prelusive "got to pay your dues if you want to sing the blues" of 'It Don't Come Easy', he'd already be hostage to the beat of its introductory fanfare that had been counted in while he waited in the wings and the tension mounted.

Like a parody of Beatlemania, libidinous middle-aged women rushed down aisles towards the little fellow "like Yasser Arafat impersonating a Krishna" in his ponytail and the sunglasses that he'd declared were "from Elton's safe". For the second half, he'd steal on in a different jacket from a wardrobe that included ones in bright pink, silver lamé (with tails) and Chinese silk, all dragons and tassels.

From his acned years as a would-be Teddy Boy, he still believed that you wouldn't guess that he was no Mr Universe, if his apparel was sufficiently gaudy. His emergence up-front from behind the kit with The All-Starrs demonstrated that he was also no Mick Jagger. Moreover, he got the giggles occasionally and effected a "champion" handclasp above his head whenever a number went down especially well.

Much of his patter became predictable to the syllable as every recital yielded "the best audience yet", particularly after they'd bought the badges, T-shirts and other durables that he'd always inform them were for sale during the interval. Charming some and sickening others, he'd enquire, "What do you think of it so far?" and, several times, "What's my name?", raising a titter with "I love that bit" when everyone bawled "Ringo!" back at him.

Because he was Ringo, he got away with these enthusiastic inanities and deporting himself as if he had all the time in the world. The *LA Times* critic rubbished him at first, but then concluded, "Ringo was a smiling, delightful neo-vaudevillian who capered about joyfully while making all the hokey moves that fell flat earlier seem somehow full of life" as he attacked each opus "like a drummer by shifting his weight from side to side and singing each word on the beat". Getting braver as the tour progressed, he began to experiment with diction and phrasing, but not enough to mar the good old ones played in approximately the good old way, despite feet-finding false starts, cluttered middles and miscued endings. Yet, for all the carefree mistakes that only old pros could make, The All-Starrs went about their business without pomposity, "a little loose, a little ragged and a whole lot of fun".

On the grounds of his light, friendly mood on and off the boards, Ringo had come to terms with his past and present situations by concentrating on the possible with what *The New York Times* lauded as "the better kind of nostalgia tour", and although some of his antics had been a bit crass he hadn't milked audiences as much as some might have anticipated. Of course, he'd have been lynched if he hadn't done Beatles numbers, but he'd practised a grace-saving constraint exemplified by equating 'Honey Don't' with Carl Perkins – not *Beatles For Sale* – in its preamble and in his refusal of a big-time chauffeured ride to Vancouver's Pacific

Colosseum from the airport in the psychedelic Rolls Royce that had once belonged to John.

He'd select only one Lennon-McCartney composition ('I Wanna Be Your Man') for the concert album issued by Christmas 1990 – by EMI, of all labels – to combat bootleggers who still profiteered from anything on which an ex-Beatle even breathed.

Assumptions that Ringo would never feel his way out of his Beatles-nostalgia rut were strengthened as, one by one, reissues of his solo albums on compact disc were deleted. There'd been little point in Ringo putting out even a single in 1990, as, despite the pencilling-in of dates in Europe, he postponed another All-Starrs adventure until the following August amid rumours that Todd Rundgren and Keith Emerson had been drafted in to replace those unavailable from the 1989 personnel. Scheduled to perform once again in North America "in the same places", Starr advocated for this market consolidation a prudent change of format, with probably 'Octopus's Garden' and other favourites excluded from 1989, plus a track or two from a brand-new album. Because he'd shown that he meant business by his willingness to reach his public again – even if it was the same public as last time – someone had finally seen no harm in "taking a chance on us" in the form of a 1991 recording deal with Private Stock, signed largely because Ringo had got on well with Taj Mahal's producer, Skip Drinkwater, who ventured forth on an immediate quest for songs for his new client, before being superseded by Jeff Lynne, who had steered both George Harrison and Roy Orbison back into the charts.

Thus Ringo's life settled into the next stage of what has become almost a set pattern for biographies of famous 1960s pop musicians. After the years of struggle, the climb to fame, the consolidation, the decline and the "wilderness years" comes, hopefully, the qualified comeback. In nearly all examples, too, the repercussions of the initial breakthrough – in Ringo's case, the flush of chart strikes with The Beatles – yet resound, having gouged so deep a wound on pop that it gives the decades left to the artist a certain irrelevance, regardless of latter-day commercial or artistic windfalls.

Ringo Starr was to have a necessary hand in an excavation and even a surprise exhumation of The Beatles, but other than that his professional undertakings in the 1990s and since have stemmed, more or less, from that first nostalgia trek with The All-Starr Band. Certainly, there have been no more films, although he was the voice on middle-of-the-road 'You Never Know' from the soundtrack of a flick entitled *Curly Sue*; and, of course, there was his "appearance" in US cartoon series *The Simpsons* in 1991.

When The All-Starrs crossed the Atlantic in summer 1992, perhaps the most eagerly anticipated stops were those at the Montreux Jazz Festival(!) for the recording of a second live All-Starrs album, the Stadtpark in Hamburg, London's Hammersmith Odeon and, especially, the Liverpool Empire, after Cavern City Tours announced limited weekend package trips to see him there. BBC Radio 4's early-morning magazine programme *Today* made a big fuss, and the show was to be filmed for the Disney Channel, along with location sequences in the city centre. By one of these coincidences that occupy many an idle hour amongst Beatle disciples, Pete Best and his group were working the new Cavern on the very evening – 6 July – that The All-Starrs were on at the Empire.

A disaffected onlooker's angle might have been that, other than a few local references during announcements and Ringo dedicating an opus to his mother, it was just like any other evening on the tour. Although Starr rattled the traps as expected, he was more like a featured singer than anything else, sometimes vanishing into the wings as one of the others took over with an item, often half remembered at most by the audience. Give him credit, though. Ringo wasn't playing it so safe this time around. Mixed in with the yellow submarines and help from his friends – and a bold instrumental version of 'Lady Madonna' – were items from his new studio album, *Time Takes Time*.

As Ringo had aged, so had most of the topics tackled by either him or his wordsmiths. In a realistic conversational flow, parenthood (in 'Golden Blunders'), the passing time, regrets about past foolishness *et al* were filtered through clever arrangements and technological jiggery-pokery that somehow made the LP too pat, too dovetailed, too American for my taste, but that's the feeling of someone who would far prefer to find some scratchy old 45 by The Troggs in an Oxfam shop to receiving, say, the latest CD by Bruce Springsteen as a Christmas present.

What the hell do I know? A million Bruce Springsteen fans can't be wrong. Nor could a million fans of Ringo Starr back in 1973. However, moving the clock forward nearly 20 years from 'Photograph' and 'You're Sixteen', was either *Time Takes Time* or its spin-off single, 'Weight Of The World', a hit? You guessed it. However, its failure probably had less to do with its polished quality than with a chart climate that begs the question, who wants proper songs any more – even those as unremarkable (if pleasant) as 'Weight Of The World', with its Byrds-like jingle-jangle? Nevertheless, if I'd gone to an All-Starrs recital, what would I have wanted to hear? Ringo didn't become a contemporary challenger again partly because his fans, old and new, will always clap loudest for the sounds of yesteryear.

Two years after the All-Starrs' Liverpool show, Harry Graves passed away at the age of 87. Shortly after his stepson attended the funeral, another with a principal role in the Ringo Starr story was gone, too. Despite a bone marrow transplant from her elder son, leukaemia took Maureen Tigrett – Starkey as was – in a cancer-research clinic in Seattle in December. Her children and their respective fathers were all present at the final moments.

Tragedy almost struck the family again when Ringo interrupted an All-Starr tour that August after Lee – diagnosed as hydrocephalic – was rushed from the London garden flat that she shared with Jason to an operating theatre, where keyhole surgery relieved the pressure of excess fluid on the brain and thus saved her.

Ticket holders were sympathetic rather than angry about the cancelled dates of what was – for the US faithful, at least – the most value-for-money All-Starrs thus far, containing as it did Billy Preston, Felix Cavaliere from The Young Rascals, Grand Funk Railroad's Mark Farner, Randy Bachman of Bachman-Turner Overdrive, and, on bass, John Entwistle, The Who's second-string composer.

Around this time came talk of the Fab Three recording new material for their protracted *Anthology* project of CD boxed sets of hitherto-unissued Beatles tracks, a correlated TV documentary series and an autobiography of transcribed tape-recorded ruminations. When asked to participate in a connected news feature for London's Capital Radio, I ventured the opinion that all they'd be doing was incidental music. Writing in *The Daily Mail*, *Melody Maker*'s former editor, the late Ray Coleman, hoped that it wouldn't go any further than this, arguing – with none to disagree – that it wouldn't be the same without Lennon and fuelling Ringo's truism, "There were four Beatles and there are only three of us left."

After a fashion, Starr, McCartney and Harrison's efforts weren't without Lennon. Sessions at Paul's studio in Sussex and George's in Oxfordshire yielded the grafting of new music onto stark performances of 'Free As A Bird' and other compositions by John on home tapes provided by Yoko. "It was just a natural thing which gradually evolved," explained Ringo. "It actually took about three years for all this to happen."

'Free As A Bird' took shape as a sort of mordant 'A Hard Day's Night'. Although it was 'Ticket To Ride' that he was describing as "uplifting and sad at the same time", Beatles admirer (and imitator) Noel Gallagher could have said the same about 'Free As A Bird'.

"It's great, and I'm not just saying that because I'm on it," enthused Ringo. Well, to quote Mandy Rice-Davies, he would say that, wouldn't he?. Naturally, it sold millions. Revenue from every aspect of the *Anthology* project certainly swelled the participants' bank accounts. Well before 1996 was out, Starr would be indexed among Britain's richest 500 in an annual survey conducted by *The Sunday Times*.

18 "I'll Be Fine Anywhere"

Recently it's been more or less business as usual for Ringo –
and quite big business, too. In spring 1996, for instance, he
banked half a million pounds for uttering just one line in a
Japanese television commercial for Ringo Suttar natural juice.
Into the bargain, he didn't even have to go to Japan to do it,
merely board a first class flight to Vancouver to be filmed in
front of a photograph of Mount Fuji.

Not so lucrative, however, would be Starr's hitherto-
unissued revival of 1971's 'Power To The People', John
Lennon's fourth solo 45, sharing vocals with Billy Preston
and, apparently, Eric Burdon for the soundtrack of *Steal This
Movie*, a biopic of 1960s political activist Abbie Hoffman.
Ringo agreed to do it out of the goodness of his heart, because
all that he had to do these days was sit back and let the
royalties from the ongoing Beatles industry roll in.

Rather than his customary million pounds or so per
annum from his cut of sales of the four's back catalogue,

dividends from 1996's renovated *Yellow Submarine* – with additional footage, remixed soundtrack CD, video and DVD and associated clothing, memorabilia and toys – reduced even the Ringo Suttar money to a sideshow. More was to come – up to £5 million more in a single tax year via the publication of *The Beatles Anthology* autobiography in 2000. Despite a £35 cover price, this accrued enough advance orders to slam straight in at Number One in *The Sunday Times'* book chart, a feat duplicated across the world.

With its weight on a par with that of a paving slab, this deluxe "Beatles story told for the first time in their own words and pictures" had been several years in its gestation. Transcriptions of recent ruminations and fallible reminiscences by Harrison, Starr and the lately knighted McCartney and archive spoken material by Lennon – plus a treasury of photographs, documents and further memorabilia – were edited by Genesis in consultation with fellow travellers of the ilk of *Sir* George Martin.

Overall, a likeable and sometimes courageous account – and an intriguing companion volume to this one – passed the litmus test of any pop life story, in that it provoked a compulsion in the reader to check out the records. Nevertheless, it was flawed, mainly because there is little if any anchoring text for that Tibetan monk who still hasn't heard of the wretched group, and while the surviving Beatles were often painfully honest about events that occurred up to 50 years earlier, it was an autobiography aimed at fans who prefer not to know too much about what kind of people their idols are in private life. Too many illusions will be shattered, and the music may never sound the same.

As serious a fault was that, like the televisual *Anthology*, it lacked the perspectives of other living key dramatis personae, such as Pete Best, Tony Sheridan, Kingsize Taylor, Cilla Black – you name 'em. But where do you draw the line? By including all of the acts on the same label? Everyone who ever recorded a Beatles song? The factory hands who pulped the trees to make the paper on which they were written?

Anthology remained a bestseller while a four-strong team at Apple – now run from one of the white townhouses encircling central gardens in Knightsbridge – helped co-ordinate EMI's biggest-ever marketing campaign. Its budget was between £1 million and £2 million in Britain alone, and eight million copies of *1* – titled originally *Best Of The Beatles*, a compilation of The Beatles' 27 UK and/or US chart-toppers – were shipped around the world.

The fastest-selling CD ever, *1* was just that in Britain, Japan, Spain, Germany and Canada within a week of its issue in autumn 2001, with over 400,000 customers stampeding into Japanese record shops during the first day. At home, it outsold the latest by Oasis four to one.

Whether looking forward to the past is a healthy situation for any artist is open to conjecture, but it was hard fact that Joe Average was more intrigued by the corporate Beatles than Ringo Starr or any other individual locked in their orbit. If Paul and George weren't yet ready to go gently into that good night, Ringo's acceptance of the situation was manifest in his continued trans-continental treks with The All-Starr Band and the first 12-track volume of *The Third All-Starr Band Live*, with all of the usual suspects delivering their vintage goods, notably US Number Ones in The Rascals' 'People Got To Be Free' and – all from 1974 – Billy Preston's 'Nuthin' From Nuthin", Bachman-Turner Overdrive's 'You Ain't Seen Nothing Yet' and Grand Funk's rehash of Little Eva's 'The Locomotion'. Britain held her own, however, with John Entwistle doing creepy 'Boris The Spider' (the discerning Jimi Hendrix's favourite Who opus) and new recruits Simon Kirke – once Free's drummer – giving 'em 'All Right Now' and Procol Harum's Gary Brooker 'A Whiter Shade Of Pale', 'Conquistador', 'The Devil Came From Kansas' and 'A Salty Dog'.

Although his portfolio bulged with more crowd-pleasers than any of them, the All-Starrs' leader understood, too, that few – apart from regular readers of *Beatles Monthly*, *Beatlefan* and suchlike – could speak with any authority or interest about a cossetted life divided domestically between Monaco, California and – for however many weeks per annum ordained by Britain's tax laws – a country estate in Cranleigh, Surrey. These days, Ringo Starr's name was far less potent an incentive to hold the front page, unless he pulled some eye-stretching stroke such as getting half killed, like George Harrison would be by some Beatlemaniac (from

Liverpool, of all places) late in 1999. That had been far bigger news than a new or recycled disc by any ex-Beatle that a journalist might or might not have been aware as he cobbled together an editorial tirade about the government's vacillation about curbing the increase of violent crime in these distracted times.

Slotted somewhere towards the backs of most national newspapers in May 1998 was a story concerning the most successful of Ringo, George and Paul's attempts to contain the industry of illicit Beatles merchandise, which was thriving as if the *Anthology* albums had never been. There was even a US magazine – *Belmo's Beatleg News* – devoted to unforgiving hours of everything (and I mean everything) on which The Beatles, together and apart, ever breathed. Germane to this discussion is an item like Lost And Found, which contained the Chips Moman sessions and, rubbing salt in the wound, an excerpt from Ringo's spell in the witness stand during the hearing in Atlanta to stop their over-the-counter release.

At what sort of lunatic were such products targeted? Who had the patience to sit through six takes of the same backing track, a fractionally shorter edit of some Italian B-side, a false start of 'Act Naturally', one more fantastic version of 'It Don't Come Easy' and then spend infinitely less time actually listening to something like Lost And Found over and over again than discussing how "interesting" its contents were?

The overall effect of eavesdropping on such conversations was akin to overhearing a prattle of great aunts comparing ailments. Yet, to The Beatles' most painfully committed fans, the intrinsic worth and high retail price of a bootleg hardly mattered and, displayed between, say, *The Koto Music Of Japan* and *Aznavour Sings Aznavour Volume Three*, it serves as a fine detail of interior decorating and a handy conversational ice-breaker.

Beatles talk became more animated among the faithful in 1998, when a borderline case – *The Beatles Live At The Star-Club*, Germany, 1962 – reared up again when Lingasong, a company of no great merit, announced its intention to reissue it on lavishly packaged CD. Reviewing it the first time round, a now-defunct UK pop journal had noted contemporary implications in the back-cover photograph of 1962 teenagers congregating beneath the club's attributive neon sign, "Treffpunkt Der Jugend" ("youth rendezvous"), before concluding waspishly, "The Beatles couldn't play, either." That's as may be, but Billy Childish, a leading light of the 1980s Medway Town's pop scene, had considered it "their finest LP". The artists concerned, however, lacked Billy's objectivity about both the alcohol-fuelled playing and a muffled sound, despite further expensive studio doctoring.

So it was that, on a midweek day in May 1998, The Beatles and Apple forced Lingasong before the High Court in London. Leaving his Southport butcher's shop to take care of itself for the day, Kingsize Taylor would swear that he'd been granted verbal permission by John Lennon to tape The Beatles' late shift at the Star-Club, "as long as I got the ales in". Lennon's go-ahead meant – so Taylor had assumed – that it was OK by the others, too. The judge decided that it wasn't, and the mutton-dressed-as-lamb press-packs of the CD that had been distributed by Lingasong in false anticipation of victory became instant prized rarities.

While Starr, McCartney and Harrison presented a united front against Lingasong, team spirit wasn't as pronounced on their return to individual activities. George, for example, was to slide some bottleneck on an overhaul of Kitty Lester's 'Love Letters' on *Double Bill* by Bill Wyman's Rhythm Kings, but had been less inclined to do so on in-one-ear-and-out-the-other 'I'll Be Fine Anywhere' and pleasantly funereal 'King Of Broken Hearts' during sessions for Ringo's album of summer 1998, *Vertical Man*.

"He wasn't in the mood," sighed Ringo. "Two weeks later, I phoned him up from LA just to say, 'Hi,' and, 'What are you doing?'

"'Oh, I'm in the studio, playing with the dobro.'

"I go, 'Oooh, a dobro would sound good on my album.'

"So he goes, 'Oh, all right. Send it over, then.' I really wanted that slide guitar. His soul comes out of that guitar. It just blows me away."

Produced by Mark Hudson, singing guitarist with The Hudson Brothers – a US act signed to Casablanca in the mid-1970s – 13-track *Vertical Man* embraced what Beatle-ologists might have interpreted as more than a little offhand breast-beating. Was its very title a reference to Ringo's recovery from alcoholism, or to Atouk the Caveman becoming *Homo erectus* when, inadvertently, he cracks his bent spine into an upright position? Furthermore, for unmitigated audacity alone, Starr's trundling and artistically pointless retread of 'Love Me Do' – with Aerosmith's Steven Tyler on harmonica – deserved attention.

"I think I've got the hang of it now," laughed Ringo. Perhaps it was a symbolic laying to rest of the ghost of Andy White, now aged 71 and a resident since 1983 of New Jersey, where he teaches children to play in Scottish-style pipe-and-drums bands. As he was on the same land-mass at the same time as Starr, maybe he should have been hired for the new 'Love Me Do' to please the more perverse amongst us. Instead, Ringo stuck with more negotiable studio guests such as Brian Wilson, Tom Petty, Steve Cropper, Alanis Morrisette – a young Canadian whose debut album, 1995's *Jagged Little Pill*, had sold millions – and, crucially, Paul and George.

Paul was loud and clear on 'What In The World', one of the majority of items co-written by Ringo himself. Conspicuous among the exceptions was his 'Drift Away', a US smash in 1973 for Dobie Gray, best known previously for Mod anthem 'The In Crowd'. 'Drift Away' was also tried by The Rolling Stones early in 1974, but it wasn't included on their then-current LP, *It's Only Rock 'n' Roll*, probably because, like Ringo's version, it wasn't up to the fighting weight of the original. In Ringo's this was partly because he chose to hover in the background of what amounts to a duet by Alanis Morrisette and Tom Petty, both technically more proficient but less distinctive vocalists.

When to the fore and singing his own lyrics, Ringo comes over as a kind of Scouse Socrates in the sloganising optimism of 'Mindfield' and the title track, although he's not quite so chirpy on ambitious 'Without Understanding', with passages scored for a fusion of operatic contralto with tablas and wiry sitar. A breath of the Orient is exhaled for two bars only in 'Mindfield', which, while alluding to Dylan, actually mentions the Maharishi. Similar biographical references crop up more subtly in period "pudding" tom-toms throughout; psychedelic babble in 'I Was Walkin'', embracing possibly the most delightful drum fill in Starr's entire career; 'I Am The Walrus'/'Fool On The Hill' mellotron peeping out on 'King Of Broken Hearts', along with George's fretboard careen; 'Free As A Bird' blat-blat snare to kick off 'Vertical Man' itself; and a 'She's Leaving Home'-esque string arrangement for 'I'm Yours', a ballad as uxorious in its way as any of Lennon's paeans to Yoko.

Elsewhere, you can pick out a riff reminiscent of the early Kinks in 'What In The World' and respective touches of Cropper's Booker T And The MGs and Elvis Presley's 'Got A Lot O' Livin' To Do' in 'Puppet' and 'I'll Be Fine Anywhere' – but, welded together, the contents of *Vertical Man* were more absorbing than any Starr album since *Ringo*. However, so counter was it to the turn-of-the-century pop climate of rap and interchangeable boy bands that it begged the question, who wants proper songs anymore? Least of all ones like *Vertical Man*'s first spin-off single, 'La De Da'?

While the libretto to this lightweight but attractive ditty was a propos of nothing in particular, that was fine by me. 'La De Da' certainly sounded like a hit, and I should imagine that Ringo would have had no trouble working it up into a rowdy singalong with All-Starrs audiences. Yet it wasn't considered a worthwhile marketing exercise in Britain, and its promotion in the United States was dogged by ill luck. A planned video shoot at Shea Stadium at a convenient moment during a major-league baseball match was scrubbed when rain stopped play. Undeterred, Ringo and the camera crew then took to the sidewalks of New York with Hanson, a blond trio, then the latest pre-teen sensation.

The resulting clips were seen in North America on *Entertainment Tonight* and *MTV News*, and Ringo was there in person on other programmes, such as a sofaing beneath sweaty arc lights on *The Regis And Kathie Lee Show* and on ABC TV's *The View*, actually giving 'em 'La De Da', 'Photograph' and – over closing credits – 'With A Little Help From My Friends'. 'La De Da' alone was intended for the more prestigious *Tonight* show with Jay Leno (a sort of US Terry Wogan), along with a pre-recorded interview with both Ringo and Paul during a break in the *Vertical Man* sessions. Even if the black carnival in the immediate wake of Frank Sinatra's sudden death – the US equivalent of that of the Queen Mother – in Los Angeles on the day of transmission hadn't put paid to this, Ringo Starr still couldn't have got a hit with 'La De Da' to save his life, partly because the USA's love affair with British pop was now at its most distant since Sinatra's optimum Hot 100 moments in the 1950s.

Two days before the passing of Old Blue Eyes, Ringo had fronted The Roundheads at New York's Bottom Line on 12 May 1998, his first club date since The Beatles. As the presence on the boards of Joe Walsh and Simon Kirke indicated, outlines dissolved between The Roundheads – centred on Mark Hudson and his brothers – and the latest incarnation of The All-Starr Band, although this time Starr monopolised the lead vocals, giving 'em all the expected favourites plus highlights from *Vertical Man*.

With the promptness of a vulture, this recital was made available on CD straight away by Mighty Fishy Records. It was less a roots-affirming engagement – similar to those to which the Stones were partial in the midst of global stadium tours – than a dress rehearsal for the next day's filming of *Storytellers* at Sony Studios for VH-1 television. This special concert spawned a damage-limiting official album, but this was less important than the broadcast itself, the heftiest push there'd ever be for *Vertical Man* and 'La De Da'.

Neither were mentioned a week later when Ringo attended an auction in aid of Elizabeth Taylor's AIDS charity in the Moulin De Mougins restaurant as part of the Cannes Film Festival. His onstage spot with Elton John and actress Sharon Stone was memorable for someone pledging $90,000 if the three would perform 'Great Balls Of Fire'. Capping this, another pudgy millionaire – carried away by the jubilee atmosphere but unsure which member of that English combo everyone used to talk about was up there – promised a further $90,000 if they did 'Twist And Shout'.

The next two months were filled with preparations for the next All-Starr Band tour. The mid-August agenda included the Moscow Sports Complex on 25th August 1998 – when Starr became the first Beatle to chance a performance in Russia – and London's Shepherd's Bush Empire, which was poignantly appropriate, given that the All-Starrs now contained the highest percentage of Britons thus far, namely Peter Frampton, Simon Kirke, Gary Brooker and Jack Bruce. Putting his more avant-garde leanings on hold, Bruce – Cream's former bass player – replaced John Entwistle, who, with Zak Starkey now on drums, was embroiled in Who projects.

If not as constant a travelling minstrel as Bob Dylan, forever on the road with his appositely named Never Ending Tour, Ringo – finding the pace energising – had an All-Starrs on the road for each subsequent year, mostly back and forth across the Land of the Free.

It was to US consumers only – or, perhaps more specifically, to watchers of repeats of *Shining Time Station* and those too tough to admit that they did – that Ringo's 1999 album was pitched. Out in time for the December sell-in, *I Wanna Be Santa Claus* was a perennial record-industry strategy. The tradition stretched back to the very dawn of 33rpm long-players. Since Bing Crosby shifted a million of his *Merry Christmas* in 1947, the disparate likes of Mantovani, Elvis Presley, The Beach Boys, The Partridge Family and Max Bygraves have been among countless artists trying their luck with albums freighted with seasonal evergreens.

On paper, Ringo seemed no different from everyone else, in his commandeering of 'Rudolf, The Red-Nosed Reindeer', 'Little Drummer Boy' (as inevitable as Valentino's recording of 'Kashmiri Song') and all the rest of them. He even exhumed 'Christmas Time Is Here Again', doggerel from a Beatles fan club flexidisc disguised as a "proper" song (with bagpipes), and dared to take on 'Blue Christmas', an Elvis Presley A-side from 1964. Nevertheless, Ringo and his team clothed these in idiosyncratic musical vestments such as a quasi-military Gary Glitter-ish drive to 'Winter Wonderland', a pseudo-reggae jerk and Hawaiian guitar solo on 'White Christmas' and a spoken interlude in 'Rudolf...'.

There were also a commendable number of cleverly arranged Starkey-Hudson originals including 'Christmas Eve' (albeit expressing the same downbeat sentiments as 'Blue Christmas'); charitable 'Dear Santa'; 'The Christmas Dance', which veered from an ostinato on loan from Elvis via Arthur Crudup's 'My Baby Left Me' to an ersatz Viennese waltz and the finale, 'Pax Um Biscum (Peace Be With You)', in which a tuning-up orchestra segues into lyrics that are as succinct as a haiku and backing that emulates a celestial Indian bhajan.

Although he acquitted himself admirably on *I Wanna Be Santa Claus*, Ringo's non-Beatle income hinged mainly on earnings on the road with the All-Starrs. While the troupe was to reach Australasia in 2000, it was for North America that it was always designed. Sponsored by something called the Century 21 Real Estate Corporation, the last tour was 29 US cities long and began with a press conference in New York's Plaza Hotel, where The Beatles had been under siege prior to their *Ed Sullivan Show* debut in 1964. Now there was no shrieking tumult kept at bay by mounted policemen outside but, instead, a few dozen journalists and fans unscreened by security, receiving a sober greeting from besuited Steve Salvino, senior vice president of marketing, who introduced the firm's next TV commercial – in which Ringo (in cameo, as part of the deal) spoke two lines – and pointed out that proceeds of century21.com's online auction of artefacts donated and autographed by the stars would be donated to charity. To help him keep abreast of this and other matters – such as a series of real-time web chats from various stops – to do with the tour, Ringo was presented with a laptop computer with Internet access, but confessed, "I've sent three emails in my life, and my wife, Barbara, typed two of them."

When Salvino unveiled the 2000 edition of the All-Starrs, the most famous new face – in New York, anyway – was Eric Carmen. Four years after his Ohio garage band, The Choir, warmed up for The Yardbirds in 1966, he'd formed the more prosperous Raspberries. On leaving the group in 1974 – that year again – he scored a global million-seller in 'All By Myself' and a two year run of lesser US hits, but hits all the same. While his stint with the All-Starrs was "an honour, a wonderful thing", it was also an avenue of welcome exposure for his latest album, *I Was Born To Love You*, which, if not adventurous, was at least competent. The same could be said of nearly every disc by another member of the entourage, Dave Edmunds, both before and after the *Carl Perkins Rockabilly Special*.

Commensurate with this was Ringo's promise that the band would be "out there doing the songs that people know and love. That's what the All-Starrs is all about. We go out for a couple of months, have a lot of fun and do all the hits. We've more or less settled on 90 per cent of what we're going to be doing. For me, the rehearsal part is always the worst. We all have to get to know each other again so that I'm really comfortable when we do the show."

19 "I Go Along With Whatever Is Happening"

In April 2003, the latest Ringo Starr album, *Ringo Rama*, was unleashed. Almost all reviews were favourable, noting that he'd written or co-written every track himself, and that it was an artist doing something he was good at, even if he was too old to learn new tricks. *Record Collector* concluded that "this effort deserves a much higher chart placing than the one it will probably get."

How different could his life have been? Ringo himself once agreed that, "If I hadn't taken the chance and gone to Butlins and then joined The Beatles, I'd still be on the shop floor as a fitter. I'm not really a strong-willed person. I go along with whatever is happening." Possibly, he'd have stuck with Rory Storm to the bitter end or else joined some luckier local outfit, thereby recouping more than golden memories from the Merseybeat craze before drifting back to Liverpool, privately relieved, perhaps, to return to normality.

RINGO STARR

What if King Harold had won the Battle of Hastings? What if Adolf Hitler had been strangled at birth? What if Elvis had been cross-eyed? What if The Beatles had passed their Decca audition? Let's concern ourselves with facts. When the graph of Richard Starkey's life gave a sharp upward turn in 1962, he blossomed as if made for the success that, in the long term, denied him maturity. In the teeth of the uncritical adulation of Beatlemania, never was his character tested more thoroughly and found sound. More important to The Beatles than his drumming, acting and singing was his graduation from passenger to the one who kept them on the rails. To the late Bob Wooler, the Cavern disc jockey, he was their "only working-class hero. That lad was still living in the Dingle when he was a hit parader. Lennon, on the other hand, was a very privileged person." With his millions, Ringo behaved much like any other disadvantaged lad who'd won the Pools: the Rolls, the flashy clothes, the diamond rings, the champagne, the sexy model, the tax exile in Monte Carlo. When The Beatles went sour, he spent less time on anything constructive than on just mucking about – albeit "with extraordinary panache" – becoming but a footnote in social history.

If it matters to him, he can die easy in the knowledge that his will remain the name most likely to trip off the tongue whenever pop percussionists are discussed by lay people – and, if ever a ballroom is built on Mars, you can bet even money that soundchecking drummers there will still be hailed "Oi, Ringo!" by its janitor.

Songography
By Ian Drummond

All songs composed by Richard Starkey, with co-writers appearing in brackets. Listed by artist/band and then in chronological order of composition. All dates refer to album and single releases unless otherwise stated.

THE BEATLES

'What Goes On?' (Lennon-McCartney)	*Rubber Soul* (Nov 1965)
'12 Bar Original' (Lennon-McCartney-Harrison)	*Anthology 1* (Nov 1995)
'Flying' (Lennon-McCartney-Harrison)	*Magical Mystery Tour* (Dec 1967)
'Jessie's Dream' (Lennon-McCartney-Harrison)	*Magical Mystery Tour* film (Dec 1967)
'Christmas Time (Is Here Again)' (Lennon-McCartney-Harrison)	'Free As A Bird' B-side (Dec 1995)
'Don't Pass Me By'	*The Beatles* (Nov 1968)
'Octopus's Garden'	*Abbey Road* (Sep 1969)

'Free As A Bird' (Lennon-McCartney-Harrison)   *Anthology 1* (Nov 1995)

'Real Love' (Lennon-McCartney-Harrison)   *Anthology 2* (Mar 1996)

RINGO STARR
'Looking For The Lightning'   Tape auctioned at Christie's (Jun 1996)
'Sitting In The Back Of My Car'
'Traffic Sign Song'
'Hang On To The Roll She Gave You'

'Dialogue'   *The Magic Christian* (Dec 1969)

'Coochy Coochy'   'Beaucoups Of Blues' B-side (Oct 1970)

'Nashville Jam'   *Beacoups Of Blues* (1995)
     (Daniels-Kirby-Howard-Pickard-Reed-Shook-Kennedy-Drake-Keith-
     Huskey Jnr-Harman-McCoy-Richey-Lavender-Buchanan-Fontana)

'Early 1970'   'It Don't Come Easy' B-side (Apr 1971)

'Back Off Boogaloo'   Single (Mar 1972)
'Blindman'   'Back Off Boogaloo' B-side (Mar 1972)

'Down And Out'   'Photograph' B-side (Oct 1973)

'Photograph' (Harrison)   *Ringo* (Nov 1973)
'Oh My My' (Poncia)
'Step Lightly'
'Devil Woman' (Poncia)

'Oo-Wee' (Poncia)   *Goodnight Vienna* (Nov 1974)
'All By Myself' (Poncia)
'Call Me'

'Cryin'' (Poncia)   *Ringo's Rotogravure* (Sep 1976)

'Las Brisas' (Andrews)
'Lady Gaye' (Ward-Poncia)
'Spooky Weirdness'

'Gypsies In Flight' (Poncia)   *Ringo The 4th* (Sep 1977)
'Wings' (Poncia)
'Gave It All Up' (Poncia)
'Out On The Street' (Poncia)
'Simple Love Song' (Poncia)

'Party' (Nilsson)   Unreleased

'Just A Dream' (Poncia)   'Drowning In The Sea Of Love' B-side (Sep 1977)

'Who Needs A Heart' (Poncia)   *Bad Boy* (Jun 1978)
'Old Time Relovin'' (Poncia)

'Stop And Take The Time To Smell The Roses' (Nilsson)   *Stop And Smell*
The Roses (Nov 1981)

'In My Car' (Walsh-Foster-Goody)   *Old Wave* (Jun 1983)
'Hopeless' (Walsh)
'Alibi' (Walsh)
'Everybody's In A Hurry But Me' (Walsh-Clapton-Stainton)
'Going Down' (Walsh)

'Shoobedoo'   Unreleased
'Whiskey And Soda'   Unreleased

'Runaways' (Warman)   *Time Takes Time* (Jun 1992)
'Don't Go Where The Road Don't Go' (Warman-Grainger)
'After All These Years' (Warman-Grainger)
'All In The Name Of Love' (Warman)

'Angel In Disguise' (McCartney)   Unreleased

'One' (Hudson-Grakal-Dudas)   *Vertical Man* (Jun 1998)
'What In The World' (Hudson-Grakal-Dudas)
'Mindfield' (Hudson-Grakal-Dudas)
'King Of Broken Hearts' (Hudson-Grakal-Dudas)
'Vertical Man' (Hudson-Grakal-Dudas)
'I Was Walkin'' (Hudson-Grakal)
'La De Da' (Hudson-Grakal-Dudas)
'Without Understanding' (Hudson-Dudas)
'I'll Be Fine Anywhere' (Hudson-Grakal-Dudas)
'Puppet' (Hudson-Grakal-Dudas)
'I'm Yours' (Hudson-Newin)

'Come On Christmas' (Hudson-Grakal)   *I Wanna Be Santa Claus* (Oct 1999)
'I Wanna Be Santa Claus' (Hudson-Monda)
'Christmas Eve' (Hudson)
'The Christmas Dance' (Hudson-Cox-Dudas)
'Dear Santa' (Hudson-Dudas)
'Pax Um Biscum' (Hudson-Gordon)

'Eye To Eye' (Hudson-Dudas-Grakal)   *Ringo Rama* (US only, Mar 2003)
'Missouri Loves Company' (Hudson-Dudas-Grakal)
'Instant Amnesia' (Hudson-Dudas-Grakal)
'Memphis In Your Mind' (Hudson-Burr)
'Never Without You' (Hudson-Nicholson)
'Imagine Me There' (Hudson-Burr)
'I Think Therefore I Rock 'N' Roll (Hudson-Grakal-Santo)
'Trippin' On My Own Tears' (Hudson-Burr-Grakal)
'Write One For Me' (Hudson-Burr)
'What Love Wants To Be' (Hudson-Burr)
'Love First' (Hudson-Burr-Grakal)
'Elizabeth Reigns' (Hudson-Burr-Dudas)
'English Garden' (Hudson-Burr-Dudas)
'I Really Love Her' (Hudson)

BILLY LAWRIE
'Rock And Roller' (Lawrie)   *Ship Imagination* (Nov 1973)

'Where Are You Going (Lawrie)   Unreleased

PAUL McCARTNEY
'Really Love You' (McCartney)   *Flaming Pie* (May 1997)

HARRY NILSSON
'How Long Can Disco Go On?' (Nilsson)   *Flash Harry* (Sep 1980)

GUTHRIE THOMAS
'Band Of Steel'   *Lies And Alibies* (May 1976)

DORIS TROY
'I'm Gonna Get My Baby Back' (Harrison-Troy-Stills)   *Doris Troy* (Sep 1970)
'You Give Me Joy Joy' (Harrison-Troy-Stills)

George Harrison

Printed in the United Kingdom by MPG Books Ltd, Bodmin

Published by Sanctuary Publishing Limited, Sanctuary House, 45–53 Sinclair Road,
London W14 0NS, United Kingdom

www.sanctuarypublishing.com

Distributed in the US by Publishers Group West

ISBN: 1-86074-519-9

George Harrison

Alan Clayson
Sanctuary

Contents

1 The Rebel

With middle-aged candour, he'd insist, "I'm just an ordinary fellow." Certainly, the occupations of George Harrison's immediate forebears were the kind you'd expect an ordinary fellow to have. Merseysiders all, they came and went and in between they earned livings as joiners, able seamen, bricklayers, engine drivers and similarly honourable if unlettered professions.

The Harrisons had lived in the predominantly working-class South Liverpool district of Wavertree where Harold Harrison began a two-year courtship of Louise French, a greengrocer's daughter. Within a year of their marriage, in 1931, Harold and Louise were blessed with their only daughter, who was named after her mother, as their eldest son, born three years later, was named after Harold.

His job as a ship's steward being the only impediment to family stability, Mr Harrison took a chance on finding work on land in the mid-1930s' recession. For months, he drew

7

dole money until taken on as a Corporation bus conductor in 1937. Shortly after the outbreak of World War II, his wife gave birth to another child, Peter, in 12 Arnold Grove, the two-up/two-down family home within the clang of the High Street fire station.

Into this household of shared bedrooms and bathwater, 33-year-old Mrs Harrison's final confinement would produce the remarkable George – named after King George VI – on 25 February 1943, a mild, dry night. Both George and Peter took after their father, with his slim build, jug-handle ears, angular features and eyebrows that, thickening towards the nose, tinged their lopsided smiles with gravity. George inherited some Irish blood from Louise, and there was the hint of a leprechaun about him – but one that carefully deliberated its impishness. Growing from babyhood, he caught and held a dry and "common" Scouse drawl that would be with him always.

When he was six, the family moved to a slum overspill estate in Speke. 25 Upton Green was unquestionably an improvement on Arnold Grove, with a hallway, bathroom and extra bedroom. However, the youngest sons were prevented from enrolling at Alderwood Junior School, directly opposite Upton Green, because its roll was full. Instead, Peter and George were sent back towards Wavertree where stood Dovedale Church of England Primary, the only school with vacant desks, when the gaberdine-raincoated and short-trousered brothers' formal education began.

George had cringed with embarrassment when, after delivering him for his first day at school, Louise had lingered outside with the other mothers. The next morning, he implored her to let him and Peter walk the mile from home to school unescorted. Even at five, he resented any personal intrusion that her gossiping at the gate with other parents might precipitate.

He was also given to roaming the farmland, woods and marshes of the Cheshire plain to the east on foot or bicycle: "There's a part of me which likes to keep quiet, and I do prefer wide, open, quiet spaces to traffic jams."

He endured plenty of those after he started at Liverpool Institute High School For Boys in September 1954. Self-conscious in the regulation uniform of black bomber shoes, grey flannels, blazer, white shirt and tie, the first-former boarded the number 86 bus to school from the stop on Speke Boulevard for a trek which, in the morning rush hour, took just under an hour to reach the dropping-off point within earshot of the cathedral bells.

The Institute was adjoined by a sister school, the Dance and Drama Academy and the grimy looking Art College – and perhaps its proximity to these establishments and the city's Bohemian oasis bestowed upon it an attitude less shrouded in the draconian affectations and futile rigmarole prevalent in newer Merseyside grammars such as the Collegiate or Quarry Bank over in Calderstones, nicknamed "the Police State".

George Harrison was little more to Jack Edwards, the Institute headmaster, than a name in a register. As a second former, George was remembered by another teacher as "a very quiet if not even introverted little boy who would sit in the furthest corner and not even look up. I'm not saying he was unintelligent, but Harrison hardly ever spoke." In the previous year, George had settled down almost eagerly to schoolwork, but soon came homework copied shakily off someone else on the bus, orders to spit his chewing gum into the classroom litter bin and a report that concluded that he "seeks only to amuse himself".

The signature on the chit supposedly confirming that his parents had received the report was forged by the obliging mother of Arthur Kelly, a friend in the same class. With such allies in delinquency, George "found the wit, not the brain" to cheek even the head boy, "Pontifical Pete" Sissons – later a well-known television broadcaster – during Sissons' harassed efforts to enforce school rules in lunch queue and quadrangle.

Not standing when he could lean, that Harrison boy, with his bad attitude, "would not have wanted to be a prefect" in the understated opinion of Jack Sweeney, head of modern languages, "because he was against everything. I think George may have felt lost in the academic environment."

His extra-curricular pursuits had little bearing on what he was meant to be learning at the Institute. To afford them, he'd taken on a Saturday morning delivery round for Quirk's, a local butcher. For George, the longest lasting of his diverse hobbies was motor racing. Attracted by a poster advertising the 1955 Grand Prix at the Aintree circuit, he journeyed by bus and internal railway almost twice as far as school to see the great Argentinean driver Fangio and his team-mate Stirling Moss dominate the event. With help from their father and eldest brother, driving was second nature to George and Peter long before they were officially entitled to take a car on the public highway.

George's enthusiasm also extended to motorcycle scrambles, and as far as he ever had a boyhood sports hero it was Geoff Duke, perhaps the best professional biker of the 1950s. If short of cash, George would watch the kick-starting panorama from the railway embankment adjacent to the race course with a packed lunch at his side.

In most of his pastimes, he was a spectator rather than a doer. When truanting, George's gang would frequently seek refuge at the Jacey Cinema in Clayton Square. They were particularly fond of the more escapist horror flicks about outer space "things". This period also saw the apotheosis of Hollywood's film noir and its Ealing Studios antithesis of hello-hello-hello policemen, monocled cads, kilted Scotsmen and happy endings. "I liked the way things looked in those 1940s films," said George, "when the streets weren't crowded and the chemist shops had nice signs over them."

In a haze as rosy, he would hark back also to the time "when I used to go to the Liverpool Empire. It used to be ninepence up in the back upstairs, and I'd watch all the variety shows – whatever came in there." The Harrisons went regularly to the city's most ornate theatre, whether to Christmas pantomimes or to those presentations that marked the passing of the music hall. Usually the bill would contain an entirely musical act – a singer, more often than not. In those days, you'd be less likely to be serenaded with 'Danny Boy' or 'The Road To Mandalay' than 'How Much Is That Doggie In The Window?', 'Mambo Italiano' or something else from the newly established *New Musical Express* record and sheet-music sales charts.

"That was my contact with the musical or entertainment world," said George of the Empire, "because it was before the days of TV – before we had TV – and the only other thing was the radio." Most of the music heard on the BBC's three national radio services before about 1955 was directed at the over 30s. Otherwise, there was Children's Favourites – record requests aired by "Uncle Mac" – on the Light Programme.

Disturbing Uncle Mac's red-nosed reindeers and Davy Crocketts as that year drew to its close was a disc by Bill Haley And The Comets, a North American dance band. Like all but the most serious-minded children of the 1950s, Peter and George Harrison were superficially thrilled by the metronomic clamour of 'Rock Around The Clock'. A more profound impression was created by Elvis Presley's hillbilly-blues shout-singing that the USA only dared televise from the waist up. Presley was not married and paunchy like Haley, but, as the first photograph of him published in Britain testified, a hoodlum type whose brilliantined but girly cockade was offset by sideburns down to his earlobes. Unlike Haley too, he made no apologies for his onstage frolics, which involved hip-swivelling, doing the splits and rolling about as if he had a wasp in his pants.

"At school, there was all that thing about Elvis," George enthused. "You never wanted to go to school; you wanted to go out and play or something. So when some record comes along like Elvis's 'Heartbreak Hotel' and you had this little bit of plastic… It was so amazing. Now, it's hard to realise that there are kids like I was, where the only thing in their lives is to get home and play their favourite record."

Even wilder than Presley was shrieking black Little Richard in billowing drapes, beating hell out of a concert grand in the movie *The Girl Can't Help It*, which arrived in Liverpool in 1957. Every week seemed to bring another American rock 'n' roll wildman into the British hit parade – Chuck Berry, with his crotch-level electric guitar; Jerry Lee Lewis, a piano-pumping fireball from Louisiana; crippled Gene Vincent, "the Screaming End". Britain hung onto the new craze's coat-tails with such as Tommy Steele, England's answer to Elvis, who was "just as talented or just as revolting, according to the way you feel".

Thus spake *Everybody's Weekly* in an article entitled, "Are we turning our children into little Americans?" Still a principal port of embarkation for the Americas, Liverpool was more prone to such a metamorphosis than other cities.

Many teenagers within the Merseyside hinterland knew transatlantic seamen – "Cunard Yanks" – who would import Davy Crockett caps, otherwise unobtainable records, checked cowboy shirts and other treasures long before they filtered even to London. George's source was Arthur Kelly's sister, Barbara, whose fiancé, Red Bentley, was a ship's engineer.

For a while, a crew-cut like Red's bristled on George's scalp, but eventually he adopted a closer-to-home look. On desolate estates like his and down in the docklands, pedestrians would cross streets to avoid fearsome clusters of hybrid Mississippi riverboat card sharps and Edwardian rakes out for more than boyish mischief. The first Teddy Boy murder had taken place in 1954.

At the Liverpool Institute, boys were still supposed to dress like little men, men like English master Alfred J "Cissy" Smith, very smooth in his 1950s "quiet" style of dark business suit with baggy trousers. Mr Smith's white hair was thin, matted and actually quite long at the back, which is why it was odd that he should poke fun at Harrison's lavishly whorled Teddy Boy quiff. Actually quite short at the back – cut in a "Boston" – George's oiled coiffure was not the sole butt of teachers' sarcasm. Just short of openly flaunting school rules, he'd customised his uniform to seedy-flash Ted standards. He seemed top-heavy on thin legs that, from a distance, gave the illusion that they'd been dipped in ink.

His father had eventually seen the funny side of George's enterprise in drainpiping a pair of new flannels on Louise's sewing machine. For a blazer, he'd dyed one of his eldest brother's cast-off box jackets black, although to his glee the check pattern was still discernible. From Harold, too, came a custard-yellow waistcoat that alternated with a black double-breasted one with drape lapels. With his Quirk money, George bought a white shirt, as ordained, but it was pleated down the front and was stitched with black embroidery. On his feet were winkle-pickers of dark-blue suede and, costing nine shillings and sixpence, fluorescent socks with a rock 'n' roll motif.

Oblivious to the jibes of both wrinkled senior master and trainee on teaching practice, he lounged in the back row, dumbly insolent and indifferent to logarithms and the Diet of Worms. In reciprocation, he was ignored by most teachers, as long as he didn't disturb other pupils. Relieved when he was absent, they were just as anxious for him to leave the Institute as he was.

Academically, George may have coped better with the comprehensive system's concept of "education for all", then so new that schools of this ilk were comparatively unknown north of Birmingham. So open-minded was the outlook in some comprehensives that skiffle – a British offshoot of rock 'n' roll – was seen not as a plague but as a more effective means of arousing adolescent interest in music than parallel fifths and Brahms' *German Requiem*.

Although it was derived from the rent parties, speakeasies and dustbowl jug bands of the American Depression, skiffle had never gripped the imagination of young America. Rockabilly, its closest American equivalent in primeval rowdiness, employed conventional rather than home-made instruments. While retaining a thimbled washboard for percussion, even those British skiffle outfits that made the hit parade tended to abandon the makeshift, too, thereby adulterating the form for purists, who were still divided over the policy of London's Chris Barber Jazz Band, in which an ex-serviceman named Lonnie Donegan had been allowed to sing a couple of blues-tinged American folk songs.

Donegan was, more than Tommy Steele, a British "answer" to Elvis in his vivacious processing of black music for a white audience. Sung in an energetic whine far removed from the gentle plumminess of other British pop stars, his first hit, 'Rock Island Line', was from the repertoire of walking musical archive Huddie "Leadbelly" Ledbetter. Backed by his Skiffle Group, Lonnie bossed the form throughout its 1957 prime as he brought a vigorous alien idiom and transmuted it into acceptability onto an impoverished and derivative UK pop scene.

George Harrison had been aware of pop since his infancy but, Elvis apart, had had no real allegiance to any specific star, but "Lonnie and skiffle seemed made for me. It was easy music to play, if you knew two or three chords, and you'd have a tea chest as a bass and a washboard, and you were away... [sings] 'Oh, the Rock Island Line is a mighty good road...'"

Some of the fellows George knew at school had been bitten as hard as he was by the skiffle bug. Two older lads with guitars, Don Andrew and Colin Manley, had their own group, The Viscounts. Another boy, Ivan Vaughan was among the mutable pool of players that made up The Quarry Men, formed by his friends at Quarry Bank. They were a cut above a lot of groups, in that they had a drummer with a full kit.

While appearing casually knowledgeable, George drank in accounts of his contemporaries' progress. Fired by envy, he'd turned over an idea of starting a skiffle group with Peter. As his brother had a guitar, George wondered aloud about the humble washboard while trailing along with Arthur Kelly and his grandmother on a shopping expedition in the city centre. Passing through Cazneau Market, Arthur's soft-hearted grandma paused at a hardware stall to hand over a threepenny bit for George Harrison's first musical instrument.

This kind gesture was much appreciated, until George expressed a longing for a guitar by tracing its shape in the condensed vapour on windows and in illicit doodlings at school. Through overspending on his provocative clothes, George had nothing saved up when someone at the Institute offered him a second-hand guitar with f-holes and a movable bridge for half its cost price of £5.

His mother came to the rescue with the required cash transfusion, but George then made two depressing discoveries. Firstly, the instrument – ill-made, anyway – could only be restrung so high above the fretboard that holding down a barre chord was painful and single-note runs were impossible on high frets. Secondly, like the rest of the family, George was no natural musician. He was, however, handsomely endowed with a capacity to try, try again. Boosted by his mother's jocund encouragement, he laboured over his guitar late into the evening, to the detriment of even that modicum of homework necessary to avert a detention the next day. Positioning yet-uncalloused fingers on the taut strings, he'd pore over exercises prescribed in *Play In A Day*, a tutor book devised by Bert Weedon, guitarist on Tommy Steele's records.

After commendable effort, George moved on to a more advanced manual. His fingertips hardened with daily practice, it occurred to him – and Louise, egging him on over the ironing – that he'd become a better guitarist than Peter. He might even be not that far behind Colin Manley and Don Andrew, or even Johnny "Guitar" Byrne of The Texan Skiffle Group, whom he'd seen in action at a dance in Garston, a grim Liverpool suburb a couple of bus stops from Speke. With help from Louise again, George scraped up enough for an electric model from Hessy's, a central Liverpool music shop that boasted "our easy terms are easier". Compared to his first guitar, George's new £30 Hofner Futurama cutaway was as a fountain pen to a stub of pencil.

George fed his new purchase through an amplifier of unspecifiable make mounted on an unpainted chipboard speaker cabinet when the skiffle outfit he'd dreamed of leading made its first public appearance. Arthur Kelly and Peter were the other guitarists, with the remaining personnel being two other lads on mouth organ and a tea-chest bass. They called themselves The Rebels, a name duplicated by other groups throughout the country, including one that recorded for Parlophone, a subsidiary of EMI, one of London's four major record labels.

George's Rebels had no such aspirations, but with two songs at their command they began at the bottom by procuring an audition at a British Legion club, a few hundred yards from Upton Green. At the moment of departure, George advised that they sneak from the house, crouching with their instruments behind the hedge before dashing down the road one after another. In case their debut was a flop, he wanted the least possible number of people to know about it.

At the Legion Hall, a surprise awaited them: the booked act hadn't materialised. Clutching at straws, the social secretary bundled The Rebels on stage and hoped for the best. Courageously, they stretched out their limited repertoire for the whole evening, the bass player's fingers bleeding by the finish. Cheered for their youthful nerve, The Rebels tumbled through the Harrisons' front door afterwards, wild with excitement, each recounting the eventful engagement at the top of his voice and flourishing the ten-shilling note he'd been given from the grateful club's petty cash.

The Rebels didn't spoil the greatest night any of them could ever remember with a repeat performance. Besides, Peter was fed up with the guitar, and Arthur's parents didn't want him to think of skiffle as a career. George, too, conceded that it had lost its flavour on the bedpost overnight. Even Donegan, the genre's figurehead, had hacked "Skiffle" from the name of his group, and in the teeth of much criticism was broadening his appeal with 'Knees Up Mother Brown' and other music-hall gems, scoring his third Number One with an adaptation of the Liverpool folk ditty 'My Old Man's A Fireman On The Elder-Dempster Line'.

At the end of skiffle's brief but furious reign, some of its exponents turned to traditional jazz. On Merseyside, however, there was a greater tendency to backslide via amplification to classic rock and an increasingly more American Top 20. "I think a lot of people dropped the idea of being musicians," commented George, "but the ones who didn't, like the washboard players, progressed into snare drums, and the tea-chest players bought bass guitars." To reflect their new leanings, groups re-emerged with new handles – The James Boys, for example, were now Kingsize Taylor And The Dominoes and Gerry Marsden's Skiffle Group evolved into Gerry And The Pacemakers. The remnants of The Texan Skiffle Group wasted no time in relaunching themselves as just The Texans, and auditions for new members had been held at leader Alan Caldwell's home.

When George Harrison went to try out for The Texans, he was already a familiar figure to the Caldwells. After his first girlfriend, Ruth Morrison, moved to Birmingham with her family, he had paired off with Alan's sister, Iris. This became a foursome when Arthur Kelly dated her best friend. Violet Caldwell apparently nicknamed the two boys "Arthur and Martha".

It was her duty to tell 14-year-old Martha that, for all his experience as a Rebel, he was too young to quit school and go professional, as The Texans intended to do at the earliest opportunity. This had been a foregone conclusion for her son and Johnny Byrne, no matter how well George played and sang the ballad 'Wedding Bells' – Gene Vincent's 1956 arrangement – for them.

George was less concerned with The Texans' impression of him than with Jack Edwards' testimonial, which each leaver received as he filed out on his last day at the Institute. An inkling of what George's would say was detectable in Edwards' acidic remark that he'd "made no contribution to school life". Sure enough, George read on the bus home that the headmaster "cannot tell you what his work is like because he hasn't done any". A postscript to George's bursting free of the Institute was his return in September to repeat the "O"-level year, so some mortified teachers assumed. Only an hour in class, however, convinced him that slacking until the following summer among boys a year his junior was an uninviting prospect that would give him no more time to find an opening as a musician than if he followed his father's advice to get proper work.

He submitted half-heartedly to a written test for eligibility to work for the Liverpool Corporation. Botching this, he then underwent a humiliating interview at the Youth Employment Centre, and was sent to Blackler's, a largish department store, where there was a vacancy for a window dresser. While George was sauntering over there, however, it went to someone quicker off the mark.

This was probably just as well as, in order to publicly adorn dummies in sober clothing, you have to dress soberly yourself. Nonetheless, he was found a job under Mr Peet, Blackler's maintenance supervisor, as a trainee electrician. Although George had failed at the Institute, his Dad was delighted at his respectable overalled apprenticeship. In George's stocking that Christmas was a magnificent set of electrical screwdrivers. With young Harold a mechanic, Peter a welder and George an electrician, Mr Harrison's daydreaming ran to a family business – a garage, maybe.

Window-gazing in Blackler's, George realised how far removed his own notion of self-advancement was to one who'd borne the brunt of the Depression. Rigging up Santa's Grotto in December or laying cables in the firm's Bootle warehouse had been among few highlights of a workaday routine as dull as school. Already he'd absorbed habits of his idler co-workers, stopping the service lift between floors for a quiet smoke or enjoying rounds of darts on a board hung in the basement. During an under-age drinking session one lunchtime, he showed the others what a hell of a fellow he was by managing – so he bragged later – to hold down two hamburgers, three rum and blackcurrants and 14 pints of ale.

2 Carl Harrison

The audition with Alan Caldwell's Texans hadn't been George's only attempt to "be in a band, as opposed to having a job". Along Hayman's Green, a leafy thoroughfare in West Derby village, was the Lowlands, a skiffle club in uncertain transition, where he'd scraped acquaintance with some lads more his own age who were forming a group. One of its guitarists, Ken Brown, was committed enough to invest in a Hofner and a new ten-watt amplifier. He and George became the instrumental backbone of The Les Stewart Quartet, with Les taking most vocals and hacking a third guitar.

Regular bookings at the Lowlands seemed to be the fullest extent of the Stewart combo's ambitions. Therefore, while religiously attending rehearsals, George had no conscience about playing with other musicians whose outlook might prove more attractive. Around the time that his school career began its decline, he'd discovered that another boy who boarded the number 86 at Speke also had a guitar. This Paul

McCartney was in the year above George, but could exculpate himself from criticism of hob-nobbing with a younger pupil as Mrs Harrison had once met him on the bus and had lent him the money to pay his forgotten bus fare. From then on, Paul felt obliged to be civil to her son George.

The two began playing together, usually with Paul singing to his acoustic as George picked at his Futurama. Discussions during these sessions drew to light George's liking for Carl Perkins, a rockabilly artist from Tennessee whose harsh guitar style was as cutting as his singing on his best-remembered hit, 'Blue Suede Shoes'. Much admired, too, was Chet Atkins, heard on countless Nashville country-pop recordings, including some by Elvis Presley.

As far as he could, McCartney modelled his appearance on Elvis, particularly after he became a Quarry Man in July 1958. Through Paul, George came to join the group too. It was led by an art student named John Lennon. He had been in the same form as Peter Harrison at Dovedale Primary, but George was first aware of Lennon as a rather sharp-featured boy who lived in one of the posher houses on his meat round.

Among reasons why Lennon accepted the younger boy as a Quarry Man was, as Paul McCartney pointed out, "George was far ahead of us as a guitarist...but that isn't saying very much, because we were raw beginners ourselves." In addition, George's training at Blackler's ensured that overloaded amplifiers with naked wires would be rendered less lethal and less likely to fall silent midway through a number. Furthermore, George's dad was such a power on various depot social committees that he could swing it for The Quarry Men to play in clubs like the one in Wavertree where he and Louise taught ballroom dancing.

Even with George in their ranks, however, such engagements were few and far between, despite The Quarry Men's willingness to perform for as little as a round of drinks. In the months before they disbanded, bookings were confined mainly to "a few parties at night. Just silly things – John, Paul and I, and there were a couple of other people who kept coming and going."

Matters were becoming so desperate that George felt better off with Les Stewart, even if the Lowlands was about to close. Through Ruth Morrison, the Quartet had become known to the brothers Pete and Rory Best, who, with a team of helpers, had spent most of the summer of 1959 converting the spacious basement of their family home into a coffee bar-cum-club.

At 8 Hayman's Green, just up the road from the Lowlands, the club was to be like the Gyre and Gimble, the 2I's and also like London venues where Harry Webb and Reg Smith used to sing before changing their respective names to Cliff Richard and Marty Wilde. When Pete, Rory and their friends began spending hours listening to pop records in the basement, it was their mother, Mona, who suggested turning it into a club. It was she too, who christened it "the Casbah Coffee Club".

Partly because Ken Brown and George Harrison had assisted in the redecoration, The Les Stewart Quartet were asked to play on the Casbah's inaugural evening on Saturday 29 August, when a huge attendance was expected. A week prior to this engagement, the four met at Stewart's house to run through the set. A tense mood came to a head when Les rounded on Ken for missing rehearsals. The accused guitarist protested that the group would have nothing to rehearse for if it wasn't for the time he'd put in at the Bests'.

Lines were drawn as the quarrel boiled down to Stewart washing his hands of the Casbah. Keeping his peace throughout, George elected to side with Ken. Outside Stewart's banged front door that afternoon, he tried to assuage worries about letting Mrs Best down with the idea of amalgamating with "two mates I sometimes play with". For two hours, Ken fretted in the Casbah until George reappeared with Paul and John. That evening, The Quarry Men played before a full house of 300.

What Les Stewart's unit had been to the Lowlands, The Quarry Men were to the Casbah for several weeks, until a dispute with Mrs Best and Ken Brown – present but unable to perform through illness – over the division of one night's fee. Ken had been the key to the Casbah, but he wasn't missed when the remaining three took their brief turn under the Empire's proscenium in a "Search For Stars" talent contest organised by Carroll Levis, spiritual forefather of fellow Canadian Hughie Green, of *Opportunity Knocks* fame.

Although it's debatable whether or not The Quarry Men's decision to change their name made a difference, the fact remains that Johnny (Lennon) And The Moondogs qualified for the next and then final round of the contest, which was held at the Manchester Hippodrome. Up against such disparate acts as a blindfolded knife-thrower and Three-Men-And-A-Microphone comedy impersonators, the Liverpool trio went down sufficiently well to eat their hearts out when obliged to catch the last train back to Lime Street before they could be judged by volume of applause in the finale.

Although John let George duet with him on Buddy Holly's 'Words Of Love', Johnny And The Moondogs' principal asset was the vocal interplay between Lennon and McCartney. Fans attempting to describe it found it simpler to say that it sounded like The Everly Brothers. That power structure, in which George was subordinate to John and Paul for as long as they stayed in the same group, was founded not so much on vocal compatibility as the handshake that had formalised the Lennon-McCartney songwriting partnership during John's last term at Quarry Bank. Between the two older boys, it was understood that, should the group fold, they would make a go of it together.

For an audible but private gauge of John and Paul's efforts alongside that of professionals, they and George committed 'Hello Little Girl', 'The One After 9.09', 'You Must Lie Every Day', 'I'll Follow The Sun' and others into McCartney's Grundig tape recorder. On a muffled tape of one such session, the three guitarists are anchored by the plonk of a simplistic bass line supplied by Stuart Sutcliffe, a gifted painter in John's year at college whom he had lately befriended.

Prior to Sutcliffe's arrival, Paul had thought of taking up bass himself, as, no matter how contrasting his and John's chord shapes could be, the group had one rhythm guitarist too many. On the likely conjecture that the greater number of lead vocals, the higher a member's rank in the group hierarchy, Paul was several cuts above George, who was well ahead of Stuart, who had only 'Love Me Tender' to sing. As well as a handful of Perkins, Holly and Presley favourites, George – with a voice not long broken – was now carrying the tune of 'Three Cool Cats', a gift from John, who, with Paul, just harmonised on key lines. Lennon had gone off the song after the trio of Marty Wilde, Cliff Richard and Dickie Pride had massacred it on *Oh Boy!*, a BBC television pop series.

Hank B Marvin, of Richard's backing quartet, The Shadows, remains the most omnipotent of British lead guitarists, given those fretboard heroes like Jeff Beck and Ritchie Blackmore, whose professional careers started in outfits who copied The Shadows. While their line-up – lead, rhythm and bass guitar plus drums – consolidated the pop group stereotype, few assumed that there were openings for The Shadows and their imitators beyond instrumentals and accompanying some pretty boy like Cliff. The main attraction of being in a group was, perhaps, the implied camaraderie. Also, glancing at four-eyed Hank and stunted fellow Shadow Jet Harris, you didn't have to be a Charles Atlas to join one.

Sniffing the wind, Johnny and his Moondogs began rehearsing more instrumentals. In the forefront of these was George, loud and clear on 'Ramrod' and Bert Weedon's 'Guitar Boogie Shuffle'. Trickier, but with as little scope for improvisation, were several group originals like 'The Guitar Bop', developed from a passage in Chuck Berry's 'Brown-Eyed Handsome Man'.

Almost as strong an influence as Berry was Eddie Cochran, a multi-talented Elvis from Oklahoma. Co-starring with his pal Gene Vincent, his first "scream-circuit" tour of the country reached Liverpool's Empire in March 1960. Although all of Johnny And The Moondogs attended, George – with his working-man's wage – was able to follow Eddie to other northern cities to learn from a distance what he could of the American's terse, resonant lead-guitar technique. Joe Brown, an English intimate of Cochran's, later told George about Eddie's practice of using an unwound, extra-light third string. This was the secret of his agile bending of middle-register "blue" notes.

The indigenous supporting bill included Billy Fury and other charges of noted British pop svengali Larry Parnes, and it was through Larry's contact with Allan Williams, a local agent, that Vincent and Cochran were scheduled to return to Merseyside on 3 May to head a three-hour extravaganza at a 6,000-seat sports arena near Prince's Dock. A handful of local outfits were added to the bill by Williams after Eddie Cochran couldn't make it, having died in Bath's St Martin's Hospital nearly three weeks earlier.

Pulled from the same car crash was Gene Vincent, who, despite broken ribs and collar bone, plus injuries to his already callipered leg, insisted with characteristic obstinacy on honouring existing British dates. On 3 May, Larry Parnes had been sufficiently awed by both the local boys' impact on the frenzied audience and Allan Williams' competence as a promoter to discuss a further – albeit less ambitious – joint venture. He wanted Williams to procure backing groups for Scottish tours by Parnes's solo acts.

Though Johnny And The Moondogs were of lesser standing locally than the groups he'd procured for the Gene Vincent spectacular, Williams was prepared to let them try out for Parnes. Lately, they'd renamed themselves yet again. They were to trade as "The Silver Beatles" or "The Silver Beetles" for several months before settling on just plain "The Beatles". They'd also acquired a seemingly permanent drummer in Tommy Moore, a forklift truck driver at Garston Bottle Works.

Tommy was late for the group's make-or-break ten-minute spot during auditions held a week after the Vincent show for Larry Parnes. Prudently, they concentrated mainly on instrumentals and, if nothing else, they weren't slick to the point of sterility, like other units Parnes surveyed that day.

"Silver Beetles – very good," he jotted on a pad. "Keep note for future work."

"Future work" came sooner rather than later. On 14 May at Lathom Hall, a dilapidated Victorian monstrosity in Seaforth, they'd completed their first true semi-professional engagement. Less than a week later, the group began an eight-day tour of Scotland, backing a square-jawed hunk on whom Larry Parnes had bestowed the *nom du théâtre* Johnny Gentle. A-twitter with excitement and childish swagger, the three youngest Silver Beatles straightaway gave themselves stage names too, George's being "Carl" Harrison, in recognition of Carl Perkins. While the stratagems Stuart "de Stael", Paul "Ramon" and John Lennon used to obtain release from college and school were not entirely honest, all Tommy had to do was take an early summer holiday from the bottle works, while "Carl" – who'd never acknowledged that he'd one day be a department supervisor like Mr Peet – went the whole hog by resigning altogether from Blackler's.

Only the swiftest rehearsal was feasible before star and group trooped on at Alloa Town Hall to entertain with mutually familiar rock 'n' roll standards. Johnny was delighted with The Silver Beatles as musicians, especially George, and said as much when he called Parnes with progress reports. The story goes that he presented George with one of Eddie Cochran's old shirts.

The light-heartedness of such a gesture was typical of the prevalent atmosphere of the tour, which after Alloa zigzagged along the northeast coast with its brooding sea mists and dull watchfulness when the van in which the party huddled stopped at lonely petrol stations. The spurious thrill of "going professional" gave way to stoic cynicism as each man's £18 for the week's work dwindled. Rumbustious repartee became desultory and then suddenly nasty as, led by John, Paul and George – swimming with the tide – poked ruthless fun at whomever of the other two seemed likelier to rise to it.

Well, it helped pass the time as they trudged around Scottish venues where Gentle headlined over a diversity of local acts. The most northerly engagement, Fraserburgh Town Hall, was notable for Moore drumming with his head in bandages, fuzzy with sedatives and missing several teeth. He'd been the sole casualty when the van had crashed into a stationary Ford Popular earlier in the day. Not of Gene Vincent's "the show must go on" persuasion, Tommy had been semi-conscious in hospital when the group and hall manager barged in as showtime approached. They weren't laden with grapes and sympathy either.

Larry Parnes had a homily that ran, "Take care of the pennies and the lads can take care of themselves." Well before they steamed back to Liverpool after the final date, Tommy Moore – with only £2 left to show for his pains – had had more than his fill of being a Silver Beatle. They all had.

3 Das Liebschen Kind

"The Germans were just coming to the end of their jazz era," remembered Dave Dee, "and the American rock 'n' roll thing had really taken off. For the Germans to bring in all these stars from America would have cost a fortune, and there they had, just across the Channel, these English blokes that were copying the Americans and doing it very well. So it was easy to bring them in for 20 quid a week and work them to death, so all the English bands were in Germany doing two- or three-month stints."

One of the first West German impresarios to put action over debate was an ex-circus clown called Bruno Koschmider, who, in spring 1960, set off with his interpreter for London and the Soho coffee bar that seamen visiting his Hamburg clubs had assured him was still the shrine of British pop. From the 2I's, Herr Koschmider raked up a ragbag of out-of-work musicians to transport across the North Sea for re-assembly as The Jets on the rickety stage of his Kaiserkeller, a nightspot

down a side street in the Reeperbahn area, notorious as the
vice capital of Europe.

The Jets were licked into shape by the better of their two
singing guitarists, Tony Sheridan, an ex-art student who'd
flowered momentarily on *Oh Boy!* Seizing songs by the scruff
of the neck and wringing the life out of them, Tony and the
other Jets were an instant and howling success with a clientèle
for whom the personality of the house band had been
secondary to boozing, brawling and the pursuit of romance.

Rival club owners cast covetous eyes on Koschmider's
find, and soon Tony and his boys were administering their
rock elixir at the Top Ten, a newer and bigger night spot,
where they were protected by its manager's henchmen from
any reprisals for deserting the Kaiserkeller.

Bruno returned to London armed with a cast-iron
contract for any attraction likely to win back the many
customers who'd followed Sheridan to the Top Ten. Through
one of those chances in million, he and Allan Williams froze
in mutual recognition across the kidney-shaped tables of
the 2I's.

Earlier that year, Williams had visited the Grosse Freiheit,
and, with amused contempt, had listened to the inept
Kaiserkeller band who were destined to be displaced by The
Jets. Before the night was out, Williams and Koschmider,
entrepreneur to entrepreneur, had had an exploratory talk
about the possibility of bringing to Hamburg some of the
Merseyside outfits held in esteem by no less than Larry

Parnes. The discussion ended on a sour note, however, when a tape of the fabulous groups in question that Allan proudly threaded onto the club recorder had been rendered a cacophonous mess through demagnetisation, probably as it passed through customs.

Back in Liverpool, Williams shrugged off this embarrassing episode to concentrate on the possible. However, one story goes that, thanks to Allan's string-pulling, a Liverpool outfit, Derry And The Seniors, gained a spot at the 2I's, over the edge of the world in London. Koschmider chanced to be there too, and after Derry *et al* had showed him what Scousers could do with such unbottled exuberance, they were on their way to Germany before the week was out.

To Reeperbahn pleasure-seekers, Derry And The Seniors proved a comparable draw to Sheridan. With the Kaiserkeller thriving again, Bruno's thoughts turned to the Indra, his strip club at the dingier end of the Strasse. With only a few onlookers there most nights, it could only be more profitable to put on pop.

Now convinced that The Beatles were no longer, as George would say, "hopefully messing around", Allan Williams told them the Indra contract was theirs, if they could enlist a drummer. They found one back at the Casbah, where Pete Best's adoring mother had bought him an expensive drum kit. Following a cursory audition at the Blue Angel, Best became a Beatle and, to many who heard him play with them, would always remain so.

Pete packed his case with Mona's blessing. With no ties, academic or otherwise either, George met hardly any opposition from his parents for this, his first trip abroad, although Harold was still a little reproachful about his losing a chance to Make Good at Blackler's. Unlike his big brother on National Service, George would have no old job waiting for him when he got back to the real world. His mother, who'd seen the group play, felt that, if he kept at it, he might just make a reasonable living as a musician.

The Kaiserkeller was vaster and plusher than any club or ballroom The Beatles had ever played in Liverpool. It was therefore a huge disappointment when Mr Koschmider showed them next around the tiny Indra, which had the tell-tale signs of having known better days: the dusty carpeting and heavy drape curtains; the padded wallpaper peeling off here and there; the depressed forbearance of its staff.

The Beatles endured the Indra for seven weeks, six hours a night, an hour on and 15 minutes off, before being moved uptown to the Kaiserkeller.

After a week's petrified inertia on the expansive Kaiserkeller podium, The Beatles slipped into gear when Allan Williams' exasperated yell of "Make a show, boys!" was taken up as "Mach schau!" by club regulars. This chant – later corrupted to "Let's go!" – infused each of the group's front line with the desire to outdo each other in cavortings and skylarks. John made the most show of all, with much bucking and shimmying, like a composite of every rock 'n' roller he'd ever admired, an act that – so they and other outfits observed – always elicited a wild response.

Driven by the new fans' enthusiasm, as well as the fizz of the amphetamines available in nearly every all-night establishment on the Reeperbahn, The Beatles' last hour each morning was often as energetic as the first had been at 7pm. Now that they had the knack, there was no stopping them, although, as George would recall, "All we really were was thump-thump-thump."

Seventeen-year-old Harrison's appeal as *Das Liebschen Kind* – "the lovely child" – of The Beatles was demonstrated by the hoisting of a placard daubed "I love George" – the first of its kind – and shouts for him to take a lead vocal. Waved in by Lennon, George would evoke desultory screams with Presley's throbbing 'I Forgot To Remember To Forget' or Carl Perkins's 'Your True Love', singing close to the microphone with concentration on every phrase lighting his face.

Sending frissons through more nervous systems was Pete Best, toiling at his kit. Though an improvement on Tommy Moore, Pete's hand in The Beatles' on- and offstage frolics was dutiful, rather than hedonistic. They'd remember later the longer conversations he had with fellow drummers such as The Seniors' Jeff Wallington or, from the group who replaced them, Ringo Starr of Rory Storm's Hurricanes.

Whilst fraternising more with the Storm combo than they had with the rather supercilious Seniors, The Beatles also became friends with certain of Hamburg's bohemian elite – the "exis" (existentialists) – who had dared to trespass into the Kaiserkeller to see The Beatles.

The first German existentialists – nicknamed "exis" – to stumble on The Beatles were an illustrator named Klaus Voorman and his photographer girlfriend, Astrid Kirchherr.

For them, the most enigmatic Beatle was not Pete but Stuart, the tortured artist whose eyes were usually hidden behind sunglasses unnecessary in the overcast German autumn. It was no coincidence that bass guitar was the instrument that Klaus began to teach himself. He also felt no loss of face or admiration for Stuart when Astrid and the younger Stuart became lovers.

Like everybody else, including the lad himself, Astrid acknowledged that George was the "baby" of The Beatles. After she presented John with an edition of the works of de Sade for a Christmas gift, George enquired whether his contained comics. Of George's own age among the exis was another photographer, Jurgen Vollmer, who was also the maker of the "I love George" sign. Vollmer's most abiding memory of the youngest Beatle was of adolescent narcissism, after George had to be roused for an afternoon's boating on a Hamburg lake. While understanding his guest's need to stay dry, Jurgen was amused at how much persuasion was required before, in order to stabilise the vessel, George would remove his long winkle-pickers, which were stuffed with cardboard so that they didn't curl up. Back on shore, he carefully combed his wind-blown hair into place before he and Vollmer caught the tram back to the Freiheit evening.

Jurgen's *pilzenkopf* ("mushroom-head") hairstyle, commonplace in Germany, would be emulated by Stuart and then George during a second trip to Hamburg, although the latter restored it to its old shape before he went home. Funny looks from Kaiserkeller Rockers and open laughter from the other musicians were bad enough, but, within a year, said McCartney, all of The Beatles bar Best would get Vollmer "to try and cut our hair like his".

Questions of haircuts may have been as yet unresolved, but at the club George reckoned that, "We got to be very good as a band because we had to play for eight hours a night. We got together a big repertoire of some originals, but mainly we did all the old rock things." The monotony of stretching out their Merseyside palais repertoire up to four times a night at the Indra had been sufficient impetus to rehearse strenuously even the most obscure material.

Because it had been recorded rock 'n' roll style by US comedian Lou Monte in 1958, The Beatles even had a go at the vaudeville novelty 'The Sheik Of Araby', with Harrison on lead vocal. Neither had they inhibitions about deadpanning standards such as 'September Song' and – an eternal favourite of George's – Bing Crosby and Grace Kelly's 'True Love', from the 1956 movie *High Society*.

In the days when vocal balance was achieved by simply moving back and forth on the mike, the three-part harmonies of John, Paul and George were hard won but perfected in readiness for what lay ahead. Even John's rhythmic eccentricities were turned to an advantage. "We learned to live and work together," said George, "discovered how to adapt ourselves to what the public wanted and developed our own particular style – and it was our own. We developed along the lines we felt suited us best."

Musical progress didn't correlate with personal relationships between The Beatles and Bruno Koschmider. In the face of Bruno's reprimands, the group's increasingly frequent visits to the Top Ten had gone beyond merely watching The Jets. When The Beatles joined them on stage during Kaiserkeller breaks, Top Ten proprietor Peter Eckhorn heard not casual jamming but a new resident group, after The Jets' stint ended on 1 December. As well as higher wages, Eckhorn also offered bunk-bed accommodation above the club that, if plain, was palatial compared to that provided by Koschmider. Furthermore, The Jets found Peter an affable employer from whom bonuses and other fringe benefits could be expected when business was brisk.

Reading Eckhorn like a book – and an avaricious publication it was – Koschmider acted swiftly. Firstly, The Beatles were given a month's notice and reminded of a contractual clause that forbade them from working in any other Hamburg club without his permission, which he withheld. Aware that Eckhorn could grease enough palms to circumvent such legalities, Bruno struck harder by withdrawing whatever immunity he'd arranged concerning the youngest Beatle's nightly violation of the curfew forbidding minors from frequenting Reeperbahn clubs midnight.

With less than a fortnight to go at the Kaiserkeller, The Beatles were ordered to present their passports for police inspection. As George was a good three months short of his 18th birthday and had so flagrantly disregarded the law, he was to be deported from West Germany forthwith.

He spent much of the day before his exile giving Paul and John a crash course in lead guitar the Harrison way, as they seemed quite willing to continue in his absence. Only Astrid and Stuart saw him off from Hamburg railway station. Bewildered, subdued and very young, George flung his arms around the couple before heaving his suitcase, amplifier and guitar into the second-class compartment of the long, high, foreign train.

Many hours later, he walked stiffly from the ship with his luggage across the concrete desolation of the customs post at Newhaven. After the connection to Liverpool jolted forward, he may have slipped into the uneasiest of slumbers, now that he was more assured of getting home. Near the taxi rank of Lime Street station, newspaper vendor in his kiosk barked the headline of Tuesday 22 November 1960's edition of *The Liverpool Echo*.

4 The Cave Dweller

Over a few days' convalescent sloth, George pondered. With every reason to believe that The Beatles would remain indefinitely in Europe, who could blame him if he joined another local group? Most were in it for beer money and a laugh with a "Bert-can-play-bass" attitude. However, as their hire-purchase debts at Hessy's demonstrated, some meant business, among them The Remo Four, who, emerging from Don Andrew and Colin Manley's Viscounts, were recognised as Liverpool's top instrumental unit.

No more an amateur, George might have been welcome in a band of like status, but such a consideration proved academic as, by the second week of December 1960, all of The Beatles except Stuart Sutcliffe – by now betrothed to Astrid – had come home, their Top Ten enterprise scotched when Best and McCartney were ordered out of the Fatherland on a trumped-up charge of arson, which had been created courtesy of Herr Koschmider.

Because of their sojourn in Hamburg, the "successful German tour" of pre-engagement publicity, they were an unknown quantity locally, but not for long. They were a last-minute addition to a bill at Litherland Town Hall on the 27th, and John Lennon would recall The Beatles "being cheered for the first time" in Liverpool after a casually cataclysmic performance that their spell in Hamburg had wrought.

You couldn't deny The Beatles' impact on the crowd yet musically they were a throwback, now that pop was at its most harmless and ephemeral. "In England," recounted George, "Cliff Richard And The Shadows became the big thing. They all had matching ties and handkerchiefs and grey suits, but we were still doing Gene Vincent, Bo Diddley and Ray Charles things."

John, George, Pete and Paul could also deliver distinctive arrangements of The Marvelettes' 'Please Mr Postman', Barrett Strong's 'Money' and other records on Tamla-Motown, a promising black label from Detroit that had manoeuvred its first fistful of signings into the Hot 100. Of all Tamla-Motown acts, George listened hardest to The Miracles, whose leader, Smokey Robinson, had an "effortless butterfly of a voice" that he would never bring himself to criticise in the slightest.

The Beatles were particularly adept too at adapting songs by US girl groups to a different set of hormones such as The Orlons' 'Shimmy Shimmy' and 'Boys' from The Shirelles, a favourite with the ladies because it was one of Pete Best's infrequent vocal outings. However, certain songs might be so worthily executed by this or that Liverpudlian pop outfit that it would be shunned by rivals. Few, for instance, were assured enough to take on The Merseybeats' gauchely sentimental 'Hello Young Lovers' and black vocal group The Chants' arrangement of The Stereos' 'I Really Love You'.

Allegedly, it wasn't until Paul McCartney noticed Earl Preston's TTs performing a self-penned song that The Beatles risked any Lennon-McCartney originals in their stage repertoire. Other Merseybeat musicians also came up with items superior to some of their respective groups' non-originals, while The Big Three knocked together 'Cavern Stomp', immortalising the club where The Beatles were to perform more than 200 times over the next two years.

On one chronicled occasion, George slipped Cavern doorman Paddy Delaney a few shillings – "but don't tell her I gave it to you" – to pass on to an impoverished fan loitering with vain hope outside. George must have been unusually well heeled that day, because his average turnover was only "a couple of quid a week". Church halls, social clubs, village institutes, pub function rooms, ice rinks and even riverboats now offered beat sessions. George Harrison's earliest remark in the national music press was, "You know, we've hardly done any touring in England. Working in and around Liverpool keeps you busy throughout the whole year."

Yet, thanks largely to Mrs Best's badgering and Peter Eckhorn's assurances of their good behaviour, the West

German Immigration Office allowed firebugs Paul and Pete back so that The Beatles could begin a four-month season at the Top Ten in March. Paul had transferred to bass guitar at last because Stuart – now a student at Hamburg's State Art School – had, for all practical purposes, left the group.

The most piquant memory of The Beatles' first, truncated residency at the Top Ten was an extra-long extrapolation of 'What'd I Say' with Sheridan's departing Jets. The undisputed Presley of the Reeperbahn, Tony had had no fixed backing band, using instead whoever happened to be also playing the club. Most felt honoured to be on the same stage, learning the tricks of the trade from one nicknamed "the Teacher". Throughout the spring of 1961, the Teacher's star pupils were The Beatles, who'd been on stage with him when they were heard by Alfred Schlacht, a publisher associated with Deutsche Grammophon, with whom Sheridan had signed in Germany.

At Schlacht's urging, Bert Kaempfert, a power on Polydor, the company's pop subsidiary, invited the thrilled Beatles to be one of two groups – both to be called The Beat Brothers – who'd cut tracks with Sheridan from which a single and probably an album could be selected. Therefore, one May morning, after snatching a little rest from the night's Top Ten shift, Tony and The Beatles were transported to their first session. Each number was punched out in three takes, at most, but the mood was sufficiently relaxed for Kaempfert to lend critical ears to some of Paul and John's songs and an instrumental that George had composed with John's help. It

sounded much like a Shadows out-take, and Kaempfert
allowed The Beatles to record it as one side of a possible
single in their own right. Given a title and enlivened with
barely audible background yelling, 'Cry For A Shadow' thus
became the first Beatle original to be released on record,
appearing in June 1962 on Sheridan's *My Bonnie* LP, named
after the 45 that had taken him high up in the German charts.

The final weeks at the Top Ten became very long,
simmering as The Beatles were to get back to Liverpool to
impress everyone with their marvellous achievement. Calling
on Arthur Kelly, George and Paul had literally danced with
excitement, leaving footmarks on the freshly scrubbed kitchen
floor. To Barbara Kelly's deflationary scolding, Paul's riposte
was that she'd regret her blunt words when he was famous.
With John assuming Tony's lead vocal, The Beatles rubbed
it in onstage. Bob Wooler plugged 'My Bonnie' relentlessly,
for all it signified rather than its sound. He'd received his
copy from George, who'd made sure his relatives and friends
got one as well.

For the Harrisons, home would shortly be 174 Mackett's
Lane, a council house again but this time the other side of
Woolton from the McCartneys and a more select area than
Speke. That three of the group lived so near each other was
handy for the van pick-up for bookings. The Beatles' first
true road manager was Frank Garner, who doubled as a
Casbah bouncer. He was also their official driver, but, since
both Harrison and McCartney had just gained their licences,

they would clamour for a turn at the wheel, the older Paul bullying his way most often into the driver's seat.

There was a degree of unpleasantness among them all that was representative of the discord and intrigues that make pop groups what they are. Unspoken as yet was the desire of John, Paul and Ringo to be rid of Pete as soon as someone more suitable came to light. His dismissal in August 1962 may be ascribed to an inability to conform to the mores of his peers, shown by his maintenance of a shaped cockade instead of what became known locally as a "Beatle cut". More serious was his continued refusals of the amphetamines consumed by the rest during their Reeperbahn residencies. Neither did he contribute much to the group's studentish restricted code, superstitions and folklore.

Pete didn't have to try as hard as the less well-favoured Paul, scuttling to and from microphones, and John, who, scoffed Bob Wooler, "gave the impression of being so hard". Brought forward for his 'Sheik Of Araby', George might have cultivated a Cheeky Chappie persona, but, said his mother, he "never used to say anything or smile. George used to say that it was because he was the lead guitar. If the others made mistakes through larking about, nobody noticed, but he couldn't make any."

George didn't always look glum but he was no natural show-off. His main and most imitated stage gesture came to be "the Liverpool leg", a rhythmic twitching of the said limb as if grinding a cigarette butt with the heel. All the same,

John McNally affirmed, "You'd think somehow George would get left behind, but he didn't, and he developed his own style – a bit shy – and the girls really liked that."

This was noticeable during The Beatles' third Hamburg season – this time at the new Star-Club, which had given no quarter during a ruthless campaign to outflank the Top Ten as the district's premier night spot. During The Beatles' seven weeks at the Star-Club, they warmed up for three visiting US idols: Ray Charles, Little Richard and the ubiquitous Gene Vincent. George hit it off straight away with Billy Preston, Little Richard's 15-year-old organist, but, as far as George was concerned, they were only likely to meet again if Preston found himself on Merseyside or the Reeperbahn – which, for The Beatles, was all there was.

Of the two stamping grounds, Hamburg seemed the better financial bet, but rather than modestly coming into their own on foreign soil, The Beatles preferred to return to Liverpool, even if some groups there had overtaken them on certain fronts. Derry And The Seniors, for instance, had just released a debut single, while The Remo Four had broken into the US airbase circuit. On the plus side, they were "the biggest thing in Liverpool", estimated Ringo Starr – to which George Harrison added, "We were recognised there, too, only people didn't chase us about." Copying their repertoire and off-hand stagecraft were units like the younger Merseybeats, who, as their Tony Crane admitted, hired a second guitarist "to make the band more like The Beatles".

As unaware as his interviewers were of The Beatles' distant thunder, US balladeer Roy Orbison – in London in 1962 – conjectured that "you don't seem to have the kind of rhythm groups that we have in the States, and I'm sure that is what the kids want: strong, beaty rhythms that make them jump". Nobody at Roy's press conference could predict that soon native British "rhythm groups" would be jumping up the hit parade in abundance. One of them would end 1963 as arguably more popular than Cliff Richard And The Shadows, with records as competent and attractive but played with guts, like.

5 The Mersey Beatle

The Beatles had taken local impact to its limit. Campaigns for engagements beyond Merseyside yielded little beyond a further Hamburg residency. It wasn't back to square one, however, because The Beatles' undimmed ring of confidence had caught the eye of Brian Epstein, a local businessman, who had followed his father into I Epstein & Sons, beginning as a trainee salesman. 1961 found him in charge of the record department of the city-centre branch of NEMS (North End Music Stores), named after a smaller suburban shop taken over by the firm during his grandfather's time.

Far from thinking of records as mere merchandise, this Mr Epstein was more conscious than he needed to be of the artistic and entrepreneurial aspect of their creation and marketing. Indeed, he'd gone as far as attending a Beatles' Cavern session in his conservative suit, sensible shoes, briefcase and "square" haircut. Much has been written about Brian's homosexuality and his erotic attraction to The Beatles, but what struck him first was that the four louts up there in their glistening leathers sounded like nothing he'd ever heard. Hitting all their instruments at once at a staccato "Right!", they'd barged into a glorious onslaught of pulsating bass, spluttering guitars, crashing drums and ranting vocals. Brian, over his initial shock, tuned into the situation's epic vulgarity as The Beatles walked what seemed to him to be an artistic tightrope without a safety net. Dammit, they were great! When they stumbled off after exacting their customary submission from whoever hadn't wanted to like them, what could Brian do other than struggle through the crowd to congratulate them?

After the second set, Epstein pondered the laconic question that a Beatle – George, it was – had put to him when he'd poked his head into the bandroom: "What brings Mr Epstein here?" He'd know why when he was drawn back to another Cavern sweatbath a few days later. For reasons that included vocational boredom and frustrated aspirations to be a performer himself, Brian decided he wanted to be The Beatles' Larry Parnes.

The group weren't as nonchalantly indifferent as they appeared to the overtures made to them by this "executive type". Three had arrived late but arrived all the same when Brian suggested a formal discussion with them at NEMS after one Wednesday half-day closure. Finally, all four assembled for a second meeting where Brian was informed by leader Lennon that he was the man for them. Determined on the utmost correctness, Brian then called on each Beatle's parents to affirm his own sincerity and faith in the group. The Harrisons had fewest reservations about him, reassured that such an elegant, nicely spoken gent was taking their youngest in hand.

As Larry Parnes would have advised him, Brian's first task was to make the group altogether smoother pop entertainers. They had to be compelled to wear the stylish but not-too-way-out uniform suits he'd bought them. Playing to a fixed programme, punctuality and back projection were all-important. Stage patter must not include swearing or attempts to pull front-row girls.

Their new manager scuttled about like a mother hen, bringing about and enforcing the transformation, being met with irritated shows of resistance. These lessened after Epstein's position as a major retailer caused Dick Rowe, Decca's head of A&R, to send his second-in-command, Mike Smith, to the Cavern in mid-December 1961 to judge The Beatles. Smith thought them a lively enough act in their natural habitat, but only his boss could decide whether they'd come over on vinyl. Could the boys come down for a test in Decca's West Hampstead recording studio? Shall we say 11am on New Year's Day?

The Beatles weren't at their best when, for a tardy Mike Smith, they ran through 15 songs selected by Brian to demonstrate their versatility as "all-round entertainers" rather than their individuality as a group. Blotting out the solemnity of the occasion, George was inspired to sing Bobby Vee's latest hit, 'Take Good Care Of My Baby', with an edge that was missing from the original. He also injected the required humour into 'The Sheik Of Araby' and 'Three Cool Cats'. Furthermore, while fright muted the others, garrulous George came across to Smith as the Beatle with most "personality".

With as many vocal showcases as John, George might have been more of a prime candidate for election by Rowe and Smith as the group's figurehead, for, when British records charted in the early 1960s, it was usually with solo stars. Perhaps the notion of "George Harrison And The Beatles" flashed across Smith's mind.

Such a suggestion proved hypothetical, however, as among Dick Rowe's critical prejudices was that the last thing anyone – from a teenager in a dance hall to the director of the Light Programme – wanted to hear was a home-made song, and The Beatles had included three. Composers have to start somewhere, but, apart from B-sides of no real musical value, the possibility of a group developing songwriting to any great extent was unheard of. How, then, could Rowe appreciate how formidable the Lennon-McCartney partnership had become by 1962? After Decca joined EMI in turning them down, criticisms other companies gave The Beatles were just as blinkered.

Even without a record deal The Beatles were now a cut above most other Merseybeat outfits. They'd moved up to the ballroom circuits controlled by leisure corporations that had belatedly clasped rock 'n' roll to its bosom. Thus they became a dependable draw as their work spectrum broadened to Yorkshire, Wales and as far south as Swindon.

John and Paul sang most of the weightier material, leaving comic relief and no less than three Joe Brown numbers – including an embarrassed 'I'm Henery The Eighth I Am' – to George. When dancers wanted something from the charts, it would be George who'd give 'em passing joys like Tommy Roe's 'Sheila'. Nevertheless, John had handed him Chuck Berry's 'Roll Over Beethoven', and he'd been permitted to slow things down with 'Devil In Her Heart' by The Donays.

George was rarely allowed a lead vocal for less run-of-the-mill events, such as The Beatles' first radio broadcast, recorded before an audience at Manchester's Playhouse on 7 March 1962. Afterwards, the four were mobbed by libidinous females not much younger than themselves. Most were after Pete, who, pinned in a doorway, would lose tufts of hair to clawing hands. Watching the frenzy sourly was Paul's father, who would unjustly berate the drummer for stealing the limelight.

For a long while, Best and his pushy mother had been unconscious victims of sardonic *bons mots* by the McCartneys and Lennon. George too joined in the underhanded dissection of Pete. Brian Epstein was another scapegoat. By mid-1962, he still hadn't landed that elusive record deal. With John's wilful sarcasm pricking him, Brian embarked on one more traipse round the record companies of London.

Two days after arriving, he was sitting opposite George Martin, of the one EMI subsidiary that hadn't given The Beatles a thumbs down. What Martin heard of Epstein's group didn't excite him much, but they weren't obvious no-hopers and Brian himself was more believable than others who'd pressed their clients on Parlophone. It would do no harm, George supposed, to record The Beatles in one of EMI's St John's Wood studios.

After they'd done so, George Martin pondered. All four songs they had taped were fairly mordant and at odds with the group's hilarious corporate personality. He'd have to grub around publishers' offices for a vehicle to project this. The notion of drafting in an outsider to be their Cliff Richard was dismissed.

When they returned to record their debut single in September, The Beatles had done some structural tampering on their own account in the heartless sacking of Pete Best. The vexation of his many devotees had spilled over into "a lot of trouble", as George wrote to a girl fan. This embraced a very real riot as The Beatles entered the Cavern with their new member. George's appearance onstage that day with a black eye, however, resulted not from the Best affair but a jealous swain's vendetta caused by jealousy because of his girlfriend's inordinate fondness for The Beatles.

The bruise still hadn't healed in time for the publicity photographs taken during the group's second visit to Abbey Road, and he compounded this blemish with a sullen expression for the first that Britain at large would see of George Harrison. More welcoming was the wan smile on the homely visage of Ringo Starr, who'd been one of Pete's deputies and then his successor.

At the second session for the group's single, Ringo was dejected when George Martin hired a more experienced player to ghost the drumming. At console assistant Ron Richards' insistence, George Harrison left out most of the repetitive guitar phrases in an opus entitled 'Love Me Do', a harmonica-led Lennon-McCartney original that The Beatles preferred to the perky and "professional" 'How Do You Do It' that Martin thought tailor-made for them.

Not long after the release of 'Love Me Do' on 4 October 1962, a few scattered airings crackled from Radio Luxembourg. Tipped off about the night but not the time of the first of these, George sat up to listen. His mother waited, too, until she could scarcely keep awake. She rose from bed, however, at George's shout when 'Love Me Do' finally filled the airwaves. As his wife and son crouched downstairs, straining to hear the guitar work, Harold groaned. He had to be at the depot, fresh and alert for the early morning shift.

Spurred on by plays on the Light Programme and the buzz from the northwest, 'Love Me Do' began its yo-yo progression to a tantalisingly high of Number 17 in the *New Musical Express's* Top 30. They'd done well, for first-timers, but who would assume that The Beatles were anything other than a classic local group who'd caught the lightning once, never to do so again? However, as 1963 got underway, a second 45, 'Please Please Me' was scudding up the charts, after they'd mimed it on *Thank Your Lucky Stars*, ITV's main pop showcase.

As pleasant a shock in its way were the considered ovations that unfurled into screams when the group were second billed to Helen Shapiro for an around-Britain tour that spring. By the final night, Helen was still closing the show, but the de facto headliners by then were The Beatles, whose debut LP had just been issued to cash in on their 'Please Please Me' breakthrough.

Over half of the album was written by Paul and John – including 'Do You Want To Know A Secret?', George's only lead vocal. Conscious that Lennon especially would knowingly warp the tunes of others to his own ends, it dawned on George that this particular opus was "actually a nick, a bit of a pinch" from The Chants'/Stereos' 'I Really Love You'.

George decided to give this composing lark a whirl too. For months, however, everything he tried sounded the same. He didn't have the confidence for the public trial and error that John and Paul endured without a thought when they pieced together The Beatles' third single, 'From Me To You', on the coach during the last leg of the Shapiro tour.

A bare week after this jaunt was finished, the group were thrust into another such trek. On the posters, their name was in smaller type than Tommy Roe and Chris Montez, Bobby-ish Americans both with singles currently in the UK Top 20

– but right from the first night, the running order was reshuffled as audience response had dictated that the home-grown Beatles play last.

Negotiations began then for The Beatles to top the bill on *Sunday Night At The London Palladium* – although, as John Lennon insisted, "We don't feel we are ready" – even though, on their third major tour in four months, The Beatles were headlining over Roy Orbison. He was no lamb to the slaughter like Roe and Montez, and the group were relieved that they could still whip up screams that were growing louder every time they played. At first, Orbison considered them pretty rough and ready, "Just a rehash of rock 'n' roll that I'd been involved with for a long time, but it turned out to be very fresh and full of energy and vitality. So I recognised it at the time."

Their tour with Orbison was causing scenes as uninhibited and contagious as those that had accompanied concerts by Johnnie Ray back in the 1950s. The national press noticed too that here was was a human-interest story of Poor Honest Northern Lads Who'd Bettered Themselves. Furthermore, they were good copy – plain speaking, coupled with quirky wit delivered in thickened Scouse.

John and Paul's comedy act had long been a diversion from the daily grind of road, dressing room, stage and hotel. George was on more solid ground when able to steer discussions with journalists away from "what's-your-favourite-colour" trivia to music, but there were moments when he exploded with succinct repartee. In fact, some of his backchat was even erroneously attributed to John. Joined by comedian Ken Dodd for an interview on ITV, The Beatles were invited by Dodd to think up and earthy forename for him, as he wished to become a rock 'n' roller. "Sod?", suggested George the second the commercial break started.

Every recording manager outside EMI was watching with nitpicking hope for the remotest indication of The Beatles' fall. They'd surely had enough revenge on those who'd spurned them when at last they agreed to star on *Sunday Night At The London Palladium*. Could anyone get more famous than that?

The next day, the media was full of the "overnight sensation" and its aftermath as a police cordon with helmets rolling in the gutter held back hundreds of clamorous fans who'd chase The Beatles' getaway car into Oxford Street. A pressured journalist chronicling the mayhem came up with the word "Beatlemania". The phrase stuck, but Beatlemania as a phenomenon was to have less to do with the group itself than with the behaviour of the British public, who, once convinced of something incredible, would believe it with an enthusiasm never displayed for mundane fact.

6 The Moptop

Virtually every other track on autumn 1963's *With The Beatles* album was covered by another artist. All were either Beatles' arrangements of non-originals from their concert repertoire or new Lennon-McCartney compositions. The one exception was 'Don't Bother Me', rehashed for Pye by Gregory Phillips with an "oo-aah" girlie chorus, the only digression from Beatle precedent. This opus was the first published solo composition by George Harrison.

He didn't follow up speedily on this tentative exercise in composition, undeserving of inclusion in the stage act. Instead, he fell back to his accustomed role of being one of Paul and John's sounding boards, one whose advice wasn't taken as seriously as that of George Martin. Nonetheless, they'd let him have three *With The Beatles* lead vocals to Ringo's one. "In The Beatles days, I was always very paranoid, very nervous, and that inhibited my singing," George said, but still he managed a painless 'Devil In Her Heart'. Although smoother than Lennon's might have been, his 'Roll Over Beethoven' emerged as a single – and hit, to boot – in many foreign parts.

It was a year when The Beatles could have topped charts with 'Knees Up Mother Brown'. Some listeners, however, weren't that snowblinded. At this most public and prolific phase of the four's recording career, it was easier for journalists and photographers to infiltrate the sessions regulated by the Musicians' Union that The Beatles were yet to challenge by running over into the small hours. When outsiders were scheduled to be present, George would forsake his usual jeans and open-necked shirt for clothes less casual. However, no amount of sprucing up for the cameras could prevent George Martin from stopping run-throughs to point out errors. In front of one scribbling reporter, he criticised the guitar tuning, "and you, George, should be coming in on the second beat every time instead of the fourth." "Oh, I see," replied Harrison, his hackles rising slightly.

Also noted were the jumbled solos that George would insert into some backing tracks. Those ignorant of advancing recording techniques might or might not be told that George had invented them on the spot for reference only. Later, he'd re-record the parts in less public circumstances, combining his and, most of all, George Martin's further thoughts about them.

Self-contained enough to disassociate the instrument from Martin's schoolmasterly perseverance, "A day doesn't pass without me having a go on the guitar." He picked the song very prettily when 'Till There Was You', a song from a film musical, was second in the group's subdued four-song segment in the *Royal Variety Show* in November. On the boards, however, he wasn't generally so hot. An indifferent improviser, he'd often double up with John, as plainly heard on 'I Saw Her Standing There' during five October days in Sweden, the group's first true overseas tour. In his defence, however, it must be stated that, at that particular recital in Stockholm, George was about to be almost yanked offstage by rampaging fans.

On their homecoming from Scandinavia, just over 1,000 teenagers on half-term holiday had ignored the heavy drizzle to converge on Heathrow Airport's upper terraces just for a glimpse of them. From their morning flight, the baffled quartet were met by the unison banshee scream that they'd mistaken for engine noise on touchdown.

Beatlemania was pop hysteria at its most intense. Other unhappy artists on the same bill would soldier on as the eclipsing howls and chants for The Beatles welled up to a pitch where you drowned in noise. Somehow, the already ear-stinging decibels climbed higher when The Beatles sauntered onstage, outwardly enjoying their work. The girls went crazy, tearing their hair, wiping their eyes, rocking foetally and flapping scarves and programmes in the air. The volume rose momentarily to its loudest, as if they'd all sat on tin-tacks, when Paul and George appeared.

Absorbing this accelerating adulation, George was initially the Beatle least unsettled by it all. For a while, he remained his old, selectively amiable self, although "old" was a little inappropriate. Some of those reporters who'd figured out which one was which would refer to him as "young George". He didn't yet behave older than his years. To the group's long-serving publicist Tony Barrow, he lagged behind the other three "in terms of physical appearance and general sophistication". He was the one sighted most often preening himself before dressing room mirrors, perhaps applying lacto-calamine lotion to spots that no hit record could prevent from appearing on an otherwise comely adolescent complexion.

Nevertheless, "society" Londoners were often intrigued to meet him and other real "wackers" now that Liverpool was where more happened than just dock strikes. More fascinating was that some of them were suddenly rich enough, like George, to "get a Ferrari and bomb about".

He could also afford well-deserved breaks in faraway places. On 16 September 1963, George was the first Beatle to set foot in the United States, when he flew via New York and St Louis to stay for a fortnight with his married sister, then living in Benton, Illinois. Naturally, Louise had been kept posted about George's exploits with his group and had collected all of their Polydor and Parlophone records, plus the two or three issued in North American on labels of no great merit. Through her, some had been played on local radio, but these few spins had the impact of a feather on concrete in a continent whose wavelengths were overloaded with yapping disc jockeys with lurid *noms de turntable* – Wolfman Jack, Murray the K, Magnificent Montague – all unmindful of whatever was gripping a backwater like Britain.

"I don't know. What do you think?" was the spirit that pervaded the eventual unleashing of 'I Want To Hold Your Hand' by EMI's American outlet, Capitol. Although this ensured a better chance of airplay than earlier Beatles singles had with smaller companies, the group and Epstein could not yet assume that they'd be much more than a strictly European phenomenon, like Cliff Richard.

Always they expected it to end. By 1964, preceding them on a British stage was less onerous "now that The Beatles have found their own level" – so said the most frequent of their guest stars, Kenny Lynch, in an article headlined "Is The Beatles Frenzy Cooling Down?"

Supporting Lynch's argument that "The Rolling Stones may be just as big as The Beatles now" was the sense of impending hangover in Liverpool. As the record companies weren't coming around so much any more, far-sighted Merseybeat musicians realised that their very dialect was shortly to be a millstone around their necks. More than one Scouse group attempted to dilute their accents and pass themselves off as Londoners.

The Beatles had become a London-based outfit when NEMS Enterprises uprooted itself late in 1963. George began his metropolitan domicile by renting briefly a *pied à terre* in

Green Street, just off Park Lane and handy for West End nightclubbing. By the time 52 sacks of mail were dumped on his parents' doorstep the day he came of age, he and Ringo were sharing what became an untidy flat beneath Brian Epstein's mews apartment in Whaddon House, Knightsbridge – a target for graffiti and marathon vigils by fans.

7 The Serious One

Like any backstreet lad abruptly rich, George's consumption was more conspicuous than those for whom wealth was second nature. Though he'd later rein in his extravagance, purchasing a succession of flash cars was beyond rapture for a youth who for too long had had his nose glued to showroom windows.

Chronologically, he'd grown to man's estate, but there remained a strong streak of the adolescent in him. At a party, he got so giggly over a quip about "pack up Mick Jagger in your old kit bag" that he had to write it down. On an edition of *Juke Box Jury* showcasing the whole group, he switched the name plates so that, for years, my friend Kevin was under the misapprehension that George was John.

No Beatle was baited by the others as Stuart and Tommy had been, but George was often treated with less than respect by John and Paul. Sometimes he asked for it. One of his most irritating traits was butting into their conversations with some flat line as if trying to imprint his importance to the group on outsiders. Interrupting Paul and a *Melody Maker* interviewer, George "was thinking, 'How about something like Little Richard's "Bama Lama Bama Loo"?'" "You just write daft things, George," snapped Paul before turning back to the reporter. "As I was saying, about writing a rocker – I'd liken it to abstract painting..."

Since 'Don't Bother Me', George had composed not a single "daft thing". Yet his undervalued guitar style was as rich a legacy for other artists as any other Beatle innovation. Because his solos and riffs were constructed to integrate with the melodic and lyrical intent of each song, they seemed unobtrusive – even bland – in contrast to those within the year's crop of groups who'd ditched Beatle winsomeness for denim taciturnity. Musically, the main difference lay in the lead guitarist, who, unlike Harrison, would step forward into the spotlight to react with clenched teeth and intellectual flash to underlying chord patterns rather than the aesthetics of the song.

Containing such an exquisite, The Yardbirds secured a support spot at The Beatles' 1964 Christmas season at Hammersmith Odeon. While sharing the self-immolatory tendencies of some of his black icons, lead guitarist Eric "Slowhand" Clapton was steeped more than most in the note-bending dissonance of the blues. This distinction did not register with George Harrison, who passed the time of day with the Yardbird along backstage corridors "but didn't really get to know him".

For as long as Clapton, Jeff Beck and other would-be virtuosi fermented hitless in the specialist clubs and college circuit, George would continue to win polls as top guitarist. Deservedly, he – and The Searchers – can be credited for introducing the 12-string guitar to the common-or-garden pop group: "It's gear. It sounds a bit like electric piano, I always think, but you can get a nice fat sound out of it." From an actor friend of Bob Dylan, he learned the rudiments of playing it finger-style, but he always reverted to the plectrum. While it was still a novelty at home, George had procured a Rickenbacker semi-acoustic model – with the four lowest sets of strings tuned in octaves – during The Beatles' first trip to the States. Limited as a solo instrument, its uniquely circular effect powered a flip-side, 'You Can't Do That', on which John played lead, although George's new 12-string took the resounding *bis* passage in the title song on *A Hard Day's Night*.

After the USA had capitulated, the rest of the world was a pushover. Despite torrential rain, The Beatles were welcomed in Australia by the biggest crowd since aviator Amy Johnson landed there after her solo flight from England in 1932.

This tour had been negotiated by Brian Epstein even before the trip to the States. For his "boys" – his surrogate children – he did whatever energy and willingness could do to help their careers, to make him prouder of them and them of him. He took their gratuitous insults, their piques, their flagrant cohabitation with their girlfriends and their headline-making misbehaviour like the loving father he should have been.

George and a new girlfriend – a model named Pattie Boyd – accompanied Brian to the south of France. Solicitous as usual, he deferred to the couple's wishes about how they spent their leisure but could be relied upon to suggest diversions. A bull fight in Arles, however, wasn't a wincing George's notion of a pleasant afternoon.

Fun for all the family, however, The Beatles' TV appearances back home were always special, and Christmas wouldn't be Christmas without the "Fab Four" at Number One. Under parental pressure, some West Country headmasters reshuffled lunch hours so that senior pupils might rush to railway stations to glimpse The Beatles when they were shunted to and from Paddington and Devon for four days for some of the train scenes in *A Hard Day's Night*.

A romantic sub-plot had been on the cards briefly, until producer Walter Shenson realised how much the group's female following might resent it. Visualised for this role had been 16-year-old Hayley Mills, a pert, snub-nosed miss who'd been in films since the late 1950s. George was the Beatle who'd drawn the short straw for the pleasure of squiring her to the Regal in Henley-on-Thames for a showing of the Hitchcockian *Charade*. At this charity midnight matinee, he was as impressed with the cinema's Art Deco interior as he was with *Charade* and Miss Mills.

A one-off date was enough to set tongues wagging about Harrison and Hayley, but rumours about him and Pattie Boyd had infinitely more substance. Pattie was then consistent with George's taste, which "runs to small blonde girls who can share a laugh with me". Their backgrounds, nonetheless, were poles apart. The eldest of six children, Patricia Anne Boyd was born in Somerset in 1945, but one of her father's RAF postings obliged the family to move to Kenya four years later. By 1962, however, anyone peering through the window of a certain Wimbledon hairdressing salon might have seen her putting the finishing touches to some aged crone's blue rinse. Noticing Pattie's willowy figure and avalanche of wavy hair, another customer – a writer for a women's magazine – asked if she'd ever thought of becoming a photographic model.

When she met George, she was in the same mini-skirted league as Twiggy, Celia Hammond and Jean Shrimpton, the new face of *Vogue*, *Seventeen* and the fashion pages of Sunday supplements. Mary Quant, Shrimpton's haute couture Diaghilev, noted how mandatory it had become for 1960s dolly-birds "to look like Pattie Boyd rather than Marlene Dietrich. Their aim is to look childishly young, naïvely unsophisticated, and it takes more sophistication to work out that look than those early would-be sophisticates ever dreamed of."

It was fitting, therefore, for 20-year-old Pattie to land a bit part as a schoolgirl in *A Hard Day's Night*. With her and three other uniformed and giggly girls as the audience, The

Beatles mimed 'I Should Have Known Better' in a studio mock-up of a guard's van. "I could feel George looking at me," recalled Pattie, "and I was a bit embarrassed. Then, when he was giving me his autograph, he put seven kisses under his name. I thought he must like me a little." At first, George, the unencumbered bachelor, came on as the rough, untamed Scouser, but this brash outer shell, Pattie discovered, contained surprising gentleness and sensitivity.

After pairing off with Pattie, George became less of a West End clubman, but his record collection still reflected an advanced awareness of the American soul music that forever filled the downstairs disco's deafening dark at the Scotch Of St James, London's trendiest night spot. Nevertheless, George would never be snooty about mainstream pop. His tastes again were largely North American, running to the post-surf Beach Boys, The Byrds and New York's Lovin' Spoonful, who had roots in rural blues and Memphis jug bands. Both The Byrds and the Spoonful had been classified as "folk-rock", as was Bob Dylan, who'd also offended folk purists by going electric in around 1965. Because it exposes a point of view, even 'Can't Buy Me Love' may be construed as political, but Dylan sang stridently through his nose about myriad less wistful topics.

Lennon and McCartney weren't in complete agreement on the issue of Bob Dylan. While Paul had reservations, John's moptop was often covered at this time with a denim cap like Dylan's, and some of his newer songs – especially 'I'm A

Loser', from *Beatles For Sale* – betrayed an absorption of the American through constant replay of his albums. The time would come when George would be even more hooked on Dylan than John. "Even his stuff which people loathe I like," he'd boast, "because every single thing he does represents something that's him."

As an individual, Dylan was "the looniest person I've ever met". This George had surmised when The Beatles were first introduced to him in a New York hotel suite during their first North American tour. Soon Dylan would grow as heartily sick of explaining his songs as The Beatles were of answering questions about haircuts and how they found America ("turn left at Greenland"). "They asked one question eight different times," George snorted after another mind-stultifying press conference. What kind of a world was this, where hotel chambermaids would sell their stories to journalists before the group had even checked in?

When interruptive fans in restaurants spoiled too many meals, the four took to "ones where people are so snobby they pretend they don't know us". Even an R&B jamboree in Richmond was no sanctuary, as an excursion by George and John to see The Animals there fired an outbreak of Beatlemania and the pair's hasty departure. "We can't go window shopping," shrugged Harrison, "We can't browse around a department store. We'll have this for four or five years or a few more. In the meantime, we'll wait, and it's not bad, really. We're making money while waiting."

There are worse ways of making a living, but for George performing was becoming the most onerous obligation of Beatlehood. In concert, they heard the relentless screaming no more than a mariner hears the sea. As far as guesswork and eye contact would allow, they adhered to recorded arrangements, but, sighed George, "It was impossible to know which song they screamed for most." Because George had mentioned in *The Daily Mirror* that he was partial to them, jelly-babies would shower The Beatles in Britain. As different from these sweets as hailstones are to snow, their harder equivalents would hit them overseas. Through the medium of *Melody Maker*, George begged "a favour for us. Write down that we've had enough jelly-babies now. Thank the fans very much, but we'd like them to stop throwing them."

Up there, they endured the mixed blessings of their vulnerability by jesting amongst themselves. For devilment, they'd mouth songs soundlessly or slam deliberate dischords. For the wrong reasons, concerts could still be a laugh. "We must have been hell to work with," George would smile in another decade. "We'd always be messing about and joking."

Who could keep a straight face in the madness? Socialites, civic dignitaries with their hoity-toity children and everyone who was anyone were falling over themselves to be presented to four common-as-muck Liverpudlians. Cassius Clay and Ringo would spar playfully. Zsa Zsa Gabor would have her picture taken with George, who concluded, "Meeting everybody we thought worth knowing and finding out they weren't worth meeting, and having more hit records than everybody else and having done it bigger than everybody else – it was like reaching the top of a wall and then looking over and seeing that there's so much more on the other side."

Soon to disappear was the jubilant youth who, clad only in a bath towel, waved at worshipping masses from a hotel balcony in Sydney. What had been the point of travelling so far and seeing nothing but what he could remember of, say, a stolen afternoon driving a borrowed MG sports car in the Dandenong Mountains or a bowling alley somewhere in Quebec, re-opened for his private use at midnight? He'd seen only glimpses of the places where his blinkered life with The Beatles had taken him. When asked what such-and-such a city had been like, he was damned if he could even find it on a map.

8 The Member Of The British Empire

Indifferent to success rather than celebrating it, George had been seeking – as he'd articulate later – to "try to stop the waves, quieten them down, to make myself a calm little pool". Rather than joining John, Ringo and Mr Epstein in their Weybridge stockbroker's estate, he'd chosen instead a place called Kinfauns, an exclusive property in wooded Claremont Park in Esher, a few miles nearer the metropolis. Surrounded by high walls, it was not as exposed to fans' attentions as his Knightsbridge flat, but George was, nevertheless, the first Beatle to equip himself with electronically operated gates.

Very much the junior partner in the group, George's songwriting explorations thus far were of less value than the power he gave to Lennon and McCartney's patterns of chords and rhymes. Neither of the two albums that had passed since *With The Beatles* contained additions to the Harrison portfolio. Lyrics were almost always "the hardest part for me. When the thing is finished, I'm usually happy with some parts of it and unhappy with others, so then I show it to John and Paul, whose opinion I respect."

Lennon lent the most sympathetic ears when George presented two possibilities for inclusion on the soundtrack to the next film, *Help!*. A week prior to the recording dates in February 1965, John and George spent most of the night polishing up 'I Need You' and, with a country-and-western tinge, 'You Like Me Too Much'. "Well, it was 4.30 in the morning when we got to bed," enthused George, "and we had to be up at 6.30. What a fantastic time!"

To fans, George was as much the public face of The Beatles as John, and matters had gone far enough for any fears of him going the way of Pete Best to vanish. Although he was no match for John as a verbal intimidator or Paul as a diplomat, the concept of a Beatles without him or Ringo was now unthinkable. Nevertheless, the chemistry of the four interlocking personalities apart, he was expendable. In 1966, George could still be made to do as he was told.

In the studio, Norman Smith witnessed how Lennon and, especially, McCartney treated the other two as mere tools for their masterworks, "because George would have done two or three takes that seemed perfectly all right but Paul wouldn't like it and he'd start quoting American records, telling George to play it like it was such and such a song. We'd try again, and then Paul would take over and do it himself on the left-handed guitar he always brought with him. Later I found out that George had been hating Paul's guts for this but didn't let it show. It says a lot for George that he took so much stick from Paul."

Yet the promotional clips on television still paid lip-service to John on rhythm, Paul on bass, George on lead and Ringo on drums, even though the latest single, 'Ticket To Ride', had Paul on both bass and lead.

The single's B-side, 'Yes It Is', and 'I Need You', taped at the same session, were more taxing for George, as they kept his feet as well as hands and voice occupied. Mistaken in a *Music And Musicians* critique for a harmonica were the tearful guitar legatos achieved by George on both songs with a volume pedal.

Their camouflage nets sparkling with dawn dew, Centurion tanks guarded The Beatles as they mimed George's 'I Need You' for film cameras on Salisbury Plain scrubland. Only a mild exaggeration of the protective bubble surrounding the group in real life, this scene was to be Harrison's big moment in *Help!*.

'You Like Me Too Much' was placed on the non-soundtrack side of *Help!*. Lyrically more substantial than 'I Need You', it might have described one of the tiffs that punctuated the otherwise happy domesticity with Pattie at Kinfauns. The jealous character assassinations and physical threats that had fanfared Pattie's public entry into the Beatle "family" had abated by now. George's female fans still envied her but could now stomach Pattie's wasp waist, her lisping confidence and her finger on the pulse of fashion.

As George Harrison's girlfriend, she'd be commissioned to write a regular "Letter From London" for *16*, a US magazine that never probed deeper than her favourite *color*, and what food she served when the Lennons visited.

Pattie would recall "so many laughs". The idiosyncratic humour that had sustained George and the others before she knew them was still potent. On the Madrid stop of the 1965 European tour, they pulled swimming trunks over their heads to greet ballet dancer Rudolf Nureyev, another hotel guest, who met fire with fire by deadpanning the subsequent platitudes. Such diversions were to George "always the best bit about being in a band, rather than like Elvis, who, being one, suffered things on his own".

They might have been offhand with Nureyev, but The Beatles were speechless at first when taken to Presley in his Beverly Hills mansion late one evening in August 1965. Because of some now-forgotten quarrel that day, George was in a foul mood when he arrived with the others for the audience with the King. However, according to Presley's stepbrother, David Stanley, Presley thought, "George Harrison was all right. Harrison was a seeker of truth, just as Elvis was, and that gave them a special bond." In 1972, George was to insinuate his way backstage to pay respects after an Elvis show in New York. "I had my uniform – the worn-out denim jacket and jeans – and I had a big beard and long hair down to my waist. He was immaculate. He seemed to be about eight feet tall and his tan was perfect. I felt like this grubby little slug and Elvis looked like Lord Siva."

Lord Siva is a Hindu demigod. The journey to a George Harrison almost unrecognisable from the yeah-yeah-yeah moptop had started a few months before that first meeting with Elvis in 1966. The turning point had been an occasion when George and Pattie had, as usual, paired up with the Lennons. A mischievous dentist with whom George was friendly – "a middle class swinger", reckoned John – concluded an otherwise pleasant evening around his house by slipping into his guests' coffee a mickey finn of LSD.

The effects of LSD vary from person to person, from trip to trip. George compared it to a mystic purging akin to an extreme religious reverie: "Up until LSD, I never realised that there was anything beyond this state of consciousness, but all the pressure was such that, like the man [Dylan] said, 'There must be some way out of here.' I think, for me, it was definitely LSD. The first time I took it, it just blew everything away. I had such an overwhelming feeling of well-being, that there was a God and I could see Him in every blade of grass. It was like gaining hundreds of years' experience in twelve hours."

Media interviewers couldn't help but perceive the change in George. Although his replies to questions were unfailingly to the point, any witticisms were oddly sour and would provoke but a puffy smile where there used to be a chuckle. More than any in the entourage, George begrudged

Beatlemania. Even before LSD worked its questionable magic, "I was fed up. I couldn't take any more but resigned myself to suffering it for another year." Fledgling journalist Philip Norman was admitted to one backstage sanctum in late 1965, where he found the group "perfectly friendly and pleasant – all but George Harrison. He was rather withdrawn, but the others just talked away."

Others mistook George's frequent brown studies for sullenness, but during a final tour of Britain those in the know might have attributed them to his longing for the sanctuary of Kinfauns and Pattie. Just before Christmas, not so much a proposition as a discussion – involving Brian, too – led the couple to tie the knot as quietly as they were allowed at Epsom Registry Office on 21 January 1966. "I got married because I'd changed," George explained at the unavoidable press conference the next day.

Beatlemania had not merely robbed him of privacy but had also stunted him artistically. As he cranked out the same 30 minutes' worth of stale, unheard music night after artless night, he weighed up the cash benefits of being a Beatle on stage against his self-picture as a musician. In any case, tracks from their newest LP, *Rubber Soul*, were difficult to reproduce with the conventional beat group line-up, although some sections could be approached by using Paul or John's skills on the Vox Continental electric organ that now travelled with the guitars and drums. One that couldn't, however, was the sitar played by George on 'Norwegian Wood'.

George had stumbled upon one among props strewn about the set of *Help!*. He treated it as if it were some fancy guitar until, with deceptive casualness, the Indian sitar virtuoso Ravi Shankar came into his life at a mutual friend's London home in the late spring of 1966. Ravi was only vaguely aware of his new acquaintance's stature, but Harrison "seemed so different from the usual musicians I meet in the pop field. He was so simple and charming and kind, and he showed his desire to learn something." Ravi put him right about the folly of teaching yourself sitar. Ideally, it was best to be accepted as a shishya under a master like himself. Thus began a lifelong amity akin to that of a liberal-minded teacher and a waywardly earnest pupil. In his realisation that "through the musical you reach the spiritual", George was beyond the first rung, but, insisted Ravi, he must visit India, not only for more intensive training but also to get the rhythm of life there under his skin and thereby slip more easily into his new musical tongue. As his Beatle duties beckoned until autumn, however, George would have to get by with Ravi's tape recorded correspondence course.

The Beatles traversed an Earth that was rapidly becoming less and less eye-stretching. A luxury hotel in Belgium was just like one in Tennessee – the Coca-Cola tasted exactly the same. Everywhere was the same. If it's Monday, it must be Manila.

Manila, however, would always be remembered. Unaware that they were required to pay a courtesy call on the family and friends of the Philippines' autocratic President Ferdinand Marcos, the group slept through the arrival and ireful departure of presidential lackeys who had been commanded to bring them to his palace. George recalled his bafflement when, over a late breakfast, somebody "turned on the television and there it was, this big palace with lines of people and this guy saying, 'Well, they're not here yet,' and we watched ourselves not arrive at the party."

On the following day, the expected crowd of fans at Manila International Airport were puzzled that no security measures had been laid on. Close enough to be touched, their agitated idols lugged their baggage up static escalators a few steps ahead of an angry mob of adults who stopped just short of open assault when their prey threaded slowly and in a cold sweat through a customs area resounding with jack-in-office unpleasantness and every fibre of red tape that Philippino bureaucracy could gather. "They were waiting for us to retaliate," said George, "so that they could finish us off. I was terrified. These 30 funny-looking fellows with guns had obviously arranged to give us the worst time possible."

This jubilant oppression had started the previous evening, when incessant interference contrived by station engineers had wiped out every word of Brian Epstein's televised apology for his Beatles' unknowing insult to the hallowed person of Ferdinand Marcos. Sent on their way by boos and catcalls from the tyrant's creatures, never had George's arguments against continued touring made more sense, but even the Manila incident would be a trifle when compared to what awaited them on the final leg. Prophetic, then, was his flippant "we're going to have a couple of weeks to recuperate before we go and get beaten up by the Americans".

A psychological rather than physical battering started when US journals picked up the story that Lennon had "boasted" that The Beatles were more popular than Jesus Christ. If anything, John in the original *London Evening Standard* article had seemed to be bemoaning the increasing godlessness of the times, but more sensational was the North American interpretation of "blasphemy".

As the ripples of backlash and moral opprobrium spread, so did real fear of an assassination attempt on Lennon and perhaps the other three, too. Engagements in the north passed without incident. Nevertheless, a firework that exploded on stage in Memphis gave all four a horrified start, following a telephoned death threat that afternoon. Recalling an evening in 1964 when "a kid in Brisbane threw a tin on stage and it freaked him right out", an eye-witness theorised that "George has an incredible fear of being killed—" who hasn't, sport? "—which possibly accounts for the shell he withdrew into".

At San Francisco's Candlestick Park on 29 August 1966, they downed tools as a working band. No better or worse than any other concert they'd given on the tour, they ran through this final half-hour any old how, with George fluffing his guitar runs as Paul tried to make a show of it.

George's would be the most quoted remark from the flight back to England. "Well, that's it," was his succinct and strangely dejected elegy. "I'm not a Beatle any more."

9 The Shishya

George's hard listening to Ravi Shankar came to the fore in 'Love You To' from *Revolver*. A backing track of himself on sitar and a certain Anil Bhaghat hired to tap the tablas set the mood with a slow alap ("introduction"), but rather than sustain this serenity, as Ravi would, they snapped into feverish tempo. Only the English lyrics and, down in the mix, the electric bass and fuzz guitar gave 'Love You To' any semblance of Western pop. The common chord reasserted itself in other Harrison compositions, such as 'Taxman', the rhythmic bounce of which belied a libretto dark with dry fuming at the ravages of the Inland Revenue. George's tally of three songs on *Revolver* was the highest so far on any album. Delivered from the treadmill of the road, his consequent flowering as a songwriter contributed to The Beatles' eventual self-destruction, but on *Revolver* they were at their most effective as a team.

As yet, George didn't miss the stage, though he still attended recitals by other groups – such as Cream, a trio whose appeal hinged not so much on looks but virtuosity demonstrated in lengthy improvisations of selections from their debut album. The loudest cheers – not screams – were for the over-amplified flash of Eric Clapton, who had been the subject of graffiti claiming "Clapton is God" while with John Mayall's Bluesbreakers.

Both *Fresh Cream* and *A Collection Of Beatles Oldies* were released in December 1966, but the former climbed higher in the charts than the latter, and Clapton became, with newcomer Jimi Hendrix, the most worshipped of pop guitarists. To *The Sunday Times*, however, George Harrison was only "a passable guitarist (say among the best thousand in the country)".

Such slights on George as an instrumentalist were unfair, as The Beatles' stylistic determination left little space for any extensive extrapolations of the kind popularised by Hendrix and Cream. Nonetheless, George must have warmed to Clapton, who, in *Disc* magazine, praised the lead-guitar playing on *Revolver*. This accolade was deserved, if only for the technical accomplishment demonstrated by George's idea of superimposing two backwards – and tuneful – guitar overdubs on top of one another to create the apt "yawning" solo and obligato on Lennon's 'I'm Only Sleeping'. This attractive enveloping sound was developed further by other guitarists, notably Hendrix on the title track of his LP *Are You Experienced?*.

It was pleasing to be liked and copied like this, but George wasn't to be as revered a guitar hero in the later 1960s as he'd been in the beat boom. Although he'd always see himself as a lesser guitarist, George was in a different rather than lower league to Clapton and Hendrix, whose fretboard fireworks were then heard night after night onstage.

For long after the armoured car had whisked George from Candlestick Park, his guitar had been played only sporadically. This wasn't because it symbolised all that he'd recently and gladly relinquished; it was simply that as once he'd laboured over *Play In A Day*, so, from Indian script, he was practicing the sitar hour upon hour, day after day

Two weeks after Candlestick Park, he had flown to India for further study under Ravi Shankar in Banares. Ravi found George to be "an enthusiastic and ambitious student because he realises that the sitar itself is an evolvement from Indian culture. It might take a lifetime of learning, but, if he progresses in the same way that he has been doing, his understanding will lead to a medium of greatness on the sitar."

To his shishya, Ravi Shankar was more than a music teacher; he was also a spiritual guide and something of a father figure. He may not have cut much ice with a younger George in the fleshpots of Hamburg, but in Banares, the holiest of Indian cities, the refugee from Beatlemania was open to religious enlightenment. Thus his Cook's tour of Hinduism took in religious festivals in temples towering over narrow alleyways and on the banks of the Ganges, the steps to which were worn as smooth as the the Blarney Stone by pious feet descending into the grimy but purifying bathing ghats, each one dedicated to a different deity.

All good things must come to an end, and Harrison returned to Britain's unusually rainy autumn with a rakish Imperial beard and doctrines and perceptions of deeper maturity than before. Both he and Pattie had embraced vegetarianism, and George had even gone through a phase of eating with his hands, Indian style. As well as the expected nut roasts and meatless curries, the Kinfauns kitchen also served dishes that, while common in Banares, were exotic in Esher.

However scrumptious these meals were, the fact that a Beatle was tucking into them was splendid news for stockists of Indian goods in the West. In provincial Britain, where the 1950s hadn't ended until 1966, a Beatle fan might waste hours outside a record shop debating whether or not to spend three week's paper-round savings on Ustad Ali Akbar Khan's *Young Master Of The Sarod*, for which George had supplied sleeve notes.

Over in San Francisco, "raga rock" was an ingredient in the psychedelic brew being concocted by The Jefferson Airplane, The Grateful Dead and other acts in a city about to become as vital a pop Mecca as Liverpool had been. Like The Big Three's homage to the Cavern, hit records in 1967 by both Eric Burdon and Scott McKenzie paid tribute to San Francisco's new eminence. Each performed in June of that year at the Monterey International Pop Music Festival a few miles down the coast. Among many other highlights was an afternoon set by Ravi Shankar, which confirmed the larger public's acceptance of him and his instrument.

Ravi's association with The Beatles had done him a lot of good. Ticket sales for his concerts were guaranteed to pick up if there was a hint that George might be attending. A sizeable representation of Fleet Street lying in wait at Heathrow would disperse happily after noting the amusing spectacle of George in flowing Indian garb greeting a disembarking Shankar wearing a Western business suit.

Ravi was, however, disappointed by The Beatles' use of psychedelic drugs as an artificial means to greater awareness. When he had sat on the Monterey stage, his Beatle shishya and cohorts assembled at Lennon's house to join him in spirit: "We just took acid...and wondered what it would be like."

At Kinfauns, garish psychedelic patterns had been painted all over the outer walls under the direction of four Dutch theatrical designers whose mediaeval fancy dress matched their work and tradename, The Fool. This amalgam also submitted a frontage that was turned down as too hackneyed for *Sgt Pepper's Lonely Hearts Club Band*, the LP that followed *Revolver*.

The photo montage of characters on the LP consisted mainly of each Beatle's all-time heroes. Almost all of George's were Eastern gurus and religious leaders. As John's choices of Hitler and Christ were vetoed by EMI, so was George's of

Gandhi, although escaping the airbrush were Yogananda and Orientals even more unknown to the average Joe.

Just as erudite were those souvenirs of India with which George fairy-dusted passages of *Sgt Pepper*, among them tamboura and the swordmandel, a cross between a zither and an autoharp. Otherwise, he remained as dispensably in the background of John and Paul's creations as Ringo. During the media blitz commemorating the 20th anniversary of the album's release, perhaps it was fortunate that George wasn't present to hear McCartney remark nonchalantly, "George turned up for his number and a couple of other sessions but not much else."

It was true that George had absented himself once to attend a Ravi Shankar concert, but this could be excused as fieldwork for the orchestration of 'Within You Without You', his sole *Sgt Pepper* composition and, interestingly, the only one on which just one Beatle appeared. It was also the longest and most complicated piece on the album. Scored for an assortment of Indian instruments and superimposed violins and cellos, its three changes of time signature were unprecedented in a body of work that, since The Beatles' inception, had rarely deviated from straightforward 4/4.

Lyrically, it touched on matters spiritual. As orthodox pop is as devotional in its boy-girl way as sacred music, the chasm between 'Don't Bother Me' and 'Within You Without You' was not unbreachable, as George had discovered: "Singing to the Lord or an individual is, in a way, the same."

After "getting religion" in 1966, George's ideals would compound rather than alter. When the Kinfauns pond metamorphosed from clear tap-water to duckweed and wriggling animation, a visiting Epstein associate, Alistair Taylor, was drawn into a discussion that "veered off the subject of the pool... With George, everything leads to the cosmic meaning of life". The cruel manner of an older Beatle's passing years later would hurt, but death itself "doesn't really matter. He's OK, and life goes on within you and without you."

In Haight-Ashbury, the flower-power district of San Francisco, *Sgt Pepper* was a code for life. "Beatle readings" were as much part of the pageant of its streets as mime troupes, palmists, dancers, painters, spiritual healers (who gave instruction on how to write to archangels), poets and vendors of journals such as *The Psychedelic Oracle*.

"Wow! If it's all like this, it's too much," George remarked politely when he descended on Haight-Ashbury one August afternoon in 1967. As his coming was unheralded, he was just another sightseer for a few yards, before someone cried out, "Hey, that's George Harrison!" As the beglamoured girl panted up to him with her tongue-tied laudation, other passers-by gathered around, "then more and more people arrived and it got bigger and bigger". Fearful of the growing commotion, he and his retinue hastened back to the car with as much grace as they could muster after just over half an hour in the hippy capital.

He had surprised the hippies with his refusal of ingratiating tabs of LSD and tokes of marijuana as he strode past. Many of them had only "turned on" in the first place because they'd read that The Beatles had. As they were more than pop stars now, the group reacted to pressure from the world's youth to find "the truth", and, judging by the hollowed-eyed young derelicts that littered Haight-Ashbury and elsewhere, it wasn't LSD. "We're influencing a lot of people, so really it's up to us to influence them in the right way," admitted George. Although individually they either continued or resumed the habit, when The Beatles publicly repudiated the taking of illegal drugs, they never again made an issue of it.

George did not regret his experiences: "It showed me that LSD can help you to go from A to B, but when you get to B, you see C." Notable junctures on his and Pattie's pilgrimage to C were a climb up a Cornish tor one night after digesting a book about cosmic communication. Several hours passed with no sign of any extra-terrestrials.

In February, a friend of Pattie's had persuaded her to attend a lecture at London's Caxton Hall on "Spiritual Regeneration". There, the orator had stressed that his words were but a pale sketch onto which only the movement's founder, Maharishi Mahesh Yogi, could splash more vivid hues.

There remains bitter division about the Maharishi. Was he a complete charlatan or a well-meaning sage sucked into a vortex of circumstances that he was unable to resist?

Definitely he was smarter than the average yogi. Styling himself Maharishi ("great soul"), the mere mortal, born Mahesh Prasad Varma in 1918, had travelled to London in 1959 to set up a branch of the International Meditation Society, which had garnered a British membership of some 10,000 by the time Pattie brought her intrigued spouse to a meeting. Like a Charles Atlas course for the mind, the society promised increased productivity, less need for sleep, greater alertness and sharper distinction between the important and the trivial.

The overall aim – via short, daily meditation sessions – was to eradicate piecemeal all human vices and ego until a pure state of bliss was reached. Moreover, such washing of spiritual laundry was possible without forsaking material possessions (bar the society's membership fee) and, within reason, worldly pleasures. This seemed an excellent creed to a millionaire Beatle.

A few had been led to believe that a tutorial on 24 August at the Park Lane Hilton was to be Maharishi Mahesh Yogi's last before he disappeared back to his Indian fastness. Dragged along by the Harrisons, Paul, Jane Asher and the Lennons stole into the hushed hotel functions room like children to Santa's grotto. He so lived up to George and Pattie's spiel that, directly afterwards, The Beatles buttonholed the Great Soul and wound up promising to join him the next day at the Society's ten-day initiation course at a university faculty in the seaside resort of Bangor.

For people who'd viewed the world from the Olympus of stardom since 1963, it was perhaps too much of an adventure. Unused now to actually paying for things with hard cash, they were at a loss the following night when handed the bill after a meal in a Bangor restaurant. George was the first to realise why the waiters kept hovering about the table, and it was he, too, who settled the matter with a roll of banknotes he happened to have about his person.

Neither this imposition nor the hard mattresses in their hostel accommodation on the late-Victorian campus could deflect the pop stars from their iron purpose. Yet, during the press conference that Varma's public relations agent had set up in the main hall, most journalists didn't appear to take The Beatles' preoccupation with meditation very seriously.

One or two sick jokes started to circulate among the press corps awaiting them on Sunday afternoon, as they learned that Brian Epstein's life had ended suddenly in London. As the coroner would conclude later, he'd been killed through "incautious self-overdoses" of over-prescribed tablets he took compulsively to sleep, to stay awake, to calm his nerves, to lift his depressions.

As twilight thickened, The Beatles brushed past a pitiless whoomph of flashbulbs, their mouths moving mechanically as they walked from the university building into a black Rolls Royce. Its interior was their last sanctuary before they'd be obliged to respond fully to their manager's death. "We didn't know what to do," shrugged George later. "We were lost."

10 L'Angelo Mysterioso

Brian's most tangible legacy was The Beatles' new deal with EMI, which gave them a royalty rate higher than that of any other recording act. All they had to do in exchange was produce 70 tracks for release before 1976. This they would do well within the limit, both as individuals and, to a diminishing degree, collectively.

Four new tracks were unloaded onto the soundtrack of *Yellow Submarine*, which, inspected halfway towards completion, had been a pleasant surprise. This cartoon portrayed The Beatles as *Sgt Pepper*'s bandsmen in surreal encounters during a "modyssey" from Liverpool to Pepperland. So charmed were the real Beatles with this epic cartoon that they agreed to appear in cameo for the last scene.

However, as 1967's flowers wilted, so did their enthusiasm for *Yellow Submarine*. Significantly, half of the cheapskate tie-in album consisted of George Martin's incidental music and the cancelled 'Only A Northern Song'. The only new items that The Beatles bothered to add were, as they realised themselves, just inconsequential fillers. From George's quill had dripped 'It's All Too Much', in which a wide-ranged melody and laughably pretentious symbolism stayed afloat amid a roughcast, noisy backing with a vignette from Purcell's Trumpet Voluntary chucked in for good measure. In 1975, it was to be revived by arch-hippy guitarist Steve Hillage.

Favourable critical reaction to *Yellow Submarine* served to obscure memories of *Magical Mystery Tour,* a laboured film project, which wasn't perhaps suitable viewing for a nation sleeping off its Yuletide revels. It had been a development of McCartney's pretty idea of a journey with no known destination or outcome. Although the bulk of *Magical Mystery Tour* was drawn from this excursion, many interior scenes were filmed elsewhere, mainly back in London. Putting new moral objections on hold, George sat woodenly next to John in the front row of Paul Raymond's Revue Bar. Before him, a stripper entertained to the accompaniment of The Bonzo Dog Doo-Dah Band.

Magical Mystery Tour wasn't Citizen Kane, but its music was a winner. Proof of this was the grapple for UK chart supremacy between their latest single, 'Hello Goodbye', and a double EP for the film's six numbers, which cost three times more. Occupying a whole side of this novel package was George's repetitive 'Blue Jay Way', after the boulevard of the same name where the Harrisons stayed while in Los Angeles. As fog encircled their rented house, a still jet-lagged George had picked out its tune on a small electric. It wasn't much of a song, really, but it conveyed the requisite misty atmosphere. So, too, did the clouds of incense that shrouded the 'Blue Jay Way' sequence in the film, with the composer squatting in a lotus position, his swirling image refracted.

In *Yellow Submarine*, too, he'd been caricatured as a hazy mystic, and it was no surprise to Joe Public when George emerged as the most vocal supporter of this meditation caper.

Since Bangor, a retreat for further study to one of the Maharishi's two yoga-ashrams ("theological colleges") in the forested foothills of the Himalayas had been on the cards. This trip had been postponed twice owing to *Magical Mystery Tour* commitments, but George had maintained contact with His Holiness, mainly by telephone, although he had taken a day trip to Sweden with Ringo to confer with him and, with John, accompanied the Great Soul to a Shankar concert in Paris.

The media uproar during The Beatles' curtailed sojourn in Bangor had brought home to Varma what a catch he'd made. Like Ravi Shankar before him, he'd been unaware of the group's stature, but, armed with the relevant records, he underwent a crash-course in their music and began to illustrate his talks with quotes from their lyrics. Flattered though they were, The Beatles were unconvinced by his argument that, if they were sincere about meditation, they ought to tithe a percentage of their income into his Swiss bank account. Because they hadn't actually said no, the Maharishi assured

American investors that the four would be co-starring in a TV documentary about him. "He is not a modern man," explained George, as much to himself as anyone else. "He just doesn't understand such things."

Shelving their stronger misgivings, Paul, Jane and the Starkeys followed an advance guard of the Harrisons and Lennons to India, in February 1968, where all were both relieved and disconcerted that the meditation academy was not a compound of mud huts but whitewashed, air-conditioned chalets fully equipped to US standards, with an attached post office, laundry and dining hall.

"It'll probably turn out like a Butlin's holiday camp," George had remarked to *Melody Maker* before he left, and so it did for Maureen and Ringo, who went home early. The remaining seekers of nirvana would assemble clothed against the morning heat in the open-air amphitheatre for lessons that included practical demonstrations, such as the apparent suspended animation that His Holiness induced in one of his staff. He also spoke of levitation, but no Beatle would be around long enough to witness any. Gradually, the talks became shorter and periods for individual contemplation lengthened. Later, George bragged of being entranced for a 36-hour period.

Shortly after the celebration of Pattie's 23rd birthday, Jane and Paul threw in the towel and returned to London. A Beatles hanger-on named Alex Mardas, meanwhile, was torn between his own boredom with ashram life and his desire to maintain his position at John's ear. His problem was resolved three weeks later, when he'd accumulated enough tittle-tattle to speak to Lennon and Harrison of Varma's clandestine scheming for the downfall of an American nurse's knickers. With the manipulative Alex urging him on, Lennon confronted the Great Soul with this infamy. Deaf to all the protestations of innocence, John announced his immediate departure.

Not knowing what to think, the Harrisons chose to wash their hands of the Maharishi, too, although George preserved a vestige of regard for one who'd orchestrated "one of the greatest experiences I've ever had". Still a believer in the soundness of the too-human guru's teachings, he confessed, "It's just that we physically left the Maharishi's camp but spiritually never moved an inch. We still meditate now. At least, I do."

He broke the journey back to England to look up Ravi Shankar. At a press conference the previous August, he'd been addressed as "George" and Ravi had been "Mr Shankar". This was commensurate with the respect held for each as a sitarist. Starting too late in life, and with his pop career precluding daily hours of practice, Ravi admitted that George "realised it demands the whole time, but he still continues to learn from me as much as he can about Indian music, which he uses in his own work as inspiration". For years afterwards, "George Harrison (sitar)" would crop up in the Miscellaneous Instruments sections of music-press polls. "People put you in a bag,", he groused, "and nowadays all I've got to do is the slightest unusual rhythm and they say, 'There he goes, all Indian again.'"

There was, however, stark evidence of this when George was commissioned to provide the soundtrack to an oddity of a cinema film entitled *Wonderwall*. Aware of the publicity value of Beatle involvement, director Joe Massot felt that any old rubbish would do, as long as the words "George Harrison" could be printed on the credits.

As it turned out, George's music would be cited as the saving grace of a film graphically condemned by one leading critic as "a right load of codswallop". Issued some months before the film, the associated album was the first LP to be released via EMI on Apple, The Beatles' own record label. The label's name had first been tossed around during the *Revolver* sessions, to the extent of giving provisional fruity titles to tracks yet to receive one. 'Love You To', for instance, began as 'Granny Smith'.

Records, however, would be only one division of an "Apple Corps", with tentacles in other spheres such as film, electronics and tailoring. With their own struggles niggling still, "We had this mad idea of having Apple there," said George, "so that people could come and do artistic stuff and not have a hard time."

In April 1968 – the beginning of the tax year – advertisements appeared in both national and underground journals soliciting the public to bring "artistic stuff" to the new Apple Foundation For The Arts in London, "We had every freak in the world coming in there," groaned George.

"If you want George to listen to your tape, you're doing it all wrong," shouted one Apple employee when the first Beatle to arrive that day was smothered in kisses by some French-Canadian girl. A doorman was appointed to keep out riff-raff like that, but, behind that closed door, no one Beatle felt responsible for straightening out a venture that had taken a mere two months to snowball into chaos.

No more qualified to run a business than Brian Epstein had been to play guitar, George was the Beatle least interested in any Apple function beyond making records. A Harrison composition was heard by the public as the A-side of the third Apple single, although not as often as 'Hey Jude', which had a more appetising title than 'Sour Milk Sea'. With George at the console, this jittery rocker, taped at a "glorified jam session", was sung by ex-Undertaker Jackie Lomax.

Hardly any of Lomax's work on Apple was exceptional, but Eric Clapton gave him a relic to guard for life, the Gibson SG heard on Cream's double album *Wheels Of Fire*. Since *Fresh Cream*, the trio had gone from their native turf to grander, more impersonal venues in North America, where their musical sensitivity and subtle ironies were corrupted when "We were not indulging ourselves so much as our audiences," reflected Eric, "because that's what they wanted." The trio's calculated disbandment in November 1968 was no surprise to George, who'd arrived at a similar artistic impasse in 1965.

Cream had planned a final LP, *Goodbye*. Most of it consisted of in-concert tapings from the last US tour, although each member also agreed to donate a new composition. Songs had never come as readily to Clapton as they had to bass guitarist Jack Bruce and drummer Ginger Baker. Under pressure because the others had finished their *Goodbye* numbers, Eric now felt close enough to George to seek his assistance. George was only too pleased to collaborate, viewing Eric as "one of those people I get on so well with it's like looking at myself".

Other than a plain chord strummed after each verse, 'Badge' had no discernible hook line; much of its appeal lay in the interplay of Bruce's bass lope and the chopping of guest rhythm guitarist George Harrison, under the *nom de guerre* "L'Angelo Mysterioso".

Following Cream's disbandment, Clapton with drummer Ginger Baker amalgamated with Steve Winwood of Traffic and Rick Grech from "progressive" group Family, to form Blind Faith, a "supergroup" who, so a letter to *Melody Maker* wrongly predicted, would achieve "almost Beatle status". Rather than an expected stylistic hybrid, there'd be strong evidence of Eric's fondness for an LP of insidious impact, *Music From Big Pink* by The Band, a group from upstate New York. The album demonstrated a True West blend of electric folklore that had been nurtured over many a rough night spent in hick Canadian dance halls before the musicians landed a job backing Bob Dylan.

As John's enthusiasm for Dylan had rubbed off on George, so did Clapton's for The Band, whose professional relationship with Bob Dylan had not ceased during his convalescence, as they recorded with him in the basement of their communal pink house in West Saugerties, not far from Bob's own rural home in Bearsville.

Beginning with an invitation from Band guitarist Jaime Robertson to call on Big Pink, George became a frequent guest at Bearsville where he and Dylan formed a desultory songwriting team that would bear sparse, half-serious fruit.

George's cultivation of Dylan's friendship may have been interrelated with the behaviour of Lennon since his confrontation with the Maharishi. Shortly after their return to England, John had left Cynthia and Julian to move in with Yoko Ono, a Japanese-American who was to art what Screaming Lord Sutch was to politics. She had found a niche too in the more distant extremes of avant-garde jazz, walking a highly strung artistic tightrope without a safety net. In the company of respected figures such as Ornette Coleman, she used her voice like a front-line horn, interjecting screeches, wails, nanny-goat vibrato and Nippon jabber into the proceedings.

A writer to *Beatles Monthly* expressed the widespread view that Cynthia and John's subsequent divorce eroded The Beatles' magic even more than the absence of the usual Christmas single in 1966. Annihilating completely any cosy illusions such traditionalists had left was the first of a trilogy of non-Beatle albums by Lennon and Ono. The ordinary fan's shocked reaction to its cover photographs – of the couple unclothed – was best articulated in the topical disc 'John, You Went Too Far This Time' by Rainbo, alias Sissy Spacek, who was then a struggling starlet.

The next Ono-Lennon LP, *Unfinished Music No 2: Life With The Lions*, was one of but two albums that appeared on Zapple, Apple's only subsidiary label. Intended as a platform for the spoken word and experimental music, "It seized up before it really got going," sighed George, "as with so many other things at Apple."

With commendable honesty, George has said that "both of the albums that did come out on Zapple were a load of rubbish". Alongside Yoko and John's second soul-baring episode was George's own *Electronic Sound*, which were exactly that: "All I did was get that very first Moog synthesiser, and I put a microphone into a tape machine. Whatever came out when I fiddled with the knobs went on tape."

It rose no higher than Number 191 in the US chart, and was on a commercial par with an album that George had brought back from the States the previous year. *Krishna Consciousness* featured the chanting of disciples of Swami Prabhupada, who had arrived in New York from India in 1965 to bring the maha-mantra to the West. Although disadvantaged by poverty and advanced age, he worked up a small following of acolytes dedicated enough to wear the order's citrus-coloured saffron robes, mark their faces with the white clay tilak sign of a servant of God and, if male, plane their scalps to a bare stubble, bar a dangling hank at the back. In crocodile procession, these bhaktas would jog the main streets of the Big Apple and, with finger cymbals keeping time, chant their endless Hare Krishna mantra. According to the pamphlet they distributed *en route*, continual repetition of Krishna's name would build up the chanter's identification with God, thereby drawing upon divine energy.

As the *Krishna Consciousness* LP whirled for the first time in Kinfauns, "It was like a door opened somewhere in my subconscious, maybe from a previous life." George began chanting himself, once keeping it up non-stop while driving from France to Portugal. When he listened to George's new album, John didn't go that far, usually chanting only when he was with George.

The group's authorised biographer, Hunter Davies, blamed "the arrival in John's life of Yoko Ono" for the end of The Beatles. Harrison may have hoped that, if they ignored Yoko, she would go away. In reciprocation, "She wasn't particularly interested in us, anyway," said George. Because of Yoko, The Beatles were less to Lennon now than the artistic bond with her that was making him a laughing stock.

One day at Savile Row, George could no longer contain his resentment of Yoko's intrusion. He burst into the couple's office and came straight to the point. Naming Dylan among those with a low opinion of uncool Yoko, Harrison complained about the present "bad vibes" within The Beatles' empire that were co-related with her coming. "We both sat through it," said John. "I don't know why, but I was always hoping that they would come around."

Having let off steam, George did try to come around. He and Pattie, of all the other Beatle couples, were most supportive of John and the soon-to-be second Mrs Lennon. With all pretensions of the Beatle four-man "brotherhood" gone, Pattie joined Yoko at the microphone for backing vocals on 'Birthday', a track destined to open the third side of the long-awaited successor to *Sgt Pepper*. George and John were the only Beatles heard on Lennon's unreleased 'What's The New Mary Jane', which, though it had lyrics and a tune, was closer to the eight challenging minutes of 'Revolution 9' than it was to 'Birthday'.

Although it encompassed the odd segue and reprise, all that the new record did was spotlight the talents of each separate Beatle. "And that," said George, "was when the rot started setting in, really. I was starting to write loads of tunes, and one or two songs per album wasn't sufficient for me."

Already, Paul and John had unbent enough to allow a Harrison number to grace a Beatles B-side. His last "Indian" song for the group, 'The Inner Light', parcelled a delightful melody over one of the Bombay backing tracks and a marginal adaptation of a Chinese poem. The fact that he'd so freely lifted lyrics from another's work fuelled George Martin's long-held and deflating view that "an awful lot of George's songs do sound like something else. There actually was a song called 'Something In The Way She Moves', a James Taylor song, and that was written a long time before [Harrison] wrote his 'Something'."

To be fair, most of 'Something' had occurred to George before 'Something In The Way She Moves' was released. "I sort of just put it on ice," he'd recall, "because I thought, 'This is too easy. It sounds so simple.'" Momentarily, George considered passing it on to Jackie Lomax, but gave it instead to Joe Cocker, who'd scored a recent UK Number One with an overhaul of 'With A Little Help From My Friends' from *Sgt Pepper*. Figuring that it'd stand a better chance with a hit act than a lost cause like Jackie, George put 'Something' Joe's way "about a year before I did it, and then it took him that long to do it".

The workshop ambience of Abbey Road permitted George to tape demos of 'Something' and other new compositions that were now streaming from him, such as 'Old Brown Shoe', 'Isn't It A Pity?' and, from a stay at Dylan's, 'All Things Must Pass', which was inspired by the "religious and country feel" of The Band's 'The Weight'. Not meant for public ears, these weren't much more than guitar-and-voice sketches, but superior to the issued version was such a take of 'While My Guitar Gently Weeps', rated by many as George's greatest recording.

He expected an enthusiastic response to his new song from John and Paul but "went home really disappointed". There, he concocted an answer to this and future instances of artistic frustration. He was going to bring in an outside party of such eminence that – like a vicar in a BBC situation comedy – his mere presence would compel the other three to bite back on their nonsense.

This would require delicate handling, though, and so, after mentally rehearsing what he would say, George telephoned to ask Eric Clapton if he'd mind giving him a lift to the next evening's session. Taken aback by his friend's next request, Eric's gut response was, "I can't come. The others won't like it." Nevertheless, turning a thoughtful steering wheel as they neared Abbey Road, he relented. Within minutes, he realised that there was something rotten in the state of the group. Nothing was seen of John during the entire seven hours that Eric was there. Ringo and Paul, however, "were as good as gold", smiled the crafty George as they and their distinguished visitor laid down a version of 'While My Guitar Gently Weeps' that was to be among the high points of the double-album that they'd now decided to call just *The Beatles*.

A more dubious accolade for Eric on *The Beatles* was George's 'Savoy Truffle', which was notable for the purpose for which it had been composed, which had been "to tease Eric. He's got this real sweet tooth, and he'd just had his mouth worked on. His dentist said he was through with candy, so, as a tribute, I wrote, 'You'll have to have them all pulled out after the Savoy Truffle.'"

Why did 'Savoy Truffle' and, as much of a muchness, 'Long Long Long' make it onto The Beatles when stronger

Harrison material didn't? Possibly a green-eyed monster whispered to McCartney and Lennon, when he thought about it nowadays, that George – heaven forbid – might catch up on either of them as The Beatles' most self-contained and commercial force. And why not? "He was working with two brilliant songwriters," reasoned John, "and he learned a lot from us. I wouldn't have minded being George the invisible man." Of the new, clever music coming from inside the old Harrison, George Martin justified his previous condescension towards the baby of the group: "He'd been awfully poor up to then, actually. The impression is sometimes given that we put him down. I don't think we ever did, but possibly we didn't encourage him enough."

11 The Gravedigger

Although the United States took them as seriously as ever, The Beatles had become less pin-ups than favourite – if slightly dotty – uncles in Britain. Nevertheless, they weren't so far above the adoration of schoolgirls that they didn't have recent group photographs available on request for *Jackie* and *Fabulous 208*. The folded arms and unsmiling demeanour of each detached individual reflected the mood that had permeated sessions for *The Beatles* and beyond. George wasn't even in the country when Lennon and McCartney recorded 'The Ballad Of John And Yoko' as The Beatles' final British Number One.

Paul and John's congeniality as they piled up this single's overdubs had been at odds with "the most miserable session on earth" – Lennon's words – a few months earlier. This vain endeavour to get back to their Merseybeat womb had been precipitated by McCartney's raising of the subject of touring again – though George preferred the notion of a residency like the ones they'd had in the Cavern and Hamburg. "Then you've got your amps and drums set up and got used to the one sound." From the perspective of security and experience gained since 'Love Me Do', he and the other mellowed Beatles hoped to "get as funky as we were in the Cavern". Instead, they only hastened their sour freedom from each other.

They spoke less often of where it would take place, but preparations for a concert began in January 1969 in Twickenham Film Studios. Killing two birds with one stone, a film crew was on hand to document every unforgiving minute. The best bits were stuck together to make *Let It Be*.

They warmed up every day to whatever anyone began to play. Spanning 15 years, numbers with all the standard chord changes and others long learnt by rote accumulated on footage and tape. Sometimes they'd peter out, if bedevilled by a forgotten middle eight or words that the vocalist couldn't be bothered to la-la any more. Anything went – 'Three Cool Cats', 'The Harry Lime Theme', 'Michael Row The Boat Ashore', 'You Can't Do That', 'Love Me Do'...

Any euphoria that these ambles down memory lane had wrought would fade when they came up against each other's new compositions. McCartney was so purposefully confident about his that, moaned Harrison, "you'd have to do 59 of Paul's songs before he'd even listen to one of yours. The very first day, Paul went into this 'you do this, you do that, don't do this, don't do that', and I thought, 'Christ, I thought he'd woken up by now.'" Frustrated to the point of retaliation,

George was no longer prepared to studiously avoid confrontation or continue to be Paul's artistic pawn.

It took a week for him to up and quit the chilly encampment with mains leads fanning out in all directions across the hollow chamber. "I didn't care if it was The Beatles," he said. "I was getting out." None of the others thought to either remonstrate or plead with him to return, although Ringo called with a reminder of the following week's business meeting.

It was not, however, conducted as if nothing had happened. Paul and John looked at George with new respect. Who'd have thought it? This was George with an unprecedented glint in his eye, George making a stand, George without his thumb in his mouth.

The disagreement's most beneficial outcome was a transfer to the half-finished but cosier studio in the Savile Row basement. The strained atmosphere, however, could only be alleviated by George employing his 'While My Guitar Gently Weeps' strategy, "because having a fifth person there, it sort of off-set the vibes".

Instead of a guitarist, George's eyes fell on Billy Preston, whom Ray Charles had predicted "will follow in my footsteps". It was after a Royal Festival Hall concert with Charles that Billy renewed his acquaintance with George Harrison. There was an amicable exchange of telephone numbers and an invitation from George to drop in at Savile Row. On 22 January, he and Paul were about to descend into the Apple basement when "Billy walked into the office. I just grabbed him, and brought him down to the studio."

Preston's coming did, indeed, lift the strike-happy depression. The ideal conclusion to the film had to be some public spectacle. Therefore, with less than a day's notice, cameras and sound equipment were made ready for a Beatles performance on Apple's flat roof. Unannounced, they and Preston shambled onto this makeshift stage to impinge upon the hearing of those as far away as Oxford. Some within earshot weren't aware that they were being treated to something they could tell their grandchildren about. They weren't square, but there was a time and a place for this sort of row.

Nevertheless, this episode had cleared some of the air and, if anything, The Beatles' drifting apart seemed less inevitable than it had when the mayhem that was Apple had been at its most uproarious. Not that far from the truth would be a scene from 1978's spoof Beatles film biography *All You Need Is Cash*, in which a thinly disguised Apple Corps' is pillaged by its employees while, in the foreground, its press agent chats to a television news commentator (played, incidentally, by George Harrison).

Enough of the Money Beatle of old remained for George to worry about drainage of the company economy. A letter from the group's accountant disabused George that his financial means were infinite. Since the loss of Brian Epstein, some of The Beatles' antics had given their investors pause for agonised wonder. For some, the supreme folly had been the appointment of Allen Klein as their business manager on 3 February 1969.

Although he'd been the first to champion the new administrator, Paul was the only dissident. To disentangle Apple's disordered threads, he'd advocated his own father-in-law, a New York lawyer named Lee Eastman.

The Harrisons had been unable to attend Linda Eastman and Paul's wedding celebrations on 12 March. Armed with a search warrant, a squad of Scotland Yard officers and Yogi, a sniffer dog, had reason to believe that Kinfauns was being used for the consumption of controlled drugs, contrary to the provision of the 1966 Dangerous Drugs Act, section 42. Unconvinced by Pattie's air of fluffy innocence, Yogi and his colleagues executed their duties under the direction of plain-clothes Sergeant Norman Pilcher, who had busted John Lennon the previous October. National treasures or not, The Beatles weren't above the law any more.

Charged with possession of 570 grains of cannabis and a quantity of cocaine, the Harrisons pleaded guilty, and were fined £250 each. The more trivial tabloids also stressed the irony of a dog called Yogi bringing the most spiritual Beatle to book.

On the afternoon following the court appearance, George had received a conveyor belt of press in his Apple office. During his audience, the *Music Echo* correspondent logged the presence in the white room of "members of a quasi-religious cult calling itself the 'Khrishna [sic] Consciousness Society'".

"I was never with the Hare Krishna movement," George would insist later. "I was just friends with them." Nonetheless, from George's purse had poured the means for founding and provisioning many temples and yoga-ashrams, as well as the printing of Krishna books, some of which contained Harrison forewords and interviews. "All part of the service," he reckoned of his astounding feat of steering the mantra into the Top 20 in September 1969.

Most of the accompaniment – harmonium, bass, percussion and guitar – on The Radha Krishna Temple's accelerando 'Hare Krishna Mantra' on Apple was manufactured by George just before a session for *Abbey Road*, The Beatles' next album. If the strangest act ever invited to be on *Top Of The Pops*, their irrepressible 'Hare Krishna Mantra' encroached on public consciousness to a degree that the milkman whistled it, and a rendition was a punch-line in a *Crackerjack* sketch on BBC's children's television.

More satisfying than these dubious accolades were the full houses at the movement's free initiatory evenings. Some attendees arrived in anticipation of seeing George Harrison, but there were many new converts and an even bigger increase of sympathisers who no longer regarded a line of Hare Krishna chanters down Oxford Street with sidelong scepticism or contemptuous amusement.

Doing no harm either was the follow-up single, 'Govinda' – Krishna reincarnated as a shepherd boy – which was an actual verse-chorus song rather than a repeated chant. Its

Sanskrit lyrics aside, with its muted but driving beat 'Govinda' it didn't sound out of place on the juke box in the greasiest café any more than it did on the sound system at the Society's museum in Los Angeles, where the Harrisons ordered a life-sized fountain-cum-statue of the demigod Siva to be delivered to their new home when they found it.

All four Beatles had been house-hunting of late. Ringo had moved from Surrey to Highgate after purchasing the home of a friend, Peter Sellers, with whom he was co-starring in *The Magic Christian* in his first major film role. Assisting Sellers with the screenplay had been fellow humorists John Cleese and Graham Chapman, who were on the team of *Monty Python's Flying Circus*, then in the midst of its maiden series on BBC2. Watching the first show, George "couldn't understand how normal television could continue after that." As was his expensive habit then, he sent a telegram straight away to Broadcasting House: "Love the show. Keep doing it."

George's enjoyment of this programme was a minor comfort during a year beset with more than just Beatle traumas. His marriage had floated into a choppy sea, partly because of Pattie's increasing disinclination to play Yoko to George's John. Her personality precluded as deep an engrossment in spiritual pursuits as her husband. She wanted a bit of frivolity, for a change – and there were others after a bit of frivolity, too. George had become rather sanctimonious about certain London theatre presentations since the abolition of stage censorship in 1968. Nevertheless, Pattie took her seat in the Roundhouse on the opening night of *Oh! Calcutta*, a musical with much nudity and explicit language. With George's blessing, male companions such as Eric Clapton accompanied her on this and like occasions almost like 18th-century *cavaliere servantes*. Clapton, however, tired of always meeting her in public.

George confided the dilution of his marriage to a favoured "Apple Scruff", his nickname for a constant loiterer around its steps. A handful had clogged the pavement for so long that, in this less hectic phase of The Beatles stardom, they'd understood how privately ordinary, even boring, were the icons they'd once worshipped from afar. Adoration, however, would be years a-dwindling. In February 1969, after George's tonsillectomy at University College Hospital, its switchboard had been jammed with requests for the gruesome excisions.

Harrison was still as prone to idolatry as the most devout Scruff, often spinning over and over again the same records by Electric Flag, Stoneground or whatever new US combo had captivated him – none more so than a workmanlike group led by Deep South guitarist Delaney Bramlett, which also included his wife Bonnie, and a faction of Los Angeles session musicians nicknamed "the blue-eyed soul school". That faintly sickening word "funky" was used to describe the economic tightness of their rhythm section.

Eric Clapton was keen enough about Delaney and Bonnie and Friends to finance a European tour in December. He'd be their lead guitarist and, they hoped, a passport to fame.

Their freewheeling Southern ebullience was so infectious that George "just grabbed a guitar and an amp and went on the road with them. With his re-grown beard, drab denims and lank hair centre-parted and splayed halfway down his back, no one in the crowd knew who the extra guitarist was until he was introduced near the finish. Only then was he the cynosure of all eyes. This wasn't a record cover, television or a pin-up; George Harrison of the superhuman Beatles was actually there.

While crossing the North Sea for dates in Scandinavia, Delaney And Bonnie crept into the UK Top 30 for the first and only time. Strongly in evidence on 'Coming Home' was the departed Dave Mason's bottleneck-guitar obligato. It made sense to plug this single *en route* round England, and George was asked to supply the missing element: "Delaney gave me this slide guitar and said, 'You do the Dave Mason part.' I'd never attempted anything before that, and I think my slide-guitar playing originated from that."

During the earlier week of the Delaney And Bonnie jaunt George had confined himself to a passable solo on 'Coming Home' before dropping back to hack rhythm for the rest of the set. Gaining confidence, however, he gradually inserted more bottleneck and less rhythm. After this practical experience, he continued to teach himself at home, "thinking maybe this is how I can come up with something half decent".

In Sweden, during the Friends tour, he'd written his first bottleneck song, 'Woman Don't You Cry For Me', which strode a tightrope between skiffle and the country-and-western end of pop. During the band's three nights in Copenhagen, he started another opus, 'My Sweet Lord'. As all artists do sometimes, he borrowed from and disguised his source of inspiration, in this instance by tampering with the chordal accents of 'Oh Happy Day', an 18th-century traditional spiritual that had itself been overhauled to chart-climbing effect in the previous summer by US gospel choir The Edwin Hawkins Singers. Although George removed it many degrees from 'Oh Happy Day', something else about 'My Sweet Lord' remained infuriatingly familiar.

Present in Scandinavia at George's invitation, another temporary Friend, Billy Preston – now a born-again Christian – liked the finished 'My Sweet Lord' enough to want to record it. Perhaps because the final result bore too much of a melodic resemblance to 'He's So Fine', a 1963 hit by US vocal group The Chiffons, it was released as a single only in Europe, where it became a medium-sized hit. It might have spared George much grief if the 'My Sweet Lord' saga had ended there.

Sales of Billy's 'My Sweet Lord' earned George mere pin-money compared to those for 'Something', his first Beatles A-side. It was heard too the following summer, when it was given a second lease of life in the British Top Ten by Shirley Bassey in one of nearly 200 cover versions – as supermarket muzak, in the tinklings of Liberace, by James Brown, Smokey Robinson, Elvis, Bert Kaempfert, Booker T's MGs and, yes, Ray Charles. 'Something' was also the only Beatles number to be recorded by Sinatra, who hailed it as "the greatest love song of the past 50 years".

George would cite later compositions as equal in quality, "but they might not be as popular, because it was The Beatles who made 'Something'". This blueprint sliced to Number One in the States like a wire through cheese. Pop, however, obeys no law of natural justice, which is why, in the UK, 'Something' was stopped in its tracks during the usual Yuletide silly season.

This petty dampener on George's triumph could be ascribed to Allen Klein's adherence to US procedure of issuing a single off an already successful album. George's second *Abbey Road* composition, 'Here Comes The Sun' sparkled with finger-picked acoustic Gibson and, in light-hearted verses about melting ice and smiling faces, caught the moment of emergence after a winter cocooned indoors. "You can almost feel the rays of the sun," *Melody Maker* exclaimed of the *Abbey Road* original while damning with faint praise its cover by a chap called Paul Munday, who was poised to trouble the forthcoming decade as "Gary Glitter". A younger glam rock executant than Glitter, Steve Harley's better timing would put his version of 'Here Comes The Sun' into the British Top Ten during 1976's extraordinarily warm July.

That George's *Abbey Road* songs were subjected to the most widespread syndication reflected both his commercial peak as a composer *per se* and his ascendancy over both Lennon and McCartney. The duo that had soundtracked the swinging '60s wouldn't be able, as solo songwriters and ex-Beatles, to so minister to the '70s, even if the illusion of reconciliation that was *Abbey Road* still fooled the public into believing that The Beatles had saved not the world, perhaps, but themselves. It was, as Debussy said of Wagner's Das Rheingold, "a glorious sunset mistaken for a dawn".

12 The Ex-Beatle

The most emphatic twitch in the death throes of The Beatles was 'Something'. Of its singer, George Martin predicted, "I think it's possible that he'll emerge as a great musician and composer next year. He's got tremendous drive and imagination, and also the ability to show himself as a great composer on a par with Lennon and McCartney."

While Paul and John's first respective post-Beatle offerings were either barrel scraping, slap-dash or luxoriously self-centred, to George was afforded the luxury of sifting through a backlog of around 40 songs – "and some of them I think are quite good" – for a new album, a double if he felt like it. As it turned out, it'd be – after the *Woodstock* soundtrack – pop's first triple album, named after one of the songs previewed in the *Let It Be* film – *All Things Must Pass*.

The first and biggest-selling 45 to be lifted from the album, 'My Sweet Lord' was at the top in Britain within a fortnight of its release. By February 1971, it was Number One virtually everywhere else, too. Every silver lining has a cloud, however, and the vast exposure of 'My Sweet Lord' threw the song's stomach-knotting similarity to The Chiffons' 'He's So Fine' into sharper focus. Allen Klein brought to George's notice a revival of The Chiffons' opus by Jody Miller, onto which was faithfully grafted every detail of the 'My Sweet Lord' arrangement, even the plainly strummed acoustic guitars that had replaced Billy's jazzy keyboards on the introduction and the background chants where The Chiffons' doo-lang-doo-lang-doo-langs had been.

This bad karma, however, was at arm's length as the falling 'My Sweet Lord' collided with the catchy 'What Is Life?' on its way up. Belying its pensive title, this second single from *All Things Must Pass* seemed to be a straight, lovey-dovey pop song. Unissued as an A-side in Britain, where it had already appeared on the flip of 'My Sweet Lord', the rise of a version by Olivia Newton into the Top 20 was, like Shirley Bassey's 'Something', a wooing of a parallel dimension of pop turned off by all this religious nonsense that hippies liked. George's infiltration of this area by proxy continued with 'Isn't It A Pity', which, when sung by Ireland's Dana as the storm brewed in Ulster, was more poignant than either his own or Matt Monro's version.

If George was on top of the world as the most commercially viable ex-Beatle, Eric Clapton was heading for the bottom. A heroin addict now, he could make no long term plans. His descent into this abyss was hinged on what had now become an infatuation with Pattie Harrison. So far, she'd spurned his advances, which even his friendship with her husband would not rein – and even as her marriage muddled on because neither she nor George had enough motivation to finish it. In January 1970, their year of searching for a dwelling that would combine privacy without without imprisonment, and close proximity to London had ended with the purchase of Friar Park, the estate above Henley-on-Thames that was to be as synonymous with George's name as the Queen's with Windsor Castle.

For several months, Friar Park was open house to Swami Prabhupada and his disciples until they were able to decamp to Pickett's Manor, the mock-Tudor theological college – renamed Bhaktivedanta Manor – in Hertfordshire that was to become the most popular Hindu rallying point in Europe. Footing the bill for these 17 acres near Letchmore Heath, was George, who felt "fortunate enough to be able to help at the time".

George's most memorable charitable gesture in the early 1970s, however, was co-ordinating what would stand as his finest hour: The Concerts For Bangladesh. Like most occidentals, he was "not interested in the politics of the situation" which had emerged in March 1971, four months after East Pakistan – now Bangladesh – had been devastated by a cyclone, General Yahya Khan amassed a Moslem army mighty enough to eradicate the Hindu majority who opposed his military dictatorship. Prostrated by the tempest's aftermath of homelessness, lack of sanitation, cholera and starvation, the East Bengalis were further traumatised by this reign of terror. Carrying their pathetic bundles, millions of refugees stumbled towards the safety of India, which had received hardly a tenth of the foreign aid needed to cope with the disaster.

Ravi Shankar's own family and friends were among the ceaseless fatalities and exiles. In California, during these unhappy months, from Ravi's distraught helplessness came the notion of a modest fund-raising concert. When George arrived in Los Angeles in late June, a better answer clicked in Shankar's mind like a key sliding into a lock: "He gave me all this information and articles on what was going on in Bangladesh, and I slowly got pulled into it. I started getting carried away with the whole idea of doing something good, maybe making $10 million."

Holding at bay misgivings about treading the boards again, George instructed Allen Klein to book no less a venue than New York's 20,000-capacity Madison Square Gardens, where no Beatle had gone before. The most convenient date was Sunday 1 August, which left George just enough time to recruit and rehearse whatever musicians he could muster.

To share his lead guitar functions, who better than Eric Clapton. To many, the essence of the show was Harrison and the thrillingly unrehearsed Clapton breaking sweat on duelling guitars during 'While My Guitar Gently Weeps', one of the rare "blowing" numbers. Others were more impressed by Ringo Starr's singing of 'It Don't Come Easy', endearing in its distracted clumsiness. George took it down with 'Here Comes The Sun', and was unsure what would follow this lull. On the set list sellotaped to his guitar, "Bob?" had been written, "so I just looked 'round to see if there was any indication if Bob [Dylan] was going to come or not, and he was already there. He was so nervous, and he had his harmonica on and his guitar in his hand, and he was walking right on stage. It was, like, now or never, and so I had to say, '[I'd] like to bring on a friend of us all – Mister Bob Dylan.'"

A movie of the event would win no Oscars, but the album earned a Grammy and spent most of 1972 in the Hot 100. Its picture sleeve mentioned the Bangladesh Disaster Fund organised by UNICEF, for whom was earmarked the $243,418.50 generated by the show plus the greater amounts accrued by record, film and other by-products. However, although record companies might have waived royalties theoretically owing to their artists, George discovered that "the law and tax people do not help. They make it so that it is not worthwhile doing anything decent." The show might have been over, but as turgid bureaucracy on both sides of the Atlantic dissected the Bangladesh millions with unhelpful slowness, George contemplated riding roughshod over official interference by travelling personally to India to ensure delivery of what he'd describe in a 1973 B-side as "the rice that keeps going astray on its way to Bombay".

With The Concerts For Bangla Desh shipwrecks as his sea markers, Bob Geldof would be knighted for Live Aid after

1985, but, further back on pop's road to respectability, George was recipient of a UNICEF citation on US television. In his acceptance speech, it was beneath him to vilify those who, in frozen ledgers and computer run-offs, had super-taxed the starving, the diseased and the huddled masses fleeing from the terror.

13 His Lectureship

The Bangladesh spectacular was *the* George Harrison moment, never to return. During the 15-month hiatus between the film's première and his next album, no time would have been better for a world-wide barnstormer. Dollars danced before his eyes, but the so-called Money Beatle, his own man at last, "wouldn't really care if no one ever heard of me again".

All the same, he recorded a new album, *Living In The Material World*, which contained another hit single in 'Give Me Love', and, in 1974, began thinking aloud about a North American tour as in interview he deadpanned the usual inane and damned impertinent questions. Mr Harrison, are The Beatles getting back together? Are you getting divorced? No, that's as silly as getting married. Is Eric Clapton going to be in your backing band?

It wouldn't take long for the scum press to flesh out the Harrisons' domestic upheavals. When at last Eric confronted George with his feelings about Pattie, there was less anger than amusement, with George offering to swap her for the latest of Clapton's long-suffering girlfriends. Because George's disarming wit and rationalisation had defused what might have developed into an ugly showdown, the path to a formal dissolution of the Harrisons' dead marriage on 7 June 1977 began. With retrospective honesty, Eric would discourse to his eulogists of his winning of Pattie's hand. Verified by friend and actor John Hurt is a story of Harrison challenging Clapton to a guitar duet over the woman, trading licks rather than using them as clubs, although this may have been a joke.

A combination of fame, wealth and religious education had rendered unto Harrison a greater certainty than before about everything he said and did. Old at 31, a crashing bore and wearing his virtuous observance of his beliefs like a sandwich board, he was nicknamed "His Lectureship" behind his back. Visitors to Friar Park tended not to swear in his presence. Along corridors where portraits of bearded gurus gazed haughtily, you would just as often bump into a robed ascetic as a Dark Horse session musician.

"Compared to what I should be, I'm a heathen" seemed, therefore, a strange admission. There had been rare excursions to catch prurient films like *Last Tango In Paris*, but the greatest paradox during this most cerebral phase of his life was that George was boozing quite heavily. Much of it was connected with business problems.

Headlines like Rolling Stone's "Did Allen Klein Take The Bangladesh Money?" were not reassuring.

However unfounded the story, it sparked off an intense and unwelcome interest by Messrs Harrison, Lennon and Starr in their manager's handling of their affairs. Klein's dogged streamlining had, indeed, recouped a fortune from disregarded record-company percentages to the smallest petty-cash fiddle, but where was it – and Klein – when George was challenged with a tax bill that had snowballed over 15 years of international stardom?

Like never before, George "needed someone to organise me out of all that mess. I wanted someone to help me with my present and future, but unfortunately he would have to get involved with my past." Such an apparent paragon materialised in a beanpole of a Los Angeles financial consultant, Denis O'Brien, who was temperamentally and physically everything that the portly, brash Allen wasn't. Although he'd appreciated that The Beatles had been a cut above the usual bilge, he'd never been crazy about pop, "and the stories I'd heard of record people, I thought they'd crawled out of the gutter".

Whether or not O'Brien and his new client anticipated more than a practised but detached professional relationship, there grew between them a friendship as each came to know what made the other tick. Outsiders might have assumed this mutual admiration to be a collision of opposites. Even Eric Idle, one of the Monty Python crew, generalised that it was "a balance between George as an amateur saint and Denis an amateur devil". As Harrison wasn't a drug-crazed boor nor O'Brien an unsmiling pedant, there was enough common ground between the Money Beatle and his business advisor for each to be prone to both thrift and extravagance, as well as frequent distribution of alms to outstretched hands.

Although overshadowed by the Concerts For Bangla Desh, a not-inconsiderable percentage of the takings and all proceeds from programme sales for the long-awaited US tour were annexed for all manner of charities. Yet however demonstrative George's giving, the purpose of his sold-out tour was the same as that of any other rock singer. As such, he was to be judged and, by some, found wanting.

Rehearsals on a soundstage at A&M studios didn't run as smoothly as expected. Unaccustomed to singing for so long and having to instruct a crack Los Angeles session team, his vocal cords weakened to a tortured rasp: "I had a choice of cancelling and forgetting it or going on and singing hoarse." Like a trouper, he took the latter course.

As the tension built on opening night, a backstage security guard might have glanced at a set list that promised an equilibrium of Beatles numbers and solo hits since. It looked like George didn't intend to renege on his past, even if – perhaps to counteract the continuing 'He's So Fine' debate – George was to hasten a not immediately recognisable 'My Sweet Lord' out of the way at breakneck speed.

He also included tracks from a new album *Dark Horse* – which contained only nine tracks that included a non-original and an instrumental that went in one ear and out the other. However, this apparent writer's block didn't prevent more than a little off-hand breast-beating to intrude. Most blatant was his liberty-taking with The Everly Brothers' 'Bye Bye Love' with sly lyrical digs at Pattie and "old Clapper". Nevertheless, *Dark Horse* also contained the wonderful 'It Is He (Jai Sri Krishna)'. Over an accompaniment with pulsating wobble-board to the fore, the repeated chorus was so uplifting that it scarcely mattered that it was sung entirely in Hindi.

Apart from a couple of passable numbers and the startling 'It Is He', *Dark Horse* was a comedown after the less derivative *Living In The Material World*. Nonetheless, beneath the premeditated carelessness, the hurried meticulousness and yawning ennui was a non-Beatle, as well as an ex-Beatle in uncertain transition. For that reason alone, *Dark Horse* – an artistic *faux pas* – is worth a listen.

Adapted from the logo of an Indian paint firm, a seven-headed dark horse had reared up throughout the tour – on the stage backdrop, on the T-shirt, on belt buckles and on necklaces. As well as the album, it also signified Dark Horse Records Limited, a label founded by George in May 1974. As EMI had buoyed up Apple, so Dark Horse was under the aegis of A&M.

George's nine-year contract with EMI/Capitol wasn't due to expire until 1976, but he doubted that he'd re-sign, owing to what he saw as the company's avaricious dithering over the Bangladesh album and certain royalty discrepancies.

Needless to say, EMI/Capitol refuted this sullying of its good name. Swallowing its ire at his accusations, its representative joined the queue of other major labels submitting their bids to Harrison, who at that time was still hot property. Looking for a new record company was as chancy as looking for a new girlfriend. Partly because Billy Preston got on well with A&M, George tested the water by leasing to the label via Dark Horse "a lot of things I was working on".

The jewel in Dark Horse's crown was Splinter, a duo from South Shields. Whatever their feelings about the end result, Splinter seemed in awe of George's working "for 24 hours straight" at sessions for their debut album. Their mentor played at least four superimposed instruments on their 'Costafine Town', which scrambled to Number 17 in the UK hit parade, the same position as 'Love Me Do'.

No 'Please Please Me' equivalent was forthcoming as Splinter's follow-up, 'Drink All Day', slumped well outside the Top 50. To be blunt, it wasn't a masterpiece of song. Neither were Splinter the new Beatles. They were, however, appropriate to the mild, harmless nature of mid-1970s pop.

Although Dark Horse stumped up a Splinter-sized budget to launch Jiva, a California soul band, their solitary album for the label failed to set the world alight. It was the same with a black vocal quartet, The Five Stairsteps. The title of their only Dark Horse LP, *Second Resurrection*, was only wishful thinking. Lead singer Keni Burke tried again with what chanced to be the penultimate album by Dark Horse, which by then was no longer affiliated to A&M.

At A&M Studios when it was still all smiles, George had fulfilled his last commitment to EMI/Capitol, as well as the final album release for Apple as *Wonderwall* had been the first. Like a tenant paying overdue rent with bad grace, he turned out "a grubby album in a way. The production left a lot to be desired as did my performance."

The content of this artistic nadir could not be divorced from the weighty personal misfortunes that split his concentration. 'Grey Cloudy Lies', for example, "describes the clouds of gloom that used to come over me, a difficulty I had". It slopped over into media interviews, too. On Radio 1, he intoned dolefully, "People who were never really keen on me just really hate my guts now. It has become complete opposites, completely black and white."

He was inflicted with such inflexible polarity himself. Once a hero, Allen Klein was now a villain of the darkest hue. The auditors appointed by the three Beatles had unravelled enough evidence of "excessive commissions" from Klein's mazy balance sheets for a court case. Going in fighting, Klein counter-sued for an eight-figure sum, with a cunning card up his sleeve for the specific trumping of George. Mr Klein, George would discover, was not a gentleman – but perhaps he never had been in the first place.

14 The Jewish Man In The Kitchen

During one of his last interviews, John Lennon sighed, "Well, he walked right into it. He must have known, you know. He's smarter than that. George could have changed a few notes and nobody could have touched him, but he let it go and paid the price." Found guilty of "subconscious plagiarism" on 7 September 1976, John's former colleague had been ordered to pay just over half a million greenbacks – and in days when half a million was worth something – to settle the 'He's So Fine'-'My Sweet Lord' business after Allen Klein, scenting a financial killing, had, said George, "bought the case". For a while, "it made me so paranoid about writing that I didn't even want to touch the guitar or piano in case I touched somebody's note. Somebody may own that note." Fortunately, George was able to home in on the humorous aspects of what had been a humiliating episode. After all, it wasn't the only song he'd ever written or would write. Who could weep for a composer for whom 'Something' would always provide a regular income?

Not as big a hit, yet still a hit all the same, was the therapeutic 'This Song', which was penned in the aftershock of the lawsuit. It unburdened itself with lines like, "This song ain't black or white and, as far as I know, don't infringe on anyone's copyright."

'This Song' was the first of two moderately successful US singles and one flop to be taken from the delayed new LP *Thirty-Three And ⅓* (George's age, see). The album kept rock's FM radio in tasteful focus, but a reviewer in punk-rock Britain dismissed it with "Of course it's not rock 'n' roll. Whatever gave you that idea?"

To George, punk was "rubbish, total rubbish. Listen to the early Beatles records – they were innocent and trivial but still had more meaning than punk music, which is destructive and aggressive." Punk was also the start of his own – albeit temporary – farewell to pop.

No incentive for any withdrawal was apparent, however, when the new Harrison album qualified for a golden disc within weeks of its release in time for Christmas 1976. Although it found enough home buyers to flit briefly into the LP charts, "I get the impression from time to time that England is not particularly interested".

Thirty-Three And ⅓ had been issued not by A&M but the mightier Warner Brothers conglomerate. Having ploughed nearly $3 million into Dark Horse, A&M had hoped that, by cross-collateralisation, *Thirty-Three And ⅓* would transfuse what had become a disappointing investment. Stipulations in

Harrison's contract forbade such a ploy, so they sought to recoup what they could, even if it meant losing their ex-Beatle, who – if Extra Texture was anything to go by – was past his best, anyway.

As Warners' out-of-court reimbursement of A&M's Dark Horse money was part of the deal, George was delighted to announce, "We're very excited about our new affiliation." To show willing, he'd subjected himself to an extensive publicity blitz, which included a five-city promotional tour of the States. Patiently puffing a Gitane, George gave the media unblinking copy, clarifying the album's more obscure lyrical byways, and retelling the old, old story of The Beatles for the trillionth time. Yes, he'd pencilled in a world concert tour for summer 1977, "but I would pace it better." It would embrace, he promised, neglected markets in Japan and Europe, "because they keep shouting about it." When the campaign actually reached Europe, he wasn't so sure.

After doing his *Thirty-Three And ⅓* duty, George, with Olivia Arias – formerly his personal secretary at A&M – spent four days in southern India for the wedding of Kumar Shankar, Ravi's nephew. On to Los Angeles, George and Olivia, now regarded as his intended, looked in on Prabhupada, then at the city's Krishna centre.

Olivia – five years younger than George – was a self-possessed, California-reared Mexican whose easy smile showed off her fine teeth. Despite her Aztec forebears, she was not unlike her Liverpudlian suitor, both facially and in her slim build. She and George plighted their troth on 2 September 1978 in an unpublicised ceremony at Friar Park. Among the few witnesses was their son, Dhani, who had been born the month before in a Windsor nursing home. Called after the notes dha and ni from the Indian music scale as much as for the name's phonetic proximity to the English "Danny", the infant would be so removed from public gaze that, when he was older, he would be able to walk around Henley unnoticed.

Appropriately clad in a Union Jack coat, Dhani's father had dared a sortie down the hill to a street party during 1977's Royal Jubilee. For greater distances, it was safer to drive. Nevertheless, George was sighted on more than one occasion knocking back a quiet brown ale in one or other of South Oxfordshire's more far-flung pubs or eating in a favoured Indian restaurant in Caversham Park Village, on the outskirts of Reading.

From the stultifying humidity of a Thames Valley summer, the Harrisons could escape to the purer air of an opulent Maui spread called Kuppaqulua, separated by two miles of gravelled track from the fern-edged coastal road. Escaping from the facile superficiality of showbusiness, it was most agreeable to mix with the 60 or so islanders who populated nearby Hana, where Hasegawa's General Store served the more immediate needs of stomach and household. Hana's only other major public facilities were a garage, a hotel and a plant nursery, whence George would furnish Kuppaqulua with silversword, poinsettia and other local flora.

Both 'If You Believe' and 'Love Comes To Everyone' on 1979's *George Harrison* album were finished on Maui, as was the pretty-but-nothing 'Dark Sweet Lady' – dedicated to Olivia – which introduced the harp to Harrison's canon. More obviously born of Kuppaqulua was 'Soft Touch', which transmitted the blue curvature of the ocean via the swoop of a Hawaiian guitar, while the lengthy intro to 'Your Love Is Forever' had a subtler Polynesian flavour. 'Soft-Hearted Hana', however, screamed its origin, its background hubbub taped directly from Longhi's restaurant in Lahaini, only two miles from Hana.

As his less intense media junket for *George Harrison* intimated, records were not much of a concern. George was now looking beyond music for fun and profit. Scoring only one vote against Ringo's 60 in a 1966 *Melody Maker* poll for best actor in *Help!*, George always seemed the Beatle least likely to involve himself in films. However, after the final series of *Monty Python's Flying Circus* in 1974, among the more successful correlated ventures was Eric Idle's BBC2 series, *Rutland Weekend Television*. On one programme, in December 1975, George was roped in to back Idle on 'The Pirate Song'. Riddled with excerpts from 'My Sweet Lord', the track had an Idle-Harrison composing credit.

As a spin-off from *Rutland Weekend Television*, a parody of The Beatles – The Rutles – was elongated for the silver screen. Premièred in March 1978, *All You Need Is Cash* ran the gauntlet, from an Arthur Scouse sending The Rutles for a season at Hamburg's Rat Keller, their rise to fame, Sergeant Rutler's Darts Club Band, formation of Rutler's Corps, and the split following *Let It Rut*. Get the picture? While Idle cast himself as the heart-throb "Paul" character, the part of "Stig O'Hara" (ie George) went to a musician, Rick Fataar, a latter-day Beach Boy. Mainly in cameo were other of Idle's pop-star pals, including George himself.

So began George's transition from maker of curate's-egg albums to paladin of the British film industry. In with the Python crowd, he'd stayed informed about the follow-tip to their feature film *Monty Python And The Holy Grail*. Originally called *Jesus Christ: Lust For Glory*, *Life Of Brian* trod on thinner ice with the scriptures than The Rutles had with the Fab Four. God might have been able to stand the joke, but during pre-production the film's nervous investors elected to wash their hands of it on the grounds of blasphemy.

Rather than jettison *Life Of Brian*, the Python team investigated other possibilities for raising the budget required. Chief of these was Idle's bit-part player George Harrison. Amused by Eric's ideas for the film, Harrison, in conjunction with Denis O'Brien, "pawned my house and the office in London to get a bank loan – and that was a bit nerve-wracking".

With his own property as collateral, George was mightily relieved when *Life Of Brian* grossed in excess of $15 million in North America alone. Thus heartened, Harrison then ventured further into the celluloid interior with the official formation of HandMade Films in 1980, named "as a bit of a joke" following George's outing to the British Handmade Paper Mill at Wookey Hole in Somerset.

The maverick firm developed an adventurous policy of taking on what a major backer would most likely reject or, at best, severely edit. On the strength of a two-page synopsis, for example, Monty Python's American animator, Terry Gilliam, got the go-ahead for the *Time Bandits* family fantasy, while HandMade's first US film, Tony Bill's *Five Corners*, came about because Harrison "liked his restaurant in LA. We'd had a good meal there, and then he came up to the table and said he'd like to make a film for us."

Although his new position as movie Big Shot had novelty appeal, George was too long in the tooth to harbour pretensions far beyond that of money lender and lay advisor. He'd tool along to an odd day's shooting, but ultimately, "I'm just this lad who happens to be standing around watching them make a movie." As with Alfred Hitchcock, the sharp-eyed viewer might espy George in minor roles – like "the Jewish man in the kitchen" in the *Life Of Brian*. More pertinent to his calling were soundtrack contributions, like 'Only A Dream Away' – with an insidious nonsense chorus – for *Time Bandits*.

As if in late consolation for his poor showing in *Melody Maker's Help!* tabulation, the placing of *Time Bandits* at Number Three in its Film section was the sole Beatle-associated entry in the magazine's 1979 popularity poll. The only other Beatle still in the running was the irrepressible Paul, who was happy to bask in the limelight of what were often hit singles. As much Mr Showbusiness in his way was Ringo, who had actually been close to death in 1979 with an intestinal complaint. Those who read about it felt sorry for him but were no longer buying his records. Until his final weeks, nothing as public could cajole John from his reclusive sojourn as Yoko's house-husband. Now blessed – like the Harrisons – with a son, the Lennons were based in New York's exclusive Dakota block. Only the rare postcard filtered between George and John. Other than these, Harrison now knew Lennon only via hearsay and tales in the press of him as the Howard Hughes of pop. The same as any other fan, George was "very interested to know whether John still writes tunes and puts them on a cassette, or does he just forget all about music and not play the guitar?".

A chance encounter with John in a Bermudan night club made one newshound report that the Lennon songwriting well was not as arid as might be imagined. This was confirmed a month later in August 1980, when John and Yoko booked sessions in a Big Apple studio to cut enough material for two LPs, the first of which was later scheduled for release in autumn.

New records from George, however, were not big events anymore. Maybe he also needed to absent himself from pop for years on end, for – as Ringo was already aware – an old stager's album was now less likely to be accepted without comment by a record company's quality control. Unnerving was executive reaction in October 1980 to Somewhere In England, George's proposed third album for Warner's. "If George wants a million-seller," moaned company president Mo Ostin, "it's not on here."

Ostin desired not a promotional single that might or might not chart but an unmistakable worldwide smash like 'My Sweet Lord' had been. George had had a good run since then, but now – even in the States – only by pulling such a stroke could he reverse what was an undisguisable downward spiral. Amid these glum reflections, an occurrence as the Yuletide sell-in got under way would give Warner Brothers a miracle.

A US Number Two, and placed in most other Top Tens, the lyrical connotations of "All Those Years Ago", and the affinity of its writer to its subject had bequeathed unto this singalong canter an undeserved piquancy. 'All Those Years Ago', you see, was about John Lennon, who had been shot dead outside the Dakota in a travesty of legitimate admiration by Mark David Chapman, described in the song as "the Devil's best friend". Everybody remembers the moment they heard. In Friar Park, Olivia had told George after being wrenched from sleep by a long-distance call from her sister-in-law just before dawn. "How bad is it?" he inquired dozily. "A flesh wound or something?" With phlegmatic detachment, he turned over and "just went back to sleep, actually. Maybe it was a way of getting away from it."

When the world woke up, John Lennon still hadn't recovered from being dead. Cancelling the day's recording session, George withdrew indoors with Dhani and Olivia. By late afternoon, he was collected enough to parry calls from the media with a prepared opening sentence: "After all we went through together, I had – and still have – great love and respect for John." He and Paul had each suffered derogatory remarks from John during the promotion of *Double Fantasy*, but his waspishness – as both its targets and Lennon himself realized – could be shrugged off.

John seemed wounded, however, by the "glaring omissions" of him from George's autobiography, *I Me Mine*, published earlier that year. The roots of what its author admitted was "a little ego detour" lay in a conversation in 1977 with two representatives of Genesis, a publishing concern. Not any old publishing concern, Surrey-based Genesis specialised in beautifully made books of creamy vellum, coloured inks, gold leaf and hand-tooled leather bindings. Limited by cost, it was good going if an edition exhausted a run of a couple of thousand, as did a facsimile of HMS Bounty's log, a snip at £158 apiece.

George warmed to the notion of Genesis reproducing his lyrics as a joy forever, "because how it's made was almost more important than what's inside". Derek Taylor, then HandMade's publicist, was commissioned to write a scene-setting introduction, but confessed, "I couldn't, though I'd known him for 15 years. I didn't know enough. I decided

that it should be the story of his life as he chose to tell it."
Interspersed with Taylor's narrative, therefore, were
transcriptions of George's taped reminiscences.

This filled but 62 pages. A photograph section then led
to Part Two, which took up the remaining two thirds of the
"autobiography". Here, George's original scribblings of
rhymes and chords are printed alongside his commentary on
each. With the fly-leaf signed by George himself and – via
some outlets – sold at a knockdown £116, what discerning
fan could resist investing in *I Me Mine*?

Easier on the pocket in mass-market paperback, seven
years on, its value in my research was not as great as you'd
think as *I Me Mine* is not so much a serious study of his life
as a good read. There's little space for in-depth estimation
of motive or weighing of experience, but the surfacing of
some unfamiliar anecdotes and the recounting of the old
yarns in the subject's own laconic words is as relaxed as a
fireside chat.

15 The Hermit

It was income from HandMade – which by now averaged three or four films annually – rather than royalty cheques from *Somewhere In England* that kept the wolf from the door nowadays. The company had gone from strength to strength, from Bob Hoskins' BAFTA Best Actor statuette for *Mona Lisa* to George and Denis receiving from the Duchess of Kent an award for HandMade's services to British film. Before millions of BBC viewers, a jubilant George planted a kiss on the royal cheek.

Such Fab Four-ish sauciness was absent on ITV a few months later, when News At Ten showed George among protesters at an anti-nuclear rally in Trafalgar Square. This was one of the less anonymous manifestations of his and Olivia's concern about pressing environmental and human issues that had passed him by during the ebbing bustle of the 1970s.

Of all of George's interventions in more parochial affairs, none were as intensely public as those concerning the

threatened demolition of Henley's Regal Cinema. To a howl
of rage from the 7,000 who signed an opposing petition, the
Regal was to be levelled by bulldozers in order to extend the
adjacent branch of Waitrose supermarket and create a mall
of 18 shops – and, if you like, a smaller cinema.

As *éminence grise* behind some of the Regal's weekly
offerings, George had needed little persuasion to join a star-
studded show of strength outside the empty cinema on a busy
Saturday morning in September 1986. Hemmed in by jotting
reporters, George snarled further about Waitrose's "Orwellian
cynicism" and "concrete monsters", evoking Dylan and
Liverpool during a debate that simmered on even after
Environment Secretary Chris Patten decided against calling
a public enquiry in October 1989.

Also pitching in were Joe Brown from neighbouring
Skirmett, Dave Edmunds and Jon Lord, who, as squire of
the acres round Yewton Lodge, could well afford the thousand
quid he put into the "Save The Regal" kitty.

They and other members of the Henley Music Mafia
played together, either in the privacy of their own homes or
on stages like those in Watlington's Carriers Arms or the Crown
in Pishill, with a rambling selection sprung from "old twelve-
bars, The Everly Brothers and the odd bit of Django
Reinhardt". From these casual unwindings came more palpable
liaisons. George composed 'Flying Hour' with Nettlebed
guitarist Mick Ralphs – former mainstay of Mott The Hoople
– and 'Shelter Of Your Love' with Alvin Lee from Goring.

For George, Jon Lord manipulated synthesiser on 1982's *Gone Troppo*. This album, so George would disclose, would be his last. From now on, there'd be just the perverse joy of creating uncommercial music: "I've never stopped writing songs, and I've made hundreds of demos." He also added to a multitude of credits on the LP jackets of others. As well as Ringo's latest and film soundtracks, he was also heard on albums by Gary Brooker and Mick Fleetwood, drummer with Fleetwood Mac and husband for many years of Jenny Boyd. In contrast, George's was the slightly throaty vocal refrain – in Hindi – on the title tack of Ravi Shankar's eclectic *Tana Mana* album, which also contained a track entitled 'Friar Park'.

Confining such favours to fellow old soldiers, George also allied with other guest musicians for a TV special starring one whose songs about clothes, lust and violence had captured George's adolescent imaginings. *Carl Perkins And Friends: A Rockabilly Special*, broadcast on 21 October 1985, was before an audience of Teddy Boys, who might have preferred a more typical Perkins recital, unimpeded by the contemporary stamp of approval of his illustrious helpmates. Carl was who they'd mob afterwards.

The Teds were appeased, however, by the homely pub-like ambience as the players switched on small amplifiers. With grey-haired Perkins close enough for everyone to see, among those waiting in the wings were Eric Clapton, two of the revivalist Stray Cats and Ringo Starr, who was to rattle the traps while singing 'Honey Don't' and, with Carl, 'Matchbox', two Perkins items that had thrust him into the main spotlight with The Beatles.

No one was surprised when George ambled on in a baggy grey suit for 'Everybody's Trying To Be My Baby'. However, as his spot progressed with less familiar pieces from the Silver Beatles era, many were struck by his animated enthusiasm and obvious pleasure in performing again.

George guaranteed himself a more pronounced stake in the proceedings when he booked Perkins as entertainment for a televised celebration of HandMade's first decade in business. Master of ceremonies Michael Palin's after-dinner speech had concluded with glasses raised to the founder of the feast. Following this toast, George's opening sentence, to sycophantic titters, had been, "Thank you all for coming. Now fuck off."

A couple spared this amicable vulgarity were Madonna and her then husband, Sean Penn. Since completing their roles in *Shanghai Surprise*, an adaptation of Tony Kenrick's novel *Faraday's Flowers*, George hadn't "seen them from that day to this". After sinking £10 million into *Shanghai Surprise*, HandMade had been "damn lucky to get our money back and not lose our shirts."

George blamed this close shave on "a combination of her thinking she's a star and the way the press was gunning for her". Penn and his wife's Garbo-esque refusal to be interviewed was a provocation to Fleet Street, which disgraced itself from the moment the pair arrived at Heathrow *en route* to the filming location in Hong Kong. More than anyone, George could sympathise with the brusque Penns' plight and said so at a London press conference in March 1986. Most questions were directed at George throughout the 45-minute grilling, which ended with Madonna proclaiming, "We're not such a bad bunch of people, are we? Byeeeeee."

Hoping the newspapers might agree, executive producer and stars then split like an amoeba, he to Henley and they to Hong Kong with the press in close pursuit. To the glee of breakfast-table readers everywhere, the situation worsened. Juxtaposed with misappropriated *Shanghai Surprise* stills were both true and untrue tabloid stories of "Poison" Penn's bodyguards assaulting a photographer; a make-up girl's sacking for asking Madonna for an autograph and frightful quarrels that could be heard all over the set.

A despairing George was compelled to jet eastwards to sort out the mess. Later, he'd laugh off this "bloody nightmare", but, when first he reached Hong Kong, "[Sean and Madonna] weren't being very nice to the crew. It's hard work [for the crew], dragging equipment 'round places where it's freezing cold for hours. And while she's in a warm trailer, the crew are trying to drink a cup of tea to keep warm, and a little 'Hello, good morning, how are you?' goes a long way in those circumstances. So when I got there, the crew hated them."

The executive producer's descent into their midst stripped the Penns of enough hauteur for Madonna to propose humouring the malcontented underlings with a party. Disgusted, George had already gauged that such tardy sweetness and light wouldn't wash, "because, to tell you the truth, nobody would show up." For the second time that year, he submitted himself to another paparazzi ordeal for Madonna's benefit. Although he bore himself with his accustomed self-assurance, clicking shutters froze a thunderous countenance in marked contrast to Mrs Penn's smirk.

Harrison also rendered unto *Shanghai Surprise* a soundtrack, which went unreleased "because the film got slagged off so bad". Madonna had been mooted to duet with George on the main title theme, but the job went instead to the more affable Vikki Brown, wife of Joe and cabaret star in northern Europe.

Of more long-term import was the assistance elsewhere on the soundtrack of Jeff Lynne, whose bond with Harrison was to prove considerably more productive in the months to follow. Though he'd overseen his Electric Light Orchestra's explorations of the more magniloquent aspect of The Beatles' psychedelic period, 39-year-old Lynne's attitude towards recording seemed to have gone full circle.

While they were getting to know each other, George confessed a dislike of automation in music. He wished for "all these whales stuck in ice – namely the music industry – to release all these people from feeling guilty for not using a synthesiser and not being able to programme it," which forthright Lynne crowned with, "Don't even bother learning; just play the bleeding piano."

In Jeff, George found "the perfect choice", while if Jeff "could've picked one guy I wanted to work with, it would've been George." With the compatible Lynne, George prepared to contradict his 1982 retirement statement with a new album.

This was all very well, but was a comeback actually tenable? Although George had been quite actively consolidating his other professional and recreational interests since *Somewhere In England*, when he'd materialised to defend Madonna it was as a ghost from the recent past, reinforcing the press-inspired concept of him as "the Hermit of Friar Park".

Nevertheless, although his so-called seclusion had been aggravated in part by the horrible release of John's spirit, fear for his own safety had mutated to a blithe fatalism that enabled him pop out to shops around Henley and even from HandMade's office to Chelsea emporia. The years away from the public at large had helped in that. "Thankfully, today's generation really doesn't know much about me or what I look like. Now I reckon I could walk down the high street and there would be very few people who would recognise me, and that's a great feeling."

Prominent in a citrine pullover, he was conducted round Shiplake College, midway between Henley and Reading. It had been recommended by Jon Lord, whose children had gone there. Had Dhani's parents been of Paul and Linda

McCartney's self-consciously homely bent, they might have considered one of Henley's state institutions, instead of such a slap-up, fee-paying seat of learning with vast grounds cascading down to a Thameside marina that swelled with supervised aquatic activity during jolly boating weather.

While providing their boy with the best of everything, George and Olivia hoped that "we can instil the right values in our son. It is his nightmare that he should grow up spoiled. No child likes to be singled out." Yet, although it wasn't stressed at home, Dhani couldn't help but become aware of his sire's celebrity, even if George's "retirement" granted his handsome offspring more paternal attention than most. Most of George's familiars agreed that fatherhood suited him.

Best illuminating the balanced content of the Quiet One in middle life was his authorship of brief forewords to both *Chant And Be Happy* – a learned history of the Hare Krishna movement – and Joe Brown's chirpy autobiography, *Brown Sauce*. With the imposition on his privacy at its lowest level within the parameters of his fame and means, he had "gone about my life like a normal person. Every so often, I see a newspaper saying I'm this, that or the other, but, as Jeff Lynne says, 'It's tomorrow's chip-paper.'"

16 The Trembling Wilbury

From the beginning of 1986, George Harrison's re-emergence as an entertainer became more perceptible. A performance in Birmingham's National Exhibition Centre involving Jeff Lynne was a welcome break during sessions for his new album. Not quite a year later, he was up on the boards again whilst on a business trip to Los Angeles in connection with his now-completed album, entitled *Cloud Nine*. Mixing work with pleasure, he was in the company of Bob Dylan and John Fogerty, being serenaded by bluesman Taj Mahal in the Palomino Club on Sunset Strip. Emboldened by a few can beers, the party clambered onstage to delight the other 400 drinkers with an amused rendering of Creedence Clearwater hits, old time rock 'n' roll and Dylan's 'Watching The River Flow', the latter sung by George. A few months later, George was less sure of the words to 'Rainy Day Women' as he intoned them at Wembley Arena during a ragged encore on the last night of Bob's European tour.

George was no stranger to Wembley. On 6 June 1987, 25 years to the day after The Beatles' Parlophone recording test, he made a more formal appearance there among star acts assembled for a show organised by the Prince's Trust, one of the heir to the throne's charities. Endearingly nervous, in between 'While My Guitar Gently Weeps' and 'Here Comes The Sun', George saluted his ad hoc backing quartet of Eric Clapton, Jeff, Ringo, Elton John and Ultravox's Midge Ure on bass. A handshake from the Prince of Wales afterwards had possibly less intrinsic value than "You were good, Dad, you were good" from a round-eyed Dhani, for whom the extravaganza was his first experience of his father as a stage performer.

As the tide of his musical career continued to turn, it wouldn't be long before George Harrison would wash his hands of HandMade, after a falling out with Denis O'Brien. Moreover, because George had been so busy on *Cloud Nine*, many of the exotic plants and shrubs in Friar Park that had been destroyed in an unforeseen hurricane were not immediately replaced.

The console labours related to this marginal neglect were not in vain. Released in 1987, *Cloud Nine* brought much of the aura of a fresh sensation to those young enough not to have heard much of George Harrison before – especially as he was unmarred by baldness and obesity, and had lately shaved off a scrappy beard. When he walked into a Burbank record shop, a teenager near the counter cried, "Look! There's that singer!" Turning their heads, her companions saw neither a dotard nor the oldest swinger in town.

Warners' executives had passed *Cloud Nine* as "a killer sequence of tracks". Pulling from all elements in his musical past, George had come to terms with both The Beatles and his present situation. Other than one more obvious and calculated stroll down Memory Lane, you'd pick up on this "oh yeah", that ascending guitar riff from *Revolver*, a gritty *All Things Must Pass* horn section and a sweep of *Gone Troppo* bottleneck.

One of the spin-off singles, 'When We Was Fab' was a happier invocation and exorcism of The Beatles than the selfish 'Ballad Of John And Yoko' or 'All Those Years Ago'. Musically, it leaned most heavily on the *Magical Mystery Tour* age, with its ELO cellos, a melodic quote from 'A Day In The Life', effervescent 'Blue Jay Way' phasing and a psychedelic coda of wiry sitar, backwards tapes and 'I Am The Walrus' babble. The mock significance of 'When We Was Fab' might have overshadowed companion pieces that had more to say, such as 'Devil's Radio', a swipe at tittle-tattlers by one who'd long been one of their victims.

He risked providing the press with more gossip by an active participation in the promotion of *Cloud Nine* – which was nudging the higher reaches of the US chart when George mounted the podium in New York's posh Waldorf-Astoria Hotel after The Beatles had been inducted by Mick Jagger at the third Rock 'n' Roll Hall of Fame ceremony. Representing what was left of the group, too, were John's widow and Ringo. In the opening sentences of his speech, George made light of McCartney's absence.

Paul also backed out of an apparent agreement to appear in videos for the *Cloud Nine* singles. George had been slightly disappointed that the non-original 'Got My Mind Set On You' was chosen as the first of these. Nonetheless, it touched a British high of Number Two. Over in the States, it went one better, the first Harrison 45 to top a national chart since 'Give Me Love'.

Not as gigantic a smash was 'When We Was Fab'. Jeff Lynne had had a cameo in its video. With his part in steering the former Beatle back into the spotlight recognised, Jeff was much in demand these days. A considerable accolade for him was a contract to produce most of *Mystery Girl*, the LP that restored Roy Orbison to the charts.

Jeff had suspended work on *Mystery Girl* to oversee one final and trifling detail of his prior commitment to Harrison, a bonus number for the European 12in of 'When We Was Fab'. Roy Orbison was on the conversation's edge when the two Englishmen discussed this over luncheon in Los Angeles. George was elated when the jovial Orbison volunteered to sing with him on this extra track. It wasn't worth booking anywhere expensive, so George – impressing Roy with his proud familiarity – telephoned the Santa Monica home of Bob Dylan, whose "little Ampex in the corner of his garage" was available the next day.

Duly rolling up late the following morning, Roy shook hands with Tom Petty, whom Jeff and – to a lesser extent – George had assisted in his production of a Del Shannon album in 1987, after Petty's group had backed Dylan on the tour that had terminated at Wembley.

From initially merely providing refreshments, Dylan later lent a hand when Harrison – with his B-side only half-finished – said, "Give us some lyrics, you famous lyricist." By the evening, flesh had been layered on the skeleton of 'Handle With Care'. George had added what he called "a lonely bit" for Orbison, who'd long been stereotyped as a purveyor of woe, while Dylan wheezed his trademark harmonica on the fade-out. At this juncture, the gathering was not intended as any permanent "supergroup", that most fascist of all pop cliques. Orbison spoke for everyone when he said, "We all enjoyed it so much. It was so relaxed. There was no ego involved and there was some sort of chemistry going on."

On the next day, Roy left for a one-nighter in Anaheim, near Long Beach; Bob carried on preparing for a summer tour and George slipped over to Warners with the new tape. There it was pronounced too potentially remunerative to hide its light under a 12in 45. In conference with Jeff afterwards, the idea of cutting a whole LP with the 'Handle With Care' quintet surfaced. When the two skidded up to his house with the plan, Petty jumped at the chance while, over the phone, Dylan's affirmative was blunter. That evening, Jeff, George, Tom and their wives drove down the coast to Anaheim to put it to the Big O. "Roy said, 'That'd be great,'" remembered Petty. "We watched Roy give an incredible concert and kept nudging each other and saying, 'Isn't he great? He's in our band."

When intelligence of this new combination spread, other musicians in the Harrison circle wondered why they hadn't been invited to join in, but the album – attributed to "The Traveling Wilburys", and completed over the summer of 1988 – "worked because it was so unplanned," estimated Orbison. Despite a "Volume One" tag on the cover, no second Wilbury LP was then on the cards, partly because, as Roy explained, "We couldn't repeat the ploy on the record companies the second time 'round."

Out of step with the strident march of hip-hop, acid house, *et al*, the release of *Volume 1* was like a Viking longship docking in a hovercraft terminal. After the songs had been written, only ten days could be set aside for the taping, owing to Dylan's forthcoming tour, but any lifting of this restriction might have detracted from the proceedings' rough-and-ready spontaneity and endearing imperfections. Close in execution to skiffle or rockabilly, the items on *Volume 1* were for George a V-sign at all that he detested about 1980s mainstream pop: "They represent the stand against this horrible computerised music."

When *Volume 1* was finished, the personnel returned to individual projects – although, bound by the Wilbury "brotherhood", each performed services for the others.

Mystery Girl, for example, was completed at Friar Park, with George on acoustic guitar. He also assisted on both Tom and Jeff's first solo albums. Bob offered a song for the follow-up to *Mystery Girl*, but it was never recorded owing to the ill-starred Roy's fatal heart attack in December 1988.

It was to be expected that the morbid publicity would boost the Top 40 placings of both the slipping 'Handle With Care' single and the LP. Whereas the video for 'Handle With Care' had had all five grouped around an omni-directional microphone, in the one for 'End Of The Line' Roy's spiritual presence was symbolised by a guitar propped up in a vacant chair. In April 1990, Harrison, Lynne, Petty and Dylan were recording together in a rented house in Bel Air for what was presumed to be Volume Two but was actually entitled *Volume 3*.

George's first post-Orbison Wilbury release was 'Nobody's Child', a skiffle standard. This was taped after Olivia had asked her husband to consider recording a number for the appeal she'd set up after the Romanian earthquake in May 1990. In further support of the compassionate Mrs Harrison's Romanian Angel Appeal was a compilation LP – with 'Nobody's Child' the title track – organised by George and featuring mostly his old musical confreres, among them Clapton and Starr.

Far less likely than a bona fide new Harrison album was George's full-time return to the stage. Such weapons as programmable desks and graphic equalisers in the war against adverse auditorium acoustics couldn't erase George's memories of touring in 1974, and the perturbing psychological undertow compounded by an admirer "going absolutely bananas" feet from the stage at the Prince's Trust bash: "He was so fanatical and kept staring at me with this manic glint in his eye." With gun-toting Chapman and his sort shadowing his thoughts, George had decided that, "even if I had been considering coming back to do large shows, the sight of this guy made me think twice."

Similarly ugly occurrences of cold terror did not thwart Paul or Ringo, who in 1989 each chanced their first tours since John's slaughter. George, however, didn't "really see myself as being out there like the George Michaels or the Mick Jaggers. I'm not putting them down, but they have performing built into them. Well, I just don't have a desire to be a pop star. I just want to be a musician, somebody who writes songs and makes music."

17 The Anthologist

Things went as quiet as they had during the post-*Gone Troppo* period. In the years that followed, George put his head above the parapet rarely, if memorably.

In November 1991, there was a 12-date tour of Japan with Eric Clapton, a country second only to the USA in the intensity of its passion for the Beatles. With no new record in the shops, the lion's share of George's part of each night's proceedings was fixed unashamedly on nothing that wasn't in either The Beatles' or his solo portfolio of hits. Into the bargain, Clapton – whose "name and likeness can be no larger than any other sidemen's", according to a memo from his record company – slipped 'Badge' and his 1977 paean to Pattie, 'Wonderful Tonight', into his four songs at the central microphone. "Here's another one of the old ones for you" was a sentence that seemed to recur during continuity by George that was more effusive, witty and relaxed than customers who recalled *The Concerts For Bangla Desh* movie might have expected.

There was to be no falling off in quality, either, during what amounted to his first full-scale UK concert as an ex-Beatle when it was announced on 1 April 1992 that he'd be heading a surprise extravaganza entitled "George Harrison And Friends: Election Is A Celebration" six days later at the Royal Albert Hall.

He was doing it to raise funds for – and sharpen the profile of – the Natural Law Party (NLP), an organisation that had smouldered into form in the previous month after the Prime Minister had called a general election. Its manifesto promised "a disease-free, crime-free, pollution-free society", epitomised by transcendental meditation on the National Health and the cross-legged yogic flying that is the best-remembered sequence of the party political broadcast that delayed BBC1's *Nine O'Clock News* one evening as the population prepared to cross its ballot papers.

In case you haven't yet realised, the proposals of the NLP were traceable to the Maharishi Mahesh Yogi, now in his 80s, and again in favour with George, whose testimonial on behalf of the party explained, "I want a total change, and not just a choice between left and right. The system we have now is obsolete and is not fulfilling the needs of the people." Hear, hear! 60,000-odd people voted Natural Law when the time came, but not a solitary one of more than 300 NLP candidates fielded was to make a maiden speech in the House of Commons.

Harrison declined an invitation to stand for a Merseyside constituency, perhaps recalling Swami Prabhupada's advice that he'd be more useful as a musician. Against a backdrop of the NLP rainbow symbol and amid a heavy fragrance of joss-sticks, George was accompanied at the Albert Hall by personnel drawn mainly from Eric Clapton's backing group, still warmed up enough by the Japanese expedition to need few rehearsals.

Before an audience with a preponderance of over-30s – who nonetheless weren't above odd outbreaks of screaming – George drew spontaneous salvos of applause for specific couplets in 'Taxman', its topicality emphasised with an updated libretto name-dropping notable national and world figures. Less political than sentimental, however, was a clearly moved George calling up Ringo from a balcony box for the encores, 'While My Guitar Gently Weeps' and a reprised 'Roll Over Beethoven'.

Among the assembled cast for this finale had been Dhani, now very much a young adult. He had also become a proficient guitarist, so much so that he joined his nervous father for 'In My Little Snapshot Album' as a contribution to a George Formby Appreciation Society convention in March 1991 in Blackpool. Places where Beatle-spotters would have been more likely to find George were on the stage at London's Hard Rock Café, where he sat in with Carl Perkins – and at Madison Square Garden, where, on 16 October 1995, he was prominent in the jubilee atmosphere of a Bob Dylan tribute concert.

Others with principal roles in the story of the Quiet One had not left its latter-day orbit, either. The Shankar family holidayed with the Harrisons in as recently as 1995, and George instigated the resurrection of the Dark Horse label in the following year to issue *Ravi Shankar: In Celebration*, a lovingly compiled four-CD boxed retrospective spanning different aspects of the now quite elderly Padma Bhushan's recording career, from the post-war decade to 1995.

George also turned up at the home of George Martin, to be interviewed for a June 1992 edition of ITV's *South Bank Show* that marked yet another anniversary, marking the quarter-century of the release of *Sgt Pepper's Lonely Hearts Club Band*.

It always boiled down to The Beatles. Yet, nearly two years earlier on BBC2's *Rapido* pop series, George had not only poured coldest water on any idea of a Beatles reunion but had also underlined his boredom with the ceaseless fascination with the wretched group, a fascination that was to escalate with the runaway success in 1994 of *Live At The BBC*, a compilation of early broadcasts. This prefaced an official proclamation of a coming anthology of further items from the vaults. These were to be hand-picked by George, Paul and Ringo themselves for issue over the period of a year on nine albums (in packs of three) as companion commodities to a six-hour documentary film to be spread over three weeks on ITV and presented likewise on foreign television.

Then came talk of the Fab Three recording a new single for the project in the teeth of George arguing – with no one contradicting him – that it wouldn't be the same without

Lennon. After a fashion, Harrison, Starr and McCartney's well-documented regrouping in the mid-1990s *wasn't* missing Lennon as they grafted new music onto John's stark demos of 'Free As A Bird' and other numbers on tapes that were provided by his widow.

Yet, for all the amassing of anticipation via no sneak previews, a half-hour TV special building up to its first spin over a remarkable video and the multitudes willing it to leap straight in at Number One, 'Free As A Bird' stalled in second place in Britain's Christmas list. The follow-up, 'Real Love', reached the Top Ten more grudgingly, having been dogged by exclusion from Radio 1's playlist of choreographed boy bands, chart ballast from the turntables of disco and rave and Britpop executants like Supergrass, The Bluetones, Ocean Colour Scene and, most pointedly of all, Oasis.

Oasis, The Bluetones and all the rest of them were inclined to be more impressed by Lennon and McCartney compositions than anything by the Other Two. Yet Oasis borrowed the title of George's *Wonderwall* soundtrack for their best-known song – and the influence of Harrison in general was heard most blatantly in the grooves of Kula Shaker, the most exotic of all the new Top 40 arrivals of the mid-1990s. This London combo's fourth single was 'Govinda', complete with Sanskrit lyrics. Its B-side, 'Gokula', lived so obviously in a *Wonderwall* guitar riff that permission to use it had to be sought by Kula Shaker from Northern Songs via a direct appeal to the composer himself.

Kula Shaker were a further acknowledgment that, as both a Beatle and ex-Beatle, George Harrison's entries in *The Guinness Book Of Hit Singles* count for less than his inspiration for pop musicians to dip into non-Western cultures. The impact of Oriental music only seems to hold less allure these days because of the fine line between its ear-catching extraneousness and the real danger of it sounding like a parody of George Harrison.

Beyond pop, where would the Krishna Consciousness Society be without the invocation of George's name and money? Without him, how many of its tracts would be screwed up unread or perused with the same scornful amusement reserved for Flat Earth Society's pamphlets? In a mugger's paradise like Reading, why else is there enough interest for chanting bhaktas to process down its main streets on Saturday afternoons now and then and to hold weekly meetings in a church hall also used for judo and amateur dramatics?

Conversely, George was grateful that "The Beatles enabled me to be adventurous. It saved me from another mundane sort of life." What as? An electrician at Blackler's? A "good, medium-weight business executive", as *The Sunday Times* once suggested? A latter-day Swinging Blue Jean instead of Colin Manley?

Just as fond of hypothesising is George himself, who "would've probably been a better guitarist than I am now, because the fame made me end up playing the same old stuff for years". He'd tell you himself, too, that he "can't write

brilliant lyrics – though occasionally some are half-decent –
and I can half-decently produce something, but I've never
really had any cards to play".

18 The Alien

On Wednesday 29 December 1999, a chilly twilight fell on the small village that is Friar Park. Within the parameters of a remarkable life, it seemed like an unremarkable night for George Harrison. The mother-in-law had already gone to bed. He and the wife watched some video or other. Olivia lost interest and retired, too. George joined her just after two o'clock.

Whatever the nature of the film and its effect upon his nocturnal imaginings as he climbed the stairs, how could he possibly have suspected that, by dawn on Thursday, his own gore would be splattered and drying on the surrounding walls and carpets, that he'd be half dead in hospital and that Olivia would be raised to unlooked-for heroine status?

The horror came to Henley in the likely looking form of Michael Abram, a 34-year-old paranoid schizophrenic – from Liverpool, of all places. If diagnosed as psychotic, this had been dismissed as curable as soon as he stopped malingering and found the self-discipline to cease his drug habit. Then he borrowed his mother's Beatles tapes, and his destiny was taken from him.

The local Mister Strange would roam the shopping precincts ululating Beatles numbers to himself while lost in misery, paranoid self-obsession and lonely contemplation. Who were, he pondered, the four phantom menaces, spreading global consternation and plague, as predicted by Nostradamus? Clinging desperately to his fantasies, he attracted comparatively little hostile attention as a seemingly harmless if unsavoury part of the parochial furniture.

If such a condition can be quantified, the solar eclipse in August 1999 correlated with gradually more profound insanity. Michael had convinced himself that he was possessed by McCartney, deconstructing the title of 'Let It Be', for example, as "L" for "hell", "et" for "extra terrestrial" – and "It Be" an indication that he (Abram) was about to contract tuberculosis.

By October 1999, he was focusing his persecution complex on George, seeing the line "It's going to take money" from 'Got My Mind Set On You' as a reference to the £80,000 he understood that someone he knew owed a drug dealer. After the game was up, Michael informed his solicitor, "The Beatles were witches, and George was the leader, a witch on a broomstick, who talked in the Devil's tongue, an alien from Hell."

As the incarnation of St Michael the Archangel, Abram had been sent to execute George Harrison by God, with

whom he was overheard arguing in a police cell on one of
the three occasions that he'd been arrested for minor public-
order offences since the eclipse.

On 16 December, Michael bought a railway ticket to
Henley. Keeping his dark reflections to himself for now, he
peered through Friar Park's concealing shrubbery over a
section of disrepaired wall that was neither as high nor as
thickly razor-wired as elsewhere and turned away. In front
of the Town Hall, he burst into ranting song, hoping to stir
up an uprising to lay "the House" to siege. "Which house?"
asked a bemused onlooker.

"Which house?" or "Witch House"? Fixating on the
latter, the wheels of the universe came together for Michael
Abram. He hoped, nevertheless, that something would prevent
him from boarding the train for his second and final journey
to Friar Park. He carried about his person a two-foot length
of cord and a black-handled knife. While his prey's awareness
of his role in the tragedy was totally irrelevant, Michael
himself was certain that Harrison knew what was coming to
him. As it had been with the Crucifixion, the world would
be saved by the sacrifice of a divine victim in his prime, be
he angel or demon.

Spurred on by a voice in his ear as clear as a bell telling
him that "God is with you", Michael affected entry to Friar
Park in the graveyard hours of 30 December, undetected by
the infra-red sensors, the closed-circuit television cameras
and further state-of-the-art installations.

Not long after three, Olivia was jerked from slumber by what she'd describe in court as "the loudest crash of glass imaginable". Had a chandelier fallen? In case it was something more sinister, she broke into George's dreams. He toiled groaningly out of bed and, clad in dressing gown, pyjamas and sockless boots, semi-groped his way down the two flights of a wide stairway. A whiff of cigarette smoke and a blast of colder air from the crack under the kitchen door told him that it was no shattered chandelier.

With throat constricting, skin crawling and heart pounding like a hunted beast – which he was – the head of the household hastened back upstairs, where Olivia was attempting unsuccessfully to telephone the entrance lodge, where the video surveillance equipment was supposed to be under constant observation. However, another member of staff was contacted and instructed to ring the police and try to activate the floodlights. Olivia then dialled 999 herself.

Venturing to the balustrades overlooking the hall, George, frowning with astonishment, caught the crunch of footsteps on shards of glass. With a stone lance from a statue of St George and the Dragon in the conservatory, Michael Abram had smashed the double patio doors of the kitchen. Now, his leather-jacketed, black-gloved shape stood glaring into the gloom above as his victim's face smouldered into form.

His voice should have been shrill with fear, but George asked almost matter-of-factly the identity of the intruder. In contrast came a bawled "You know! Get down 'ere!"

As he had in that hair-raising flight to New York in 1971 and other ugly moments, George let slip a "Hare Krishna" or two. For a split second, Abram was dumbfounded before interpreting these exclamations as a curse from Satan. Furiously, he breathed hard and charged onwards and upwards to George.

Aware of the peril a beat before an eerily silent and strong assailant fell upon him, "My first instinct was to grab for the knife," Harrison was to inform the Crown prosecutor. "I tried to get into a room, but the key was stuck, so I decided to tackle him by running towards him and knocking him over. We both fell to the floor. I was fending off blows with my hands. He was on top of me and stabbing down at my upper body."

The commotion drew Olivia out. Freeze-framed for the blink of a bulging eye, Olivia held her husband's bewildered gaze, "one I had never seen before". The slow moment over, she seized the nearest blunt instrument to hand, a small brass poker, and waded in. A snatch at his testicles sent Abram into a unbalanced half-spin, but, boiling over with pain, he sprang like a panther at Olivia, who dropped the poker and fled vainly into the sitting room next to the sleeping quarters. Abram's grip on the back of her neck slackened as George leapt on her pursuer, "but he continued to strike out and he got the better of me".

George and Michael tumbled, wrestling, onto meditation cushions. Beyond the knobbles of the latter's spine, George saw Olivia grab a weighty glass table lamp and bring it down with all her force. "Even as I was swinging," she later recalled, "I was aware and amazed that I was doing so without a drop of malice in my heart."

"Don't stop!" yelled George. "Hit him harder!"

Heaving violently like an erupting volcano, Abram took a few more indiscriminate blows while fumbling for the light's flex, whipping it around the woman's hands and gashing her forehead in the process. Panting too, George "felt exhausted. My arms dropped to my side. I could feel the strength drain from me. I vividly remember a deliberate thrust of the knife into my chest."

Warm liquid welled up inside his mouth. Blood. Lower down, the knife had missed his heart by less than an inch, but a twice-punctured lung collapsed, and so did its owner. "I believed I had been fatally stabbed," he said later. But, even as the blade had penetrated his flesh, he understood that he would be genuinely mourned by Olivia.

With facial wounds that needed stitching, the fight had gone out of Abram as well. "He slumped over me," Olivia later recalled. "I again took hold of the blade of the knife and wrenched it from his grasp."

At that point, two Thames Valley constables – PC Paul Williams and, only six months in the job, 33-year-old Matt Morgans – turned up, not exactly in the nick of time. "The house was in total darkness," so Morgans related to both his sergeant and *The Henley Standard*. "We jumped out of the car and PC Williams went up to the huge set of front doors while I went around the side to see if someone had broken in there. My first thought was that, in my training, we were told you shouldn't touch anything, but then I heard the screaming, so I shouted for PC Williams and went through the window."

There, in a red haze, a bruised and bloodstained Olivia was staggering to the bottom of the hallway stairs.

"I was so new in training, I just went into automatic mode," gasped Matt. "Since then, people have asked me why I didn't call back-up or put a stab-proof on. I met her, and she said the man was upstairs, trying to kill George. He was my immediate priority.

"I saw a guy running across the landing. I thought he was wearing a mask, but it was just the blood running down his face and in his hair from where Olivia had hit him. He was a bit streaky and wild. I shouted to the man to stay where he was and get down on the floor, which he did. I stood over him, and then saw the bedroom light and George Harrison lying behind the door. I left PC Williams to handcuff the intruder and restrain him.

"George was in a right mess. He had been kicked, punched and stabbed. He was conscious, but his main concern was for his wife. He thought the man thought he was finished and had gone after his wife. I put him in the recovery position and did enough first aid so that he didn't croak."

The officers then checked elsewhere for any accomplices, but there was only Michael Abram, whose ravings you could have heard down at the police station in Falaise Square. "You should have heard the spooky things he was saying, the bastard," he shrieked, before "I did it! I did it!" several times in succession.

Next on the scene was Dhani. He knelt by his prostrate father and was "immediately covered in blood". As well as the lung, the knife had left its mark in George's thigh, cheek, chest and left forearm. "He was drifting," noticed Dhani. "I honestly believed he was going to die. He was so pale. I looked into his eyes and saw the pain. Dad kept saying, 'Oh Dhan, oh Dhan.' He looked even paler in the face, and he was groaning and saying, 'I'm going out.' He made little sense, and I knew he was losing consciousness. It was about ten to twelve minutes – although it seemed like a lifetime – before the paramedics arrived."

Both victim and attacker were rushed to the Royal Berkshire Hospital in Reading. The truth that he may have refused to avow at first inflicted itself on Dhani at this point: "As [George] was taken away in a stretcher chair, he looked back and said, 'I love you, Dhan.' My father's spoken words were broken with coughing and spluttering. He said, 'Hare Krishna,' and closed his eyes. At this point, he drew a very strange breath. It was deep and what I would describe as a death breath. His mouth was puckered, his cheeks were drawn in and he sucked at his bottom lip. I shouted, 'Dad! Dad!

You are with me? Listen to my voice. It is going to be OK. Stay with me!' His face was contorted and he had not taken a breath for some seconds. As I finished shouting, he breathed out and opened his eyes. I have never seen another human being, whether dead or alive – and I have seen my grandfather in his coffin – look so bad."

Sooner than expected, George was off the danger list by the following afternoon. He was then transferred to Harefield Hospital, on the edge of London, where he saw in AD 2000. Gruesomely hilarious remarks and relayed witticisms hid the shaken man beneath to everyone but Olivia and Dhani, to whom he still had every appearance of being seriously unwell – despite assurances that he was on the mend.

For Olivia, fright had turned to rage towards one who "owes us a thank you for saving him from the karma of murder. We do not accept that he did not know that what he was doing was wrong. We shall never forget that he was full of hatred and violence when he came into our home."

When George's old smile was back by mid-January, she accompanied him on a brief convalescence in Ireland as a prelude to a longer stay with Dhani and a lately widowed Joe Brown in a rented holiday home in Barbados, the expensive facilities of which were less important than the ex-SAS militia who patrolled the grounds around the clock.

From less exotic surroundings, Michael Abram, on remand, sent a letter of apology "for having to face a lunatic like me in their house". Via the Crown Prosecution Service, this reached

Friar Park the day before his case came up the following November. Olivia, for one, was not impressed: "I didn't read it properly. What I did read sounded like it wasn't written by him. Given the timing, it sounded convenient."

The next day, in Oxford Crown Court, Abram was smartened up beyond recognition in a pinstripe suit and John Lennon swot spectacles, his hair trimmed to a short crop. A vision of poker-faced sobriety, he denied two counts of attempted murder, causing grievous bodily harm, unlawful wounding and aggravated burglary. Through the oratory skills of his barrister, the jury were persuaded that Society Was To Blame, and in measured tones the defendant was to thank Mr Justice Astill, after being found not guilty of the charges on the grounds of insanity.

The summit of his life conquered, Michael was escorted away by two male nurses for the first stage of a journey that would terminate in a psychiatric hospital in rural Merseyside. He was to be detained indefinitely, meaning that he'd be eligible for release if ever a mental health tribunal decided that he was no longer a risk to the public. The Harrisons' plea to be informed if this should happen was rejected, but Justice Astill intimated that there might be "other channels" they could try.

This was food for thought, as, flanked by bodyguards in the building's forecourt afterwards, Dhani Harrison read a statement to the gentlefolk of the press. Its most crucial sentence was, "The prospect of him being released back into society is abhorrent to us."

Newspaper reports on what amounted to 22-year-old Dhani's first public address were accompanied by photographs that accentuated his close resemblance to his father at the same age.

Dhani had preferred not to stand up in court, but his mother had resolved from the start to testify in her own voice rather than "have my statement read by a male police officer in a monotone". Via a half-page interview in *The Independent On Sunday*, she also expressed hopes that "the growing violence in society is controlled and ultimately replaced by the goodness of most people in the world" before putting a full-stop on the affair, with a dramatic "The line is drawn under it all when I hang up this phone."

Yet it wasn't as easy as that. Death threats from other Beatlemaniacs continued to reach George Harrison and unfounded media speculation that he was planning to leave Friar Park because it now had "bad vibes" reawakened parochial opinion that he intended to offer the place to the Krishna Consciousness Society.

"Mr and Mrs Harrison are not merely victims but continuing targets" was the thrust of hired QC Geoffrey Robertson's argument on behalf of George when approaching Home Secretary Jack Straw, one of Judge Astill's "other channels". Straw assured Robertson that to "put victims back at the heart of the justice system has been my guiding preoccupation as Home Secretary. When I read and hear of the experiences of those like George and Olivia Harrison, it intensifies my determination. I believe victims of crime have a right to know that those who have offended against them are released and I propose to introduce new laws to do just that."

These fine words in the run-up to 2001's general election have been thus far the most far-reaching repercussion of the Michael Abram incident, although the amassed publicity did help to pave the way for the release schedule of re-mastered CDs of George's solo back catalogue, complete with tacked-on alternative takes, hitherto-unissued songs and a recent remake of 'My Sweet Lord' on the 2001 boxed set of *All Things Must Pass*.

This double CD's topping of *The Henley Standard*'s Top Ten was reflected to a lesser extent in lists throughout a wider world. This boded well for CD re-promotions of the more attractive *Living In The Material World* and the *Dark Horse* catalogue, which had now reverted to its maker. Jumping to the front of the queue, however, would be an album of fresh material that had exhausted two working titles already, *Portrait Of A Leg End* and *Your Planet Is Doomed, Volume One*.

In the aftershock of Michael Abram's homicidal campaign, George had sent a grateful bottle of champagne to the police station in Falaise Square, and both Paul Williams and Matt Morgans had been awarded with commendations for bravery. "We're not heroes," shrugs Matt. "We just happened to be on the right shift. People did say to me afterwards, 'Weren't you the one at George Harrison's house?' I'd reply, 'Well, yes, I was. But you still get your parking ticket.'"

For George, the experience faded, and according to Nick Valner, his London lawyer, he was "in the best of spirits and on top form – the most relaxed and free he has been since he was attacked". This was part of a statement relayed to the press in May 2001, shortly after George Harrison underwent a second operation in three years to remove a cancerous growth on a lung. From his bed in the Mayo Clinic in Rochester, Minnesota, George blamed smoking – a habit he gave up when the condition was first diagnosed.

While George convalesced in Tuscany with Olivia, Valner assured the public that "the operation was successful and George has made an excellent recovery. Although *All Things Must Pass Away*, George has no plans right now and is still *Living In The Material World*, and wishes everyone all the very best."

19 The Artist Dying

George Harrison could not permit himself the luxury of hope after a syndicated photograph from Tuscany reached the media. He smiled his old smile, but, ashen-faced and grey-haired now, he seemed to have aged shockingly. Those well-wishers in closest contact – including Ringo and Paul – became as uneasily aware as George was that there might be less than six months left. As if blowing sparks of optimism, he marshalled enough energy to record 'Horse To The Water', a new opus by himself and Dhani. Yet outward evidence of respite from gathering infirmity ended when a brain tumour developed, requiring weeks of chemotherapy in a specialist clinic in Switzerland. Prescribed a course of drugs and avoidance of stressful situations, he convalesced in Kuppaqulua – where he continued to practice guitar and tease songs from nothing more than the ghost of a lyric or melody.

Being awash with medications for a debilitating illness wasn't the soundest footing from which to consider another

Cloud Nine-sized comeback. A final desperate strategy was an admission to New York's Staten Island University Hospital for what George had been convinced was a "revolutionary" new radiotherapy technique that had bought time for other cancer sufferers. There was, however, little that could be done.

Coming to terms with what was inevitable, George resigned as director of Harrisongs, a publishing company that had existed since 1963, and, with characteristic black humour, created "RIP Ltd", an outlet for 'Horse To The Water' and other latter-day compositions. He also affirmed a wish to be cremated without ceremony, and for the ashes to be scattered on the Ganges.

A further onslaught of symptoms brought him to UCLA Medical Centre in Los Angeles for care rather than cure. The light was fading, but he discharged himself and took refuge in the house of Gavin de Becker, head of the most proficient Hollywood security service money could buy. As it had been in Switzerland and New York, there wasn't a newspaper editor on the planet who wouldn't promise a fortune for a Harrison exclusive or an up-to-date picture. Nevertheless, de Becker's home was as off-limits as Howard Hugues's Las Vegas penthouse. For George Harrison, it was there, with imposition on his treasured privacy as low as it could be, that the light went out in the early afternoon of Thursday, 29th of November 2001.

Songography
By Ian Drummond

All songs composed by George Harrison, with co-writers appearing in brackets. Listed by artist/band and then in chronological order of composition. All dates refer to album and single releases unless otherwise stated.

THE BEATLES

'In Spite Of All The Danger' (McCartney)   *Anthology 1* (Nov 1995)
'Cry For A Shadow' (Lennon)

'Don't Bother Me'   *With The Beatles* (Nov 1963)

'You'll Know What To Do'   *Anthology 1* (Nov 1995)

'I Need You' (by George Harrison)   *Help!* (Aug 1965)
'You Like Me Too Much'

'Think For Yourself'   *Rubber Soul* (Nov 1965)
'If I Needed Someone'

'12-Bar Original' (Lennon-McCartney-Starkey)   *Anthology 2* (Mar 1996)

George Harrison

'Taxman'   *Revolver* (Aug 1966)
'Love You To'
'I Want To Tell You'

'Within You Without You'   *Sgt Pepper's Lonely Hearts Club Band* (Jun 1967)

'Only A Northern Song'   *Yellow Submarine* (Jan 1969)
'It's All Too Much'

'Flying' (Lennon-McCartney-Starkey)   *Magical Mystery Tour* (Dec 1967)
'Blue Jay Way'

'Jessie's Dream'   *Magical Mystery Tour* film (Dec 1967)
     (Lennon-McCartney-Starkey)

'Christmas Time (Is Here Again)'   'Free As A Bird' B-side (Dec 1995)
     (Lennon-McCartney-Starkey)

'The Inner Light'   'Lady Madonna' B-side (Mar 1968)

'Piggies' (demo)   *Anthology 3* (Oct 1996)

'While My Guitar Gently Weeps'   *The Beatles* (Nov 1968)
'Piggies'
'Long Long Long'
'Savoy Truffle'

'Not Guilty'   *Anthology 3* (Oct 1996)

'For You Blue'   *Let It Be* (May 1970)
'Dig It' (Lennon-McCartney-Starkey)

'Something' (demo)   *Anthology 3* (Oct 1996)
'All Things Must Pass' (demo)
'Old Brown Shoe' (demo)

'Old Brown Shoe' 'The Ballad Of John And Yoko' B-side (May 1969)

'Something' *Abbey Road* (Sep 1969)
'Here Comes The Sun'

'I Me Mine' (McCartney?) *Let It Be* (May 1970)

'Free As A Bird (Lennon-McCartney-Starkey) *Anthology 1* (Nov 1995)

'Real Love' (Lennon-McCartney-Starkey) *Anthology 2* (Mar 1996)

GEORGE HARRISON
'Microbes' *Wonderwall* (Nov 1968)
'Red Lady Too'
'Tabla And Pakavaj'
'In The Park'
'Drilling A Home'
'Guru Vandana'
'Greasy Legs'
'Ski-ing'
'Gat Kirwani'
'Dream Scene'
'Party Secombe'
'Love Scene'
'Crying'
'Cowboy Music'
'Fantasy Sequins'
'On The Bed'
'Glass Box'
'Wonderwall To Be Here'
'Singing Om'

'Under The Mersey Wall' *Electronic Sound* (May 1969)
'No Time Or Space'

'I'd Have You Any Time' (Dylan) *All Things Must Pass* (Nov 1970)

GEORGE HARRISON

'My Sweet Lord'
'Wah Wah'
'Isn't It A Pity?'
'What Is Life?'
'Behind That Locked Door'
'Let It Down'
'Run Of The Mill'
'Beware Of Darkness'
'Apple Scruffs'
'Ballad Of Sir Frankie Crisp (Let It Roll)'
'Awaiting On You All'
'All Things Must Pass'
'I Dig Love'
'Art Of Dying'
'Hear Me Lord'
'Plug Me In'
'I Remember Jeep'
'Thanks For The Pepperoni'
'Out Of The Blue'

'I Live For You'   *All Things Must Pass* (Jan 2000)

'Bangla Desh'   Single (Jul 1971)
'Deep Blue'   'Bangla Desh' B-side (Jul 1971)

'Miss O'Dell'   'Give Me Love' B-side (May 1973)

'Give Me Love'   *Living In The Material World* (Nov 1973)
'Sue Me Sue You Blues'
'The Light That Has Lighted The World'
'Don't Let Me Wait Too Long'
'Who Can See It?'
'Living In The Material World'
'The Lord Loves The One'

186

'Be Here Now'
'Try Some Buy Some'
'The Day The World Gets Round'
'That Is All'

'I Don't Care Anymore'   'Ding Dong' B-side (Dec 1974)

'Hari's On Tour Express'   *Dark Horse* (Nov 1974)
'Simply Shady'
'So Sad'
'Maya Love'
'Ding Dong Ding Dong'
'Dark Horse'
'It Is He'

'You'   *Extra Texture* (Sep 1975)
'The Answer's at The End'
'This Guitar Can't Keep From Crying'
'Ooh Baby (You Know That I Love You)'
'World Of Stone'
'A Bit More Of You'
'Can't Stop Thinking About You'
'Tired Of Midnight Blue'
'Grey Cloudy Lies'
'His Name Is Legs (Ladies And Gentlemen)'

'Pirate Song' (Idle)   Written for *Rutland Weekend Television* (Dec 1975)

'Woman Don't You Cry For Me'   *Thirty-Three And 1/3* (Nov 1976)
'Dear One'
'Beautiful Girl'
'This Song'
'See Yourself'
'It's What You Value'

'Pure Smokey'
'Crackerbox Palace'
'Learning How To Love You'

'Mo'   *Mo's Songs* (US release, Dec 1994)

'Not Guilty'   *George Harrison* (Feb 1979)
'Here Comes The Moon'
'Soft-Hearted Hana'
'Blow Away'
'Faster'
'Dark Sweet Lady'
'Your Love Is Forever'
'Soft Touch'
'If You Believe' (Wright)

'Blood From A Clone'   *Somewhere In England* (Jun 1981)
'Unconsciousness Rules'
'Life Itself'
'All Those Years Ago'
'Teardrops'
'That Which I Have Lost'
'Writing's On The Wall'
'Save The World/Crying'

'Sat Singing'   *Songs By George Harrison* (Feb 1988)
'Life Itself' (demo)
'Lay His Head'
'Tears Of The World'
'Flying Hour' (Ralphs)

'Wake Up My Love'   *Gone Troppo* (Nov 1981)
'That's The Way It Goes'
'Greece'

'Gone Troppo'
'Mystical One'
'Unknown Delight'
'Baby Don't Run Away'
'Dream Away'
'Circles'

'Shelter In Your Love' (Lee)   Unreleased

'Cloud Nine'   *Cloud Nine* (Nov 1987)
'That's What It Takes'
'Fish On The Sand'
'Just For Today'
'This Is Love'
'When We Was Fab'
'Devil's Radio'
'Someplace Else'
'Wreck Of The Hesperus'
'Breath Away From Heaven'

'Zig Zag'   'When We Was Fab' B-side (Jan 1988)

'Ride Rajbun' (English)   *The Bunburys* (Oct 1992)

'Cheer Down' (Petty)   *Lethal Weapon 2* soundtrack (Sep 1989)

'Poor Little Girl'   *Best Of Dark Horse* (Oct 1989)
'Cockamamie Business'

'Any Road'   *Brainwashed* (Nov 2002)
'P2 Vatican Blues (Last Saturday Night)'
'Pisces Fish'
'Looking For My Life'
'The Rising Sun'

GEORGE HARRISON

'Marwa Blues' (Instrumental)
'Stuck Inside A Cloud'
'Run So Far'
'Never Get Over You'
'Rocking Chair In Hawaii'
'Brainwashed'

THE TRAVELING WILBURYS
(with Bob Dylan, Jeff Lynne, Tom Petty and Roy Orbison)

'Handle With Care'   *VOLUME 1* (Oct 1988)
'Dirty World'
'Rattled'
'Last Night'
'Not Alone Any More'
'Congratulations'
'Heading For The Light'
'Margarita'
'Tweeter And The Monkey Man'
'End Of The Line'

'She's My Baby'   *VOLUME 3* (Oct 1990)
'The Devil's Been Busy'
'Where Were You Last Night?'
'Wilbury Twist'
'Inside Out'
'If You Belonged To Me'
'Seven Deadly Sins'
'Poor House'
'Cool Dry Place'
'New Blue Moon'
'You Took My Breath Away'
'Maxine'   Bootleg only
'Like A Ship'   Bootleg only

DAVID BROMBERG
'The Hold-Up' (Bromberg)   *David Bromberg* (Jun 1972)

ERIC CLAPTON
'Run So Far'   *Journeyman* (Nov 1989)

'That Kind Of Woman'   *Romanian Angel* (Jul 1990)

CREAM
'Badge' (Clapton)   *Goodbye* (Feb 1969)

JESSE ED DAVIS
'Sue Me Sue You Blues'   *Ululu* (Jan 1972)

JIMMY HELMS
'Celebration' (Moran)   *Water* (Jan 1985)
'Focus Of Attention' (Moran-Clement)

JOOLS HOLLAND
'Horse To The Water' (D Harrison)   *Small World, Big Band* (Nov 2001)

ALVIN LEE AND MYLON LEFEVRE
'So Sad'   *On The Road To Freedom* (Nov 1973)

JACKIE LOMAX
'Sour Milk Sea'   *Is This What You Want* (Aug 1968)

GARY MOORE
'That Kind Of Woman'   *Still Got The Blues* (Mar 1990)

BILLY PRESTON
'Sing One For The Lord' (Preston)   *Encouraging Words* (Sep 1970)

RONNIE SPECTOR
'Tandoori Chicken' (Spector)   Single (Apr 1971)

RINGO STARR
'Photograph' (Starkey)   *Ringo* (Nov 1973)
'Sunshine Life For Me'
'You And Me Babe' (Evans)

'I'll Still Love You'   *Ringo's Rotogravure* (Sep 1976)

'Wrack My Brain'   *Stop And Smell The Roses* (Nov 1981)

DORIS TROY
'Ain't That Cute' (Troy)   *Doris Troy* (Sep 1970)
'Give Me Back My Dynamite' (Troy)
'Gonna Get My Baby Back' (Troy-Starkey-Stills)
'You Give Me Joy Joy' (Starkey-Troy-Stills)

RON WOOD
Far East Man (Wood)   *I've Got My Own Album To Do* (Sep 1974)